BORN
TO BE
KILLERS

A Warner Book

This first edition published in 2004

ISBN 0-7513-3589-3

Produced by Omnipress, Eastbourne

Printed in Great Britain

Time Warner Books
Brettenham House
Lancaster Place
London WC2E 7EN

CONTENTS

INTRODUCTION

Born to be Killers is a study of the chilling complexity and sometimes irrational twists that takes a crime beyond understanding. It studies the cases of children and adults alike, in which the cold-blooded cruelty, the cunning scheming and callous lack of reason in a killing, takes a crime into a different perspective.

This book also tries to get inside the disturbed minds of the people that commit these heinous acts. What possesses them to rape or kill someone in cold blood? Do they really believe they will not get caught for such abominable crimes? These are just some of the questions forensic psychologists and scientists are constantly trying to answer where the violent criminal is concerned. The only way to get any sort of an answer is to try to get inside the minds of such criminals. Scientists need to find out everything they possibly can about the way the criminal mind works, and what factors contribute to make them the way they are – that is no easy task and there is no simple way to go about it.

The background of violent criminals can very often help the police catch offenders before they strike again. By using information gathered from offenders already in prison regarding their preferred methods of killing, it is becoming ever more possible to catch violent criminals.

Serial killers are the most dangerous of all violent criminals. They not only kill until they are apprehended, but they also have a psychotic reasoning that makes it very difficult to catch them. However, there do seem to be many physical similaries in serial killers. Some of these include ritualistic and compulsive behaviour, suicidal tendencies, a history of serious assaults, hypersexuality, a history of drug or alcohol abuse, alcohol or drug-abusing parents, cruelty to animals, and finally a unnatural liking for firearms. Mind you it would not be accurate to say that a person who may have one or more of these traits is a serial killer, of course. But, conversely, a serial killer will have some, if not all, of these characteristics.

There are also emotional behaviour signs which may not be obvious to the layman. It is known that many serial killers suffer from chronic depression, feelings of powerlessness or inadequacy, abuse as a child, a rollercoaster of emotions during childhood and a masking of one's sanity. When interviewed, a vast majority of serial killers did not have recollections of a happy childhood. Many of them suffered emotional and/or physical abuse from either their parents or step-parents and suffered serious neglect as a child.

Violent offenders who rape their victims fall into different categories. There are different types of rapists, who rape for different reasons and do it in different ways. Profiles have been created for each kind of rapist and these are often used in an effort to track down and punish the contrasting types of rapists.

One example is the 'Power Reassurance Rapist' and this is probably the most common type. Normally, this type of rapist will carry a weapon, or at least claim to have one. However, the offender will not normally use the weapon or any more force than is necessary to fulfill his fantasy. His main objective is to express his power through sex, not physical injury. This offender will spend quite some considerable period of time with the victim, may even compliment her on her appearance, and possibly going as far as to apologize for his actions.

The *Power Assertive Rapist* primary concern is to show just how 'manly' he is through extreme violence. This rapist is not remotely concerned with the extent of suffering he causes his victim and usually employs more force than necessary to overpower her.

The *Anger Retaliatory Rapist* is even more aggressive. This type of offender has a deep hatred towards women and consequently takes out his revenge on his victim, and as a result many of his victims will require hospitalization.

The *Anger Excitation Rapist* or sexual sadist is sexually stimulated by the amount of suffering his victim endures and he is definitely the most dangerous type of rapist.

The *Opportunistic Rapist* will rape someone while another crime is taking place, for instance, during a kidnapping or possibly a robbery. This type of rapist will not spend very long with his victim and is usually either high on drugs or drunk during the ordeal.

Mass murderers are extremely menacing because they act without any reasoning at all. Very often one single traumatic episode will spark off a violent rage in the offender. Acting completely on impulse, the murderer will go into a public area like a park, restaurant, or office building, and immediately open fire on any innocent person who happens to be in the vicinity. He does not expect to come out alive and tries to kill as many people as possible before he is eventually killed himself. This is very worrying because the murderer does not consider the consequences. The only thing on his mind is death, and so there is no limit to the extent of his destruction. These situations are highly unpredictable and probably the hardest to prevent.

Scientific studies have recently found a strong connection between the development of the brain and the nature of violent offenders. Extensive studies have proved that many offenders had previously suffered strong blows to the head, which may have damaged the brain. The damage may be severe enough to alter the control over emotional and certain sensory organs. As a result of this damage, certain people are unable to feel remorse or control their aggression. Another contributory factor is that after many years of emotional abuse, the brain becomes used to it and creates a defence mechanism. People who have suffered from this kind of abuse tend to shut off from other people, becoming antisocial, and when they are confronted often become very hostile. This is their only way of coping with everyday life and the turmoil they feel from it.

Although there is no way to prevent violent crimes from happening, hopefully with new technology we will eventually be able stop it as soon as it begins. Born to be killers – or maybe just born with the natural instinct to kill!

PART 1

CHILDREN WHO KILL

What Makes Them Kill?

In February 1993 the world was shocked by the news that two ten-year-old boys had murdered two-year-old Jamie Bulger. The two boys, Jon Thompson and Robert Venables were branded as 'evil monsters' and 'savages' and people still reel at the concept that this kind of horrendous act could ever have taken place.

THANKFULLY, cases like this one are extremely rare. Over the last two-and-a-half centuries in Britain there have only been thirty-one recorded cases of people under the age of fourteen killing. Perhaps it is because that children are normally perceived as being innocent and good, that crimes committed by juveniles appear all the more horrendous. The public are generally so shocked and appalled by these crimes, that they immediately want to label the offenders as being 'freaks of nature'. In the sixteenth century children were seen as being 'born evil' and needing to be trained or forced to be good.

Although there is a great deal of resistance to the idea of branding children as sexual offenders, there does appear to be a growing problem of sexual abuse of children by children. This is a great worry to the authorities, as it appears that children who have been sexually abused themselves will frequently become sexually reactive and begin to sexually abuse others. Of course, not all children who become sexually aggressive have necessarily been abused themselves. It may be the result of having been exposed to explicit sexual material and violence. Sex and violence become linked in their minds and, as they develop their sexual identity during puberty, they find it hard to differentiate between the two.

It is quite fair to say that children who abuse nine out of ten times grow up to be adults who abuse. Although the rehabilitation of adult sex offenders is often ineffective, it is a proven fact that children are far more resilient and the trauma that causes them to become abusive can often be alleviated if it is treated early enough. Again and again, the children who kill or sexually abuse another person are merely re-enacting the violence that was done to them. These children may have been the victims of abuse for years and years before they finally snapped and became the perpetrators themselves. In some cases they would kill the family that caused the suffering, but more often than not they would take out their revenge on an innocent victim.

One such example of this is Mary Bell. During her childhood her mother had attempted several times to poison her, had attempted to give her away to a stranger, and then when she was only four, involved her in sado-masochistic prostitution by holding back Mary's head so the clients could ejaculate into her mouth. With such a background it is hardly surprising that by the time she was eleven she was a deeply disturbed child who had murdered two boys.

A more up-to-date case is that of Brenda Spencer. On January 16, 1979 who positioned herself outside the Cleveland Elementary School and waited for the headmaster to open the building. As soon as the children started arriving at the school, Brenda opened fire. For a total of twenty minutes she took out her revenge on the children and teachers alike, and in which time Brenda managed to kill the Principal and school caretaker, also injuring nine children aged between six and twelve. Once she tired of the game, Brenda went home and waited for the police. She eventually gave herself up after two hours of questioning. For her it had all been worth it, for she had gained twenty minutes worth of attention, something which she greatly lacked at home.

Another really shocking case was that of the sixteen-year-old Jessica Holtmeyer, who hanged a learning-disabled girl in Pennsylvania and then hit her about the face with a rock. Read the full story further in this book.

All of these children certainly have a character disturbance. They devalue others and lack a sense of morality. Events as those described above have made it ever more clear that psychopathy is not something that is exclusive to adults. In fact, certain child development experts believe that childhood psychopathy is increasing at quite an alarming rate. Their main concern is that these 'young and inexperienced psychopaths' will become increasingly more dangerous as they get older. Although they might not necessarily resort to the act of killing, they could learn how to manipulate, deceive and exploit others for their own gain. Because they have failed to develop any bonds of affection during their youth, it does not allow them to empathize with another person's pain. Instead, they develop traits of arrogance, dishonesty, an unhealthy admiration of themselves, shamelessness and last, but by no means least, callousness.

Children can become wary, distressed, distrustful, resistant or even angry if not securely attached by the first nine months of their life. Studies show that securely-attached children tend to be far more competent and well-adjusted in their later life. This means that childhood psychopathy most probably forms at this crucial early stage of development, especially if the child is prone to a lack of behavioural inhibitions and sensation-seeking. While a born psychopath may have neurological disorders that defy everything we try to do, it may still be possible with the right nurturing to redirect such children before they become truly dangerous.

DEVELOPING SOCIAL SKILLS

It is very obvious from the studies carried out that children who grow up around violence are at risk in their pathological development. It is vital that infants and toddlers develop trust and a feeling of safety in order to have a healthy psychological development. It is quite apparent that if they don't have a good bond with their parents, they will have a much tougher time outside the home environment.

School years are the time when children develop their social skills and learn how to function as adults, but violence can seriously impair this progress. Studies made of children with violent tendencies has shown that:

- Lack of safety harms cognitive performance;
- Children who live in fear will often repress their feelings, which hinders their ability to be in tune with their surroundings;
- Children who are regularly exposed to violence tend to lack the ability to concentrate;
- Children who are constantly abused are prone to feelings of helplessness;
- Constant stress in the home can produce symptoms of Post Traumatic Stress Disorder

There is certainly a proven connection between certain factors and the risk of violence among adolescents:

- Past violent behaviour
- Substance abuse
- Aggressive peers
- Family aggression
- Social stress
- Character or mental disorders
- Access to weapons,
- Focused anger
- Low degree of resilience

16

Self-worth, resilience, hope, intelligence and empathy are all essential factors in the building of a healthy character – effective control of impulses, anger management and conflict resolution. Without these skills, children cannot form rewarding relationships with community systems.

Children who kill to solve their problems in fact solve nothing. Society needs to understand the fact that children can form intent to kill, whether or not they understand what they're doing. They can kill without knowing that it is final, so this point needs to be impressed on them during the early stages of their development. Any signs of lack of empathy or value of another person's life needs to be caught early and treated, not ignored.

THE EFFECT OF TELEVISION

Do violent television and videogames play a significant role in conditioning our children to become violent without teaching them the consequences? Every day, children are bombarded by messages and images from the media – messages about how to behave, what choices to make and what to think. Children even try to emulate what they learn from television, video games and the Internet. They are far more susceptible to these messages than adults because they haven't developed the skill of judgment or indeed the ability to process the information they are given.

According to over thirty years of scientific studies violent television programmes and computer games do appear to desensitize children to violence. While the murder rate doubled between 1957 and 1992, the aggravated assault rate – that is the rate at which people are attempting to maim or kill one another – has multiplied many times more.

Although only a few children may actually act out such violence, it is becoming apparent that brutality is rapidly becoming an acceptable part of our existence. Sensational visual images showing hurting as being powerful and domination of others as permissible, are undoubtedly dangerous to juvenile minds. We are, in short, teaching them that killing is natural. As adults we know that it is something that does not come naturally and, even with trained soldiers, only a percentage of them can bring themselves to actually kill in situations other than self-defence. Many of the training methods used in the military to prepare soldiers to kill are used in violent media programming.

From very young ages, children are trained to accept violence as the norm. Even cartoon characters aimed at the very young, are constantly knocking each other about. In the early 1990s *The Journal of the American Medical Association* published a definitive study on television violence. They compared regions with television to those without and, keeping most other factors the same, it was proved that where television was introduced, there was an explosion of violence on the playground. Within fifteen years, the murder rate had doubled, which is '. . . how long it takes for the brutalization of three- to five-year-olds to reach the prime crime age'. In one particular town in Canada where television was introduced in

18

1973, there was a 160% increase in shoving, pushing, biting and hitting among adolescents.

It does not take very long before young minds come to associate violence with entertainment. They may possibly eat and drink while watching, so that violence becomes part of a pleasant daily routine. They laugh when there is violence in comedies and are eager to see violent and scary films. Interactive videogames that reward violent acts with higher scores, are teaching our children that violence is good. In certain circumstances, the stimulation associated with this type of programming is close to being erotic. They rapidly learn to point and shoot at 'targets' which appear to be human, but the consequences of actually taking a human life are never realized in such games. We are teaching our children to kill, but what is more disturbing is that they are learning to like it.

The American government carried out a study in 1999 and discovered that by the time a child reaches the age of eighteen, he or she will have seen 200,000 dramatized acts of violence and 40,000 dramatized murders. Moreover, half of the videogames that a typical schoolchild plays will have a tendency towards violence. It is through this kind of exposure that some troubled children develop a taste for violence. The difference between fantasy and reality is far more difficult for children to assess than adults and, added to the desensitization and conditioning that goes on daily from the media, it is clear that violent programmes and games do have a negative impact.

THE INTERNET

The Internet is now being accessed by younger and younger children, but what many parents fail to understand are the hidden dangers when they leave their children unsupervised at the computer.

In the wake of the tragic school shootings over the past few years, society has suddenly begun to realize what research has already shown. Children who frequently play violent computer games display more aggressive behaviour and actually teach children to kill. Parents need to carefully monitor the type of computer and inter-active Internet games their children are engaged in and help to provide constructive alternatives.

BARRY LOUKAITIS

Barry Loukaitis was one of the modern day school ground killers who was certainly influenced by the media. He was a pathetic loser with numerous problems, most of which stemmed from his upbringing. At his trial it came out that there was a history of mental illness on both sides of the family, with depression being quite common in both his parents' genes. He was even subjected to listening to his mother telling him of her plans to kill herself in front of her ex-husband and his new girlfriend on Valentine's Day in 1996. Apparently it was Barry who talked her out of it, and encouraged her to write down her anger – what a pity he couldn't follow his own advice.

For some reason Loukaitis felt the need to take

out his revenge on some classmates that must have agitated him. He planned the shootings carefully, getting his ideas from the book *Rage*, written by Stephen King, and the film *Natural Born Killers*. The book was about a high school student who takes a gun to school and fatally shoots two of his teachers. Loukaitis was also very keen on a band called Pearl Jam, and in particular, their song *Jeremy*. It would seem that young Barry took the song to heart, and for those who have never seen the video to the song – it shows a boy killing his classmates.

For Barry it all came to a head on September 2, 1996. He broke into the algebra class with a high-powered rifle and shot three students and their teacher. Two of the children died and so did the teacher. Hearing the shots, P.E. teacher, Jon Lane, decided to be a hero. He burst into the classroom, disarmed Barry and held him down until the police arrived. During questioning it came out that Barry had been having problems with another student, Manuel Vela, who had been one of the students he shot.

OTHER CASES OF SHOOTING

Barry Loukaitis was certainly not an isolated case. There has been such a spate of schoolground violence in America recently, that it is causing people to raise difficult questions about what leads a child to pick up a gun and kill another.

On 16 April, 1999, a second-year high school pupil fired two shotgun blasts in a school hallway in Notus, Idaho. No-one was injured.

In May 1998, 15-year-old Kipland Kinkel killed two fellow pupils at Thurston Hill High School in Springfield, Oregon, and then murdered his parents.

On the very same day, 320km north in Washington State, a 15-year-old boy shot himself in the head after taking his girlfriend off the school bus at gunpoint and back to his home in the town of Onalaska. He shot himself as the girl's father tried to break down the door, his 14-year-old girlfriend was luckily unharmed.

Just two months earlier, two boys opened fire on classmates at Westside Middle School in Jonesboro, Arkansas. The boys, aged 11 and 13, killed four girls and one teacher, wounding nine more girls and one other teacher.

On May 19, 1998, an 18-year-old at Lincoln County High School shot and killed a student in a school parking lot in Fayetteville, Tennessee, three days before they were to graduate. The reason, apparently, because there had been an argument over a girl.

On April 25, 1998, a 14-year-old boy opened fire on an eighth-grade graduation dance at Parker Middle School in Edinboro, Pennsylvania, killing a teacher and wounding two students and another teacher.

December 1, 1997, a 14-year-old boy shot and killed three girls and injured five others at Heath High School in West Paducah, Kentucky, while they took part in a prayer circle.

October 1, 1997, a 16-year-old stabbed and killed his mother, before going to school where he proceeded to shoot nine fellow students. His ex-girlfriend and another girl at Pearl High School in Mississippi were among those killed. Seven other students were wounded and six boys, aged between 16 and 18, were charged with conspiracy to commit murder.

THE EFFECTS OF DRUGS AND ALCOHOL

Illegal drug use among the young is on the rise and can play a significant role in their criminal conduct. Drugs and alcohol are attractive to young people for many different reasons. Firstly, as far as alcohol is concerned, drinking is seen by young people as an adult behaviour and thus a way to appear grown up. The appeal of alcohol is that it helps in social situations by making people more relaxed and uninhibited, and much the same can be said of cannabis. Of course another reason for children taking drugs is that it represents a rebellion against adult values. Finally we should not ignore the fact that hard drugs can become addictive, either because of life circumstances or because of a personality disorder.

The teen years are when many young people begin dangerous experimentation with drugs, alcohol, tobacco, sexual activity and engage in other life-threatening behaviours. Drugs can have a severely debilitating effect on the physical and psychological development of a child, not just at the time of use, but for many years to come. Continued drug use can lead to self-degradation, loss of control and disruptive, antisocial attitudes

23

that can cause untold harm to young people and their families. Children from the ages of 12 to 17 who smoke marijuana are twice as likely to cut class, steal, attack people and destroy property.

Another alarming statistic is that suicide rates jump in the teen years due to many factors, including greater access to firearms, drug and alcohol abuse, social pressures and negative family situations outside of the child's control.

STREET GANGS

Street gangs are usually formed according to ethnic or racial guidelines, although there seems to be a current trend to form gangs for more sinister reasons. The gangs discussed here are a group of people who form an allegiance for a common purpose and engage in violent, unlawful, or criminal activity. A gang may or may not claim control over a certain territory in the community. Young people (as young as nine or ten) gave the following reasons for wanting to be a member of a gang:

- to belong to a group
- for excitement
- to get protection
- to earn money
- to be with friends

Gangs thrive on intimidation and notoriety. They often find violence glamorous and a necessity in order to maintain individual and gang status. Like most groups, street gangs depend upon both individual and group participation. Unlike legitimate groups or organizations, street gangs generally do not have an identified leader. It is generally the person who is considered to be the toughest, the one who has the guns, or has the most money, that emerges as the leader, but often this status is short-lived.

Gang membership extracts a terrible toll from the lives of all who are in contact with the member. Families of gang members must be concerned for their own safety as well as that of their son or daughter who is the gang member. Friends who are not involved with the gang's activities are cast aside and soon the youth's only friends are other gang members. Belonging to a gang, even if only a temporary phase for some youths, will shape the individual's future. Formal education is discarded because it is counter-productive to the gang's objectives. Gang members who are not killed or seriously injured often develop patterns of alcohol and narcotics abuse, and extensive police records that limit their future employment opportunities.

Gang members frequently seek showdowns with rivals and the resulting violence often claims the lives of innocent victims. Gang violence can vary from individual assaults to drive-by shootings. Common gang activities are the sale of drugs, extortion, robberies, motor vehicle thefts, or other criminal activities for monetary gain. Vandalism in the form of graffiti and the wanton destruction of public and private property is often done as the sign of a gang's occupation of a territory. Abandoned houses are a favourite target for vandalism but even occupied houses do not escape. Local businesses suffer not only from property damage and graffiti, but also from loss of customers and employees.

Of greater concern is the inbred violence that is associated with gang graffiti. As mentioned previously, gang members use graffiti to 'tag' their 'turf' or 'territory'. They also use it to advertise the gang's status or power and to declare their own allegiance to the gang. When a neighbourhood is marked with graffiti indicating territorial dominance, the entire area and its inhabitants become targets for violence. Anyone on the street or in his home is fair game for drive-by attacks by rival gang members. A rival gang identifies everyone in the neighbourhood as a potential threat, and consequently, innocent residents are often subjected to gang violence by the mere presence of graffiti in their neighbourhood.

There have also been cases of murder, in which children kill children, and very often these killings are associated with child gangs. In many cases, it is an entire gang of children that decides to bully, attack and consciously or subconsciously kill other children or people. There are many potential roots of this type of violence – peer pressure, broken families, abusive parents, easy access to guns, violence in the media – in fact all the subjects that have been discussed earlier that help to develop our 'junior killer'.

FAMILY MEMBERS

What would induce a child to kill members of its own family for reasons other than an accident? Maybe it is because they feel pressured by demands, abuse, hatred, desire for gain, or even by the need of other family members. One 14-year-old enlisted his brother to help him murder their parents, and one mother provoked her son into killing his father. A fourteen-year-old in China killed his family because he thought his mother was not taking care of him properly. When he was ill one night, she ordered him back to bed. Instead of returning to his bed, he stabbed his father 37 times, his mother 72 times and his grandmother 56 times, then he washed his hair and watched a videotape as if nothing had happened. In truth, it is possible nobody will ever really know why they did what they did.

CASE
HISTORIES

Mary and Norma Bell

The body of a little boy was found covered with grass and purple weeds. He had been strangled. Nearby, a pair of broken scissors lay in the grass. There were puncture wounds on his thighs and his genitals had been partially skinned.

In the autumn of May 1968, three children were playing around in a deserted house when they came across the corpse of a toddler, who was later named as Martin Brown. Martin George Brown was only four years old. He was a popular little boy with fair hair and a mischievous face. Minutes before his death he had been seen in the local shop where he had bought some sweets. Now he lay in what had been a back bedroom with blood and saliva dribbling from his mouth.

Only a few days after the discovery of Martin's body, a vandal broke into his nursery school when it was closed and scribbled some graffiti on the walls. Written in crayon was the message, 'I murder so that I may come back'. Handwriting experts were positive it was the work of a child.

Three months later in August 1968, three-year-old Brian Howe was found strangled near his nursery school (the very same one attended by

29

Martin Brown). By now people who lived in the vicinity were becoming extremely concerned for the safety of their own children. This drove Newcastle's law enforcement officers to begin interviewing all of its 1,200 underage residents. It was during these investigations that the police arrested two suspects – Mary and Norma Bell.

A TOUGH BACKGROUND

Both the above crimes were committed in Scots-wood, a depressed area of Newcastle-upon-Tyne, in Northumberland. The question which was on everyone's mind was that if a child was so emotionally disturbed to commit such heinous crimes, surely there must have been some warning signs.

In the case of Mary Bell there were plenty. Mary's childhood was a continual nightmare of abandonment and drug overdoses. For some unknown and bizarre reason, her father pretended to be Mary's uncle. Her mother, Betty, was a disciplinarian, but not the sort of discipline that was desirable for the bringing up of a young family. She was a prostitute with a speciality, she used whips and bondage to 'discipline' her clients. Betty always felt her daughter was kerbing her activities and was anxious to get rid of her. She very often dropped her off to stay with relatives. Realizing that Mary was very unhappy at home, the family pleaded with Betty to let them keep her, but for some reason she always returned to her family home.

In 1960 Betty took Mary to an adoption agency,

giving her over to a distraught women who wasn't permitted to adopt a child as she was about to move to Australia. Mary was left with this strange woman, but luckily her aunt, Isa, who was suspicious about the whole arrangement, had followed them and soon found out the whereabouts of Mary.

Even at the age of two, Mary was having difficulty in forming any form of bond with others of her own age, and always behaved in a cold and detached manner. Mary became a little hardnut, never crying when she was hurt, lashing out violently, and once even smashed her uncle's nose with one of her toys. Her mother's constant rejections and reunions didn't help the situation and only further distanced Mary from the rest of her family.

Another fact that had a devastating effect on Mary and further retarded her ability to bond with others, was when she witnessed her five-year-old friend being run over by a bus. Mary's kindergarten teacher described her as a naughty child. She once discovered Mary with her hands around the neck of another child and when she was told not to do it, she replied, 'Why? Can it kill him?' She was a loner and was subjected to constant teasing by her classmates. She would retaliate by punching and kicking and was known to tell a pack of lies.

One of the most disturbing aspects of Mary's childhood, were the frequent drug overdoses, which were more than likely administered by her own mother. When Mary was only one year old, she nearly overdosed after taking some pills that were hidden inside the family gramophone. It seemed impossible that a baby could reach the pills and very strange to think that a child would eat so many of the very nasty-tasting pills anyway. Again, when Mary was three she and her brother were found eating 'little blue pills' together with some sweets that their aunt Cath had treated them to. Betty said that they must have taken the pills out of her handbag, which had been left nearby. Cath and her husband offered to adopt Mary, but Betty refused to let the child go and soon broke off any contact she had with the rest of her family.

The most serious overdose was when Mary swallowed numerous 'iron' pills, which again belonged to her mother. This time she became unconscious and had to have her stomach pumped. Mary, together with a young playmate, said that Betty had given her 'Smarties' that made her sick. Overdoses in a developing child can cause serious brain damage, a common trait found in violent offenders.

As if the overdoses were not disturbing enough, perhaps the greatest tragedy of all was Betty's use of Mary during her prostitution activities. Mary's case was perhaps one of the worst of child sexual abuse ever to have been uncovered, as she re-counted the horrors she endured as her mother's sexual prop. No other relatives, including her younger brother, were aware of this abuse.

All these things added together would certainly help to explain Mary's erratic behaviour. Probably it was her constant violation within her home unit that incited her to abuse her own little victims.

Norma's background, on the other hand, was surrounded by a much more sympathetic family. She was the third of eleven children and reacted to evidence and testimony with a more childlike combination of fear and nervousness. During the ensuing trial Mary showed none of these weaknesses.

THE BELL GIRLS

Both Mary and Norma Bell were eleven years old and close neighbours. Although they shared the same last name, they were in fact not related. The first time that anyone became suspicious about the darker side of Mary's nature was when the police and an ambulance were called to the Delaval Arms on May 11, 1968. Mary's three-year-old cousin had been discovered with some injuries at a nearby shed. The next day police took statements from the two girls who had discovered the injured child – Mary and Norma. Both girls told the same fabricated story, that they had heard someone shouting and on investigation discovered Mary's cousin, John G., lying on the concrete path with blood coming from his head.

This was not the only encounter the two girls had with the police that weekend. That same Sunday night a lady called Mrs. Watson made a complaint to the police about a girl who had attempted to strangle her seven-year-old daughter, Pauline, at a local sandpit. Mrs. Watson wasn't sure which one of the Bell's girls was involved.

Once again the police took statements from the two girls and again their stories were totally different. After further enquiries the police decided to take no action beyond informing the Children's Department and giving the children a 'warning' as to their future conduct.

Their next victim was little Martin Brown. Martin's body was discovered by three children who were looking for scrapwood in a derelict house so that they could build a dovecote. They made the grisly discovery shortly after 3.30 pm on Saturday, May 25. Martin had been seen only a few minutes earlier buying some sweets from a local sweetshop and, apart from some workmen summoned by the children who found Martin, Mary and Norma were the first people on the scene. In fact it was Mary and Norma who carried the news of Martin's death to his aunt, Mrs. Rita Finlay, who lived only a few doors away on the other side of the street.

'I think it's your June's bairn and there's blood all over,' said Mary.

On investigation by the police there appeared to be no sign of either a struggle or a fall, and the autopsy failed to determine the cause of the little boy's death. The only thing they could find that was out of the ordinary was a minor brain haemorrhage. The possibility of strangulation was dismissed because the pathologist could find no pressure marks. At the end of several days of inquiries, the police accepted that Martin's death had been an accident and the matter was taken no further.

Mary and Norma were not prepared to let the matter rest here and started their own form of emotional torture on Martin's poor aunt. The two girls visited Mrs. Finlay each day asking if she missed Martin, and did she constantly cry for him. Mrs. Finlay, overcome with grief, sent the girls away and informed the police of their constant pestering.

The persecution of Mrs. Finlay, however, was not to be the only sign of Mary Bell's demented mind. On her eleventh birthday, Sunday, May 26, Mary attempted to strangle a girl named Susan, who was the eleven-year-old sister of her friend Norma. Luckily, Susan's parents heard her frantic screams and came running out of the house. What they saw to their horror was Mary with both hands around their daughter's neck. Mr. Bell managed to break Mary's hands free and gave her a clip around the head, and the matter was taken no further.

The next morning teachers arriving at the nearby Nursery school discovered that it had been broken into during the weekend. Someone had managed to gain entry by removing some of the roof slates. Chalk, school books and cleaning materials had been scattered everywhere, and the police found four notes in childish writing among the debris. They said:

I murder so THAT I may come back

BAS . . . we murder watch out Fanny and Faggot

WE did murder Martain brown you Bastard

35

*You are micey Becurse we murdered Martain
Go Brown you Bete Look out THErE are
Murders about By FANNY AND and auld
Faggot you Screws*

The police decided that the notes were just a
sick joke, but as a precaution against further
break-ins, it was decided to install a burglar alarm
in the school loft.

Two days later Mary decided to turn her attention from Mrs. Finlay to her sister, Mrs. June
Brown, the unfortunate mother of the dead
Martin. Mrs. Brown told the police that Mary
knocked on her door and asked to see Martin. Mrs.
Brown told Mary politely that Martin was dead
and Mary replied with a grin, 'I know he's dead. I
wanted to see him in his coffin'. Mrs. Brown, who
was left totally speechless, just slammed the door
in her face.

On Friday of that week the newly installed
burglar alarm at the school started to ring in the
police station. Within minutes police constables
arrived at the school only to find that Mary and
Normal Bell had once again tried to gain entry by
removing slates from the roof. This time they were
charged with breaking and entering and released
into their parents' custody until their hearing in
front of the Juvenile Court.

A few weeks later Mary brought up the subject
of Martin's death while she was visiting one of the
neighbours, the Howes. She said that she knew
something that would definitely put Norma away.
When asked what, she replied 'Norma put her

36

hands on a boy's throat, and that boy was Martin Brown. She pressed and he just dropped'. However, later the same day she called on Norma's mother and apologized for what she had said. All these events showed what sort of sick and troubled mind the young Mary Bell really had.

Mary's next victim was the son of the family she had told about Norma, three-year-old Brian Howe. Brian's mother had disappeared early in his life and since then he had been looked after by his elder sister, Pat. Pat noticed that Brian was missing on the afternoon of Wednesday, July 31. She enlisted a few of the local children to help her look for him, and two of these children were Mary and Norma Bell. The children knew that one of Brian's favourite play areas was a stretch of waste ground which was nicknamed 'Tin Lizzie'. It got this name because the ground was littered with concrete blocks, oil drums, old building materials and metal tanks.

It was on 'Tin Lizzie' that the police eventually discovered his body, soon after eleven o'clock that night. His torso was covered with long grass and purple-flowering weeds, and he lay between two concrete blocks. Bloodstained froth was coming out from his lips which had turned a horrible blue colour. There were scratches on his nose, and scratches and pressure marks on both sides of his neck. A pair of scissors with one broken blade and the other one bent back, lay a little distance from his body. What looked like the letter 'N', which had subsequently been changed into an 'M', had been scratched on his belly.

One of the policemen on the case, Detective-Chief-Inspector James Dobson of the CID had a gut feeling that this case was connected somehow with the murder of the toddler Martin Brown. The medical opinion, which was based on the small degree of violence used and the playful rather than vicious nature of the marks on Brian's stomach, indicated that it was probably carried out by a child killer.

TIGHTENING THE NET

Within 24 hours of the discovery of the body questionnaires were handed out to all the homes in the area with young children. When questioned, Mary and Norma admitted to having spent most of Wednesday together, and yet their statements about what they had done and where they had been were totally different. Twice they had changed their statements, and at one point Mary had even tried to implicate an eight-year-old boy. She said she had seen him hit Brian, and that she had also seen him playing with a pair of silver-coloured scissors that had something wrong with them, 'like one leg was either broken or bent'. At the time of Mary's interview, nothing about the scissors had been released by the press, which made her a prime suspect.

By August 2, the police had eliminated just about everybody from their list of suspects, except that is, Mary and Norma Bell. On August 4, a detective called at Norma's house to try to get her to clarify some of the inconsistencies in her statement. She immediately started to cry and asked if she could speak to the policeman without her father being in the room. As soon as he left she blurted out: 'I was down Delaval Road with Mary and her dog. Mary took me to see Brian.'

Later that same day Chief-Inspector Dobson spoke to Norma again, this time with her father being present, and said he believed she had something she wanted to tell him about the death of Brian Howe.

Norma told him: 'I went with Mary Bell down to the blocks the day that Brian was lost. I tripped over something. I looked down and saw it was Brian's head. He was covered with grass, but I could see all his face. He was dead. Mary said, "I squeezed his neck and pushed up his lungs, that's how you kill them. Keep your nose dry and don't tell anybody." Brian's lips were purple. Mary ran her fingers along his lips. She said she had enjoyed it. Mary showed me a razor and said she had cut his belly. She pulled his jersey up and showed me the tiny cut on his belly. She hid the razor under a block and told me not to tell my dad or she would get into trouble.'

Norma was taken to the 'Tin Lizzie' in a police car and she produced a razor blade from under one of the blocks. She was then taken back to police headquarters where she made a formal statement.

Meanwhile, Mary Bell was taken out of her bed and escorted down to the police station for questioning. Although she was questioned for over three hours, she continued to deny it all, saying that she didn't know a thing.

Brian Howe was buried on August 7, and Mary came to watch as they bought the coffin out of the house. Chief-Inspector Dobson watched her closely as the coffin came into view. It was then that he realized that he couldn't risk leaving Mary at liberty for another day because she just stood there laughing and rubbing her hands. He knew then that he had to keep her in custody or she would, without doubt, kill someone else.

A policewoman was sent to pick up Mary at 4.30 on that afternoon. Mary arrived at the police station pale, tense and very apprehensive, as if she knew her day of reckoning had arrived. This time she agreed to make a statement, which was the complete reverse of Norma's, implicating her friend as the murderer. A nursing sister who was present during Mary's questioning said afterwards, that she was appalled by the child's callousness. 'She felt nothing. She said all those awful things they had done, but she didn't *feel* a thing.'

THE TRIAL

The trial for the two girls for the murders of Martin Brown and Brian Howe began at Newcastle Assizes on December 5, 1968, and lasted for nine days. Probably the most critical aspects of the trial was the impression that the two girls created in court, and the psychiatric evidence. Both of them stuck to their story that the other was the killer. But Norma, who appeared the more fragile, came across as truthful. In contrast Mary appeared eerily confident, bragging to the prosecution that she wrote the graffiti in the school 'for giggles' and that, 'Murder isn't that bad . . . we all die someday anyway'. She was quick-witted and very much in command of herself, and was obviously the more dominant of the two girls. There was expert evidence that Mary suffered from a psychopathic personality, with symptoms including lack of feeling, a liability to act on impulse, aggression, lack of remorse, and an inability to profit by her experiences.

As the trial continued, evidence started to build up against Mary. Firstly, how did she know that Martin had been asphyxiated as this was not general knowledge, and yet she demonstrated to the Howes how Martin was strangled? Forensic evidence also implicated Mary – grey fibres from one of her wool dresses were discovered on the bodies of both victims. Fibres from Norma's maroon skirt were also found on Brian's shoes.

Handwriting experts confirmed that the notes found at the school were written by both the girls. Every single letter had to be examined separately as Mary and Norma had taken turns to write the letters (they called it 'joining writing'). Norma stated, 'We thought it would be a great big joke'. Mary was supposed to be 'Faggot' and Norma was 'Fanny'.

The presence of Mary's family at the trial certainly did nothing to help her case. Her mother Betty constantly disrupted the proceedings by wailing and sobbing, and her long blonde wig actually slipped off her head on one occasion. Like a poorly-played character from a soap opera, she stormed out of the courtroom, only to reappear moments later. Mary's father, Billy, sat quietly ignoring his wife's amateur dramatics.

Norma was cleared by the jury on the grounds of diminished responsibility, but Mary was found guilty, not of the murder, but of the manslaughter of the two boys. She was sentenced to detention for life in a suitable juvenile detention centre and later the penitentiary.

Norma Bell was given three years probation for breaking and entering the Woodlands Crescent Nursery and was subsequently placed under psychiatric supervision.

REFORM SCHOOL

After the trial Mary Bell was detained at the Red Bank Special Unit from February 1969 until November 1973. Red Bank was a reform school which had a separate high security section. It was well-designed and offered a reasonable degree of comfort. The supportive staff were headed by a man called James Dixon, who was a former navy man and known for his strong moral influence over the inmates. Mr. Dixon helped to provide structure and discipline for Mary, and in time she came to both respect and love him. He filled the role of the benevolent, strong father figure which was so lacking in her life. Mary loved Billy Bell (who was not her biological father but who was in her life right from the beginning) but, as a thief, he was not an ideal role model for Mary.

However, Mary's time at Red Bank was by no means uneventful. In 1970 she reported that she had been sexually assaulted by one of the house-masters and, although her account was considered unreliable, there were changes in staff shortly afterwards which indicated that there may have been some truth in the matter. In 1972 she started provoking the boys and crept into their dormitories late at night. It was also around this time that she started to self-wound herself by making cuts on various parts of her body.

At the age of sixteen she was moved to a prison which was a very traumatic experience for the not only confused, but very angry, teenager. There can be no doubt that this transfer was very destructive in the rehabilitation of Mary Bell. She had to adjust from a mostly male atmosphere at Red Bank to a full women's facility at Styal. It was here that she became a very rebellious prisoner who was frequently being punished. It was while at Styal that she decided to create a 'butch' image, doing everything in her power to persuade the world that she was in fact masculine. She strutted and made up as if she had stubble on her face. She even went as far as rolling up stockings in the shape of male genitals, which she wore all the time. She later asked a doctor for a sex change, but her request was denied. 'It was the idea of not being me,' Mary later said.

In 1977 Mary was transferred to a less secure unit, but managed to escape. She was picked up, along with a fellow escapee, by two young men. In her brief time of freedom, Mary lost her virginity.

The man she slept with later sold his story to a newspaper and claimed that Mary had escaped from jail so that she could get pregnant. A few months before her parole in 1980, Mary was moved to a hostel where she met, and became pregnant by, a married man. When Mary discovered she was pregnant she suffered a moral crisis, but feeling that she would not make a suitable mother, she chose to terminate the pregnancy.

AFTER HER RELEASE

Mary Bell was eventually released on May 14, 1980 and went to live in Suffolk. Her first job was in the local children's nursery, but her probation officers felt this was inappropriate due to the nature of her previous convictions. She took waitress jobs, attended a university, but never seemed to be able to stick at anything for very long. She went back to live with her mother, and shortly afterwards met a young man and once again became pregnant. There was much concern over whether the woman who had murdered two children should be allowed to become a mother herself, but she fought for the right to keep her child, won, and it was born in 1984.

Mary claims that since becoming a mother herself she has a new awareness of the crimes she committed. She was allowed to keep the child, who was technically made a ward of the court until 1992. She eventually met a man and fell in love, settling in a small town. However, her probation officer had to inform the local authorities of her presence, and very soon the villagers were marching through the street with banners showing 'Murderer out!' signs. Apparently she had lived in constant fear of the moment when her true identity would be exposed, and her past continues to haunt her.

Medical experts do not believe that sociopaths can ever be 'cured'. They are normally resistant to therapy, which Mary proved during her internment. Some experts consider that it is possible that aggressive tendencies begin to quieten down with age – perhaps Mary is better but that is something that no one can be really sure about.

The Boy Fiend

*By the age of fourteen Jesse Pomeroy had killed two
people, one male and one female. Prior to those murders,
Jesse sexually and physically assaulted at least seven
other male children. Jesse was a cruel child who revelled
in the pain and terror of his victims.*

Jesse Pomeroy was born on November 29, 1859,
in South Boston. Jesse developed a mysterious
illness shortly after his birth which left him with a
noticeable scar in the white of his right eye, which
later helped in the capture of the miniature
madman. The absence of an iris and pupil gave
the boy an evil aura even before his ghastly acts
became public.

Because Jesse's appearance made him stand out
from other children, he was an easy target for
ridicule by others in his neighbourhood. Apart
from his almost pure white right eye, he had a
larger-than-normal sized head with overly large
ears that stuck out noticeably. Add to this the fact
that he very rarely smiled, preferred to play on his
own, and suffered from epileptic-style shaking
episodes, it was easy to see why he didn't fit in and
found it hard to make friends.

Jesse was the second son of Charles and Ruth
Pomeroy. They came from a lower middle class
family in the Chelsea section of Boston. Jesse's

home life was far from happy. His father, Charles, was a heavy drinker with a mean temper, and he was known to have violently beaten Jesse with a horse whip after he discovered his son had been playing truant from school. The young Pomeroy children lived in dread of being taken behind the outhouse in their garden, because this meant they would receive a severe beating which often ended in bloodshed. Before each beating their father would strip his children naked and this act could possibly have contributed to Jesse forging a link between sexual satisfaction, pain and punishment. Jesse later emulated his father's cruelty on his young victims.

Jesse's evil side first came out when he started to torture animals. The family had owned a couple of birds but they both mysteriously ended up dead, with their heads twisted completely off their bodies. His mother had her suspicions and after Jesse was discovered torturing a neighbour's kitten, she decided it would be unwise to allow another pet into their home. Jesse soon tired of his persecution of animals and turned his attention to human targets, apparently selecting victims that were smaller than himself. His attacks had an eerily familiar pattern – he acted out and enhanced exactly what he had experienced at home.

HIS VICTIMS

His first known victim was four-year-old William Paine. In December 1871, two men were climbing up Powder Horn Hill near the Chelsea Creek in

South Boston. As they passed a small cabin they heard a whimper. On approaching the cabin, the sound grew louder and they discovered it was coming from a small child. They went inside the cabin and were completely sickened by what they saw. Billy was hanging by his wrists from a rope tied to the centre beam of the cabin. He was half-naked and only semi-conscious. The weather was very cold at the time and his skin was very pale and his lips had turned a horrible shade of blue. Due to the blood trapped by the bindings, his hands were a deep purple, in stark contrast to the rest of his body. The men quickly cut the young boy down, and were even more horrified when they saw that his back was covered in red, ugly welts. Billy was not in a fit state to give any evidence as to the identity of his attacker, and the police were hopeful that it was just an isolated incident. Unfortunately, for the children of Chelsea and South Boston, this was not to be the case.

The next victim of Jesse Pomeroy was seven-year-old Tracy Hayden. In February of 1872, Jesse apparently lured Tracy to Powder Horn Hill with the promise of 'going to see some soldiers'. Once the two boys were on their own, Jesse set upon the hapless boy and tortured him mercilessly. Tracy's front teeth were knocked out, his eyes blackened, and his nose broken by the incensed Pomeroy. Just like Billy Paine, Tracy was stripped and whipped, leaving bloody welts on his back. The only description Tracy was able to give to the police was that his attacker had brown hair and that he had threatened to cut off his penis. With nothing more than a description of a teenage boy with brown hair, the police felt they were powerless to stop any further assaults.

In early spring 1872 Jesse struck again – this time it was eight-year-old Robert Maier. This time Jesse lured Robert across the fens with the promise of a trip to see Barnum's circus. Once again his attack followed the same pattern, forcing the young boy to strip and then beating his naked body with a stick. This time he forced his victim to repeat swear words throughout the attack, and Robert later told the police that his attacker was fondling himself throughout the gruelling ordeal. Apparently obtaining sexual satisfaction at the height of Robert's suffering, Jesse then let the youth go and threatened him with death if he told anyone what had happened.

By now the residents of Boston were both angry and scared for the safety of their children. They took their frustrations to the local police who immediately started a massive manhunt. Hundreds of brown-haired teenage boys from the vicinity were questioned, but they came up with no conclusive evidence. Parents of young boys became very vigilant and watched their movements, warning them not to talk to any strange boys. As the word spread, just like Chinese whispers, the boy's description changed dramatically. The new assailant took on a devilish appearance, with red hair and a wispy red beard – very different from the real monster, Jesse Pomeroy, who was still only twelve and had skin as smooth as that of a young girl.

Jesse's next attack came in mid-July of 1872, and a 60- to 90-day cycle seemed to be emerging. This time he persuaded an unwary seven-year-old to go with him to the outhouse on Powder Horn Hill, luring him with the promise of giving him money if he would run an errand for him. The assault was similar to the previous ones in that the boy was stripped, whipped and beaten until Jesse achieved an orgasm. Jesse then fled to the swamps, but not before threatening to kill the boy if he left the outhouse.

The offer of a $500 reward prompted vigilantes to begin patrolling the streets of Chelsea in an effort to track down the evildoer who was torturing their young boys.

THE MOVE TO CHELSEA CREEK

As the hunt for 'the fiend' started to hot up, Ruth Pomeroy decided to move her family from Chelsea to the less expensive area across the Chelsea Creek in South Boston. Although it is possible that she suspected her younger son was connected with the assaults, Ruth Pomeroy was fiercely loyal to Jesse throughout her life. In her heart she must have wanted to believe that her child was not capable of such monstrous acts. However, when she saw that the boy torturer had moved his operations from Chelsea to South Boston at the same time her family relocated, she must have been more than a little suspicious.

George Pratt, a sickly seven-year-old, was wandering along the South Boston shoreline when he was approached by an older boy who offered him some money if he would help him with an errand. The young boy, tempted by the offer of money to buy some sweets, accompanied Jesse where, like the others, he was stripped, bound and tortured. This time, however, Jesse's attack became even more violent. After beating him with a leather belt, he bit a chunk out of the boy's cheek and tore at his young body with his fingernails. Apparently not yet satisfied, Jesse then took a long sewing needle and repeatedly stabbed the child's body. Finally, he tried prying open the boy's eyelid to stick the needle into his eye, but Pratt managed to roll over onto his stomach. By now his sexual appetite satiated, Jesse left the youngster alone and fled, but not before biting another piece of flesh this time from George's buttocks.

It was clear by now that these attacks had been carried out by someone with a very demented mind and the police rounded up any youth in the area that fitted the description, but none of the victims could pick out their attacker. Local anger escalated, and the vigilantes stepped up their patrols of the streets.

Pomeroy's next two attacks showed just how depraved he had become. It was less than a month since he had molested George Pratt when Jesse kidnapped and assaulted a six-year-old boy named Harry Austin. The pattern of the assault was the same as before, after beating the boy with his belt, Jesse bound him and stabbed him under each arm with a pocket knife, and then between his shoulders. But this time it did not end there, for as Austin lay wriggling beneath him, Jesse knelt down and attempted to cut off the boy's penis. Luckily, Jesse was disturbed during the assault and ran before he was able to complete his mission.

The attacks now increased in both frequency and ferocity, despite the intense investigations carried out by the police. Just six days after Austin was attacked, Jesse lured seven-year-old Joseph Kennedy to the marshes and beat him savagely. Once again he was attacked with a knife and this time Jesse forced his victim to kneel down and recite obscenities. When Kennedy protested, Jesse slashed his face with the knife and then dragged him to the waterfront to bathe his face in salt water.

Six days later a five-year-old boy was discovered tied to the railway tracks in South Boston. His story was that he had been lured to a remote area by an older boy who had promised that he would show him some soldiers. Once again, when the pair were on their own, the boy was stripped, beaten and slashed about the head with a knife. As Jesse held the knife to the boy's throat, he was disturbed by some railway workers, causing him to flee the scene. The boy, whose name was Robert Gould, gave the police their first positive clue in the case. He described his attacker as a large boy with an eye like a white marble. With this information to hand, the police were now convinced that it would only be a matter of time before the assailant would be apprehended.

THE ARREST

On September 21, 1872, the police arrived at Jesse Pomeroy's school with one of his victims, Joe Kennedy, and started a room-to-room search. Kennedy, however, was unable to identify his attacker and Jesse narrowly avoided detection.

But then there was a strange twist in the story. For some unknown reason, on his way home from school that same day, Jesse Pomeroy walked into the South Boston police station where detectives were once more questioning Joe Kennedy. Whether Jesse was just playing a game with the police, or whether in fact he wanted to be caught no one will ever really be sure. When Jesse saw Joe Kennedy he quickly turned around and ran out of the door, but this time it was too late. Kennedy had already seen Pomeroy from across the room and excitedly pointed him out to the police. The police chased after Jesse and caught him before he had gone more than half a block.

They locked Jesse up in a cell and the police started to question him. After several hours of tough and intimidating interrogation, Jesse still stuck to his claim of innocence. The police then left him alone to think about his fate and went off to contact his mother. The police left Jesse on his own until after midnight, at which time they woke him up to try and force a confession out of him. They threatened him with a 100-year jail sentence unless he admitted to his crimes. The threats worked and Jesse broke down and confessed to the crimes.

The next day Jesse was taken to the main Boston jail where his victims each confirmed that he was the boy who had molested them. Jesse was bought before the magistrate in the afternoon, and again each of his victims recounted their story. Jesse's mother, Ruth, took the stand and wept, saying that he was a good boy who was both obedient and hardworking, but omitted to tell the Magistrate about the incidents with the animals.

All Jesse had to say in his defence was that 'he couldn't help himself,' and hung his head in shame.

HIS PUNISHMENT

The preferred method of dealing with juvenile delinquents in the late 1800s, was hard work, discipline and vocational training. The Westborough House of Reformation was the place where reprobate boys of all ages were sent if they were convicted of a crime. It was also a place where parents would send their boys if they found them too hard to handle at home.

Westborough was a cruel place where the strong preyed on the weak. The discipline was very harsh, and the inmates were expected to work the majority of the day on tasks such as brass nail making, chair caning and silverplating, on top of which they were expected to attend a four-hour school day. The discipline was along military lines and a smart, cruel boy like Jesse Pomeroy, flourished in such an environment. Most of the boys who had been sent to Westborough were non-violent offenders, their crimes usually being shoplifting, breaking and entering and the vague conviction of 'stubbornness'. Jesse soon learned that if he were to leave Westborough before his 18th birthday, he would need to show the authorities that he had reformed his ways. The records show that he was a model inmate, who avoided floggings and corporal punishment which were given for even the smallest of violations. Although Jesse was mainly left alone during his stay at Westborough, he was teased by some of the older boys and given a wide berth by the younger boys who all knew why he had been sent there.

His obedience and hard work did not go unnoticed, and it wasn't long before Jesse was taken out of his work at the chair shop and assigned as a hall monitor. He loved the position of authority, and took great pleasure in dishing out orders in his dormitory. Jesse was still a model inmate and did not even join a gang of boys when they tried to escape, taking full of advantage of the fact that someone had forgotten to lock a door.

Although outwardly it appeared that Jesse had reformed, one incident that happened towards the end of 1873, showed that he still had a sick and perverse streak inside him. He was approached by one of the teachers to help kill a snake that she had seen outside. Eager to help, Jesse snatched up a stick and followed her into the back garden. After a brief search he found the snake and began to strike it again and again, working himself up into a kind of frenzy as he reduced the writhing snake to an awful, oozing pulp.

KATIE CURRAN

All the time her son was incarcerated, Ruth Pomeroy, kept up a constant campaign to free her son, whom she still considered to be innocent of all the charges. Her argument was that he was too young to be the perpetrator of such horrendous acts, stating that the police had arrested the wrong boy. She wrote letters to the board of Westborough and to anyone else she felt might listen or, alternatively, be able to help her case.

But despite her fervent efforts, it wasn't his mother's pleas that eventually freed Jesse, it was Jesse himself. An investigator from the state had visited his home and found Mrs Pomeroy to be a hardworking, honest and very caring woman. Charles Pomeroy, Jesse's brother, was also considered to be an upstanding citizen who ran a newspaper stand outside his mother's dress shop. The Pomeroys promised to take control of Jesse and to put him to work in both the newsstand and the dress shop. Ruth was determined to keep a much closer eye on her young son, who had previously drifted around very much of his own will. Even the Boston police who, despite the severity of his crimes, were willing to give him a chance to redeem himself.

And so it was that just a year-and-a-half after his arrest, Jesse Pomeroy was released from Westborough and set loose on an unsuspecting public once again. The authorities didn't even bother to warn any of the neighbours that he had been released, and most of them thought that he had been locked away safe and sound until he was at least eighteen years old. This ignorance would turn out to have tragic consequences for the parents of two youngsters.

On March 18, 1874, only six weeks after Jesse was paroled from Westborough, he was opening up his mother's shop and brother's newsstand. It was around 8 a.m. when most children were getting ready for school. As Jesse finished sweeping the store, he started to speak with Rudolph Kohr. Rudolph was a boy around the same age as Jesse, who earned some pocket money by running errands for the Pomeroys. While the two lads chatted away, ten-year-old Katie Curran, came into the shop. She was wearing a black and green check dress, a ragged overcoat and a scarf, and she asked Jesse if he had any notebooks. Katie was looking forward to getting to school as she had a new teacher in her class. As soon as she had finished her breakfast, Katie asked for permission from her mother to go and look for a new notebook. Katie was allowed to go as long as she was back home by 8.30 a.m. so that she could take her younger sister to school.

Jesse told Katie that he did have one notebook left, but that it was a little soiled by an ink spot in one corner of the cover. 'I'll let you have it for two cents less,' he said, giving Katie a good look up and down as they spoke. Jesse asked Rudolph if he would run to the butcher's shop for a few scraps to feed the cats, and taking a few coins from Jesse the boy left them alone in the shop.

Jesse told Katie that there was a storeroom

downstairs and that there might be another notebook there, perhaps she would like to go with him
and have a look. Katie naively agreed and they
started to go down the cellar stairs. As she reached
the bottom couple of steps into the cellar she
realized that she had been tricked, but by then it
was too late. Jesse put his arm around her neck,
covered her mouth with his hand, and cut her
throat with a knife. Then he dragged her behind
the water closet and covered the body with some
stones and ashes.

When he had finished, hearing his brother
coming into the store, Jesse washed his hands at
the pipe in the water closet and ran upstairs. Jesse
carried on with his work just as if nothing had
happened.

Within an hour of Katie's disappearance, her
mother, Mary, was out in the streets frantically
searching for her daughter. She went to Tobin's
General Store where the proprietor told her that he
had sent her over to the Pomeroy's store because
he didn't have any notebooks. This news almost
caused Mary to faint, because she had heard all
about Jesse Pomeroy and she started to fear the
worst. The man at the store reassured Mary that
Jesse would not be a threat to her little girl,
because he came out of rehabilitation a completely
reformed character. 'Besides, he only hurt little
boys. He never attacked a girl.'

The police advised Mary Curran to go home,
saying that her daughter had probably only got
lost and that the authorities would soon be bringing her home. However, a day passed and the news

spread of Katie's disappearance. It was then that Rudolph Kohr came forward and told Mary that he had seen Katie in the Pomeroy's store. Again Mary went to the police.

Once more the police told Mary Curran not to worry because the Kohr boy was known to be a liar, but he would send Detective Adams to the shop to have a look around. Adams was met by a very unfriendly Ruth Pomeroy, who of course knew nothing of the body in the basement of her shop. Angry that her son was being accused once more, she begrudgingly allowed the policeman to search her shop. As he expected, Adams found nothing amiss.

As the weeks passed by, the police continued their investigations and even speculated that Katie's father had shipped the girl off to a convent. She was the product of a Protestant-Catholic marriage, and in a Protestant town like Boston, anti-Catholic feelings ran deep. When a tenable witness came forward who swore he had seen Katie being lured into a wagon, the police allegedly closed their investigation with the conclusion that the unfortunate girl had been kidnapped.

MORE BLOODLUST

Completely oblivious to the danger of being caught, Jesse Pomeroy continued in his efforts to lure young children into the fens and deserted buildings of South Boston. Most of the children were smart enough not to fall for his ploys, but one small five-year-old came very close to falling into his trap.

Jesse approached the youngster and asked if he knew where Vernon Street was. When Harry Field told Jesse that he did know where it was, Jesse offered him five cents to take him there. They walked off down the street hand-in-hand, Jesse clutching a broom handle in his free hand. When they arrived at Vernon Street, Harry asked for his money, but instead Jesse pulled him into a doorway and ordered him to keep quiet. He then led Harry through a maze of streets in search of a quiet spot to carry out his perverse crime. Luckily, though, fate was to be on Harry's side that day. As the two boys turned a corner, they came across another boy from the same neighbourhood who knew of Jesse's reputation. As the two boys started arguing, Harry managed to pull his hand free and ran home to his mother. Undoubtedly, the anonymous youth who came along just at the right moment, saved young Harry Field's life, but the next boy Jesse lured was not to be so lucky.

The Millen family had moved to Dorchester Street in April 1874. Their youngest child was four-year-old Horace, who had an almost angelic appearance. Horace loved sweets and on this particularly chilly spring morning he had managed to persuade his mother to let him have a couple of pennies to spend at the local bakery. On his way there he met up with an older boy – Jesse Pomeroy. Horace bought a small cake at the bakery which he generously shared with Jesse. Jesse innocently suggested that they take a trip to the nearby harbour, and Horace happily slipped his hand into Jesse's as they set off.

A number of people saw the two boys heading off towards the bay, and one woman even recalled the look of excitement on the older boy's face. The last witness to see Horace alive, besides Jesse, was a beachcomber who noticed that the older boy kept looking back over his shoulder as if he was being followed. But he merely shrugged and went back to scouring the shoreline for flotsam.

The two boys headed off across the marshland, eventually stopping in a swale, a shallow trough-like depression that carried water mainly during rainstorms or when the snow melted, which afforded them a little more privacy.

'Let's rest for a minute,' Jesse told Horace, who was still totally unaware of the danger he was in. As soon as Horace sat down Jesse took out his pocket knife and in a frenzied rage grabbed the boy and slit his throat. Horace was still alive after the first attack which angered Jesse even more, and he went berserk repeatedly stabbing the helpless youngster over and over again. His hands and lower arms showed signs of defensive wounds, which meant that even though he was badly injured Horace tried his hardest to fight back. Eventually Jesse succeeded in slicing through Horace's windpipe, which finally ended the wretched child's ordeal. However, Jesse's appetite for blood was not satisfied and he continued to hack at the body, particularly in the area of the genitals. He also punctured the boy's right eye through the eyelid and attempted to castrate the boy, mutilating his scrotum.

Horace Millen died in the early afternoon, but

his mutilated body was not discovered until around 4 p.m. Two brothers who had been playing on the beach, ran up the hill that hid Horace's body from sight. On reaching the top they saw what looked like a rag doll at the bottom of the small valley. The brothers called over some men who were on the marshes hunting ducks and, leaving one adult and a boy guarding the body, the others split up to go and fetch the police.

There were deep gouges in the sand made by the young lad's legs in his attempts at fighting off his attacker. But what was even more nauseating was that when the coroner examined the body the boy's fists were so tightly clenched in agony that the fingernails were embedded in the palms, indicating that four-year-old Horace Millen had died an excruciating death. The examiner knew this had to be the work of a complete madman.

Once their gruesome task was over, the coroner's jury issued a report to the many reporters who had gathered outside the mortuary in the hope of a story. It didn't take police long to identify the victim and shortly after 9 p.m. a police officer went to the Millen home to give them the dreadful news.

There was only one logical suspect – the teen with the strange eye who loved to torture young boys. The crime fitted his *modus operandi* perfectly. The only problem was – or so the press and police authorities believed – was that Jesse Pomeroy was safely locked away at Westborough Reformatory. Was it possible that there was another such evil fiend in the South Boston area?

They soon got their answer, however, when the Boston chief of detectives reported that Jesse Pomeroy had in fact been released on parole. The police were immediately ordered to go and pick him up. They found him at home and, despite his mother's protests, Jesse was once again taken into custody. Jesse reassured his mother that he hadn't done anything and it wouldn't be long before he would be back home. But Jesse Pomeroy was never to spend another night in that house on Broadway.

Jesse was subjected to harsh interrogation. He stood up to the barrage of questions fired at him for quite some time, denying any knowledge of the crime and offering explanations of where he had been all day. However, his story left big gaps that he could not account for and, more importantly, he was unable to offer an alibi for his movements between the times of 11 a.m. and 3 p.m. The officers carefully examined their suspect and his clothing was confiscated pending further investigation. When questioned as to how he got the scratches on his face, Jesse replied that he had done it whilst shaving. When asked if he owned a knife, Jesse hesitantly admitted that he had one at home. A sergeant was sent to the house to find it and returned a short while later with the evidence. The knife, with a three-inch blade, was clogged with dirt and there appeared to be dried blood on the handle.

While the coroner took the knife to see if it would fit Horace Millen's wounds, Jesse was left alone in a cell, where he promptly fell into a peaceful sleep.

The next morning, detectives went to the fens armed with Jesse's boots and Horace's shoes in an attempt to place both the boys at the crime scene. They found a meandering trail of both large and small footprints in the area, and after making a plaster of Paris cast of the prints, discovered that the larger ones matched perfectly with the shoes they had just taken from the feet of the young Jesse Pomeroy. Now, armed with the evidence that Jesse had definitely been at the scene of the crime, the officers returned to the South Boston precinct to wake up the sleeping fourteen-year-old.

Jesse continued to deny any involvement. Then Captain Henry Dyer, suggested that if Jesse was innocent, he wouldn't object to going to the funeral parlour to see Horace's body. Despite his objections, Jesse was taken down to the undertakers where, confronted with the fruits of his crime, he broke down and admitted killing Horace Millen.

'I am sorry I did it,' he wept. 'Please don't tell my mother.'

When asked if he knew what would happen to him now, Jesse replied, 'Put me somewhere so I can't do such things'.

When Jesse Pomeroy was finally called to the stand at the inquest, he once again denied everything and told a much more convincing story of how he had spent the fateful day. The evidence against him was sufficient to warrant the charges and he was indicted for first-degree murder.

The penalty in Massachusetts for murder was death by hanging, but the state had never had to execute anyone as young as fourteen. On the other hand, they had never had anyone as young as Jesse commit such a heinous crime. So, even before the case went to trial, there was a lot of discussion about what should happen to the boy.

REPERCUSSIONS

Things were going from bad to worse for Ruth Pomeroy and her son Charles, as they lived in close proximity to both the Millen and Curran families. Business at the shop and the newsstand were declining rapidly and it seemed the only people that now ventured in were curious onlookers who just wanted to see where the notorious Jesse had worked. Ruth did not make life easy for herself because, whilst still proclaiming her son's innocence, she blamed the two grieving families for the fate of her son. Ruth realized that they could no longer make a living out of the shop and decided to close the store down. Ruth and Charles left the original building in Broadway and tried in vain to eke out some sort of a living. Unbeknown to the Pomeroys, their former co-tenant in the building back at Broadway was enjoying great success in his business and decided it was time to expand. This expansion meant that the basement of Ruth's former shop needed to be refurbished, and it wasn't long before the workmen found the decaying remains of Katie Curran's body.

When her body was uncovered, Katie's head was severed from her body. The body was in such a state of decomposition that it was difficult for the coroner to assess quite how badly she had been hurt, but one thing that did come to light was that her genitalia had been a particular target of her murderer.

The police were in no doubts as to who had committed this atrocious act, but what they did need to ascertain was whether his family had known about it. Both Ruth and Charles were immediately taken into custody as accessories to murder. When confronted with the news of the discovery and the subsequent arrest of his family, Jesse seemed totally unperturbed, adding that he didn't know anything about it. The detectives gave him two days to think over what had transpired and then gave him the final opportunity to clear his mother and brother. It was then that Jesse confessed to killing Katie Curran. He recounted the details of the murder step-by-step in chillingly sharp detail, pointing out that his family knew nothing of the murder until the day the body was found.

LIFE OR DEATH?

Now Jesse Pomeroy stood accused of two murders and it looked all the more likely that Jesse Pomeroy would be the youngest person ever executed in the state of Massachusetts. The only way he could escape the gallows was if it could be proved that he was legally insane at the time he committed the crimes. This was the question that was left for Jesse Pomeroy's lawyers to prove – was their client just plain sick or was he legally insane? The outcome would mean the difference between life and death.

While the public and the press were calling for

his head, doctors started to examine Jesse to see if they could find out what was going on in his mind.

It was a Doctor John Tyler that managed to get closest to the truth when they started to examine Jesse. On their very first meeting, Jesse told the doctor all about his history of molesting children younger than himself, and blamed the attacks on 'a sudden impulse or feeling' which just came over him. He also told him that just before he committed each crime he felt a sharp pain on the left side of his head which subsequently passed to the right side and then went back and forth. It was the pain that prompted the violence, he claimed.

'The feeling that accompanied the pain was that I must whip or kill the boy or girl . . . and it seemed to me that I could not help doing it,' he told Tyler. Jesse quite freely confessed his crimes to his doctors, or that was the case until the day he received a note from his mother. Having read this note Jesse started to deny his role in the killings, saying that he had a voice in his head calling on him to stand up and defend himself. Two months before he went to trial, Jesse repudiated his confessions and in a conversation with Tyler adamantly denied having anything to do with either murder.

Tyler issued a final report which stated that Jesse 'envinces no pity for the boys tortured or the victims of his homicide, and no remorse or sorrow for his acts'. He finished his report by saying that Jesse could discriminate between right and wrong and felt that the boy was, and forever would be, a threat to society. He finished by saying that in his opinion, Jesse Pomeroy was insane.

THE TRIAL

The trial opened on December 8, 1874, before a packed courtroom in Boston. Throughout the often boring, but sometimes gruesome testimonies, Jesse sat unemotionally, with a look of boredom and indifference on his face. Jesse's lawyer laid all the groundwork for an insanity defence, and called up witnesses who could back up his assertion. The first witness was Jesse's own mother, Ruth, who, under intense questioning, told of the number of childhood illnesses that had left Jesse mentally deranged. Most notable of these was the sickness he suffered just before his first birthday, a brain fever which induced a three-day delirium followed by an unexplained shaking of the head. Following that, Jesse suffered from numerous mental ailments – insomnia, dizziness and frequent violent headaches. Other witnesses who took the stand followed with similar lines of testimony.

The prosecution, however, contradicted the two defence lawyers, stating that Jesse was cunning and deeply manipulative, and said that the boy was totally free of any mental defect.

The jury retired to ponder Jesse's fate. It took them five hours to reach a verdict – Jesse Pomeroy was found guilty of first-degree, premeditated, murder. The sentence for such a crime was mandatory – death by hanging. However, the jurors requested leniency for the boy on account of his age. This was a decision only the governor could grant, and the judge had no option but to condemn the prisoner to death.

Although capital punishment in 19th century America was usually swift, because Jesse was still only fourteen years of age, there was considerable argument against carrying out the punishment. The final decision was left in the hands of Governor William Gaston, who appointed a committee to study the case and report back to him. When the committee came back hopelessly divided, Gaston turned to the people for a public hearing.

Many weeks went by and in this time another Boston child died at the hands of a second mentally disturbed young man, this time in his twenties. This instigated a public outcry for a decision in the Pomeroy case – by this time things had reached fever pitch. Gaston reconvened his committee for further debate and a final vote. By a vote of 5–4, the committee recommended that the sentence stand and that Gaston should sign the death warrant. But Gaston remained resolute in his unwillingness to execute Jesse. It was probably this decision that cost Gaston his re-election and in 1876 Alexander Rice was appointed the new governor of Massachusetts.

Two years after the trial, in 1887, when the hunger for Jesse's blood had died down, Rice called his advisors together and discussed the fate of the boy waiting on death row. The decision was that although the punishment must remain severe, people were now distant enough from the crime to accept a lesser form of punishment. Rice was in agreement and, without causing too much attention in the press, he commuted Jesse's death sentence to life in prison. However, to make the sentence more severe due to the severity of the crime, Rice ordered that Jesse serve his sentence in solitary confinement.

Jesse was confined in Charlestown State Prison, and the only visitor Jesse ever received during his time there was his mother, Ruth, who was permitted to see him once a month. Jesse suffered a exceptionally boring existence, he ate alone in his cell, exercised alone, and was periodically allowed to bathe. He was granted access to reading material and became a voracious learner.

Over his years of confinement, with nothing more to occupy his mind, he made several attempts to dig his way out. He did on one occasion actually manage to get out of his cell, and on another he attempted to blow off his cell door by stopping up a gas line. The only people he ever saw were the guards who patrolled by his door.

Finally, in 1917, four decades after he was imprisoned in his little cell, Jesse's sentence of solitary confinement was relaxed and he was allowed to move in with the other inmates. For a while he relished in the fact that he was the prison's most notorious inmate. He loved approaching new prisoners, introducing himself and asking them what they knew about him. It pleased Jesse greatly that most of the inmates had grown up hearing of the infamous Jesse Pomeroy. But over the years when young men sent to Charlestown prison had never heard of him, Jesse became just another old face in the anonymous prison crowd.

Gradually his health began to deteriorate and he was moved from Charlestown to Bridgewater prison farm, where he could receive better medical care. It was his first and only ride in a car and he showed no sign of excitement or curiosity whatsoever in a world that had long stopped having any meaning for him.

Jesse Pomeroy died at the age of 71 after having spent 58 years of his life behind bars, almost all of it spent in solitary confinement. He was dismissed by the press as 'the most friendless person in the world . . . a psychopath'.

Jessie Holtmeyer

In Clearfield, Pennsylvania, unable to sleep the last 48 hours, Rick and Jodi Dotts watched the clock and paced the floor. Their eyes were bleary, their bodies exhausted, but they could not sit still . . .

It was Mother's Day, Sunday the 10th of May, 1998, around 5.45 p.m. Rick Dotts was driving home along a bumpy country backroad after having first stopped at the shops. He had been working long hours and was exhausted. On the front seat beside him were a dozen red roses for his wife. He was looking forward to a nice dinner with his family as his oldest daughter was coming home for a visit. All of a sudden his car hit a deer.

He stopped the car and got out to see if the deer was still alive. As he stared at the motionless doe a dark premonition replaced the nice thoughts he had been happening, and he somehow knew that something horrible was about to happen . . .

THE GANG

Jessica Holtmeyer was a second-year student at Clearfield High in a small rural Pennsylvanian town. She was a big-boned, tall and very intimi-

72

dating teenager. She loved to make fun of people at her school, especially taunting them about their clothes and hairstyles. She was both rough and tough with a frighteningly mean streak. She was known to worship the Devil, cut herself with razors, and loved to frighten other kids by pulling out a knife. She had a tattoo '666' behind her left ear which was the sign for the Devil. She had a self-tattoo on her right forearm of a pentagram, or a five-pointed star which is said to have mystical significance. She had two other tattoos, one on the back of her neck 'Kurt Cobain 1967–1994' and her boyfriend's name on her shoulder. Jessie Holtmeyer had pure evil running through her veins. In her early teens, she had killed many animals. Once she gathered six feral cats into a bin liner, set it on fire and then threw it into a river. Another time, she strangled a poodle to death with its own leash.

In 1968, when Jessie was 16, she made plans with a gang of friends to run away to Florida. The gang, six in total, gathered together late one morning on Mother's Day, May 10, and went to pick up one more member for the trip – Jessie Holtmeyer. The gang, unbeknown to Jessie, had invited fifteen-year-old Kimberly Dotts to join them. Kimmy, as she was known, was learning-disabled and badly wanted to be friends with the gang. The group arrived at the house where Jessie lived with her grandparents. They were out at church and Jessie had just started to watch the movie *Scream* when she answered the door.

Her first reaction on seeing Kimmy was to scowl and then she turned to her boyfriend, Aaron

Straw, and hissed, 'What is *she* doing here? You know I don't like her.'

Most of the gang were ambivalent towards Kimmy, but two members were adamant that she couldn't come along – Tracy and Jessica. It was left to Dawn to try and calm the situation as the tension mounted. The whole gang went into the house to watch *Scream*. Fifteen minutes into the movie, the den filled with shrieks as they watched Drew Barrymore's character being hanged by a masked killer.

'It'd be fun to hang someone,' Jessie said to the others.

When the film was over, the gang went over to Tracy's friend's house. Her friend was 22-year-old Mike Jarrett, and they intended to use his blue Dodge van to get out of Clearfield. However, before he was prepared to leave, Mike said he needed to have a sleep before the long journey ahead. He drove the gang to the nearby town of Shiloh and dropped them off while he had a rest. Their plan was that he would sleep for a few hours while they broke into hunters' campers to stock up on provisions for their excursion.

Kimmy just went along with the gang, helping them to break into a couple of trailers. They purloined some bottles of whisky, a few sparklers, and Jessie stole a length of nylon rope.

Jessie and Tracy were starting to bond over their hatred of Kimmy, and they led the rest of their crew to Gallows Harbor, which was a clearing in the woods of Shiloh. It received its name from a 19th century lynching that took place there.

Gallows Harbor was a popular place for the kids of Clearfield County to party and so Kimmy gladly followed her new friends deep into the woods.

THE INITIATION CEREMONY

When they arrived at the clearing Jessie proudly showed her friends the nylon rope that she had stolen.

Jessica ordered the 14-year-old Theresa Wolfe to make the rope into a noose, and then to place it around Kimmy's neck. All of which she did. Jessica then grabbed the end of rope and yanked Kimmy around as hard as she could. The wretched girl lost her balance and fell to the muddy ground. Jessica dragged her through the sludge. By this time Kimmy was crying, but the rest of the gang were just standing by and laughing.

Jessie removed the rope from Kimmy's neck and ordered Aaron to throw the end of the rope over a maple tree branch which was about fourteen feet off the ground.

Tracy said that anyone who wanted to go to Florida had to put their head through the noose as part of an initiation ceremony. Theresa and Dawn's boyfriend, 16-year-old Patrick Lucas, both volunteered to show that they weren't scared. One other member, a Clearfield junior named Clint Canaway, also agreed.

Patrick was the first one to slip his head through the noose, laughing nervously as he did it. Both Jessica and Aaron tightly gripped the end of the rope, but they did not pull it. Then Theresa did the same, and again Jessica and Aaron did not tug. The next one up was Clint and by now everyone was starting to giggle. Again nothing happened and Tracy's little game was becoming a good source of amusement.

'See, Kimmy,' Tracy said to her cousin, 'There's nothing to be afraid of . . . Now it's your turn.'

Trusting her friends Kimmy took her turn, but this time Jessica and Aaron pulled hard on the rope using all their strength. Kimmy was lifted off the ground and her hands instinctively grabbed to release the tightness of the rope around her neck. All the colour drained from her face, her legs kicked about erratically, and she started to convulse. Tracy, Jessica and Aaron were falling about with laughter, but the rest of the gang had fallen silent. They were uneasy and felt that the game was going too far . . .

Suddenly the gang were startled by the sound of a truck in the distance. They dropped the end of the rope and Kimmy fell to the ground with a loud, painful thud. She immediately curled up into a ball, crying and wheezing. Then, Jessica announced that she hadn't finished with her yet. It was at this point that four of the gang – Clint, Dawn, Patrick and Tracy – left. Although none of them opposed the further torture of Kimmy, they all literally turned their backs and took a walk through the woods because they didn't want to watch whatever Jessica had in store for Kimberly. It seemed they didn't really care what happened to her, it was just that they didn't want to watch.

While half the pack walked away from the

scene, those remaining resumed their entertainment. Kimmy was hanged for a second time, and this time her face turned a deathly white, then blue. Her legs thrashed about so violently that she lost both her shoes. Once again she went into convulsions but still neither Jessie nor Aaron let go of the rope. Theresa just stood by and watched in silence as Kim Dott's body stopped flailing and her body went limp. It was then that Jessie and Aaron let her fall to the ground.

Theresa walked over to the motionless body and checked for a pulse. There didn't appear to be one. Aaron picked up a stick and poked Kimmy in the stomach to see if he got a response. There was none, Jessica had won, Kimmy was dead.

The three started to cover Kim's body with brush, truly thinking she was dead, but then, unexpectedly, she twitched. Both Theresa and Aaron stepped back in shock as Kim started to cough and gasp for air. She was alive!

Jessica was not happy with that and when she saw her victim clinging to life, she picked up a large rock about the size of a basketball, stood over Kimmy, and dropped it on her face. She did this a few more times until Kimmy's head resembled a smashed cantaloupe melon.

Theresa and Aaron were motionless, their mouths agape in total shock.

'Why did you do that, Jessie? You killed her!' Theresa exclaimed.

With cold, unfeeling eyes Jessie replied, 'That's what snitches get'.

Her killers left her battered body under a pile of

twigs and branches and just walked away, vowing silence. As Theresa saw the rest of the gang walking towards them she cried, 'I wouldn't go back there, you guys. They just killed Kim.'

AFTERMATH

Within an hour of their horrific act, the gang was back in Mike Jarrett's van heading for Kim's home state. They didn't mention anything about Kim to Mike or his friend John Appleton, who had decided to ride to Florida with them at the last minute.

The Clearfield gang were safely on their way out of the district and away from the scene of the crime. All that is, except Jessica, who for some unknown reason had changed her mind about leaving. She and the rest of the gang had made a pact on leaving Gallows Harbor that not one of them would ever breathe a word about what had happened on that fateful day. They all agreed to tell the same concocted story that they had last seen Kim on Sunday morning, May 10, when they dropped her off at Sheetz's on their way down south.

On Monday, May 11, Jessica went to all her classes at Clearfield High as if nothing had ever happened. Meanwhile, Tracy, Clint, Dawn, Patrick, Aaron, Theresa, Mike Jarrett and John Appleton were halfway to Lakeland, Florida.

By the time the Dotts family were frantic and they posted 'Have you seen this child?' flyers all around the town.

On May 13, the remainder of the gang arrived in Lakeland. Appleton, Jarrett and Tracy Lewis dropped the teenagers off at one of their friend's houses and then headed back to Clearfield. It was while they were driving back that Tracy confessed to the boys that they had killed Kim.

Nine days after Kimberly Dotts was reported missing, on May 19, 1998, John Appleton called the police. Searchers looking for the missing girl were then able to go and uncover the body.

Jessie and Tracy were immediately taken into custody, while Clint, Theresa, Dawn, Patrick and Aaron were all expedited from Florida.

Twelve jurors and three alternates were chosen in Bloomsburg, 105 miles east of Clearfield. They chose out-of-county jurors because Jessica's lawyer argued that there was too much publicity in Clearfield.

THE CONVICTIONS

Patrick Lucas and Clint Canaway were convicted in August 1998. They each got six months in a juvenile facility for Hindering Apprehension, Burglary (for breaking into the campers), and Conspiracy.

In September, after four months behind bars, Dawn Lanager and Theresa Wolfe were tried separately. Dawn, the girl who had actually lured Kim into the hands of death, got off with probation. She was released the same day as her trial. Theresa Wolfe, the one who fashioned the rope into a noose and stood by while Kim was lynched, was sentenced to six months imprisonment.

Tracy Lee Lewis, who was already on parole for punching her boyfriend's six-year-old, was sentenced from five to twenty years for Reckless Endangerment and Aggravated Assault. With good behaviour, she could be free any day now.

Theresa, Clint, Dawn and Patrick are already free.

However, Jessica Holtmeyer and Aaron Straw will be spending the rest of their lives behind bars, with no possibility of parole. Jessica Holtmeyer has the parents of the girl she killed to thank for not receiving the death penalty. Shortly after the jury found Holtmeyer guilty of first-degree murder in the brutal killing of Kimberly Jo Dotts, the father said, 'I believe everybody deserves a second chance'.

Hannah Ocuish

Hannah Ocuish was the youngest person to be hanged in America, she was twelve years and nine months and described as a half-breed Italian girl. She was executed on December 20, 1786 for the murder of a six-year-old girl whom she had beaten to death following an argument.

Hannah was born on the east coast of the United States in 1774 into a very poor family. She grew up being bounced from foster home to foster home and was believed to be developmentally disabled. Her mother was a full-blooded Pequot Indian and an alcoholic. Her father abandoned the family when Hannah was only a toddler and it is well known that she had an unstable home life.

Hannah was only six years old when she had her first run-in with the police. Although still very young she was crafty enough to concoct a plan that would get her family some much-needed money. Using her wily skills she managed to convince her eight-year-old brother to join her in a robbery. Their target was a small girl, who they beat badly and then stole her locket. But the unfortunate siblings were found out and the people of the town ordered that they were made to serve a life of servitude.

When Hannah was twelve she was serving as a slave to a rich lady who lived in New London,

Connecticut. The lady was renowned for being a preteen terror and the children in her neighbourhood were said to have been scared of her overpowering nature.

In the summer of 1786 the fields of New London were full of beautiful ripe strawberries. Hannah's mistress gave her permission to go picking one lovely sunny afternoon, in a strawberry patch quite near the slave's quarters. This is where the tough little Hannah ran into a rather snooty, over-indulged girl who was about half her age. The child's name was Eunice Bolles and Hannah was determined to get her hands on her basket which was already full of lovely juicy berries. Little by little she browbeat Eunice into giving her the basket, for which Hannah was duly punished. Five weeks later – Miss Hannah Ocuish struck back!

HANNAH'S REVENGE

On her way back from school one morning, Eunice passed by the house where Hannah lived. On seeing the girl, Hannah grabbed a cloth from the kitchen and a rock from the garden. Eunice was about a hundred feet from the front porch, as Hannah ran up to meet her with a big false grin on her face. She cunningly lured the hapless Eunice into a secluded area behind a fence and proceeded to hit her a few dozen times by swinging the rock inside the kitchen cloth. With her victim already close to death, Hannah strangled Eunice with one of her shoelaces and then buried her under a pile of heavy stones. However, there is a possibility that the wretched Eunice was still alive at this point.

As soon as Eunice's family realized that she was missing they alerted the police, who immediately started to scour the neighbourhood. Her body was found the very same day. She had been very badly maimed and Hannah was an immediate suspect. Hannah's story was that she had seen four boys who she didn't recognize trespassing in her master's garden. She had shouted at the boys to leave and before they ran away she had heard the sound of crashing rocks. Eventually, however, she broke down and confessed to the murder.

She was sentenced to death by hanging, and still holds the record today for being the country's youngest female executed at the age of twelve years and nine months. She was sent by Ezra Stiles, the President, to her execution on December 20, 1786.

Yale minister, Henry Channing, was invited to speak at Hannah's execution. She was put on public display and reprimanded by the clergyman while the remainder of the community cheered. Rev. Channing then read a passage from the Bible as a terrified Hannah stepped up to the gallows to meet her gruesome fate.

'Withhold not correction from the child, for if thou beatest him with the rod he shall not die. Thou shalt beat him with the rod and shalt deliver his soul from hell.'

(Proverbs 23:13,14)

Robert Thompson and Jon Venables

Although both Jon and Robert were considered to be delinquents, nothing in their past lives indicated that they could be so viciously cruel and to someone so young.

Venables and Thompson had both been playing truant from school one chilly afternoon in February 1993. The two schoolboys were close friends, as well as being disreputable trouble-makers from broken homes.

Robert Thompson was the tough one, a pure-bred mischief-maker, with an appearance to match. He had a shaven head and was rather stocky in build. In comparison, Jon Venables was much thinner and rather fragile in appearance, and was far more sensitive and naive than his friend.

On the morning of Friday, February 12, Jon Venables left his Merseyside home for school. He had a note in his bag from his mother asking if he could take the class gerbils home so he could look after them during the school holidays. On his route to school he passed his friend Robert Thompson, who was hanging around with his younger brother.

Both Jon and Robert disliked school intensely and felt like outcasts in the classroom. They had both been kept behind a grade, which only seemed to make the matter worse, probably due to the fact that they felt ashamed and different from their fellow classmates. As a result of this they became expert at being truants.

The pair of boys decided to spend the morning at the Bootle Strand shopping centre, with the sole intention of stealing. Sales assistants watched the pair carefully, as their school uniforms were a sure sign they were bunking off school which usually meant they were looking for trouble. They lurked around the counters and waited until the sales-person turned away before stuffing anything they could into their pockets. They stole numerous items including batteries, enamel paint, pens and pencils, a troll doll, some fruit and sweets, makeup and other small trinkets. They usually threw away most of what they stole, for the stealing was the fun part.

After a couple of hours the couple became bored with their 'shopping' spree. They sat down and discussed what would make their outing more exciting and came upon the idea of stealing a 'little person'. They considered that would be much more fun.

It was a little after 3 o'clock, about the time they would normally leave school, when Venables and Thompson strolled nonchalantly through the shopping centre, looking for a small, unsupervised child. Perhaps in their poor, sick minds, they felt by doing this it would prove that they were no longer babies themselves.

While in the T J Hughes department store, a woman noticed that her 3-year-old daughter and 2-year-old son were playing with a couple of older boys. The boys, Jon and Robert, were kneeling down opening and closing purses, which held the younger children's attention. She called them back but it wasn't long before they strayed off again to join the older boys. When the woman had finished paying for her purchases, she found her daughter and asked her where her young brother had gone. 'Gone outside with the boys,' her daughter answered. In a state of panic, the woman rushed out of the shop calling her child's name. She saw Jon and Robert encouraging her son to follow them, but when Jon saw the woman following them, they froze and sent the small boy back to his mother. Jon and Robert quickly disappeared from sight and pondered on what to do next.

THE ABDUCTION

A little while later they found exactly what they were looking for, a small boy – James Bulger – playing alone with some cigarette butts in an ashtray outside of a butcher's shop in the centre. Baby James had only just wandered away from his mother's side minutes before Jon and Robert approached him. Denise Bulger was normally a very vigilant mother, she had lost her first child during pregnancy and she didn't want anything to happen to her precious son. But James was tired and had started to get fractious, and rather than have him squirming and whining in her arms, she felt it would be quite safe to leave him by the door of the butcher's shop for a moment on his own.

Denise chatted quite happily to some people in the long line of people waiting to be served, and momentarily her concentration was off her little boy. In fact it wasn't until she had completed her purchase that Denise Bulger noticed her son had gone missing. She called out for him in the shop and asked all the strangers around her if they had seen a 2-year-old with blond hair wearing a blue anorak. Denise became frantic and headed straight for the security office, who announced the disappearance of James Bulger over the loud-speakers. She made a careful description of the child saying that he was wearing a grey sweatshirt, a blue anorak, and his tee-shirt had the word 'Noddy' printed on it. Initially the security guards were not too alarmed as it was quite normal for young children to get lost in the crowds at the shopping centre. But then when no-one responded to their announcement, the alarm bells started to ring.

Denise and the guards searched for Jamie throughout the centre until 4.15 p.m., at which time they called the police to report that he was missing. By the time the police arrived to interview Denise Bulger, Jon, Robert and James were already about a mile away from the shopping centre.

Jon and Robert left the Bootle Strand and walked up Stanley Road, virtually dragging the small boy between them. As soon as James realized he was being taken away from his mother he had started crying and making a fuss. As soon as he started to whine for his mummy and tried to stop walking, the older boys would force him to go on by punching, kicking and shaking him until he could nothing but cooperate. For nearly ninety minutes Jon and Robert wandered around town with James Bulger, covering more than a two mile radius. During those ninety minutes they took James into a couple of stores, including a pet shop and a bakery. They pulled him down a grassy slope to a canal under a bridge. It was here that they first hurt James Bulger by dangling him upside down and then dropping him on his head. After a few minutes into that particular torture game, the boys decided to stop as it wasn't quite dark yet and they knew someone could easily peer down the hill and discover them hurting the little boy.

It was at this point that Jon and Robert turned away from the little boy, leaving him alone and crying by the side of the canal. A woman saw James and assumed he was with some other children who were nearby. But whatever was going on inside of Jon and Robert's heads they turned around and walked back towards the toddler. 'Come on, baby,' they called. Jon picked up the bruised and whimpering James in his arms, following Robert up the bank. They got to the top of the hill, adjusted the toddler's coat and scarf to cover as much of his swollen face as possible, then wandered around the town some more until it became dark. Again they were seen by quite a few people during this period. They must have seen that the child had a tear-streaked face, and a cut on his forehead, but although it made several people very uneasy, it appeared no one really knew what to do. Possibly if James had cried out for his mother or if the older boys had acted cruelly, then perhaps someone would have come forward to rescue the hapless child.

At around 5.30 p.m., when the boys felt it was finally dark enough, they took James to one of their favourite play areas – some railway tracks. It was here that they knocked the toddler to the ground and jumped on his belly and chest. Jon opened a jar of bright blue paint he had stolen earlier from the shopping centre and splashed it across the baby's face. Robert removed Jamie's shoes and underpants, and then callously inserted the stolen batteries into his rectum. One of the boys found a two-foot long heavy iron pipe which they used to hit him around the head, also hurling bricks and stones at his tiny body.

When the frenzy of their assault was over, Jon took hold of James by his legs while Robert carried the torso. They carried him directly over the railway tracks and laid him down so that that his upper half was off the tracks, while his naked legs were on them. They left before the train arrived.

AFTER THE EVENT

After their assault on James Bulger, the boys walked back into town as if nothing untoward had happened. They called on a friend who wasn't at home, but then hung around in front of his house waiting for him to come back. Bored with waiting, they wandered over to the video store, which was one of Robert's favourite places. It was here that Susan Venables, Jon's mother, swung through the doors in a furious rage. Susan told him that a little boy had been kidnapped from the shopping centre and that she was out of her mind with worry that they may have taken her son, Jon.

Meanwhile, Robert had run home in tears telling his mother, Ann, that Jon Venables' mother had hit him while they were in the video store. Robert's mother immediately reported the beating to the police. At the police station, the officer noticed a small scratch underneath Robert's left eye, but assumed it was from the attack by Susan Venables.

While all this was going on other detectives were studying the security camera footage of Jamie Bulger's kidnapping. Expecting the abductor to be an adult – possibly a paedophile – they were stunned when the tape showed two little boys, not that much bigger than Bulger himself, making off with the little boy.

The video, which was taken from a camera just above the shopping centre's main exit, was copied and handed out to local news stations for their broadcast the following day. The fuzzy, almost ghost-like footage showed the backs of three boys leaving the centre, but not their faces. All you could make out about the kidnappers' appearances was that the boy holding James' hand had a mustard-coloured coat, while the one walking in front of them was rather plump with a shaved head. There was no way to identify the two older boys, but the baby's clothing matched Denise's description of what Jamie had been wearing. They played the tape over and over again, watching in horror as James was led towards the exit. It just seemed totally incomprehensible, the police could understand the motives of a paedophile, but why would two young children take another child?

The next morning underwater divers grimly searched the bottom of the canal, while others organized search parties on the land. Less than 24 hours after Denise had lost her son, his body was discovered by four teenage boys who were messing around on the railway tracks. At first glance, they mistook the body for a doll, but on taking a closer look they realized that it wasn't a doll at all, but half of a mutilated toddler. The four boys found the upper body first, still clothed in the blue anorak and white scarf. A train had been by that morning and severed the baby at the waist, just as his two killers had planned. When the train struck, James' torso went flying off the tracks, while his naked lower limbs stayed in place.

The police stopped all approaching trains, roped off the tracks and shielded the scene from onlookers and reporters. The child's clothing, which had been removed from the waist down, was laid near his head. His underwear was heavily soaked in blood. Near the scene of the crime the police found a bloodstained heavy iron bar, about two foot long, and many bricks and stones also stained with blood. They also found 3 AAA batteries, and a tin of blue paint.

Even the most experienced investigators were sickened at the extent and voracity of the toddler's injuries, and decided they would withhold any details of the murder from the public and press.

Denise Bulger, who had been at the police station since her son's disappearance, sensed that something was going on. Suddenly the office had become very busy and when she heard that they had discovered a body, she became extremely distressed. There was nothing she could do but wait, becoming more and more hysterical as she anticipated the terrible confirmation that they had found her baby, James.

The local community had created a makeshift memorial for James near the railway. People brought balloons, flowers and teddy bears to place near the tracks in prayerful remembrance. Robert Thompson himself later laid a single rose at the site of the memorial.

THE ARREST

Since the video footage only showed the back of the boys, the police had no solid leads for almost a full week following the murder. However, all that changed early on February 18, when an anonymous caller reported she had a friend whose son, she knew for a fact, skipped school the day of the kidnapping. In addition to that, the witness stated that she had seen the said child wearing a mustard-coloured coat with blue paint on the jacket sleeve. She also said that he had a friend named Robert Thompson, with whom he had skipped school that day. With no other solid leads, investigators decided that Jon and Robert should be brought in for questioning.

At 7.30 on Thursday morning the Merseyside constabulary showed up on Ann Thompson's doorstep with a search warrant. When Robert realized that he was a suspect, he started to cry. They searched the house, gathered up all his clothes, and immediately noticed that there was blood on his shoes.

When they arrived at the Venables' house a search revealed Jon's mustard-yellow coat which had indeed been splattered with blue paint. It even appeared that there was a small handprint on the sleeve. When they went to take Jon away he broke down and sobbed, 'I don't want to go to prison, mum. I didn't kill the baby.'

Both boys crumbled and cried on the spot and blamed each other for all the bad stuff they had done to their victim. But despite these distressed reactions, the police were still not totally convinced that these two small boys had been the killers. They were simply making enquiries following an anonymous tip-off. There were other boys in the area who had records for violence and, besides, the boys in the videotape looked to be around 13 or 14 years old and Jon and Robert were only 10.

By Saturday, after many hours of questioning, both Robert and Jon were totally exhausted and distraught. The investigating officers knew they had enough evidence to prosecute the boys and consequently brought the interviews to an end. Although both boys had been difficult to interview, they had been informative in different ways.

Robert denied his part in the killing calling the other witnesses liars, but when he did talk, it appeared to be closer to the truth. He was definitely the more manipulative of the two boys, and only cried when it suited him. Jon, on the other hand, seemed to blame Robert for everything, but finally did admit to more than Robert had. His lies were far more elaborate lies, but he was also quicker to admit that he was not telling the truth. It was the fact that Jon became so distressed during the interviews, which hampered the police in getting to the truth of what had really happened.

On Saturday at 6.15 p.m. Jon was charged with the abduction and murder of James Bulger. When Robert was charged the same night, he simply responded, 'It was Jon that done that'.

While they awaited their trial, Jon and Robert were placed in special private quarters, isolated from all other juvenile offenders, including one another. While they were there psychiatrists examined the boys and determined they were mentally fit to stand trial.

JON'S CHILDHOOD PROFILE

Jon was born on August 13, 1982, to Susan and Neil Venables. Neil worked as a forklift truck driver but was very often unemployed. Jon was the middle child, and both of his siblings had developmental problems. His older brother was born with a cleft pallet, which led to communication problems, frustration, and frequent temper tantrums. He had to attend a special school, and Jon's parents spent a lot of time trying to control his brother's behaviour. Sometimes he would be sent out to foster families in order to give the family a break.

Jon's younger sister also had developmental problems and ended up at a special needs school as well. Jon was piggy-in-the-middle, probably feeling ignored, and possibly resentful of the extra attention his siblings received. On occasion, Jon would mimic his older brother's temper tantrums just in order to get attention from his parents.

Mr and Mrs Venables marriage was very turbulent, continually splitting up and then reuniting, which undermined any sense of security within the family unit. The household was in a constant state of upheaval and the instability affected all three of their children. Both parents had histories of clinical depression, and Susan was particularly prone to hysterics. When she became very stressed she had been seen both physically and verbally assaulting Jon, sometimes sending him to his father's house saying she was unable to cope with him. At the age of seven, Jon was showing signs of anti-social behaviour. He hated the other children in the neighbourhood because they constantly teased him and his siblings. Jon himself had a squint in one eye, which made him the subject of mockery, and an easy target because he was so easily provoked by their teasing.

Due to the fact that he was difficult to manage, Jon was transferred to another school, but was kept back for one year. It was here that he met his classmate Robert Thompson, another student who had been kept behind. Susan said he had been transferred to another school because he was the subject of bullying, but it appears that once Jon met up with Robert, they themselves became the bullies. They singled out kids who were weak or easy targets and picked on them, which probably made Jon feel good as he had been used to being the victim. With Robert as his friend, Jon felt tough and the pair took to skipping school on a regular basis.

Teachers at the school noticed how Jon and Robert seemed to bring out the worst in one another, and tried very hard to keep them apart. Although this was possible while they attended school, there was nothing they could do while the pair played truant. Although they were considered to be a pair of troublemakers, no one really saw the boys as being potentially violent.

At home, Jon's mother changed his diet in the hope that it would calm him down, but nothing seemed to work. He always seemed to be picking fights with his brother. When Jon went to stay with his father, Robert would call round but was always chased away by Mr Venables. Robert was a bad influence, Neil warned, and Jon was to stay away from him as he would end up getting the same reputation.

In some people's views it was Jon's own father who was the bad influence on the boy. Neil was very fond of renting videos and his choice of titles was even criticized at the trial. One in particular that drew particular attention was his showing of

Child's Play 3, which he allowed Jon to watch. The movie is about the soul of a serial killer that inhabits a doll named 'Chucky'. The evil doll, about the same size as James, runs around slaughtering hapless victims. In the end Chucky is killed in a haunted roller coaster/train ride. A battle ensues on the railway tracks and Chucky, who is eventually dismembered, has blue paint splattered all over his face. Although there is no proof that Jon saw the entire film, there are certainly many similarities to the crime that the two boys committed.

Jon certainly had an active imagination, but he apparently repressed a great deal of hostility. He always denied vehemently that there were any problems at home, despite his hysterical behaviour in the classroom. Although Neil certainly didn't appear to be abusive, his mother Susan certainly seems to have wielded an extreme amount of control over Jon. More than anything else, Jon absolutely feared her condemnation and rejection.

The doctor who examined Jon before his trial, believed that there was no obvious disability or brain damage that had caused Jon's behavioural problems, and she felt that he was fit to stand trial. Psychological reports assured that Jon did not suffer from any severe mental illnesses, including depression or hallucinations. He was, however, anxious, fidgety and temperamentally fragile a lot of the time, and became easily distressed when discussing any aspects of the murder.

It was important to establish that Jon understood the finality of death, which would affect his

comprehension of the severity of his crime. Jon said
that death meant that people could not come back,
and had an ideal of heaven and hell as permanent
places. He also claimed to be scared of television
violence. If there was a scene in a movie with 'blood
coming out', Jon said he would turn away from the
screen and put his fingers in his ears.

In most accounts of the James Bulger case it
would appear that it was Jon who took the lead in
trying to coax children away from their mothers.
Jon certainly had a festering temper which might
have propelled the mischievous kidnapping into a
murderous assault.

ROBERT'S BACKGROUND PROFILE.

Robert Thompson was definitely the tough one out
of the two boys, and the one everyone assumed to
be the ringleader. His aggression was more likely
to have been used for the purposes of defence as he
had been raised in a rough and brutal environment. Robert's father, who had come from a
violent family, beat his wife relentlessly and then
abandoned the family for good while the children
were still young. His mother, also from an abusive
family, married Robert's father at the age of
eighteen to escape the severe beatings she received
from her father. But, unfortunately, with the new
man in her life, came more beatings. Just like her
own father, Ann's new husband turned out to be
an aggressive alcoholic. He repeatedly beat his
wife in front of the children and Ann, out of her
own frustration and fear, hit her sons with sticks

and belts. She attempted suicide several times, but eventually turned to drink as a means of escape. Unfortunately the children, instead of protecting one another, just turned on each other showing the same violence they had experienced in their parents.

Robert was the fifth child out of six boys. At the age of four the eldest Thompson boy was placed in child protective services following a series of abuse. Another brother of Robert's became a master thief, taking Robert along with him on his escapades. One brother was an arsonist and suspected of sexually abusing young children and, although it is not certain, Robert may have been a victim himself. Another brother threatened his teachers with violence and constantly attempted suicide. The Thompson brothers were well known to the police and police workers and whenever a crime was committed, they were the first family to be questioned.

Robert, himself, tried to be a good boy and would help his mother desperately trying to please her. Robert was a poor student and frequently skipped school. His teachers always considered him to be shy and quiet, and yet a little manipulative of others. Most of the other kids in the class avoided him, and Jon was to become one of his few friends.

Unfortunately, Robert's abuse at the hands of his older brothers began to repeat in his treatment of his baby brother Ryan. But, although he intimidated his younger brother, they still shared a very strong, if not strange, bond. They liked to share the same bed at night, and would lie together sucking one another's thumb. Robert's relationship with Ryan may provide some rough blueprints to the crime against James Bulger. Robert bullied Ryan into bunking off school and made him go with him on his adventures. He once even abandoned his distraught brother by the canal – the same place in fact where Jon and Robert temporarily left James.

But, for all of his toughness, Robert still exhibited childish tendencies for which he was frequently teased. He played with troll dolls and still sucked his thumb. Jon pushed him into a hardness beyond his years and, forced to repress his own childishness, it is possible Robert took out his aggressions on an innocent baby, something that Robert was never allowed to be.

In complete contrast to Jon, Robert was quite willing to re-enact his version of the murder but through the use of dolls. The psychiatrist that met with Robert brought some dolls that represented the primary characters in the crime. There was also a railway track laid out and miniature versions of the weapons that were used in the assault. As Robert picked up the dolls and moved them through the motions of the murder, he demonstrated how the 'Jon doll' senselessly beat the 'James doll', while the 'Robert doll' tried to stop the attack. Robert showed how he tried to pull Jon away and how they fell backwards in the struggle. He was unable to explain, however, how the 'James doll' sustained any form of sexual damage. When the psychiatrist persisted in asking about any sexual abuse, Robert became increasingly defensive and agitated. He was willing to re-enact everything else, but not this part of the attack. When the psychiatrist suggested that the entire attack was sexually motivated, Robert hardly reacted at all, as if he wasn't surprised by that line of questioning. But he didn't deny or confirm this possibility.

When Robert was asked how he felt about James, he didn't have much to say except that he was a lot quieter than his own baby brother, Ben. Robert described how Jon disliked babies, and he wished that he could kick Jon's face in. The psychiatrist told him to go ahead using the dolls, and Robert acted out the scene by using one doll to beat up the other.

In conclusion, the psychiatrist reported that Robert was of above average intelligence, and exhibited no sign of mental illness or depression, but that he was currently displaying symptoms of post-traumatic stress disorder.

THE VERDICT

When the case came to trial on November 1, 1993, defence attorneys David Turner and Brian Walsh attempted to gain sympathy by giving the jury histories of the two boy's dysfunctional backgrounds. But their ploy failed and Jon Venables and Robert Thompson were both found guilty, and given fifteen years imprisonment. Their real names were exposed in the media for the first time. Jon and Robert became the youngest convicted murderers for almost 250 years. After sentencing they were housed in separate, secret locations somewhere in the north of England and were expected to stay there until they turned eighteen, at which time they would be transferred to an adult facility to serve the rest of their time.

There is little information available about their years of internment. Robert initially suffered from symptoms associated with post-traumatic stress disorder, including rashes, illnesses, nightmares and insomnia. He was frightened by his own notoriety, and worried that photographers might be waiting just around the corner in the jail. He became agitated and wouldn't leave his cell, and was frequently harassed by other inmates. Quite predictably he became involved in several fights with other inmates, for which he was punished. Robert was very slow about talking over what had happened, but in 1995 he seemed to have a sudden breakthrough. He started to talk about the murder, admitting his part in the killing. He used his time well and studied for an Open University degree. He also showed an interest in design and textiles and was said to have created an intricate wedding dress because he wanted to make 'an object of beauty'. He also developed talents in cooking, catering and computers.

Jon Venables suffered with his memories of the murder and was frequently tormented by ongoing nightmares of a brutalized James. The psychiatrists said that the first two years behind bars were very difficult for Jon. He repeatedly fantasized about bringing James back to life, and even wished that he could 'grow a new baby' inside him. Apparently Jon responded far more favourably to therapy than Robert.

His remorse and guilt will remain with him forever, but the fact that he acknowledges his responsibility has helped Jon to accept it. He spent much of his time in the institution playing video games, and became an avid sports fan. The opinion of the psychiatrists is that Jon Venables is no longer a threat to the community.

THEIR RELEASE

Although they had originally been sentenced to a term of fifteen years, in December 1999, the European Court of Human Rights decreed that the boys had not received a fair trial and awarded costs and expenses of £15,000 to Robert Thompson and £29,000 to Jon Venables. In October 2000, the newly-appointed Lord Chief Justice Woolf, with the support of the liberal European Court of Human Rights, overturned Robert and Jon's original sentences and released them in June of 2001 after they had both turned eighteen.

In the end Robert and Jon only served a relatively short sentence of eight years. Upon being freed they were placed in a government protection programme and granted new identities for their own safety. They were given fake birth certificates, passports and national insurance numbers and had money in their bank accounts. It is quite understandable, therefore, that the parents of the murdered James Bulger, feel that rather than being punished for their crime these two boys have been rewarded.

103

Willie Bosket

Willie Bosket is a petty thief with a propensity for violence. At the age of fifteen he shot and killed two men on the subway in Manhattan. Although only sentenced to five years incarceration, Willie's fate has been sealed and he is destined to spend the rest of his adult life in American maximum security jails.

It was Sunday, March 19, 1978, and fifteen-year-old Willie Bosket, was riding around on the subways of New York City, looking for someone to rob. Willie had been in and out of the juvenile courts since the age of nine, but as the penalties they issued were so minor, it had done nothing to deter his life of crime. In fact at this time he was waiting to face another hearing for an attempted robbery.

On the plus side of his life, a loving couple had started proceedings to adopt Willie as a foster child. This was something that Willie was desperately looking forward to but, as the state needed time to process the adoption papers, Willie was still free to roam around at will.

On one of his evening escapades, Willie had stolen a wallet containing $380 from a sleeping passenger on a subway train. He had used this money to buy a gun from Charles, who was the man currently living with his mother in Harlem.

104

Charles told Willie that by using a gun he would gain respect on the streets, and sold him a .22 for $65. Willie bought himself a holster and strapped the gun to his leg, and he had to admit that he felt far more powerful just with the knowledge that he possessed a firearm.

It was around 5.30 p.m. on the same Sunday in March, that Willie found himself alone in a compartment on the subway train, with the exception of one man, who happened to be asleep. The passenger was middle-aged and the first thing that Willie noticed was that he was wearing a gold digital watch. Willie kicked the man in the leg to see if he would wake up, but when he got no response he started to work the watch off his wrist. Willie also spotted that the man was wearing a pair of pink sunglasses which reminded him of one of the counsellors at juvenile detention whom he disliked intensely, and this started to irritate him.

Quite suddenly the man opened his eyes and stared directly at Willie. Willie's immediate instinct was to reach for his gun and he shot the passenger through the right eye of his pink sunglasses, penetrating his brain. The man screamed loudly and immediately put his hands up to defend himself. Willie was now in a state of panic, afraid that the man might not die and would be able to identify his attacker, he once again shot him in the temple. The man immediately fell back against the side of the train and his body slumped to the floor.

As the train reached its final stop near the Yankee Stadium, Willie removed the man's watch, stole fifteen dollars from his pocket and also slipped a

105

ring off one of his fingers. A ring which he sold for twenty dollars on his way home from the attack.

The victim was identified as Noel Perez, aged 44, who worked in a hospital and lived on his own. The press reported that it was a random mugging, and that little could be done to apprehend the assailant.

That fatal encounter on the subway train predetermined the remainder of Willie's life. He had always wondered what it would feel like to actually kill someone, and what made him feel really powerful was the fact that no-one had seen him do it. He even bragged to his sister about the murder, and feeling empowered by the fact that he appeared to have got away with the crime, told her that now he was 'bad', just like he'd told everyone he would be.

THE BOSKET FAMILY LEGACY

Willie was in effect living out a legacy that had been handed down to him from a history of violence rooted in Edgefield County, South Carolina. It appeared that almost every member of Willie's paternal family – father, grandfather, great grandfather – had been convicted at one time or another of a violent crime.

However, this is not a story of inherited genes, it is one of brutalization and injustice that was handed down from generation to generation. The story starts with slavery in South Carolina, in a county called Edgefield. It was the scene of violence and mayhem and it became nicknamed 'Bloody Edgefield'. The inhabitants of Edgefield were mainly Scottish–Irish refugees running from war and oppression. These refugees lived by a medieval code of honour and that was 'if you insulted a man, cheated him, or cast a covetous eye on his wife he would kill you'.

In 1760 the Cherokee Indians ravaged the area which caused gangs of outlaws to spring up in Edgefield. They took to abducting women and torturing planters and merchants for their valuables. This plundering led to outrage among the settlers and they formed bands of vigilantes in an effort to suppress the gangs. It was these vigilantes or 'regulators' that introduced the strain of violence that was to be the curse and fate of South Carolina. Their punishments were severe, and one recorded case was that a horse thief received 500 lashes for his crime.

Crime started to escalate in this area of South Carolina. In fact, records show that during the first half of the nineteenth century, rural South Carolina – and in particular Edgefield – had a murder rate four times as high as that of urban Massachusetts. This type of crime was white-on-white violence over topics such as ownership of land, their women, and honouring the code of conduct the original refugees had established. While all this was going on the slaves had been observing from their fields and shacks, learning the 'bloody code'. One of these slaves was Aaron Bosket, who was Willie's great-great-grandfather. His master was a man named Francis Pickens who was the Governor of South Carolina. It was Pickens who helped to kindle the Civil War by ordering his military forces to seize Federal property in Charleston. Aaron, being a slave under white masters, after the war became a sharecropper under white landowners. Despite the fact that he had been terrorized and cheated out of his rightful money from his crops, he was too frightened to actually do anything about it. His son, 'Pud', however, was a totally different kettle of fish.

It was quite normal that even up until 1910 white landlords were known to have given their black sharecroppers more than a few lashes of the whip. It was meant to be a ritual of degradation, reminding them that they were no more than slaves. But Pud, who was now twenty-one, was not prepared to endure this humiliation.

'This is the last nigger you're going to whip,' he cried, and grabbed the whip away from the landlord. Having defied a white master, Pud was turned away and was unable to get work within the area. Instead he turned to stealing from the local merchants, for which he punished by working a year on the chain gang. His hatred of the system seems to have been passed down through the generations and Pud's son, James, ended up as a robber, a kidnapper and even a child molester. In turn, James' son Butch also ended up a murderer.

As for Willie, Butch's son, he is the child of violence. Having been raised on the streets of Harlem, Willie was known to be volatile and his killings were merely a way of earning 'respect' from his fellow beings.

WILLIE'S SECOND KILLING

Willie had a cousin called Herman Spates. Herman called round to see Willie on the morning of Thursday, March 23, 1978, to find him still asleep. When his cousin arrived Willie climbed out of bed, got dressed, and instinctively strapped his gun and holster to his leg.

'Let's go get some money,' Willie said to his cousin. Willie was feeling tough and empowered, since it was only four days since he had actually killed a man.

The pair walked to the Number 3 subway train on 148th Street and Lexington Avenue. As they were crossing the station yard they noticed a man, Anthony Lamorte, carrying a CB radio. The boys knew that this radio would bring them in quite a lot of cash if they sold it on the streets, and so they followed the man.

Lamorte noticed the two boys hanging around the yard and yelled at them to get out as they were not supposed to be in there. This, however, incensed Willie – he wasn't going to be told what to do by a white man – and so he challenged him. Lamorte climbed down from the steps of the train car and started walking towards the boys. He thought Willie looked far too young to be hanging around, but as he got closer Willie pulled out his gun and demanded money and the man's CB radio.

Fearing that something bad was about to happen, Lamorte turned his back on the two boys and started to walk back to the train car. As he walked away he heard a loud bang and felt a numbness creep over his back and right shoulder. He then heard the boys run away, and staggered to the dispatcher's office where he told them that he thought he had been shot.

Willie and his cousin fled the scene of the shooting as fast as their legs would carry them. Undeterred by the fact that they could have been caught, over the course of the next three nights the pair were involved in three more violent assaults and robberies. They stole $12 from a man they had kicked down the stairs at a train station. They shot a 57-year-old man called Matthew Connolly in the hip, when he was foolish enough to try and resist them.

On Monday, March 27, Willie and Herman were out looking for trouble once again. They jumped over the turnstile on 135th Street and climbed onto the last carriage of the uptown train. There was only one other passenger in the car, a Hispanic man in his late thirties. Willie instructed his cousin to stand guard at the front of the carriage, while he demanded money from the passenger using his gun as an added threat. The man told Willie that he didn't have any money, but that was the wrong thing to say, and it made the boy very angry. Without any hesitation Willie pulled the trigger and the man slid to the floor, a pool of blood quickly forming around his inert body. Willie quickly went through the man's pockets but only found $2 in his wallet. Willie tossed the wallet into a rubbish bin and walked back home with Herman, laughing about what he had done. Willie now felt like a big-time killer and when it made front page news the next morning, he proudly showed his sister his newfound fame.

What Willie didn't know, however, was that on that same day the courts had finally given approval for him to be adopted as a foster child by the couple he had been looking forward to living with. But of course all of this was to change, as there was shortly to be a huge turnaround in Willie's fortunes.

THE CASE AGAINST WILLIE

Police investigating the recent subway killings felt that they possibly had a serial killer on the loose. When the police did a computer search the names of Willie Bosket and Herman Spates kept cropping up. They had been arrested earlier for the shooting of Matthew Connolly, but he had been unable to identify the pair and consequently they had been release. They had been called into the police station on numerous occasions, and now the police considered they should be questioned further.

Willie was still a juvenile at this time, only fifteen, and as his cousin was seventeen, the detective in question decided to go after Herman first. However, some over-ambitious policeman had already picked up Willie which meant that the detective had to move quickly. He found Herman with his probation officer and he quite willingly accompanied the policeman back to the station. He was questioned about his activities on the day of the shooting, and Herman responded by saying that he was asleep in the cinema. The detective replied that Willie had already given him up, to which Herman responded that it was Willie who had carried out the shooting. He also told the police about the earlier shooting on the subway and the whereabouts of the gun.

With this information the police obtained a search warrant and went to Willie's house. Willie's mother reluctantly showed the police where the gun was and then accompanied them to the police station where they were still questioning her son. During interrogation Willie threatened the District Attorney, and made a fatal blunder by actually admitting that he owned the gun.

Willie's previous cases had always gone before the Family Court and he was punished by being sent to a reformatory. However, as the amount of juvenile arrests had grown so dramatically in the mid-seventies, the system was in the process of being revised. In 1976 the Juvenile Justice Reform Act created a new category of juvenile crime, the 'designated felony'. This meant that children as young as fourteen, who committed violent crimes, could be given longer sentences than the original maximum of eighteen months. This meant that they could now be sent to a training school for anything from three to five years. It also allowed the presence of a District Attorney at the court sessions.

The District Attorney who acquired Willie's case was Robert Silbering. Although they had no witnesses or confession, they did have the gun and a ballistics test that linked it to the murder. Anthony Lamorte had picked Willie out of a line-up and the

DA pressurized Herman to testify against his cousin in return for a more lenient sentence.

The trial took place at the Family Court building on Lafayette Street in lower Manhattan. Willie was being charged with three different felonies – two counts of murder and one of attempted murder – this meant three separate trials.

During his trial Willie was so belligerent and foul-mouthed that on occasions he had to be restrained. He appeared to lack any sense of morality or indeed sensitivity to the families of his victims. In fact he appeared proud of what he had done and later bragged that, although he was only fifteen years old, he had committed over 2,000 crimes, 25 of them being stabbings.

As the trials progressed, Willie seemed to bore of the whole proceedings and told his shocked lawyer to enter a plea of guilty. He was told that he would have to admit guilt to all three counts, which Willie subsequently did.

Willie's sentence was passed and he was given a maximum sentence of five years with the Division of Youth, which meant by the time he was twenty-one he would be free. It appeared that even with all the evidence mounted against him, there was little the authorities could do to a juvenile even though there was every indication that Willie might very possibly kill again.

There was such public outrage at the leniency of Willie's sentence that it prompted the state legislature to pass the first law in the nation which allowed juveniles to be tried as adults for certain horrific crimes. This was called the 'Willie Bosket Law'.

WILLIE'S FATE

Willie spent the first part of his confinement at the Goshen Center for Boys and spent the majority of time in conflict with the wardens. He broke out of the Center with a few other boys only to be recaptured two hours later. What he hadn't realized when he broke out was the fact that while he was in Goshen he had actually had a birthday and was now sixteen years old, technically an adult. Escaping from any penal institute was a felony for an adult and he was consequently sentenced to four years in a state prison.

While he was in prison Willie befriended a group of black Muslims who only exacerbated his rage against the 'whites'. After serving a rather stormy four years in prison, Willie was returned to the Division of Youth and placed in another reform centre for boys until he became twenty-one years of age.

After his release, Willie was determined to stay out of trouble after meeting a girl called Sharon Hayward. Sharon already had a child and the pair decided to get married. For once Willie behaved like a normal well-adjusted adult. He enrolled in the local community college and even started to look for a job. Unfortunately, for Willie, this new-found freedom was not to last for long. One day while he was visiting his sister, he had an unfortunate encounter with a man from her building which ended up with the man complaining that Willie had tried to rob him. Willie protested and explained that the whole thing was a misunderstanding, but to him the whole thing smelt of politics. The Governor was apparently taking the brunt for Willie's quick release and it appeared that one way or another he was going to be put back inside.

It appeared that the system that had for so long had worked in Willie's favour was now starting to turn on him. He was a victim of his own criminal record and anything else that happened, however small, now seemed to add more fuel to the fire. Even though his juvenile record had been wiped clean, while he was in the institution he had developed such a bad reputation that the authorities were now clamping down on him. They set Willie's bail so high that his family were unable to raise the money, and so he had to remain in jail until the time of his trial. Willie was becoming more and more incensed at the way he was being treated, and this resentment built up inside him.

When the case went to court one of the officers put a hand on Willie to get him to move. However, when he resisted he was pushed by a further three officers, to which Willie responded with obscenities. Things went from bad to worse and Willie was pushed so violently against a table that it cracked under his weight, causing the legs to splinter off. One of the police officers hit him with one of the table legs and even though Willie's lawyer tried to intervene, Willie was charged with assault, resisting arrest and criminal contempt of court.

Willie was now a very angry young man and this was to be another turning point for him. Having decided that going straight had got him nowhere, he decided to take on the system feeling that he had nothing to lose.

When Willie eventually went to the hearing for his sentencing, he dismissed his lawyer and decided to represent himself. He put up a good act and claimed that he was not Willie Bosket but in fact Bobby Reed. The judge allowed him to put his case forward but at the end of the day decided that he was a dangerous man and gave him the maximum sentence. He still had to stand trial for his assault on the police officers, and again he demanded to be his own lawyer. This time he put on such a good show that the jury found him not guilty.

While all this was going on Willie's father Butch had been released from prison and was starting a new life. But the old Butch soon emerged and he molested a young child that was in his care. Once again he was arrested, but desperate to stay free, he tried to escape and was killed in a shoot-out with the police, taking his own life and that of his girlfriend before he could be apprehended.

Willie, on hearing this news, was elated because it restored his faith that his father was in fact a 'bad man' who had gone out in a blaze of glory.

Once back inside prison, Willie was convinced that he would never again be a free man. He started a one-man war against the system, with the prison guards being his main targets. One of his many fights with the guards resulted in him being charged with yet another felony charge. This meant that he had accumulated a total of three felony charges which, no matter how small, resulted in a twenty-five year to life imprisonment sentence under the 1965 persistent felony offender law. Willie's three felony charges were all fairly small – escape, attempted assault and assault/arson – and he could not understand how these could add up to the same sentence as someone who had committed murder.

With this in his head and his extreme hatred of the system, Willie carried everything to the extreme. He was now at war with the system.

On April 16, 1988, at around 12.42 p.m. in the visiting room of the Shawangunk State Prison in New York, prison guard Earl Porter was stabbed by an eleven-inch stiletto blade, which penetrated his chest only narrowly missing his heart. Even to this day, Willie Bosket's only regret is that he didn't manage to kill the guard.

This time Willie went to trial for attempted murder. Once again refusing counsel, Willie mounted his own defence. His legs were bound by heavy shackles, while his arms were handcuffed in front of him with the handcuffs chained to his waist, a further chain connected these chains to the shackles. He was once again given another life sentence – this time Willie was in jail for good.

WHERE DID IT ALL GO WRONG?

By the time Willie Bosket was eleven years old, he was an angry, hostile, homicidal boy who no one could seem to reach. He had a history of suicidal attempts and showed constant violence towards fellow human beings. In his head Willie had thought that violence had won him respect. His mother had distanced herself from Willie in the fear that he would turn out like his father. As he grew up he learned how to throw temper tantrums, he often hit his teachers, he stole and for the most part was left to his own devices. Added to this his grandfather had sexually abused him when he was only nine years old. Time and time again he told people that he didn't care whether he lived or died, as the future didn't seem to hold any happiness for him.

Crime and violence became a normal part of his existence, in fact he considered it to be a sport that he was very good at. He never really had to face up to any of his criminal acts against others, because as a juvenile he was considered not to be responsible for his actions. Somehow he easily worked his way through the cracks in the system and always ended up back at home.

When he was given a psychiatric evaluation they reported that Willie was suffering from Anti-social Behaviour, which was not far removed from Antisocial Personality Disorder, the diagnosis given to his father. Willie was not considered to be psychotic, but he was certainly dangerous.

Two questions still remain unanswered. Why was he so bitter? Why was he so angry towards the system? Why – most probably because Willie had been incarcerated since he was nine years old and was raised by his surrogate mother, the criminal justice system. If this is the case then Willie Bosket is purely a monster that was created by the very system that he now haunts. Willie has gone from the child that nobody wanted to the man who no jail can control. Willie is now considered the most dangerous prisoner in the state of New York. He is confined to a life of solitary confinement, in a concrete box without even the added advantage of electricity. He is denied all access to reading or recreational material and even his guards are not allowed to speak with him.

Willie's words still echo around the penitentiary: 'I'll haunt this damn system,' and indeed he does.

Tony Craven

Tony Craven was constantly ridiculed for being a virgin, but the problem was he didn't really fancy people his own age he was only comfortable around little children.

Tony Craven was considered an outcast in society, and consequently suffered much persecution. He worked at a food processing factory in Huddersfield, a northern English industrial town where he lived with his family. Tony was constantly being ridiculed by his work mates because he was still a virgin. He looked far younger than his seventeen years, looking more like a thirteen or fourteen-year-old, which only seemed to make his co-workers pick on him more. The men he worked with even resorted to bringing pornographic magazines into the factory, in an effort to get him interested in women. They would open the magazine at a particularly provocative page and taunt him with, 'What d'ya think of that one? Wouldn't ya like to have some of that?'

Tony tried his hardest to ignore his workmates, answering their teasing with, 'No, actually, I wouldn't. I don't like those women.' In fact Tony was not attracted by mature women, or even girls of his own age. The people he was most comfortable with were the local neighbourhood children who were only half his age. This was probably due to the fact that Tony felt so out of place in normal situations, that he found it easy to identify himself with the other children. One of these children was his seven-year-old neighbour, Angie Flaherty, for whom he often babysat.

'LITTLE ANGEL' GOES MISSING

On Saturday, August 10, 1991, Angela's parents called the Huddersfield police to report that their daughter had not returned home from her afternoon bicycle ride. Angie was nicknamed the 'Little Angel' because of her loving and trusting nature and her parents were worried that she may have wandered off with a stranger. It was just after sunset when the police started a thorough search of the neighbourhood.

Two helicopters searched the area from above, while 100 police officers – some on horseback – went over the land piece by piece. On the morning of August 11, just before midday, a constable on horseback noticed Angie's bright pink bicycle deep in the forest near to her home. Only minutes later, Little Angel's body was discovered in a makeshift play area used by the local children. They had built a kind of fort using some cardboard boxes and a soiled, tattered old mattress.

Angie's body was naked. Her clothes had been folded into a neat pile and were lying beside her spiritless body. There was a considerable amount of blood on the inside of thighs which indicated that the poor child had probably been sexually assaulted. They also noticed that apart from the

121

strangulation marks around her neck, her killer had crushed her skull with repeated blows. Whoever the evil person was that had killed this innocent child had wanted to make certain that his victim was dead and unable to identify him.

The detective who was assigned to this particularly appalling case was Detective-Superintendent Peter Bottomley. Right from the start Bottomley felt sure that Angie's attacker had to be someone that she knew. The tyre tracks through the forest proved that Angie had been riding her bike right up to where the attack took place, proving that she went quite willingly to the hidden play area with her murderer. From this Bottomley concluded that it was more than likely that the girl was lured by someone she trusted rather than by a stranger.

During the aftermath of the murder, Tony Craven played the part of an innocent extremely well. He offered statements to reporters who were hovering around outside the Flaherty's house. He told them that there were no words to express how he felt, and that he could not imagine what poor Angie's parents were going through. No-one suspected in the least that he was connected to the grisly attack on poor Angie Flaherty, except, that is Detective Bottomley.

Bottomley was watching Craven talking eagerly to the reporters while straddling his bicycle. He remarked to one of his partners that he thought Craven was a 'strange kid'. Tony didn't appear to be showing any signs of distress even though Angie was a close friend of his. If anything, he seemed to be revelling in the attention he was receiving from the press.

Two days after they discovered Angie's body, Bottomley decided that he would bring Craven in for questioning. Immediately, Tony revealed to his interviewer that he had some information regarding the case that might be of some use to them. He claimed that on the afternoon Angie disappeared, Tony had seen her with a balding, middle-aged man walking towards the makeshift fort. Craven said that although he had never seen the man before he felt sure that he was the one that had attacked poor Angie.

Bottomley was not convinced by Craven's story but went along with the false lead in the hope of outwitting him.

The next day Craven was called back to the police station for a second interview. Bottomley told him that he was going to arrange for blood tests to be taken from all the 9,000 males in the area in an attempt to find a DNA match for Angie's killer. Tony confidently agreed to have his own blood taken and tested, and showed no signs of concern whatsoever.

The DNA tests on Tony's blood were conclusive as they matched semen found in Angela. At last Bottomley had solid proof that Tony Craven was the cold-blooded killer. He was immediately arrested and quite openly admitted to what had happened.

TONY'S EVIDENCE

He told the police that he had grown tired of the

123

constant harassment he received from his fellow workers about his lack of sexual experience, so he decided he would go out and get some. Tony persuaded Angie to go to the fort and play with him as they had done many times before. He dared her to take all her clothes off and then forced her down on the dirty old mattress. She sobbed and shrieked as Tony raped her, and continued to cry out in pain even after he had finished.

'She just wouldn't be quiet,' Craven confessed. 'She just kept on screaming and screaming. Louder and louder. She said that she was going to tell what I had done to her. I asked her not to. But she went on saying she was going to.'

Realizing that he was going to have to kill her to keep her quiet, Tony tried at first to strangle Angie. However, the child struggled so much that he was unable to get a tight enough hold on her throat. In a last desperate effort to keep her quiet Tony grabbed her jaw with his left hand and with his right, picked up a rock and proceeded to hit her around the head until she bled to death.

Tony Craven willingly gave every detail of the attack to the police, but one thing that still bothered Bottomley was why he was so eager to let his blood be tested. Was it that he actually wanted to get caught? No, that was not the reason. Tony explained that he thought it would be safe to have his blood examined, as he never actually bled.

A LIFE BEHIND BARS

He was taken to Leeds' Armley Road Jail, where,

after only a few days, Tony Craven tried to hang himself using his bed sheets. However, he was discovered in time and sent to the infirmary. A few days later, when back in his cell, he tried once again to take his own life, but it was another failed attempt. A third attempt occurred while he was awaiting trial, but this time Tony slashed his wrists. It was obvious that he now found it impossible to live with what he had done to the poor 'Little Angel'.

In early May, 1992, Tony's case went to trial and he was sentenced to life in prison by Justice Connell at the Leeds Crown Court in England. His case will come up for parole in 2008, to see whether he is considered a reformed character who will be safe to release on the public once again.

Cheryl Pierson and Sean Pica

Patricide is a familiar theme both in real life and in fiction. It was fear and revenge for alleged sexual abuse that apparently drove Cheryl Pierson to kill her father with the help of a school friend.

Cheryl Pierson was a very popular, pretty pupil at Newfield High School in Selden, New York. She was a cheerleader and socially she was very successful, although her grades were never better than average. She was 5 ft 2 in tall, with clear skin and a typical permed 1980's hairstyle. She went out with an older Italian boy who loved to spend money and was also co-captain of her beloved cheerleading squad.

Cheryl hardly had the profile of a typical teenage killer, and she certainly wasn't a misfit in society. Nonetheless, Cheryl did have a couple of skeletons in her cupboard – namely, incest and her mother's death.

Her mother died of kidney failure in 1985, leaving her husband, James, to bring up their son and two daughters. Mr Pierson, an electrician, did his best to play the part of a good and caring father by taking his children to amusement parks and coaching his son's junior baseball team. To make up for the loss of a mother figure, James showered his two daughters with love and possessions. However, according to his eldest daughter, Cheryl, he showed just too much affection. According to Cheryl, her father sexually abused her from the time she was eleven up until the age of sixteen.

During the early years of sexual abuse, Cheryl's mother was in and out of hospital and was in a state of very frail health. She died when Cheryl was fifteen, and only two days after the funeral her father forced her to have sex in her dead mother's bed. She was forced to endure sex with her father twice every day, and if she put up any sort of a fight she was beaten into submission.

AN END TO HER SUFFERING

A few months before her mother died, Cheryl decided she had to do something about the ordeal her father was putting her through. She had often fantasized about having her father killed and her resentment and rage came to a head one day in November 1985 when Pierson and fellow class-mate Sean Pica, were sitting in the homeroom at their school. They were discussing an article in a local paper about an abused wife who enlisted someone to murder her husband. Pierson wondered aloud who would be crazy enough to undertake such a deadly commission and Pica promptly said he would volunteer – if the price was right.

Sean was sixteen years old, wore braces, and

was working towards getting an Eagle Scout badge. Both his father and stepmother were members of the NYPD.

Cheryl told Sean she wanted her father dead because he had been sexually abusing her since she was eleven years old. She promised to pay him the sum of $1,000 when he had completed his assignment, and Sean agreed to do it, not for the money, he said, but to end a good friend's suffering.

On a wintry morning on February 5, 1986, Sean Pica waited behind a tree in front of a house on Magnolia Drive in Seldon, shivering from the cold. The Boy Scout carried a .22-calibre rifle and had one thing on his mind, murder.

James Pierson emerged from his house and as he was opening his car door to go to work, Pica shot him five times in the head, at close range. James, then 42, slumped to the icy ground in his driveway. Pica walked over to the inert body and fired four more bullets into his body to ensure that he had completed his task, and then ran away. Sean ditched the gun and then went to school as normal.

Cheryl immediately rushed out of the house, acting as if she had been woken by a loud noise, and ran across the street to her neighbours. She told them she thought that her father had slipped on some ice and appeared quite badly injured. When the neighbours crossed the road and found Mr Pierson lying in a pool of blood they immediately called the police.

The next day, Cheryl, along with her boyfriend, Rob Cuccio, met up with Sean at a local pizza parlour and paid him the sum of $400. Cheryl had taken the money from her father's safe earlier that day.

NOT A **CONVINCING** ACT

The police department were not convinced by Cheryl's ham acting, and she was taken into the police station for questioning. After several hours of intense questions she succumbed to the pressure and pleaded guilty to having arranged for the death of her father.

On Cheryl's evidence, Sean was arrested and they were both charged as adults with second-degree murder. When the case came to trial the pleas were reduced to manslaughter in exchange for reduced sentences. Cheryl was sentenced as a youthful offender to six months in Suffolk County jail and served three-and-half months. Sean was sentenced as an adult to eight to twenty-four years in prison, and served sixteen.

It was nineteen months since the murder of her father that the case actually came to trial. Due to her age and the fact that she had been sexually abused, the case drew the attention of the press nationwide. Just before the case opened a sympathetic article was run in one of the local papers portraying the teenager as an innocent angle and her father as Satan. During the hearing they called on more than a dozen witnesses who confirmed that they had seen signs of abuse. The most powerful testimony of all was from her own brother, who said his sister had confided in him that she felt her kidneys were weakening from too many beatings.

When Cheryl was called to take the stand she cried throughout most of her deposition.

'When he was on top of me he used to breathe in my face,' she sobbed to the jury. 'I used to put a pillow on my face and block it out until it was all over.'

Three weeks into the trial, on October 5, 1987, Judge Sherman told Cheryl he was going to be lenient and he had received more than a hundred letters from people who had suffered from incest.

Cheryl served 106 days and was released on January 19, 1988. Her boyfriend, Ron Cuccio, who had waited for her throughout her ordeal, picked her up from the correctional centre in a white limousine. They were married in a Catholic church nine months later.

Today Cheryl Cuccio, now thirty-four, has two young daughters of her own. Cheryl and Rob celebrated their fifteenth wedding anniversary on October 9, 2003. She has worked as a beautician, a bank teller and a sales clerk in a department store.

The Pierson/Pica case came into the spotlight once again in 1989, when a TV film was made from the story, called *Deadly Silence*. Once more Cheryl was portrayed as an innocent victim with no choice but to murder her paedophile father. But what was never brought to attention was the fact that her father left an estate worth over $600,000, which Cheryl was well aware she would inherit when she hired her classmate, Sean Pica.

SEAN'S BACKGROUND

Sean was only five years old when his father first walked out on his mother. Although the Picas were reconciled, they eventually divorced when Sean was nine. His mother married again and, although Sean was fond of his stepfather, there was a dark side to the relationship. His stepfather beat his mother and then left the family after only three years. This affected Sean badly and he became a quiet, and very angry child. In an attempt to find some sort of acceptance he turned to the streets and got involved with a bad crowd of boys. He took to burglary, breaking into homes in his local neighbourhood, and also turned to the comfort of cocaine. Eventually he added murder to his list of crimes.

There were some people who believed that Sean was actually Cheryl's saviour, performing an act to put an end to his friend's suffering. On the other hand there were those who believed that Pica was nothing more than a drug addict who killed for the cash to fund his addiction. Whichever way you look at it the years that Sean spent in prison were not wasted and he managed to make something of himself.

Sean Pica served sixteen years in prison and is now 34 years old. He was paroled from Sing Sing on Friday 13 in December 2002. He was eligible for parole after he had served only six years of his sentence, but it was denied five times over a period of ten years because of the severity of his crime.

While Sean was in the New York State prison he

BORN TO BE KILLERS

managed to obtain a high school equivalency diploma. He was then sent to a prison upstate where he earned a bachelor's degree in organizational management and a master's degree in professional services. He has counselled high school pupils and college children for the past ten years.

Sean's last seven years behind bars were spent in Sing Sing, on Cellblock A, one of the toughest and largest blocks in the world, and yet he had survived and come out on top. When he was eventually released he spent a couple of months in a Catholic halfway house and then got a job as a counsellor in East Harlem for an organization called Strive. It is a non-profit organization that helps ex-convicts, troubled children, receivers of welfare and others who are not so fortunate to get and hopefully keep jobs through a change of attitude. He lives with an aunt and uncle in Pleasantville and is currently working on another master's degree at the Hunter College School of Social Work.

Although as a youth Sean Pica was seen as a drugged-up sociopath with a $200-a-day cocaine habit, but as an adult he is a respected member of society. The New York State prison houses over 70,000 men and women, most of whom get released back onto the streets with not much claim or dignity of worth. Sean Pica is one of the exceptions who managed to use the system to his advantage.

The West Memphis Three

On May 5, 1993, the Robin Hood Hills area of West Memphis, Arkansas, was the site of the brutal sexual assault and murder of three eight-year-old boys.

It was May 6, 1993, when the mutilated bodies of three eight-year-old boys were found in West Memphis. The three boys in question, Michael Moore, Christopher Byers and Steve Branch, had left their homes on bicycles early on the evening of May 5. After a couple of hours, Christopher's step-father, John Mark Byers, reported to the police that his son was missing. The police along with the families of all three boys, searched for them throughout the night and into the next morning. It was around 1 p.m. the next day that the bodies were found. They had been beaten, sexually molested, mutilated and were left for dead in a wooded ditch not far from the boys' homes.

The crime scene left a lot of unanswered questions. For a start there was no blood, even though two of the boys had apparently bled to death. Also there were no mosquito bites on their skin, even though they had been found in a damp area and that the bleeding bodies had been left there overnight. There were no obvious footprints at the scene of the crime, even though the area was exceptionally muddy and one of the children had been drowned at a creek on the site. All three of the boys had been tied up with black and white shoelaces. They all had cuts and abrasions some of which indicated that they had been forced to have oral sex. One child, Christopher Byers, had been castrated and his penis skinned – possibly the work of a master cutter.

The atrocious nature of the crime had the police determined to apprehend the victim before he could possibly do any more harm.

THE SUSPECTS

By 12.00 p.m. the following day the police were questioning their first suspect. A juvenile probation officer who was present during the investigation had come to the decision that this had all the markings of a Satanic murder and led the police to a local youth named Damien Echols. He was an eighteen-year-old who liked to read occult books, listen to heavy metal music, and always wore black. Over the years the police had blamed him for anything that went wrong in town simply because he was a little 'different'. Although there was no evidence to prove that he had anything to do with the murders, police leaked his name and rumours soon started spreading. The next day police brought Damien in for questioning for no other reason than the fact that he was different. He was subjected to intense questioning and then released.

Meanwhile a man who owned a restaurant near the site of the crime called the police station on May 5 to report a black man, covered in mud and blood, who had wandered into the ladies' toilet and remained in there for about an hour. The police went to the Bojangle's restaurant, but the officer did not bother to get out of the car and investigate. The following day, after the three boys had been discovered, a detective returned to the restaurant and took some blood samples from the said toilet. These samples were subsequently – or conveniently – lost. There was a negroid hair found on one of the boys' corpses, and yet not one of the accused boys were black.

The next suspect to be brought in for questioning several weeks later was an associate of Echols named Jessie Misskelley. He was seventeen years old and was described as being 'learning disabled'. After a long period of questioning he finally caved in to the pressure and admitted to the murders, also implicating another friend, sixteen-year-old Jason Baldwin, along with Damien Echols. He said that the three of them were fellow 'Devil worshippers' who allegedly visited cult meetings, sacrificed animals on makeshift altars and planned the brutal murder of the little boys. Jason and Damien were subsequently arrested the same day.

The media and public condemned the three teenagers even before their case went to trial. For the nine months since the attack the local press had been releasing stories of blood-drinking, devil worshipping, and sexual orgies involving demons. On January 19, 1994, Jessie Misskelley went to trial after an attempt to have his confession quelled was denied. Jessie was tried separately from the other two as it was his confession that had implicated them. The trial lasted for two weeks and, although there was absolutely no evidence to incriminate him, Jessie was convicted of one count of first degree capital murder and two counts of second degree capital murder. He was sentenced to life in prison without any possibility of parole.

The trial of Jason Baldwin and Damien Echols began on February 4, 1994. Jason, who asserted that his only crime was that he knew Damien, was convicted of three counts of capital murder. Due to his young age, he was given a life sentence plus forty years.

Damien Echols, who at eighteen was considered an adult, was found guilty of three counts of capital murder and was sentenced to death by lethal injection. Since his internment, Damien has been repeatedly beaten and raped while prison guards just looked on and did nothing about it. Echols said, 'I was sent here to die. I would just like to be left alone until that time comes.' He now spends most of his time reading and writing to his friends and family.

More than five years after these three teenagers were handed their sentences, they still proclaim their innocence and are still trying to get retrials granted due to the original lack of evidence. Although it is not unusual for guilty men to pro-claim their innocence vehemently, what is different about this case is that they are not alone in proclaiming their innocence. It appears thousands of American citizens are also convinced that Jessie, Jason and Damien were wrongly convicted and are now offering support in their fight for justice.

ANOTHER POSSIBLE SUSPECT

Another interesting fact in this case that seems to have been totally overlooked is that the victim Chris Byers appears to have been beaten by his stepfather, John Mark Byers, just prior to the boys' disappearance. During the trial it came to the fore that Mr Byers was receiving treatment for a brain tumour. The alibi that Mr Byers provided for the time in question was unstable, and he contradicted his own testimony on several occasions.

There was certainly some circumstantial evidence pointing towards John Mark Byers. He owned a knife on which had been found some blood which was the same group as that of his son and himself, and a hair found at the scene of the crime was very similar to that of Mr Byer's. Very low amounts of a drug that the stepfather used were found in the boy's bloodstream at the time of his death. The drug, Carbamazepine, depresses the central nervous system and can cause drowsiness if administered in large doses. Chris Byers also had evidence on his body of healed past physical abuse.

The Byers were both subsequently convicted of stealing $20,000 worth of antiques from a house. Mr Byers also attacked a five-year-old child in his own neighbourhood shortly after they moved away to a small town. Melissa Byers died mysteriously last year and the autopsy showed that she had drugs in her system, but apparently not enough to kill her.

Although it does seem that there were many items of evidence that could have linked John Mark Byers to the murders, he was never considered by the police as a suspect or indeed ever thoroughly investigated. It is quite interesting to note that at the time John Byers was a drug-informant for the WMPD, so maybe it was bias in favour of Byers that blinded the police to any evidence they had.

Finally, the one imprint they did find of a tennis shoe on the bank near the bodies, did not match with any shoes owned by Damien, Jessie or Jason. This fact alone should have meant that the police started investigating in another direction.

SUMMING UP

It is obvious from this brief picture that there are serious flaws in the case. The trial itself was somewhat bizarre, especially with the focus on the occult and Satanism.

The problems started right from the moment the bodies were first discovered. Due possibly to a lack of experience or perhaps professionalism on the part of the police at the crime scene, meant that the area was not properly protected and vital evidence was either destroyed or not collected at all. A prime example of this is the fact that they failed to keep the sticks which had held the boys clothing down in the creek. Also the removal of the bodies from the creek before the medical examiner had arrived, meant even more vital information was lost. But it doesn't end there. Even the incompetence of the medical examiner himself confused the investigators even further. He failed to take the temperature of the bodies at the scene and also ignored vital aspects of the victims' injuries.

Vital information regarding the case, which should have only been known by the offender, was made public knowledge. This meant that any information the police received from witnesses and suspects alike, may have only been their own information coming back to them.

In their fervour to get their man the police used many dubious tactics to obtain the corroborative evidence they needed.

The information the jury had been subjected to before the trial, i.e. what they read in the newspapers, saw on television and heard via the police, possibly reinforced their belief that this case was part of a brutal Satanic ritual.

To allow this community to feel safe again, the only course to be taken was to come back with a guilty verdict. Possibly the three boys are to blame for the deaths of three small children, but it does not seem feasible that a jury could have found them guilty beyond a reasonable doubt with the evidence that was supplied.

It takes time, around ten years, for a judicial system to reverse a guilty sentence. But possibly with extreme public pressure and outrage at the injustice of this case, the system will look within itself and acknowledge that it has weaknesses and flaws. Jessie and Jason have many years ahead of them, but it is possible that Damien's time will run out before this very slow process ever comes about.

Cindy Collier & Shirley Wolf

*'Today Cindy and I ran away and killed an
old lady. It was lots of fun'*

Cindy Collier was fifteen and Shirley Wolf was
fourteen when they first met. Although they
knew nothing about one another they were certainly two of a kind. Cindy, since the age of seven,
had been constantly molested by her stepbrother.
She had been neglected and abused by both of her
parents and by the time she was twelve she had
been arrested for assault and battery as a result of
a fist fight at school. Further arrests followed for
theft and delinquency, for which she received
several short stays in a juvenile hall, longer stays
in foster care, and numerous weekends of community service. During her stints of community
service, Cindy was renowned for running away
from the project sites and hitchhiking her way out
of the state. However, she was always caught and
returned to either the juvenile hall or taken back
into a foster group home.

The first time Cindy met Shirley Wolf was when
she had just walked away from yet another work
project and had hitched her way back to the group
home. She hoped to find a friend here from the

juvenile hall who would be willing to take to the road with her. However, her friend was not prepared to go with her, but another resident at the home, fourteen-year-old Shirley, was ready for an adventure.

Shirley Wolf was also an innocent victim of incest, and a survivor of neglect and frequent abuse. Her father had forced her into having oral sex right from the age of three and then full intercourse from the age of nine. He took photographs of her for an illicit child pornography magazine and made her go on birth control at the age of twelve.

When her mother was also subjected to a severe beating from Shirley's father, Shirley decided to tell her exactly what he had been forcing her to do. Together they contacted the authorities, who arrested Louis Wolf, and sentenced him to one hundred days in jail.

Torn apart by feelings of guilt, confusion and fear, Shirley tried to renounce her statement, but this only made things worse for her. She was then considered to be beyond hope and was sent to a series of foster homes. Meanwhile her father returned home, claiming he was free from blame. Shirley was somewhat of an outcast at school and often ended up picking fights with fellow classmates. It was due to this constant fighting that she ended up in the group home where she met Cindy Collier.

THE FATEFUL DAY

It was June 14, 1983, and the brand new best friends

Cindy and Shirley hitched back from the group home to Cindy's home town of Auburn, California.

Their spree of destruction started when they went swimming in a pool at a condominium and then dyed their hair in the pool's bathroom. Wanting to find some excitement they started prowling condominiums, knocking on doors at random to gain admittance. One elderly lady, 85-year-old Anna Brackett, was a grandmother herself and thought they looked like nice little girls and decided to let them in. She opened the door to the two young girls wearing only swimming costumes on the premise that they were going to call their parents.

Anna fetched the girls some water, and for a while they sat chatting with the old woman while they thought up a plan to steal her car. The phone rang and it was Anna's son calling to say that he was coming over. Cindy said to Shirley, 'It's time!'

Shirley grabbed the elderly woman by the neck and started to choke her. Cindy had found a butcher's knife and tossed it over to her. Shirley then wrestled the old woman to the floor and then started to frantically stab and slash at her body. In her fury and frenzy she broke the knife, so Cindy handed her a much larger one. Shirley stabbed Anna twenty-eight times in total, ignoring the old lady as she begged for her life. Cindy took a few stabs at the woman herself before they ran off laughing back to Cindy's house.

They were arrested by the police that night and confessed to the police that the murder gave them a 'kick' and that they would like to do another one as they thought it was fun. Shirley even wrote in her diary:

> 'Today Cindy and I ran away and killed an old lady. It was lots of fun.'

Cindy Collier and Shirley Wolf were subsequently sentenced to the maximum penalty for juveniles. They both stayed in prison until the age of twenty-seven and are now free.

It is obvious from this story that these two girls have a serious character disturbance. They seem to lack a sense of morality due to their lack of affectional bonds during adolescence. What they have developed are traits of arrogance, dishonesty, self-conceit, shamelessness and callousness, once again acting out the violence that they suffered at the hands of their parents.

The Murder of Shanda Sharer

Shanda Renee Sharer was one of the youngest murder victims in the state of Indiana in 1922. She was a sweet, caring, outgoing, twelve-year-old who was coaxed into starting a lesbian relationship which proved fatal for the unfortunate youth.

Shanda Sharer lived in New Albany, Indiana and attended Hazelwood Junior High. She was an outgoing girl with a sweet nature and had no problems making new friends. One of these new friends when she started eighth grade was a fourteen-year-old girl called Amanda Heavrin. They became close buddies and Amanda coaxed Shanda into having a lesbian relationship with her. The only problem was that Amanda already had a girlfriend, a very jealous sixteen-year-old named Melinda Loveless. Melinda became more and more obsessed and, over the course of six months, threatened Shanda both in and out of school. In fact her threats became such a problem that Shanda's parents moved her to a private catholic school even though she hadn't completed one full semester at Hazelwood High.

Shanda continued to see Amanda in secret. Melinda Loveless continued the threats to Shanda by telephone or by having friends pass on threatening notes. The teenage lovers Melinda and Amanda had been fighting for weeks over Shanda and the situation was starting to get out of hand and she wrote her lover, Amanda, a note saying:

'Yes I'm hurt and pissed at you! You better straighten your act up missy. You have not shown me no improvement yet. Shanda is not gone! And until she stops calling me and her name and writing is off of your shit, I'm not going to hang with you and your problem. I'm real mad at you! I feel like I need to cry! I want Shanda dead!! Love, Melinda'

But the notes and the threats were not enough to deter the developing relationship that was forming between Shanda and Amanda. Shanda continued to see and be seen out with her new lover.

MAKING PLANS

In December 1991 Amanda was introduced to a girl named Laurie Tackett through some mutual friends. The main reason she wanted to befriend Laurie was because she had heard her bragging that she would like to kill someone, simply for the fun of it. By Friday, January 11, 1992, Melinda Loveless had reached boiling point and decided that enough was enough. She decided to make plans to eliminate Shanda and she knew just the person who would be able to help her.

Melinda asked Laurie Tackett to come over to her house and she had something she wanted to discuss. Although she thought Laurie was a little strange, because she claimed she was a vampire and could raise demons, she was still a loyal friend.

On the way over to Melinda's house Laurie picked up two other friends, fifteen-year-olds Hope Rippey and Toni Lawrence. Neither Hope nor Toni knew Melinda well, but they had all lied to their parents about having a sleepover at a friend's house and they thought it would be a fun night. When they arrived at Melinda's they all went upstairs and starting talking about what they were going to do that night.

While they were chatting Melinda pulled out a large kitchen knife and told the others that she was going to use it frighten a girl. She then told Toni and Hope about the relationship Shanda was having with Amanda and that she was determined to do something about it. At this stage Laurie became angry with Melinda talking about her hatred of Shanda and said that if she really felt that way then she should get on and do something about it. The girls talked some more and devised a plant in which they could get Shanda into a vulnerable position.

The girls all got into Laurie's car and headed off in the direction of Shanda's house. They had difficulty in finding it at first, but after asking directions managed to find the right street and parked the car about half a block away. The plan was that as Toni and Hope had never met Shanda, they should knock on her door, say they were friend's of Amanda's, and ask her to come out to the car. The girls knocked on the front door and Shanda answered it. She was a little perplexed at first as she did not recognize either of the girls, but when they said they were friends of Amanda she relaxed a little. Toni and Hope explained that Amanda was waiting for her at a deserted stone building in the woods called Witches' Castle. Shanda told the girls that she was unable to come now as her parents were still up, but she would be able to sneak out around midnight after they had gone to bed.

Toni and Hope returned to the car and explained to Amanda what had happened. Initially she was angry that Shanda was not with them but calmed down when they told her that she was going to sneak out later to meet them. As they had time on their hands they all went off to see a punk rock concert that was being held at a nearby park.

As the concert didn't finish until around 12.00 p.m. the girls found they had to hurry back to Shanda's house. When they got there Laurie, Hope and Toni helped to hide Melinda in the back of the car by covering her with a blanket. Shanda was already waiting for them when Hope and Toni walked up to the side door of her house. Shanda was nervous at first but when Hope convinced her that Amanda was still waiting for her at Witches' Castle she followed them to the car. Shanda sat in the front seat while Laurie drove, Hope and Toni sat in the back with Melinda hiding on the floor of the car. Shanda became agitated and so the girls started chatting to put her at ease and told her that the Witches' Castle was a short drive away in a place called Utica and how it used to be the home of nine witches. During the drive Hope asked Shanda about her relationship with Amanda and she replied that she had been seeing her for quite a while and that she really cared for her. This was too much for Melinda, who suddenly popped up from the back seat, grabbed Shanda by the hair and held a knife to her throat. Shanda started to plead with the girls not to hurt her, but all they did was laugh. Shanda called her a bitch and continued to hold the knife to her throat until they reached a secluded part of the woods.

They dragged Shanda out of the car, who by this time was sobbing uncontrollably, and dragged her up to the Witches' Castle. Melinda tied Shanda's hands and continued to taunt her with the knife. It was rather dark when they reached the castle so Laurie decided to light a fire using a lighter and an old t-shirt. Laurie, pointing at the fire, teased Shanda and told her that that was what she would look like before long. Melinda and Laurie beat Shanda repeatedly and strangled her with a rope to the point where she passed out. But Laurie became nervous as several cars drove by the castle, and suggested that they take Shanda to a more secluded place to finish the job.

Unsure as to whether Shanda was still alive, the girls stuffed her into the boot of the car and covered her with a blanket and then headed for a petrol station to fill up the car. By this time both Toni and Hope were getting scared and, so as not to lose face with the other girls, they lied and said they were tired. Laurie offered to take them back to her house in Madison so that they could have a sleep, and the girls agreed.

Once back at Laurie's house all the girls went upstairs to her bedroom where she started to tell their fortunes by reading some strange mystic stones. All of a sudden Laurie's dog started barking and when they put their heads out of the window they could hear Shanda's screams coming from the boot of the car. Laurie ran downstairs and grabbed a knife. She ran to the car, opened up the boot and then repeatedly stabbed the distressed Shanda with a knife. When Laurie came back into her bedroom she was covered with blood and told the other girls that they needed to take a ride. Both Toni and Hope refused to go and so it just left Laurie and Melinda driving off into the night.

They drove around for a long time using side roads where they came across very few cars. Wondering what to do next, Laurie decided to stop the car and see if Shanda was still alive. The moment they lifted the lid of the boot, Shanda sat bolt upright. She was covered in blood and her eyes were rolling. She attempted to speak but all that came out was a very weak word 'mommy'. Laurie reached into the boot of the car and picked up a metal tyre iron and smashed it into Shanda's head. After the assault Shanda was quiet again and the two girls got back into the car and started driving once again.

They hadn't gone very far when they heard some strange gurgling noises coming from the back of the car. Once again they stopped and opened the lid to find that Shanda was now lying on her side completed saturated in her own blood.

Again Laurie picked up the tyre iron and hit her so violently around the head that this time a chunk of her skull actually broke off. Satisfied that this time Shanda was dead, Laurie got back into the car and started to laugh.

By now it was around seven in the morning and the girls decided to return to Laurie's house to pick up Toni and Hope. When they got back to the car both Hope and Toni asked what had happened to the little girl. With a cruel laugh Laurie replied, 'What little girl. It was all a dream'. With that all four girls got back into the car and Laurie offered to drop them off at their homes, after which the other two planned to dispose of the body in the boot. However, their plan was foiled when once again there was the sound of hitting and pounding on the lid of the boot. By now the girls were becoming quite frightened, they knew that Shanda was in a very bad shape, but were unsure how to kill her once and for all.

They made the decision to burn her and so Laurie stopped at a petrol station. As Laurie put petrol in the car she told Toni and go and buy a two-litre bottle of soda so that they could fill it up with petrol. When they had finished the girls drove off to Lemon Road. Hope knew the area quite well and suggested that it would be a good spot to finish off Shanda. They turned off Lemon Road onto a rural gravel track and stopped the car.

When the girls opened the boot of the car they were astonished to find that Shanda was still alive. There was blood and pieces of human flesh all over the boot, and yet she was still clinging to life begging them not to kill her. Toni said she did not want to take part any more and went and laid down on the back seat. Laurie, Melinda and Hope covered Shanda with the blanket and dragged her tortured body out of the boot and laid it onto the soft ground. They briefly argued about who would actually pour the petrol over her body, but it was finally agreed that Hope would do it. Laurie struck a match and threw it onto Shanda's petrol-soaked body, which immediately burst into flames. The three girls stood for a while watching, probably making sure that this time Shanda was actually dead. When they felt certain it was over, they got back into the car and drove away.

For some reason at this stage Melinda got nervous and asked Laurie to turn the car around. She said she wanted to make sure that Shanda was really dead. Once back at the scene Melinda grabbed the bottle of soda containing the remainder of the petrol and proceeded to pour it over the already burning body. She stood for a while watching and then got back into the car and started laughing, telling the girls how Shanda's tongue had been darting in and out of her mouth.

The girls were now happy as they felt the ordeal was over. Tired and hungry they stopped at a McDonalds restaurant on the way home to have egg Mcmuffins for breakfast. After they had eaten Laurie drove Toni and Hope back to their homes and then went back with Melinda to her house. Laurie was going to sleep over at Melinda's but not before they made some telephone calls to brag about what they had done that night.

152

THE GRUESOME DISCOVERY

It was a Saturday morning and two brothers, Donn and Ralph Foley decided they would like to do some quail hunting. After having a cup of coffee they loaded their hunting dogs into the back of Donn's truck and headed off to the country. As Donn turned into Lemon Road, Ralph saw something strange lying a few feet from the road in a field.

The first thing that came into his head was that it was a body, but then it looked so strange he thought it must be something else. Donn reversed the truck so that they could get a closer look. At first it was really hard to actually see what the object was. They initially thought it was a blow-up doll that someone had discarded and then burnt, but upon closer inspection the grisly reality of the situation was apparent. It was not the charred body of a doll at all, it was a human body. The body was naked apart from a pair of pants and was extensively charred from the waist upwards. The legs were stretched apart as if they had been posed, while the clenched fists were reaching out towards the sky. The sight of her face with the colourless eyes, and mouth wide open, was so horrific that it was something that would haunt the brothers for a long time to come.

Jefferson County sheriff's office received a call around 11.00 a.m. from Donn Foley. As there hadn't been a murder in the county for at least three years, Chief Deputy Randy Spry felt that it was either a hoax call, or that it wasn't a body at all that the brothers had discovered. He left for

Lemon Road and on arriving at the scene his doubts were soon erased and he realised that he was dealing with a very grisly murder.

He called back to headquarters and asked Sheriff Richard Shipley to come to the scene of the crime. Shipley was horrified when he looked down at the charred remains, he had seen many dead bodies in his time but none that had been so horrifically mutilated. He realised that his office would not be able to handle a murder of this magnitude and so he radioed the Indiana State Police to ask for their help.

The forensic expert, Curtis Wells, along with the Indiana State Police arrived at Lemon Road just after 1.00 in the afternoon. Wells recorded everything with a video camera and then took some photographs of the crime scene and surrounding area. He made a preliminary examination of the body and then took prints of various footprints and tyre marks that were near the scene. When he had finished, Wells turned the body over to the coroner and the body was removed to the State Medical Examiners Office in order that they could carry out an autopsy.

A ring that had been removed from the victim's body was a class ring from Jeffersonville High School, and it had the initials SGH inside. They went through all the missing person's reports, but none of them matched the description of their victim. What did puzzle the investigators in the case was why the body had been left in the open for anyone to find. If they had only dragged it several feet into the brush, it was possible that it wouldn't have been discovered for a long time. The only possible answer was that the perpetrator of this horrendous crime assumed that the fire would completely reduce the corpse to ashes and therefore be unidentifiable.

TONI LAWRENCE

When Toni arrived back home on Saturday evening, it was immediately apparent to her parents Clifton and Glenda Lawrence, that there was something wrong. Directly behind Toni was her best friend Hope, followed by her parents Carl and Gloria Rippey. They all had solemn faces, but before Toni's parents could ask any questions, she started crying uncontrollably and it was obvious that she was in a state of severe shock.

Clifton told his wife to take Toni into the other room while he had a talk with Hope's parents. Carl told Clifton that the girls had told him they had witnessed a murder that morning. He said that although the details were a little skimpy he did feel that the girls were telling the truth. He asked the Rippeys to come to the police station with him, but they refused and said they wanted to speak to a lawyer before taking any action. Meanwhile, Clifton called his wife and daughter back into the lounge and said they were going to the police.

The Cliftons arrived at the Sheriff's Office at around nine o'clock and as soon as Shipley heard that this family had information regarding a murder, he quickly ushered them into his office. As soon as Toni started to give details about what had happened the previous night, Shipley knew it was serious and decided to get everything recorded on tape.

THE ARRESTS

While the Lawrences were still at the sheriff's office, Shipley received a missing person's report from Clark County. Mr and Mrs Sharer had reported that their twelve-year-old daughter, Shanda, had gone missing around eight hours earlier. Shipley's stomach lurched as he listened to the description of the young girl, it matched that of the body found on Lemon Road.

It was almost two in the morning by the time that Sheriff Shipley managed to obtain warrants to arrest Laurie Tackett and Melinda Loveless. They discovered Laurie's truck at Melinda's house and decided to call there first. Melinda's mother answered the door and when asked where the girls were, she replied that they were upstairs sleeping. The two sleepy teenagers were handcuffed and taken back to the sheriff's office where they were booked and put in custody. Due to the lateness of the hour, they decided to wait until morning before they started to ask them any questions.

The autopsy revealed that Shanda had received multiple injuries including ligature marks on her wrists and several lacerations to her neck, head and legs. Cuts and bleeding around her anus indicated that she had been sodomized while she was still alive. But most horrifying of all was the fact that they found soot in her lungs which meant that she was not dead when her body was set on fire.

By now the media had got hold of the story and the public, who were in shock, demanded justice for the death of Shanda Sharer. It was not hard to build up enough evidence to bring the case to trial as apparently both Loveless and Tackett had told their story to at least three other people, two of whom were quite eager to give statements to the police. So gradually the police managed to build up a detailed report of what exactly happened on that night. Even though each of the four girls involved tried to play down their part in the murder, most of the details in the statements corroborated.

JUSTICE

On March 15, 1992, both Hope Rippey and Toni Lawrence were charged with murder, arson, battery with a deadly weapon, aggravated battery, criminal confinement and intimidation. Melinda Loveless and Laurie Tackett were charged with seven additional crimes including, child molesting and criminal deviate conduct and, a month later, an additional count of felony murder was added.

Sixteen-year-old Melinda Loveless was sentenced to sixty years in the Indiana Women's prison in Indianapolis, Indiana. With good behaviour she could be released in 2022.

Seventeen-year-old Laurie Tackett was also sentenced to sixty years in the Indiana Women's prison in Indiananopolis, and could also be released in 2022 with good behaviour.

Fifteen-year-old Hope Rippey was sentenced to fifty years in the Indiana Women's prison in Indianapolis, where she could be released in 2017 with good behaviour.

Finally, fifteen-year-old Toni Lawrence was

sentenced to twenty years in the Indiana Women's prison in Pendleton, Indiana. During the year 2000 Toni received an associate's degree which reduced her sentence by one year and, added to that good behaviour, she was released from prison on December 14, 2000 and remained on parole until December 2002. She only actually served nine years of her twenty year sentence.

Larry Swartz

Our last case in this section is one involving parricide.
Children who commit parricide are normally subjects of
physical, emotional and psychological abuse from an
early age. They frequently show signs of post-traumatic
stress disorder and hyperactive behaviour. Perhaps it is
time for society to become more aware of the abuse these
children have to bear and try and work out programmes
which will give them other options besides killing . . .

Bob Swartz grew up in Pittsburgh during America's Great Depression. In 1950 he moved to Ohio because he wanted to try and get an engineering degree. However, he dropped out of his studies to join the navy in 1952 but returned to study at the University of Maryland four years later. It was at the University that he met his future wife, Kate Sullivan.

Kate lived in Iowa and was brought up as a good Catholic girl by her parents. She was a bright pupil and achieved a master's degree in teaching at the University of Maryland. Bob proposed to Kate while they were still studying and she agreed as long as he converted to the Catholic religion.

Shortly after they were married Bob and Kate discovered that they were among the unlucky few who were unable to conceive and, after much discussion, decided they would adopt. In 1973 they adopted a six-year-old boy named Larry Joseph. Larry's blood mother was an unmarried teenage waitress and his father was an East Indian pimp. He had had a very unsettled start to his life and was frequently being shipped from one foster home to another, prior to his adoption by Mr and Mrs Swartz.

Two years later Bob and Kate decided to adopt another child, an American Indian boy named Michael, who was six months older than Larry. Then in 1979 they adopted their final child, this time a South Korean girl by the name of Annie.

PROBLEMS WITHIN THE FAMILY UNIT

Bob and Kate always considered their oldest son, Michael, to be the biggest problem. Michael never did very well at school and when he became a teenager he took to drinking and sneaking out of the house late at night. His parents decided to have an assessment carried out and through this they discovered that Michael had a learning disability. In an effort to improve his learning abilities, Michael was placed in special education classes. But, despite his fathers constant lectures and alleged beatings, his grades did not improve. By the time Michael was the age to go to high school, Bob and Kate felt they could no longer handle him and arranged to have him permanently institutionalized.

Larry, on the other hand, was the pride of joy of his adoptive parents. He always seemed eager to please them and after eighth grade, to their great delight Larry joined St. Mary's Seminary to study to become a priest. Unfortunately, after only two semesters Larry failed his exams and was asked to leave the priesthood. His parents were totally embarrassed and ashamed by his failure and on his return home they treated him with disdain. With Michael no longer living at home, Bob Swartz turned his anger and frustration towards his first adopted son.

When Larry first arrived back home his parents enrolled him at Broadneck High, Maryland, where his mother taught English. Once again he tried to win back their approval by taking part in extra-curricular activities, and even obtained the position of co-captain of his junior varsity soccer team. But all his efforts still were not good enough for his parents. Considering he had been an orphan with a very bad start in life, as adoptive parents they should have taken a far more under-standing and patient attitude towards his upbringing. Also, the fact that he had been in and out of foster homes for six years before coming to the Swartz home, lacking any sense of family bond, they should have known better than to exert such pressure on the confused boy. However, instead of helping him with love and affection, Mr and Mrs Swartz punished Larry for his poor grades by refusing to let him get his driver's licence.

BOILING POINT

By the time Larry Joseph was seventeen, he had simply had enough. On January 17, 1984, he was sitting in his room drinking rum following a violent argument with his father. At around 11.30 p.m. he came downstairs to the family room, where his mother was lounging around in her pyjamas, drinking a glass of beer and watching the television. The first thing she asked Larry, was how he was doing at his classes, to which he replied that he had flunked out of Spanish. Once again the lecturing began and while listening to the constant whining of his mother's voice he spotted an axe lying on top of some wood in front of the fireplace. Larry, in an insane rage, picked up the axe and proceeded to swing it at her head. He was so obsessed with the constant nagging that all he wanted to do was to get her to stop.

On hearing the sound of his wife's blood-curdling screams, Bob Swartz dashed down the stairs only to be met by his son, Larry, wielding a steak knife he had taken off his mother's dinner plate. Without giving him a chance to say a word, Larry went for his father with the knife, stabbing him over a dozen times in his brain, lungs, arms, stomach and shoulders. In a matter of minutes it was all over and his father's lifeless body slumped to the floor.

By this time Larry was being driven by the devil, his heart was racing, and he was completely devoid of any sense of reason. The voice in his head told him that he had to keep going, his appetite for revenge was not satisfied. Still standing over his father's corpse, Larry looked around the room only to find that his mother had gone! With the knife still in his hand, Larry ran out through the open sliding glass doors in their back yard. To his demonic delight he found his mother had collapsed in the snow, with blood still forcefully pumping out of the deep gash in her head. Larry knelt over the body and stabbed her seven times in the jugular vein with the knife that he still held in his hand.

Once he was certain that she was dead, he removed her pyjamas and proceeded to sexually abuse his inert mother. This seemed to be the final act in what seemed to be a bout of temporary insanity.

With his pulse back to normal and his bloodlust satisfied, Larry went back into the house, picked up the axe and the knife and threw them both into a swamp behind his house. Then he went back indoors, left the two bodies untouched, and made his way back to his bedroom where he fell peacefully asleep.

THE NEXT MORNING

The following morning at around seven o'clock, his kid sister Annie, woke Larry up saying that she couldn't find her mum and dad and that they weren't in their beds. When they went downstairs and discovered the butchered bodies, Larry feigned shock and called the police quite calmly to state that Bob and Kate Swartz had been murdered.

For three days Larry denied committing the murders and tried to implicate his brother, Michael. This seemed quite an appropriate line of action considering his brother was in a mental institution.

The police carried out intensive interviews on both Michael and Larry and, although they were certain it was Larry, decided to gather a bit more information before making an arrest. While the police were making further investigations, Larry actually disclosed to his lawyers that he was the one that had in fact brutally murdered his parents.

Luckily for Larry, the judge at his trial was quite a softie, and actually felt sorry for the young lad who had had such a traumatic upbringing. He told the lad that because of his age he felt that there was possibility of rehabilitation and he would be lenient with the sentence. Judge Bruce C. Williams gave Larry two concurrent twenty-year sentences and then suspended all but twelve years of each.

PART 2
MEN WHO KILL

Are These Men Monsters?

Edmund Kemper, a serial killer in the 1970s, once said: 'It was an urge . . . A strong urge, and the longer I let it go the stronger it got, to where I was taking risks to go out and kill people – risks that normally, according to my little rules of operation, I wouldn't take because they could lead to arrest.'

As no-one can really get inside the mind of a killer it is difficult to say whether they are actually insane monsters or merely the result of violence and abuse when they were adolescents. We have already seen in the previous section of this book that children will often re-enact the abuse that they received at their hands of their parents, so it is very possible in some of our case histories that this was carried on into adulthood.

For years psychiatrists have tried to discover where this strong urge to kill comes from, and why it is so overpowering, to the point of blinding the person from any sense of morality. Could it be genetic? Could it be hormonal or biological? Or could it be the result of cultural conditioning? These are all questions we would love the answers to. Maybe we all have monsters inside us, but it is our strong sense of morality and guidance that helps to keep it under control. What we are endeavouring to find out is why in the psychopathic killer does the monster not only emerge, but they seem to become slaves to its constant lust for blood.

We have the statements of various serial killers who gave very different reasons for their crimes: Ted Bundy claimed it was the responsibility of pornography, while Jeffrey Dahmer said that he was born with a 'part' of him missing. Herbert Mullin who killed thirteen people, blamed the voices that he heard in his head and when it was time to kill they told him to 'sing the die song'. Bobby Joe Long blamed a motorcycle accident for making him hypersexual, subsequently turning him into a serial lust killer. Others blamed prison, their upbringing and one murderer even turned the blame on his victims and said that they deserved to die. Whatever the reason they gave they must all surely be out of their minds.

In our normal, adjusted minds we would like to think that they are all insane, because it is hard to accept that any normal human being would actually enjoy taking the life of another. But the really chilling factor is that the majority of serial killers are rational, calculating and, as Dennis Nilsen put it, 'a mind can be evil without being abnormal'.

THE SERIAL OR ORGANIZED KILLER

The definition of a serial killer is someone that leaves a cooling off period between their murders of anywhere from days or weeks to even months or years. Their murders are always premeditated and very carefully planned, often selecting victims according to a specific characteristic. It is a known fact that nearly all serial killers are caucasian males that range between the ages of twenty and thirty-five at the time when they commit their crime. These killers feel a strong urge to try and dominate others and may be prone to violent outbursts. They generally have an unnatural fascination for pornography, bondage and indeed any abnormal sexual acts. Another strange phenomenon is they are often obsessed with material things and fascinated by anything to do with police work, uniforms and the apparatus they use.

What makes it hard for the police to track down the serial killer is the fact that he does not stand out from the crowd. They normally require very little sleep, are articulate, charismatic and are quite particular about their appearance. These traits are quite unlike those of the disorganized killer who will often appear dishevelled and very often withdrawn.

Although serial killers do not generally develop a long-term relationship, they do normally have a string of short-term sexual partners. Perhaps it is their fantasies about sex and violence that stops them from forming a successful one-to-one relationship.

Let us delve a little deeper and go into some of the childhood factors that could have had an effect on the way they behave as an adult. The order of birth seems to play quite a large part in the profile of an organized killer, since they are generally the firstborn. They will normally stand out at school either by acting the clown or become the classroom bully. Most reports on serial killers state that they come from very insecure backgrounds where they were abused and received very little affection. Often the killer will use fantasies about their childhood in order to escape the truth about their home life. These fantasies, rather than being about a better life, are generally about aggression and revenge.

The type of victim a killer chooses can also tell us a lot about the sort of man he is. There are generally three types of victim – high, moderate and low-risk. Organized killers like to target the high-risk victims like prostitutes, hitchhikers, vagrants or children. They may pick a victim because of the way they look, or possibly because they remind them of a past lover, family member, or something from his past. Organized killers always pursue the same type of victim and they often bear a striking resemblance to one another. For example: the colour of their hair, their occupation, age, height etc. Almost all the victims will be white as inter-racial killings are extremely rare.

The organized killer is perfected in the art of deception. They are very adept at impersonating either police officers, security guards or people in authority which forces their victim into a false sense of security. Another con is to lure prostitutes with the promise of large sums of money or children by the promise that they will take them home to their parents. They will usually have enough contact with their victim prior to the assault, as to make the whole matter more personalized.

Then there is the method of killing which will also have a pattern of similarities. The organized criminal will not attack his victim until he feels he is complete control of the situation. This control may be achieved by the use of various restraints including ropes or handcuffs, and they usually like the death to be slow and deliberate. They prefer a hands-on methods of killing, for example strangulation or stabbing, as this allows the killer to get closer to their victim thus exerting more control. Forensic reports will often report bite marks on the bodies of their victims, or semen in body orifices. Also the sexual attack generally takes place while the victim is still alive, as opposed to the disorganized killer who seems to prefer the inert corpse.

Finally there are also patterns that form in the serial killers behaviour both before and after they have committed a crime. In the immediate days before the organized killer commits his crime, they are very often involved in some kind of criminal behaviour. These crimes are generally of a minor nature such as, breaking into a house to steal items that for them have a sexual undertone and these are called 'fetish' burglaries. They have also been known to start minor fires or even kill pets within their neighbourhood. Some murderers may even go out to bars, car parks, gay bars or districts to choose a victim in advance, and it is not uncommon for them to consume alcohol or use drugs just prior to their crime.

Post-crime behaviour seems to fall into four categories:

1. They will often return to the scene of the crime.
2. They like to around when the body of their victim is discovered.
3. They keep trophies of their murders
4. They often participate in the investigation

It is quite common for the organized killer to return to scene of the crime so that he can relive the fantasy of his murder, kill another victim, or even to commit a sexual act with the corpse. He likes to be around when the body is discovered as this seems to give him a great deal of pleasure. The trophies that the killer will usually remove from the crime scene can be anything from jewellery, pieces of clothing or even photographs of his victim and he may use these time and time again to relive his fantasies. Also taking part in the investigation allows him to keep track of the police's progress. Although all these actions put him in jeopardy of being caught, the killer's desire to live out his fantasy is insatiable.

Of course all the generalizations I have mentioned will not apply to every single case, but they are found to be true in about three-quarter of the cases. It helps the police to build up a profile of the suspect and, even if all the information is not correct, the majority of it will help in the apprehension of a murderer.

The character of the serial or organized killer changes as soon as they are actually caught. From the calm, smart, organized exterior emerges an appearance of insanity. They will pretend to be a multiple personality, a schizophrenic, or the subject of blackouts – in fact anything that will make the police believe they have diminished responsibility. What does lie beneath the suave exterior of the serial killer?

THE DISORGANIZED KILLER

The disorganized killer is the complete opposite to the organized or serial killer. He will choose his victims at random, dehumanize or distance himself from them, relies less on torture and, after the murder has taken place, will take little or no steps to cover up his crime. Because they will more often than not leave clues behind them, the disorganized killer is generally much easier to apprehend, but are obviously no less a threat than the organized killer.

The disorganized killer is normally a loner and his murder will usually display anger. Most are of a low intelligence and suffer from some form of mental disorder. The killing is not pre-planned and is generally a spur of the moment thing.

The following are factors that are normally common to the disorganized killer. Firstly, he will usually walk to and away from the crime scene, but if he does use a car it will most probably be in a very poor condition. The murder is a spur of the moment event with no planning other than the one simple objective to kill. The killer will have no previous contact with his victim, and does not generally carry any particular 'tools of the trade'. The disorganized murderer does not rape or torture his victim before the murder. The actual act will normally be frenzied and the victim will sustain many wounds as a result of the high degree of violence. The disorganized murdered does not care whether he leaves any evidence at the scene of the crime, and will not attempt to move or bury the body. The killer will very often be involved in further acts with the corpse – mutilation, necrophilia, cannibalism, etc. – and may also take a souvenir from the body. Finally, they will take very little if any interest in the crime after it has been committed.

There are also keypoints in the disorganized killer's childhood, such as his family or school life. Very often their father may be unstable, inflicting forceful discipline upon their child. There are very often family problems due to drug and alcohol abuse, mental illness, etc. The child is usually a withdrawn, silent type who internalizes hurt, anger and pain. They usually have a low IQ and will usually bunk off from school as they are not able to keep up with the rest of their classmates.

As an adult the disorganized killer may have a very low opinion of themselves and consequently think that they are inadequate. They may have some form of disability, mental illness, or even a physical ailment. They are loners, withdrawn from society and incapable of forming relationships. They are usually incapable of having a sexual relationship or if they do may be very bad at it which only exacerbates their feeling of inadequacy. They feel inferior to other people and will either live alone or continue to live with one or other of their parents.

So the disorganized killer is a person who lacks the self-gratification to maintain a healthy mental attitude. Constantly being belittled they do not feel good about themselves and so it is all part of a terrible inescapable cycle of demented self-gratification.

THE MASS MURDERER

The majority of mass murderers are male, caucasian, traditionalist, and come from relatively stable, lower-middle-class backgrounds. They normally come from a stable home and have not been the subject of neglect or abuse. Instead, they are people who aspire to more than they can achieve, and blame other people for holding them back. They start to become outcasts and are not able to identify with large groups of people. In fact they become frustrated, angry individuals who feel helpless and hopeless about their future and start to form a homicidal hatred towards large groups of people. Very often they choose to die in an explosion of violence that is directed at the very group they feel that threatens or excludes them.

Mass murderers can be divided into three separate groups:

1. The family annihilators
2. The paramilitary enthusiasts
3. The discontented worker

The simmering rage within the mass murderer can be triggered off, therefore, by unemployment, extreme loneliness, a family breakup, or maybe just a reprimand at the workplace. Very often the murderer will save the last bullet for themselves, but those who don't are generally declared legally insane, a very different picture from that of the serial or organized killer.

Having looked at the various types of killers next we move on to look at some case studies of men who killed in different ways and for different reasons.

CASE
HISTORIES

Ted Bundy

*Attractive, ambitious and intelligent with a natural way
of blending in. What made this polite, well-dressed man
feel the need to prey on pretty, dark-haired girls over a
four-year period?*

On January 31, 1974, Linda Healey disappeared from her basement lodgings in Seattle without trace. All that was left behind were blood-stained sheets and a blood-stained dressing-gown that was hanging in her wardrobe.

Earlier that month Joni Lenz had been found by her student housemates, not asleep as they first thought, but lying in a pool of her own blood that was coming from her head and face.

When her terrified friends pulled back the bed sheets they were to find something even more horrendous – a rod from the end of her bed had been ripped off and savagely rammed into her vagina. Joni was rushed to hospital and miraculously was still alive although she lay in a coma and suffered brain damage that would be with her for the rest of her life. However, she was one of the lucky ones – one of the very few pretty dark-haired girls who survived an attack by Ted Bundy. There were countless victims, a number that have more likely than not been taken to his grave. He left behind him a trail of bloody murders that included the deaths of as many as thirty-six young women that spanned through four different states.

TED GROWING UP

Ted Bundy's life began on the November 24, 1946. He was born to 22-year-old Eleanor Louise Cowell in a home for unmarried mothers in Burlington, Vermont, USA. Bundy grew up never knowing his father. Soon after his birth they moved back in with Eleanor's mother and father who told everyone that Ted was their adopted son. Ted always though that they were his real parents and was told that Eleanor was his older sister.

Ted was extremely fond of his grandfather and they had a very close relationship. Other members of his family described Ted's grandfather as being ill-tempered and was known to be both verbally and physically abusive towards his wife. Ted's grandmother suffered badly from depression and agoraphobia, and very rarely left the house.

When he was four years old Ted moved with his natural mother to Tacoma, Washington to live with relatives. Shortly afterwards Eleanor married an army cook by the name of Johnnie Culpepper Bundy, and this was the family name that Ted would later assume for the rest of his life. A name that would later become synonymous with horror.

Ted's mother had four children with Johnnie Bundy, and Ted regularly had to spend his time babysitting for these siblings. As for his step-father they never really bonded. Even though Johnnie tried hard to treat him like one of his own,

Ted had other ideas. He was much closer to his grandfather whom he adored and who he would much rather spend time with.

When Ted started junior high school he was a shy but intelligent child. He was often teased and bullied but regardless of this he managed to keep his grades at a good level. He was active in the church and Boy Scouts, but is remembered for having an explosive temper when provoked.

Maybe now in hindsight it might have been apparent that Ted was not a completely normal child. It is quite common for children who have had unconventional childhoods to become introverted because of them – but it does not necessarily make them grow into callous cold-blooded killers. So was this murdering instinct present in Ted Bundy from the womb or was it something that happened later on in his life that triggered the reaction?

As it has been stated in psychological studies over the years, serial killers often tend to be white, heterosexual males in their twenties to thirties. While it is impossible to predict who will 'become a serial killer when they grow up' there are certain traits that seem to be apparent in many killers. These traits include cruelty to animals, bed-wetting, lying, drug and alcohol abuse, and a history of violence. The chicken and egg question is, does having these traits make you a killer or does being a killer give you these traits? And is Theodore Robert Cowell, otherwise known as Ted Bundy, a prime example of these studies?

By the time Ted started high-school, the fact

that he was shy did not seem to be a problem. It is said that he was much more popular than he was at Junior High, extremely well-dressed and a complete gentleman. His interests in skiing and politics started to take up all his spare time and even though he had a lot of female admirers he did not start dating until he went to college. All in all it seemed that his slightly unconventional childhood had not had any major effect on him as a adolescent. He was a shy but warm character with a keen interest in sport and no random morbid fascinations, or none that showed, that one would expect from a soon-to-be serial killer.

It was while in high school that Ted's interest for politics began to grow. He graduated from Woodrow Wilson High School in 1965 and won a scholarship to the University of Puget Sound. He started studying courses in Asian studies and Psychology but after just two semesters he transferred to the University of Washington in Seattle where he started studying intensively in Chinese. Ted Bundy seemed dedicated to achieving and worked in many part-time jobs to pay his way through university, although some employers are said to have thought that he was unreliable. Even though he was slack in his part-time work he was extremely focused in his university classes and always managed to obtain above average grades.

While he was studying at Washington University Ted embarked on an intense and passionate relationship that seemed to change his life forever.

In the Spring of 1967, Ted Bundy met Stephanie Brooks, a beautiful, intelligent and chic girl from a wealthy Californian family. She was tall, slender with long dark-brown hair with a centre parting. A look that would become very important in the not-too-distant future.

University friends said that Ted could not 'believe his luck', that someone from her background would be interested in someone like himself. She seemed genuinely fond of Ted and, although they had many differences, they also had some common bonding interests such as their passion for skiing. It was on one of their ski trips where the love and sexual side of their relationship really began, and Stephanie was the first woman that Ted became sexually involved with.

Ted was completely infatuated with Stephanie, he found her totally fascinating and was certainly the love of his life. One question that we could raise here is, was this love already unhealthy or was it the same as any other man embarking on his first sexual relationship?

Stephanie and Ted were like any other young, loving couple. Days would be spent taking long country walks, eating out and going on romantic skiing holidays. It seemed like the perfect balance of similarities and differences. However, problems started to surface when Stephanie admitted that she was not as infatuated by Ted as he was by her. She liked Ted immensely but was worried that he had no real direction or goals for the future. He tried too hard to impress her, to make her believe that he was the man for her, even if it meant lying, something that she detested – in a nutshell not the type of man that someone of her class and

181

upbringing could ever see spending the rest of her life with.

After graduating from the University of Washington in 1968, Stephanie finished the relationship with Ted. A break-up that he never, ever recovered from, a break-up that would put fear into all American women especially those who had similarities to Stephanie Brooks.

Following the breakup Ted lost his interest in everything including his studies and eventually dropped out of university. He became depressed and once again introverted, unable to believe that the love of his life did not feel the same way about him. Ted could not get over it, he was obsessed with Stephanie and managed to stay in contact with her through letters. Stephanie only replied out of politeness but had no interest in rekindling the relationship.

Could it be that this was the trigger that Bundy's mind seemed to need to turn him into an evil, homicidal maniac?

To add to this gigantic blow a year later in 1969, Ted learned that his 'sister' was in fact his mother and his 'parents' were his grandparents. This seemed to snap him out of his lethargy, and overnight he changed from a shy introvert into a focussed domineering man. Suddenly he wanted to prove himself to his family, his friends and, most importantly, to Stephanie. He was once again focussed enough to study and re-enrolled at the University of Washington, but this time to study psychology, a subject in which he surpassed.

With Stephanie now out of his life, he met a new

woman with whom he was to have a five-year relationship. This woman was Meg Anders, a shy and quiet divorcee with a young daughter. At first it seemed as though she had found the perfect father figure for her child, and to outsiders it appeared Ted had finally moved on from his infatuation with Stephanie Brooks. Meg fell deeply in love with Ted, even though she knew that she felt much more towards him than he ever did for her. Meg thought that she would, in time, change him and he would end up loving her as much as she loved him. This was a complete role reversal to the Ted who had – and still – loved Stephanie.

Bundy would spend a lot of time away from Meg on 'business trips' and spending many nights away from home. Although Meg never knew where he was, she didn't want to shatter her illusion of 'happy families' and consequently never questioned him. It was on one of his business trips in the autumn of 1973 that Ted met back up with Stephanie. She was surprised to find a confident, assertive man who was nothing like the shy boy she had known at university. Realising that he was a changed man Stephanie was prepared to try again.

Ted was still living with Meg at this time, and she knew nothing about Stephanie, least of all that they were seeing each other. Likewise, Stephanie knew nothing about Meg. That was the way Bundy liked it and that was the way he wanted it kept.

This time Stephanie became infatuated with Bundy and, realising that she had become totally dependent on him, Ted became distant and cold, and decided to stop having any contact with her. Just exactly what she had done to him a few years before.

Whilst becoming cold towards Stephanie the same was also happening at home with Meg. He lost interest in their sex life and more than ever before showed his dissatisfaction in their relationship. Any love that had been there – whether it had been real or not, was now gone. When, on the rare occasion, Bundy felt like having sexual intercourse with Meg it would be in the form of strange bondage fantasies that Meg detested and decided to end the relationship.

On the surface, between 1969–1972 it may have seemed to many that Ted's life was changing for the better. He started applying to law-schools and became active in local politics. He worked hard on a campaign to re-elect a Washington governor, a campaign that allowed Ted to form friendships with politically powerful people in the Republican Party. At the same time as being politically in-tune, Ted was undertaking voluntary work at a crisis clinic and even saved the life of a little boy who was drowning in a lake. All this seemed a long way from events that were about to or maybe had already started happening.

This is the biggest problem with many people who kill, especially serial killers, they are just so difficult to spot. They never seem 'mentally ill' but instead are usually charming, well dressed, highly intelligent and very pleasant company. Although this is only a generalization, Ted Bundy had all these characteristics, but so do many other men who do not feel the need to harm anyone let alone kill in cold blood. What is the factor that sets Ted

Bundy aside from other 'normal' human beings? Where was Ted's emotion and sense of right and wrong?

Other psychological studies of the serial killer have noted the importance of birth order, with many being the first born into uncaring and unloving families. This again, sounds very familiar in Ted's case. What were these demons within Bundy's mind, which on the surface were not apparent, doing to him?

HIS VICTIMS

Ted Bundy's first victim was Linda Healey in January 1974, just around the time that he stopped all contact with Stephanie.

About a month and a half after Linda Healey went missing a nineteen-year-old college student never arrived at the jazz concert she was going to and a month later a first-year University student was on her way to the cinema when she disappeared.

Over the period of two months another three young girls vanished.

Bundy had become a master of the lie and a true con artist. He would use a number of tricks to lure girls closer to him, acting out the injured party in order to get their sympathy. One such example is that he would have a fake plaster cast on his arm and then ask a passing girl to help him put something into his car.

More and more girls were going missing but at this point police were way off the trail. Ted had become a dormitory manager at the University of

Utah – he was now closer than ever to his victims and nobody had a clue. Whilst in this role, Bundy killed two teenage girls, sixteen-year-old Nancy Wilcox and seventeen-year-old Melissa Smith. It is said that he murdered at least eleven times in the states of Utah and Colorado. Still there was nothing that would link such a respectable young man with such horrendous crimes. But things were to soon start adding up.

The detectives working on the case had all the pictures of the missing girls laid out side-by-side on a table. The resemblance between them all was uncanny, in fact they could of been mistaken for sisters. Each woman was young, attractive, with dark brown, shoulder-length hair with a centre parting.

It appeared that Ted Bundy had become so good at his acts of deceit that he was starting to get bored and desired a little more excitement. He decided to start using his own name when luring his victims.

In July 1974 at Lake Sammamish people were out enjoying the warm weather and taking part in various water sports, but by the end of the day two more girls had vanished within sight of their groups of friends. One of these girls, Janice Ott, was seen by passers-by speaking to man with a sling who referred to himself as 'Ted'. Other women had apparently been approached by the same man, but they had been more fortunate. One of these women had gone with Ted to help him secure a sailing boat to his car, a tan colour VW Beetle. For some reason she became suspicious that something wasn't quite right, and she managed to get away.

The name 'Ted' was now buzzing around and

police had a good description of the man and his car. People started calling in with 'suspects' and one call in particular mentioned the name Theodore Bundy. Bundy was routinely checked along with other suspects by officers, but he appeared so above-board and clean that his name was filed away and forgotten – for the time being.

It wasn't until another girl who had a lucky escape, and remembered everything, that Bundy was to become the prime suspect.

INCRIMINATING EVIDENCE

Carol DaRonch was window shopping in Salt Lake City when she was approached by a man in his twenties who said he was a policeman. He asked her if she had left her car in the car-park and requested her registration number. The plainclothes policeman said that her car had been broken in to and she was asked to accompany the officer to her car to see if anything had been stolen.

Carol asked to see some identification and was shown what appeared to be a police badge. So she went with him to her car. On arriving at the car she noticed that nothing had been stolen – but Bundy was persistent in a very believable way. He asked her to accompany him to the station to make a statement. Still convinced he was genuine she followed him to his rusty old VW Beetle and got inside. Carol then began to panic when she smelt alcohol on his breath and noticed that he was driving, at speed, in the opposite direction to the police station.

Bundy stopped briefly in a side street and Carol tried to make her escape, but he was too quick for her and snapped a handcuff to one of her wrists. Ted then pulled out a gun but, with one hand still free, Carol's instincts took over and she managed to struggle and jump out of the car and run as fast as she could. Carol had been lucky but Bundy was frustrated and now even more determined to claim a victim. That evening, only a few hours later, seventeen-year-old Debbie Kent would become his next victim. Throughout the winter of 1974 and into the spring of 1975 more and more women were falling victim to Bundy, but the police were still not on his scent.

That is not until the summer of 1975, when a transport policeman in Utah noticed a VW Beetle suspiciously parked just outside of Salt Lake County. The policeman was local to the area and had never noticed the tan coloured car before. When he put his lights on to get a better look at the registration number the Beetle drove off at high speed. The policeman immediately started a chase and eventually managed to get the driver of the VW Beetle to pull over.

When the man in the car produced his driving licence for the officer it was in the name of Theodore Robert Bundy. The car was then searched with Bundy's permission. The passenger seat was missing and inside the officer found a crowbar, ski mask, rope, handcuffs, wire and an ice pick. Bundy was arrested and placed under arrest for suspicion of burglary.

Soon after his arrest police started to see

connections between Bundy and the man that had attacked Carol DaRonch. Police also suspected that Bundy was responsible for the disappearance of Melissa Smith, Laura Aime and Debbie Kent. There were so many similarities that they felt sure it had to be Bundy. But they still needed evidence to support their case.

In the autumn of 1975 Ted Bundy was put in an identity parade of seven men. Police were not surprised when Carol DaRonch picked him out as the man that had attacked her a year earlier. Now the police were ready to launch a massive enquiry into their number one suspect – Mr Theodore Robert Bundy.

In February 1976 Bundy was put on trial for the kidnapping of Carol DaRonch. He sat in the court room looking extremely relaxed, not appearing to be at all worried about the trial. He probably felt that there was simply not enough evidence to convict him. When Carol took the stand and gave her account of the harrowing ordeal that took place, Bundy stared coldly at her and said that he had never seen Carol before in his life. The judge spent two days reviewing the case before deciding a verdict of guilty for aggravated kidnapping and sentenced him to fifteen years with a chance of parole on good behaviour.

While Ted was serving time for the attempted kidnap of Carol DaRonch, more and more evidence was being uncovered to link Bundy to many other murders and abductions. But Bundy continued to deny any connection.

Bundy was subjected to a lot of psychological

testing and evaluation whilst in prison. The reports showed that he was neither psychotic, neurotic, a drug addict, an alcohol abuser, nor suffering from a character disorder – but they did conclude that he had an unhealthy dependency on women and seemed to suffer from a great fear of being humiliated by them.

So, did this fear and dependency on women come from his past relationships – especially that relationship with Stephanie? Why were other personality and character traits typical in such offenders not visible in Bundy? Maybe they just weren't there or maybe his superior intelligence mixed with his interest in psychology – in which he excelled at university – managed to fool other psychologists into a false reasoning of his actions?

In October 1976, Colorado police filed charges against Ted Bundy for the murder of Caryn Campbell. Her body had been found and upon examination her skull showed dents made by a blunt instrument. An instrument which matched the crow bar that had been found in Bundy's car the previous year. Hair was also found in the car matched the hair type of Caryn Campbell.

Whilst awaiting trial for this murder, Ted was moved to Garfield County Jail in Colorado and it was at this point that he decided to sack his lawyer and represent himself in the trial which was set for November 14, 1977.

Throughout his four year rampage it was quite obvious that Bundy planned everything meticulously. Perhaps one of his greatest plans was when he was granted permission to leave the prison on several occasions to use the courthouse library for the purpose of research. This plan went into action on June 7, 1977 when Bundy managed to jump from an open window in the library and escape. He was not wearing any handcuffs or leg irons and therefore he did not look any different from the rest of the people walking around the town of Aspen. He had obviously planned this escape for some time.

Ted managed to avoid capture for six days, and lived off food stolen from cabins and campers. He finally found a car which had the keys left in it and fled, but was spotted by police on his way to Aspen. After his recapture, police ordered Bundy to wear handcuffs at all times, as they could not afford to make any more blunders in a case that had already made them look rather inept. But Bundy was not going to be foiled very easily. He was still like the man that Stephanie had fallen in love with the second time – cool, calculating, and confident, with a driving ambition.

In late December Bundy attempted another escape which was far more successful. He had managed to find an opening in the ceiling of his cell which happened to lead into the ceiling of a prison warden's apartment. Once he knew the jailer had gone Ted walked out the front door to freedom.

By the time police had been made aware of his escape Bundy was on the road and by mid January he was in Florida – which would be the last state in which he would commit murder and the state in which he would die.

Ted acquired a new name – Chris Hagen – and using this fake identity managed to acquire a one bedroom flat in Tallahessee, Florida. Once again he just blended into his surroundings and was quite at home in his new lodgings just a stone's throw from the Florida State University. In the early hours of the morning on January 15, 1978, Bundy crept into the Chi Omega sorority house armed with a solid wooden club. By the time he left, twenty-one-year-old student Margaret Brown had been strangled, twenty-year-old Lisa Levy had been sexually assaulted and then beaten to death with a club, and two other girls had been beaten with the wooden club but thankfully managed to survive. When detectives arrived at the sorority house they discovered bite marks on the dead girls.

Ted Bundy continued his spree for a little while longer possibly realising that he could be recaptured at any point. On the other hand, knowing the confident sort of man he was, he may have considered himself too clever to be recaptured for a second time.

Less than a mile away from the Chi Omega house, Cheryl Thompson's moaning was heard by two girls in the flat next door. They had already heard banging and after calling her house and not receiving a reply they called the police. When the police arrived at Cheryl's house they found her sitting on the bed holding her swollen head. She was barely conscious and was half naked – in fact, extremely lucky to be alive.

At this point, Bundy was not a known criminal in the state of Florida, especially as he was using an assumed name which had no connection with

192

his past life. The evidence that was left behind at the sorority house was rather inconclusive, with the only firm evidence being the bite marks on the victims and the eyewitness account from Cheryl's flat mate, Nita Leary, who had seen the man leave.

A couple of weeks later, in early February 1978, Bundy was ready to attack again. This time his target was a fourteen-year-old girl named Leslie Parmenter. She was approached by a strange man in a white van as she waited for her brother to come and collect her. The man said that he was a fireman and asked if she went to the nearby school. Leslie felt uncomfortable and had always been told by her father, a Chief of Police, not to talk to strangers. Luckily, just at that point her brother turned up. She got inside the car and told him what had been said. Leslie's brother, Danny, followed the white van, took down its number plate and gave it to his father.

The sad thing is, that this incident was not reported to the police straight away, as a few days later Ted Bundy was to murder his last, and youngest, victim – twelve-year-old Kimberley Leach. Kimberley vanished from her school playground on February 9, 1978. The last person to see her was her best friend Priscilla Blakney who watched her get into a stranger's car. Priscilla was unable to accurately remember what the car or the man looked like, and the evidence was not sufficient to give the police a positive lead.

The evidence that did help in them recapturing Ted Bundy came about when Detective Parmenter, the father of Danny and Leslie, started to track the registration number that Danny had taken down from the white van a few days before. He managed to trace the car back to a man called Randall Regan who told Detective Parmenter that his number plates had been stolen a short while ago, but he had already been issued with new ones. Detective Parmenter then took his two children down to the police station to show them a book of mug-shots – a book that contained the face of Ted Bundy. Immediately both of his children recognised the strange man in the white van to be Bundy.

Ted was finally arrested on February 15, 1978, as he drove a stolen car towards Pensacola. Once Bundy was identified, moulds of his teeth were taken to compare with the bite marks found on the bodies of the girls in the Chi Omega sorority house. The results were conclusive – they were a perfect match.

THE DEATH PENALTY

In July 1979, Bundy was convicted on two accounts of murder for the sorority murders and sentenced to death in Florida's electric chair. Later the same month Bundy was convicted of the murder of Kimberley Leach and received a further death sentence.

However, Bundy was not quite ready to admit defeat. He continued pleading his innocence, used legal tactics to delay his execution, and offered confessions in exchange for a reprieve. Finally, after nearly ten years of denial Ted Bundy admitted his guilt but spoke of himself in the third person – describing an 'entity' within him that carried out those callous crimes.

In his final months when he agreed to be interviewed, Bundy seemed to suddenly have an answer for his actions. This answer came in the form of hardcore pornography, which he said was solely to blame for the way he was. He said that he had become obsessed with sado-masochist pornography and confessed that he had became excited when he felt he was in complete control. He said that rape had been his motive and that the killing came from the need to stop his victims testifying.

Finally the state of Florida became impatient with his stories and his legal manoeuvring and at 7 a.m. on January 24, 1989, Theodore Robert Bundy was executed.

It will never be known quite how many murders Bundy was responsible for, and this information has gone to the grave with him. It will also never be known why he did what he did. Is it possible to be too clever, so clever that a normal, everyday life is not enough to stimulate such a mind?

Bundy has even gone to his grave having the final analysis – in his long interviews on pornography it is clear that he has studied it from a psychological point of view. Pornography may be a reason why some criminals do what they do, but is it the reason why Ted did what he did?. Did Bundy make us believe what he wanted us to? Did Bundy out analyse the analysts?

The Yorkshire Ripper

Peter Sutcliffe terrorised the North of England in the late seventies and early eighties. In the space of five years he had claimed thirteen victims and was said to have been driven by God's voice emanating from a gravestone which commanded him to 'sweep the streets clean'.

Peter Sutcliffe, the killer dubbed as the 'Yorkshire Ripper' and 'Wearside Jack' was responsible for the murder of thirteen young women and the attempted murder of seven others from 1975 to 1980. The search for the 'Yorkshire Ripper' was the biggest manhunt Great Britain had ever seen, and it cost over £4m and used over five million police man hours.

So where did Sutcliffe's sordid lust begin? At what point in his life did he suddenly get the urge to kill – or had it been there the whole time?

HIS BACKGROUND

Peter Sutcliffe was born in Yorkshire, England on June 2, 1946. He was the firstborn son of John and Kathleen Sutcliffe and even though he weighed just 5lb at birth, he was a healthy baby.

Peter's father, John, was an extremely 'masculine'

man who loved both watching and participating in sport and going to the local pub with his friends for a few beers. John looked forward to the day that Peter would join him in his leisure activities.

But Peter did not grow up into the burly, confident man that his father was. In fact, Peter Sutcliffe had a completely different personality and character. Peter was a shy, quiet child who preferred the comfort of being at home reading with his mother then being outside fooling around and playing sport with his younger siblings and other boys of his age. It did not seem to appeal to him in the slightest. As a youth he felt rather intimidated by his father's masculinity and found safety in his mother's adoration for all of her six children.

This is often the way with the oldest child in a family, especially when the firstborn is a son. The boy can tend to take a step back from the rest of his siblings and let his brothers and sisters have the limelight and, instead, takes the role of the carer and helper. In many cases the oldest son may in fact be a father figure to his siblings, especially as, in a lot of cases, the father is out at work all day.

Peter also had the problem of being tiny at birth which meant he was always smaller than his peers. When he was at junior school he was never liked and never seemed to make the effort to integrate with his classmates. He would spend his break times hiding away from the other children and avoiding all the physical games that kids normally play. This was probably due to the fact he always came off worse due to his small stature and lack of strength.

Things did not improve for Peter when he got to

secondary school. He was severely bullied, which resulted in him playing truant from school for about two weeks, which went unnoticed until his parents were informed of his absence. Whereas a lot of children who play truant may utilise the time exploring the town centre or being mischievous, Peter had spent his weeks at home hiding in the attic reading books and comics by torchlight.

Once the school realised Peter was playing truant, they decided to take immediate action. Although the bullying did stop, it didn't mean that school became any easier for him. Somehow he was always seen as different and set apart from the rest of the students.

Peter started to feel the need to 'fit in' in the last couple of years of Secondary school. He took up weight training and much to his father's delight was soon able to easily beat his other brothers at arm wrestling. The change in Peter did not stop there, he started to participate in sports, but due to the fact he was only doing it to fit in, he never really excelled in anything.

Sutcliffe finally left school at the age of fifteen with no goals or idea of what he wanted to do with his life. For the next couple of years he flitted from job to job, never sticking things out for more than a few months, and finally he took a job as a grave-digger at Bingley Cementery.

It is quite common for teenagers to not really know what career path they want to take, and it is certainly not unusual to try out a number of jobs before finding something that you are good at or really enjoy. On the other hand, a common

BORN TO BE KILLERS

characteristic of a serial killer, is the inability to hold down a job. But who can say whether this part of Sutcliffe's life was to lay the path for his evil future or whether he was just having the normal teenage problem of not really knowing what he wanted to do tomorrow let alone in a few years time?

Peter absolutely adored his mother and would do anything for her, and spent a lot of time with her whilst he was a teenager. But his relationship with his father was totally different, they were so different that there did not seem to be a common bond. Peter's father was slightly happier when he took up weight training but that did not make Peter have any more time for his father. Peter believed that his father spent too much time with his friends – drinking and socialising. By the age of eighteen, Peter Sutcliffe had still not shown any interest in girls and relationships, something which was a concern to his father.

When Peter was twenty he finally approached a Czechoslovakian girl called Sonia Szurma. At first, her parents were not happy with her choice of man, but through time they grew to love Peter whom they believed to be a charming, hard working man who treated their daughter well.

In 1968, Peter was distraught to find out that his mother was having an affair with a police officer. He told his father that he understood what he was going through as Sonia had had an affair a couple of years after they had started dating.

Did this situation of the only two women in his life have a knock-on effect to what was to happen a few years later? Would something like this take all Peter's respect for women away? Did Peter now think that all women were the same and did not deserve to be treated with any respect? Did this make Peter's brain rationalise, in some twisted way, the murders he was about to commit?

THE KILLING STARTS

After eight years of dating, Sutcliffe married Sonia and for a long time managed to keep his public appearance as a shy, quiet gentleman. There were no outward signs of violence, and any such evil feelings were well hidden within his soul.

However, one person that had seen another slightly worrying side of Peter, was Gary Jackson, a work colleague at the cemetery. He recounted that Peter and Sonia had lived with her mother and father for three years before finally moving into a place of their own in Heaton, Bradford in 1977. But by this point Peter Sutcliffe was definitely not the man that his in-laws had grown to love and respect. Two years earlier, on October 30, 1975, Peter Sutcliffe had committed his first murder. Actually it was in the summer of this same year that his spree had actually started. Anna Rogulskyj had been attacked on July 5, 1975, but had managed to escape with only minor wounds. A month later there was another attack on Olive Smelt, but again she had a very lucky escape.

Wilma McCann, a twenty-eight-year-old prosti- tute from the rundown, Chapeltown district of Leeds, had not been so lucky. She had gone out on the town drinking in various pubs and clubs and by the early hours of October 30 was touting for business near her Chapeltown home.

Wilma was soon picked up by a man in a lime green Ford Capri who took her to the nearby Price Phillip playing fields and suggested that they had sex on the grass. This man was Peter Sutcliffe. As Wilma started taking her trousers off, Sutcliffe was reaching for a hammer and began battering Wilma over the head. Wilma's body was discovered later that morning by a milkman and was found to have stab wounds all over her body. The pathologist reported that the stab wounds were inflicted after she had been battered to death, either as a way of making sure she was dead, or as a ritualistic final stage of a sadist.

On January 20, 1976, Emily Jackson went to the Gaiety public house in Roundhay Road in Leeds, accompanied by her husband. It was a notorious meeting place for prostitutes and their clients. While her husband took a seat in the public house and waited for her, Emily climbed into the front seat of a Land Rover that had been waiting in the car park. Mr Jackson waited for quite some considerable time, but assuming that Emily was gone for the night, gave up and took a taxi home. However, the next morning her body was discovered by a workman. Her clothing had been removed and there were repeated stab wounds on her chest. Her head had been bashed with a hammer and overall there were at least fifty stab wounds to her neck, stomach and chest. Added to this her back had been gouged with a

Philips screwdriver.

It was from this murder that the police managed to obtain their first piece of positive evidence. The killer had left the impression of his size seven wellington boot stamped onto the right thigh of Emily Jackson's body. The modus operandi was so similar, that the police linked this killing with that of Wilma McCann.

In October 1976, Peter Sutcliffe came home to his wife with the good news that he had finally found work as a lorry driver with T. & W. H. Clark (Holdings Ltd) on the Canal Road Industrial Estate, between Shipley and Bradford.

It was five months before Sutcliffe would claim his next victim. On February 5, 1977, twenty-eight-year-old Irene Richardson left her rooming house at around 11.30 p.m. to go to a disco at Tiffany's Club. She was certainly down on her luck for her two daughters had been put into foster care and due to lack of money she had taken to walking the streets of Chapeltown to look for customers. On this night she had been walking to the disco but had never actually showed up at the club. Her body was discovered the next morning by a jogger near a sports pavilion. She was found lying face down with her coat covering her bloodied body. She had a fractured skull where her head had been hit with a hammer three times, her clothes had been removed, and once again she had multiple stab wounds. The attack was so frenzied that it had caused her intestines to spill out.

The police were now aware that they had a serial killer stalking the streets, something that had not been seen for a long time. The press issued details of the killings and gave the serial killer a name – 'The Yorkshire Ripper'. There had new evidence at the scene of his last victim – tyre tracks. With the assistance of local tyre manufacturers they managed to break it down to a possible twenty-six models of car. However, without the modern assistance of computers they had to rely on the records at the local vehicle taxation offices. The vehicles that were compatible with the tracks found at the scene was over 100,000 cars! Not much of a lead.

The next killing came on April 23, 1977. Patricia Atkinson lived alone in a small house in Bradford and had gone down to her local pub to have a drink with a few friends. She operated as a prostitute from her small flat and felt safe inside from the threat of the Ripper who always seemed to kill his women outside. Patricia was seen walking home at around 11.00 p.m. and it was soon after this that Peter Sutcliffe met the now drunk Tina. They walked together to his car and then drove back to her flat. As they went through her front door Sutcliffe struck the back of her head with a hammer, the same one that he had used on all his other victims. He then dragged her bleeding body to the bedroom where he proceeded to remove her clothes and further mutilate her.

Patricia's body was discovered the next day when some friends called round and, on finding the front door ajar, went inside and were horrified by what they found. The police were in no doubt that it was the Yorkshire Ripper as he had left the print of a size seven wellington boot on one of the bed sheets – the same print as the one left at the crime scene of Emily Jackson.

Peter's activities as the notorious Yorkshire Ripper continued to escalate. On June 25, 1977, he went down to a pub to have a drink with some friends and around 2.00 a.m. he left for home. Sixteen-year-old Jayne MacDonald was also out on that Saturday night. She had been to a dance and had gone to buy some chips with some friend in the city centre. Busy chatting with her friends she missed the last bus home and so it was around 11.50 p.m. that she began walking home with a young boy named Mark Jones. It was around 1.30 p.m. when they parted company. Jayne stopped to call a taxi but could not get an answer and so continued walking. She had not seen the figure lurking in the shadows waiting to pounce on her.

Jayne MacDonald's body was discovered by some children at around 9.50 a.m. lying by a wall in a playground. Everything about this attack was a replica of the others, with the exception that Jayne was not a prostitute.

Newspaper reports the following day stated that an 'innocent young woman had been slaughtered', sadly reflecting the attitude that prostitutes deserved what they got. Where witnesses were previously reluctant to admit any association with the murdered prostitutes, now people came from the surrounding area quite willing to volunteer information in an attempt to catch the killer.

The police were now getting desperate in their attempts to apprehend the murderer. Maureen

Long, who had survived an earlier attack by the Ripper, described his appearance as around 6 foot tall, 30–40 years of age with long hair. Only a few women actually survived the attacks of the Ripper and each time they gave a different description of their attacker, so the police were no nearer to catching their man. Meanwhile Peter Sutcliffe was able to continue to hide behind his disguise of respectability and continued his rampage of destruction.

THE FIVE-POUND NOTE

On October 1, 1977, a prostitute named Jean Jordan, accepted an advance of £5 and climbed into Peter Sutcliffe's car. He drove to some allotments near the Southern Cemetery in Manchester and as they climbed out of his car, Sutcliffe hit her eleven times with his hammer. He dragged her body into the protection of some bushes but just as he was about to continue his attack he heard the sound of a car approaching and fled the scene. One thing that played on his mind as he drove away, was the £5 he had given the girl, as he felt sure that the police would be able to trace it back to where he worked. It was a brand new note that he had received in his pay packet at T. & W. H. Clark. He waited for eight days and as there had been no news that a body had been found, Sutcliffe decided to risk it and return to the body to retrieve the £5 note. However, when he arrived at the allotment he searched and searched but was unable to find the victim's handbag. Frustrated and angry

Sutcliffe then proceeded to attack the body with a piece of broken glass in an attempt to hide his signature hammer blows.

The body was discovered the very next day by a passer-by but the body could not be identified at first because the head was mutilated beyond recognition. Her identity was later discovered by fingerprinting – she was Jean Jordan. She had not been reported as a missing person because apparently her husband thought nothing of her disappearance. The police thoroughly searched the scene of the crime and found the missing handbag. On further inspection they discovered a secret pocket which contained the new £5 note. The serial number, which was AW51 121565, was tracked through the bank to thirty possible companies, one of which was T. & W. H. Clark where Peter Sutcliffe worked. The police now had a list of 5,494 people who could possibly have received the note and one of these was Peter. He was questioned one month after Jordan's death in routine questioning, but the police felt he had a genuine alibi.

STATE OF PANIC

By now prostitutes were in a state of panic and they devised systems to protect themselves from the Ripper. Eighteen-year-old Helen Rytka and her twin sister Rita wrote down the number plate of every car that either sister got into and then arranged to meet at a designated place within exactly fifteen minutes. However, on January 31, 1978, Helen arrived at the meeting place five minutes early, when Peter Sutcliffe showed up. Probably thinking that the chances of the man being the Ripper were one in a million, she climbed into his car and then drove to a timber yard close to a railway line. Initially Sutcliffe's plan was foiled as he spotted two men working at the timber yard and so he ended up having sex with the girl. When the two men had gone and Helen moved from the back of the car into the front, Sutcliffe struck once again with his hammer. He then mutilated the body and hid it under a pile of wood.

Rita phoned the police reluctantly to report that her sister was missing, scared that she might be arrested herself for soliciting. Using sniffer dogs the police tracked down the body but found no other clues at the scene to help them get any nearer to the arrest of the Ripper.

On March 26, 1978, a body was spotted in the red light district of Bradford. It was partially hidden under an old abandoned sofa, and apparently had been killed ten days before Helen Rytka. This time the victim was Yvonne Pearson. Apparently, as with Jean Jordan, the killer had returned to the body to make it more visible. The killer had also left another clue to the date by leaving a newspaper under her arm, and the police were in no doubt that this was the work of the Yorkshire Ripper.

The ninth Ripper victim was forty-one-year-old Vera Millward. Her body was discovered by a gardener on the morning of May 17, 1978, on a rubbish pile close to a car park.

A HOAX?

In March 1978 the police received two anonymous letters claiming to be from Jack the Ripper who was threatening more deaths and taunting the police. Both letters were considered to be a bad joke as the contents were both false and miscalculated. On the 23 March a third letter was sent to George Oldfield, who was head of the investigation. This time the writer of the letter made some reference to a medical detail in the Vera Millward murder which made the police take it much more seriously. Forensic scientists took saliva tests from the envelope and this time they achieved a positive result. These tests revealed a rare blood group B, the same as that of Joan Harrison's killer. They also confirmed that all three letters came from the same source. The writer predicted that the next victim was going to be 'an old slut' who came from the Bradford or Liverpool district.

It had been almost a year since the Ripper had claimed his last victim, and the police were now convinced that like that of 'Jack the Ripper' this case would remain unsolved. Possibly he had moved on, had died, or more unlikely that he had 'retired'. However, these claims were soon shattered when he claimed his tenth victim.

This time the unfortunate girl was nineteen-year-old Josephine Whitaker. It was April 4, 1979, a little before midnight, when Josephine was crossing Saville Park in Halifax. Sutcliffe was cruising around in his Ford car looking for a suitable victim, when he spotted her. Her body was found the next day with all the usual signature marks but, again, Josephine was not a prostitute. It now became obvious to the police that this maniac would appear to attack any women who were on the streets at night.

Two months after the murder of Josephine Whitaker an envelope containing a cassette tape arrived at the office of George Oldfield. The handwriting on the envelope appeared to be the same as that of the letters and when the tape was played the voice had a Geordie accent. The message was:

I'm Jack. I see you're still having no luck catching me . . . I reckon your boys are letting you down George. You can't be much good can ya? . . . I warned you in March that I would strike again, sorry it wasn't Bradford . . . I'm not sure when I will strike again, but it will definitely be some time this year, maybe September or October, even sooner if I can get the chance. I'm not sure where, maybe Manchester. I like it there. There's plenty of them knocking about. They never do learn do they George? . . . Well it's been nice talking to you. Yours Jack the Ripper.

Two days later George Oldfield presented the tape at a press conference still uncertain whether or not the tape, along with the letters, was a hoax or not. George was now so determined to catch the Ripper that he set up a publicity campaign and roadside information points with a phone line where you could listen to the Geordie voice. Unfortunately the police relied so much on the 'Geordie Ripper' that once again Sutcliffe was eliminated from being the suspect.

209

The response by the public was enormous and the police received around 50,000 calls. By the end of only the second day they had received 1,000 calls and every lead had to be followed up. A voice expert from Leeds University announced that the voice on the tape came from a village in Castletown and a team of police officers were moved to the village to carry out interviews at every single home. But still their efforts were to no avail.

The strain had taken its toll on George Oldfield, who suffered three heart attacks and had to be hospitalised. He did not return to the investigation until the beginning of 1980.

By the end of August 1979, the police were starting to doubt the Geordie connection and it was felt that they should dismiss the letters and tape altogether.

THE FINAL MURDERS

Peter Sutcliffe shocked his workmates in April 1979 when he told them that he was having an affair with a young woman who lived in a village near Glasgow. He was the last person they would have expected to have been messing around, as he had always talked most fondly of his wife Sonia. He had met Theresa Douglas in a bar near Glasgow when he had been making a delivery to a nearby General Motors plant. He made regular visits to her village and soon won over the hearts of her parents. The family knew him as Peter Logan, a divorced man, who lived in Yorkshire. He even jokingly told them that he was the Yorkshire

Ripper when Theresa's brother said he had evil-looking eyes. But the family laughed as they though he was one of the nicest men they had ever met.

Peter had a dilemma though, he was faced with the prospect of losing his licence due to the fact that he had been stopped for driving in an erratic manner when under the influence of drink. That meant that there would be no more visits to see his beloved Theresa, but more importantly, no more cruising the streets of Yorkshire looking for his next victim. As Peter waited for his case to come before the court, his attacks continued.

On the night of September 1, 1979, Sutcliffe spotted twenty-year-old Barbara Janine Leach walking down a quiet road in Bradford. Barbara was a student at the University and lived with a group of other students in Grove Terrace. Sutcliffe had spotted Barbara from across the room at The Mannville Arms, and had watched her continuously. When the pub closed he went outside and waited in his car until Barbara came out with her five friends. Peter watched as the party headed towards Grove Terrace. At this point Barbara decided she would like to go for a walk and asked her friend, Paul Smith, if he would like to go with her. He told her he was going home, and she asked him to wait up for her, as she didn't have a key.

Peter watched Barbara walk down the road on her own and then started the car and drove it back to Ash Grove where he left it parked. Armed with the hammer and knife he walked quickly along an alleyway which he realised Barbara would soon be passing. He waited in the shadows and as she passed he sprang out and smashed the hammer into her skull. One blow and she was dead.

He then dragged her body into the shadows and dropped her body to the ground. He tore at her clothing exposing her breasts, abdomen and underpants and proceeded to stab her torso eight times. When his frenzied attack was complete, he covered her body with a piece of old carpet and left it beside some dustbins.

Paul waited up for Barbara for around an hour and, assuming she had been invited to a party, went to bed. However, when he realised she hadn't been home all night he first rang her parents and then the police. They searched the area and her body was found that afternoon.

The police were no nearer to catching the Ripper and their £1m publicity campaign had turned up no new clues or evidence. Had they realised at the time that the letters and tape were just a cruel hoax, perhaps they would have been able to stop the deaths of four more women.

By this time in the investigations Peter Sutcliffe had been interviewed on a several occasions, and his workmates had taken to calling him the Ripper because of all the apparent police interest in him. Even as late as 1980 Peter was never really considered to be a serious suspect despite the fact that he had a gap in his front teeth, his blood type was B group, he had the correct boot size and finally his car had been spotted on several occasions in the red light districts. Added to all that incriminating evidence was the fact that he was now on the much shortened list of 300 possible recipients of the £5 note. In fact the overwhelming reason that Peter Sutcliffe was not considered a prime suspect, even after nine interviews, was because he was always able to provide an alibi which was verified by his wife, Sonia. Also he was dismissed because he did not have a Geordie accent. This is a frightening indication of how greatly assumptions prejudiced the investigations, limiting the outlook of the investigating officers to the point that they are able to miss vital clues.

What seems totally inexplicable, though, is that, of all the men the police interviewed, none were given blood tests, placed under surveillance or indeed even had their boot sizes checked. Of course the procedures in the 1980s were not as sophisticated as they are today, but even so the police did not seem to use the evidence they had to hand to help them apprehend the Ripper.

His next attack was on Marguerite Walls, a forty-seven-year-old civil servant. She had been working late on the night of August 20, 1980, as she was due to go on holiday the next day and she wanted to make sure she had cleared up all her work before she left. She left her office around 10.30 p.m. to begin her short route home. To be on the safe side she went the long way round, as it was on a bus route and the streets were well lit. Peter Sutcliffe jumped out from behind a fence and hit her around the head with his hammer. She did not fall to the ground immediately, as Peter had expected, but started screaming loudly. Even a second blow to the head did not stop Marguerite from screaming, and in a panic Peter grabbed her around the neck and strangled her. He dragged her body into a driveway and through some overgrown bushes and by the time he had reached the garage at the bottom of the garden his victim was dead. His frustration and anger rose to fever pitch when he realised that he had forgotten to bring his knife with him. He tore off her clothes in a frenzy and then proceeded to hit her numerous times with the hammer. When his anger was spent, he covered her body with leaves and left for home.

After this he attacked two more women, but luckily they both survived. The first was on September 24, when Dr. Upadhya Bandara was walking down an alleyway on her way home. The second was on November 5, 1980, in Huddesfield, his victim being sixteen-year-old Theresa Sykes. Theresa survived the brutal attack but was never to totally recover, so Peter had left his mark on yet another family.

The thirteenth and final murder took place on November 17, 1980, in Leeds. Sonia Sutcliffe had resigned herself to another night on her own watching television while her husband was supposedly out making a night delivery in Gloucester. What she didn't know was that he wasn't working at all, but was in fact in Headingley. Jacqueline Hill was a twenty-year-old student who Peter spotted walking past the Kentucky Fried Chicken shop where he was sitting alone having his meal. Jacqueline had just got off the bus when she entered the dimly-lit area of Alma Road. She was only about one hundred yards from her home when she was struck on the back of the head, rendering her unconscious. Peter dragged her body onto some vacant land just behind the Arndale car park. Protected from view by some trees and bushes, he removed her clothes and stabbed her repeatedly. This time he was careless and forgot about the handbag she had dropped in Alma Road when he had first attacked her.

Her bag was discovered, only a short time after the attack, by Amir Hussain, a student from Iran. He took the bag home with him and showed it to his flat mates, one of whom was an ex-chief inspector with the Hong Kong police, Tony Gosden. Tony immediately felt alarmed when he realised that nothing had been taken from the bag and that there were a couple of fresh blood spots on the outside. At 11.30 p.m. the students called the police, but it was quite some considerable time before an investigating officer arrived. He was reluctant to do anything about the bag until the next day, but on the insistence of Amir, the police started to search of the area. However, the brief search by torchlight did not uncover the body of Jacqueline and the police left.

The next morning around 10.00 a.m. a worker at the Arndale centre discovered the body, which was lying less than thirty yards from where the police had searched the previous night.

The attack was widely publicized and for once it appeared that the Yorkshire Ripper was not only a threat to prostitutes but also middle-class citizens and the public became enraged. Feminists now took to the streets in a violent protest against their loss of the right to walk their own streets in safety.

THE ARREST

The police were inundated with letters from the public who named people they believed could be suspects. One of these letters came from a man called Trevor Birdsall. In the letter he wrote about a man called Peter Sutcliffe, who was a lorry driver from Bradford. When the police had still not questioned Sutcliffe two weeks later, Trevor walked into the Bradford police station and once again repeated his allegations. The information was fed into their system but Peter Sutcliffe still continued to be a free man.

On January 2, 1981, two policemen, Sergeant Robert Ring and Constable Robert Hydes, were patrolling the streets of Sheffield. They were driving down an area which was renowned for its prostitutes, when they spotted a woman climbing into a car. They immediately went over to investigate so that they could possibly make an arrest for soliciting. When questioned, the man in the car said his name was Peter Williams. He asked the police if it would be all right for him to relieve himself, and when the police gave him permission he went over to an oil storage tank. When he returned to the car the police ran a check on the number plates and discovered that they were false. Both the man and the prostitute, Olivia Reivers, were arrested and taken to the police station on Hammerton Road. The man was questioned and told the police his full name was Peter William

Sutcliffe, and that he had obtained his number plates from a scrapyard in West Yorkshire.

Peter was held overnight and questioned further the following morning. This time he told the police that he had already been interviewed regarding a five-pound note that the Yorkshire Ripper had left behind at the scene of a crime. This made the police suspicious, because not only had this man been found in a car with a prostitute, but he had already been questioned regarding the murders. Sutcliffe also told the police that he was a lorry driver who frequently travelled to the North-East. The police then contacted the Ripper Squad and found out that Peter Sutcliffe was in fact a possible suspect. When the police told the squad that they had Sutcliffe in custody, Detective Boyle decided to travel to Dewsbury to question the man.

When the arresting officer, Robert Ring, heard that the Ripper Squad were coming down to question the suspect, he remembered that Sutcliffe had relieved himself the night before right beside an oil storage tank. Sergeant Ring immediately went back to the site and discovered a knife and a ball-pein hammer. He rang the police station with the news of his discovery and they couldn't believe the fact that at last they were making some real headway in the case of the Yorkshire Ripper.

That night they searched Sutcliffe's house and also questioned his wife. In the house they found around thirty different weapons.

The following morning when Sutcliffe was being questioned once more by Detective Boyle, Boyle mentioned about the discovery of the knife and the hammer. Sutcliffe asked if the detective was leading to the Yorkshire Ripper and when Boyle admitted he was, Sutcliffe confessed to being the murderer. Over the next few days Sutcliffe gave a full confession and admitted to killing thirteen women, but denied any knowledge of the 'Geordie Ripper'.

THE END OF THE YORKSHIRE RIPPER

The main reason Peter Sutcliffe gave for his vicious murders was his hatred of prostitutes. He said he wanted to get revenge because one had once cheated him out of ten pounds. But later when he was being further questioned he changed his motives. The psychiatric assessment on Peter Sutcliffe was that he was a paranoid schizophrenic. He told the doctors who interviewed him that, when he was working at Bingley Cemetery he had heard God's voice coming out of a gravestone commanding him to kill prostitutes. They also carried out an analysis of his handwriting from an epitaph they found in Sutcliffe's lorry, and this also revealed that he had some schizophrenic tendencies.

Peter Sutcliffe went to court sixteen weeks later. It was now up to the defence counsel to prove that he was legally insane, and in the hope of this Peter pleaded guilty to manslaughter. On the other hand the prosecutors tried to prove that Sutcliffe was sane by providing a witness. This witness was a prison officer who said he had overheard Sutcliffe telling his wife that if he could convince people he was mentally ill he would probably only get a ten year sentence in a mental institution. They also came up with the evidence that Sonia, Peter's wife, had had a breakdown in which she heard God's voice – an act which Sutcliffe thought he could copy to fake his own schizophrenia.

On May 22, the jury found him guilty of thirteen murders and seven attempted murders. He was sentenced to life imprisonment which he would serve at Parkhurst Prison.

HIS LIFE INSIDE

In 1983 Peter Sutcliffe was attacked by a fellow inmate with a broken coffee jar. The cut required 84 stitches to his face and in March 1984 he was transferred to Broadmoor mental hospital.

Sutcliffe was once again attacked on March 10, 1997. Another inmate at Broadmoor stabbed Peter in both eyes during a fight at the hospital. The attacker was a man named Ian Kay – also known as the 'Woolworths Killer' – who stabbed him with a fibre-tipped pen. These pens were used during the drawing classes at the hospital. When questioned, Kay, who was described as an extremely dangerous man, 'In hindsight I should have straddled him and strangled him with my bare hands . . . He said God told him to kill thirteen women, and I say the devil told me to kill him because of that.'

In March, 1996, Sutcliffe was once again assaulted. This time a prisoner at the hospital tried to garrote Sutcliffe with the flex from a pair of headphones and, when asked why, the man said he 'resented being locked up with sex offenders'.

It will never really be known whether Sutcliffe faked his mental analysis, but it is said that his mental state has deteriorated quite considerably since he has been at Broadmoor. But the main question, which still remains unanswered, is how did he avoid such a huge police operation for all those years?

One piece of information that did emerge some years later was that the hoaxer, who did such a good job of misleading the police investigations, was in fact a retired police officer himself. Apparently he bore a grudge against George Oldfield who had headed the Ripper investigation. He said he sent the the letters to settle the score against George Oldfield, whom he hated. Oldfield died from a heart attack in 1985. This was attributed to an unhealthy lifestyle, but also to the fact that he became too emotionally involved in the Ripper case which he was so desperate to solve.

Today, Sutcliffe is in a state of incoherent mental health at the Broadmoor high-security mental hospital in Berkshire, but no-one really knows what turned him into such a monster.

One theory is that his hatred of women initially started over a simple case of hurt pride. Peter had met a young woman by the name of Sonja Szurma who was to eventually be his wife. During their early courting days Peter became jealous of Sonja as he believed she was seeing another man. Peter decided to get his own back and picked up a prostitute who agreed to have sex with him for the sum of five pounds.

Peter paid the prostitute with a ten pound note and for some reason he was unable to achieve an erection. The prostitute ridiculed Peter and then had her pimp chase him off, without giving him his five pounds change.

About three weeks later Peter met the same prostitute in a pub and demanded that she give him his five pounds change. But instead of giving him the money she ridiculed him once more in front of everyone in the pub. Peter was seething and after leaving the pub waited for the prostitute outside. When she came out he pounced on her and hit her over the head with a rock contained inside a sock. The prostitute was unhurt, other than being stunned, but still reported the matter to the police. The incident was downplayed and Peter only ended up receiving a caution. But could this have been the start of his revenge killings?

The Brides in the Bath

*George Joseph Smith first married the women he
murdered, and then made sure they left him all their
money in their will. His method was to kill them
in the bath – that was until a simple bar of soap
gave the game away.*

It was a cold winter evening in the year 1914. A
middle-aged man sat by his flickering gaslight
playing a hymn on his harmonium – Nearer My
God to Thee. On hearing the mournful sound one
could have been excused for thinking George
Joseph Smith was a religious man. However, what
the neighbours didn't realise was that, directly
above George's head in the bathroom, lay the body
of his bride.

Margaret Lofty was a thirty-eight-year-old
vicar's daughter and had only been married to
George Smith for one day. Smith had only
drowned his wife minutes before and was now
using his music as an alibi. This was done in an
effort to convince his landlady that he was in fact
downstairs at the time of his wife's death.

This was typical of the cool facade that George
portrayed. Underneath he was a serial bigamist, a
ruthless seducer who married and murdered three

wives, all purely for financial gain. Added to these murders he managed to swindle many others out of money, but they were lucky and managed to escape with their lives. George Joseph Smith was also known by the names Oliver George Love, Charles Oliver James, Henry Williams and John Lloyd and was certainly one of the most cold-hearted and notorious killers of the twentieth century.

HIS BACKGROUND

George Joseph Smith was born on January 11, 1872, in Bethnal Green, in the East End of London. Smith was a typical cockney, full of charm and wit, with a wicked sense of humour. But this cockney had a darker side. As a youth he was a petty criminal, and at the age of nine was sent to a reformatory for stealing. At a very young age, Smith learned how to manipulate women in order to make money.

His first, and only legal marriage, was in 1898. But the marriage broke up when his wife was put in prison for stealing, I might add at the request of her husband. From then on he had a string of bigamous marriages to women whom he robbed and then left penniless. He could always spot the combination of wealth and vulnerability and frequented seafronts and pleasure gardens in his search for his next prey.

Once such victim was widow Florence Wilson, who was typical of the type of women he would woo. She met him in 1908 whilst walking along the seafront at Brighton. They had a whirlwind romance and he married her in London after first demanding she take out her life savings from the Post Office. But her honeymoon was short-lived, just a one-day visit to the White City Exhibition. George settled his new wife down on a park bench while he went off on the pretence of buying a newspaper. While Florence sat waiting for her husband to return, George had gone back to their lodgings to remove her valuables and money, and was never seen again.

Although this happened to many other women, they only lost their money and probably their faith in men. What happened to his next three 'wives' was far more gruesome.

WHERE IT ALL STARTED

His first victim was the thirty-three year daughter of a bank manager, Beatrice (Bessie) Mundy, in the year 1913. She met her future husband when she was out taking a walk in Clifton, Bristol, in 1910, when he introduced himself as Henry Williams, a restorer of pictures. Within days Bessie knew this was the man she wanted to marry and the wedding took place in Weymouth.

Bessie was a wealthy woman and her money was held in trust by her uncle, who was determined to protect it from Bessie's new husband. Somehow, Smith managed to persuade Bessie to make a will in his favour, and in so doing she signed her own death warrant.

Smith visited their local ironmongers and haggled over the price of a bath, which was supposed to be a present for his new wife. He convinced Bessie that she had been having fits which she had no recollection of when she came round. Acting out the part of a very concerned husband, Smith called out the doctor on several occasions. If his little plan worked, the fits would be given as the reason for her death while taking a bath. The doctor could find very little wrong with Bessie, but he had no doubt that Smith was telling the truth and prescribed some mild tranquillizers. The doctor heard nothing for a few days and then, on July 13, 1913, received a hastily scribbled note:

'Can you come at once? I am afraid my wife is dead.'

On arriving at the house the doctor was met by a very distressed George who immediately led him up to the bathroom where Bessie was lying completely inert in the bath that Smith had recently bought for his dear wife. She was partially submerged in the water and her face had turned blue. While pretending to be very upset, Smith told the doctor that he had been out shopping while his wife had been taking a bath. On his arrival home he had gone upstairs to see how she was getting on, only to find her dead.

Before he wrote to Bessie's relatives telling them of the shocking news, George decided to wait until after the inquest so that it would be too late for them to ask any awkward questions. Everything went exactly as he had planned. The coroner's jury came to the conclusion that Bessie had indeed suffered a fit whilst taking a bath and had no option but to return a verdict of death by misadventure. Bessie died leaving a large inheritance of £2,500 (about £150,000 today) to George Smith, who showed very little gratitude to the woman who had just left him a small fortune. He refused to even allow her the dignity of a private grave, and so Bessie's body was laid to rest in a common plot. As if that wasn't enough he even had the effrontery to return the bath to the ironmonger, saying that he no longer had any use for it, for which he received a full refund.

However, unbeknown to Smith, Bessie was to have her revenge. When she died she was holding a small piece of Castile soap in her right hand. Her fingers were clamped tightly around the fragment of soap when she was killed, and this would later prove to be a vital piece of evidence at Smith's future murder trial. For the time being, though, he was a free man – free to kill again.

ALICE BURNHAM

George Smith did not take long before finding himself a new wife. In October, 1913, he met Alice Burnham, who was a pretty, if not a little plump, nurse of twenty-five, in Southsea. Again, using his charm, Alice not only agreed to marry George within a few days, but also had her life insured for the sum of £500 and made her will over to him.

Alice was over the moon when George suggested they take a honeymoon in Blackpool. What she didn't know was that he needed to distance himself as far as possible from the scene of his last murder, so as not to attract too much suspicion.

One week after their wedding, on Friday, December 12, their landlady noticed that there was some water dripping from the ceiling in her kitchen. To give himself an alibi, Smith appeared downstairs and started chatting with his landlady. Next he went upstairs to the bathroom, only to discover that his wife had died whilst taking a bath.

When the doctor arrived, he found Smith tenderly holding his wife's head above the water. But something about this worried the doctor, for he noticed that he had actually bothered to roll up his shirt sleeve – hardly the gesture of a grief-stricken husband. This was a careless mistake on the part of Smith, but at the time there didn't seem to be any reason to suspect foul play. Again the coroner came back with the verdict – death by misadventure.

Smith, having carried off two murders successfully and accruing a nice sum of money to boot, became rather over-confident, which would eventually lead to his downfall.

MARGARET LOFTY

It was little more than a year later when Smith met Margaret Lofty in the city of Bath. Margaret was a spinster and worked as a ladies companion. She was a prime target because she had recently suffered a 'disappointment' in love. George, now calling himself John Lloyd, posed as a moneyed land agent. Perhaps because she was upset by her lost love, Margaret soon succumbed to the wily charms of George. A few days after meeting her new man, Margaret wrote to her sister to say that she was going to look after a lady in London for a few days. In fact, the truth of the matter was, she was preparing for a clandestine wedding.

As soon as George had talked Margaret into taking out a life insurance for £700, the couple were married and took lodgings at Highgate in London. However, Margaret did not have very long to enjoy her married life, for within thirty hours of leaving Bath, she was dead.

Their landlady was called Miss Louisa Blatch. On December 18, 1914, at around 7.30 p.m. Louisa heard the sound of splashing coming from the bathroom, followed by the sound of wet hands sliding down the side of a bath, and then a strange sigh. She was not perturbed at the time and just assumed that it was that nice Mrs. Lloyd moving around in the bath. Minutes later she heard the sound of the harmonium being played. Next she heard a knock at the front door. When she opened it it was her lodger Mr. Lloyd who claimed he had been out to buy some tomatoes for his wife, but unfortunately he had left his key behind.

Next, he went upstairs and, on entering the bathroom, cried for help. He went through the facade of trying to resuscitate his wife, whom he was positive was dead just forty-five minutes earlier.

Once again Margaret's death was recorded as misadventure, and Smith went about the business of collecting his insurance money. He had now accrued a small fortune of £3,500 (£190,000 today) and was very probably congratulating himself, when he was approached by two policemen.

Margaret's death had been widely publicized, and had drawn the attention of Alice Burnham's father and the landlady of her Blackpool lodgings. When they read the newspaper articles about Margaret, they contacted the police and an investigation was started. To prove that Smith alias Williams alias Lloyd were one and the same person required unprecedented cooperation between police forces all around the country. They requested that the bodies of all three murdered women were exhumed. At the Old Bailey they produced 112 witnesses, 264 pieces of evidence including the bathtubs used in the murders. But the key piece of evidence was the fragment of Castile soap that Bessie Mundy had clasped in her hand at the time of her death. With this vital piece of evidence they could disprove the theory that she died while having a fit in the bath. If that had been the case her hands would have relaxed and consequently she would have dropped the soap.

With that problem solved the next question to be answered was how did Smith manage to murder his victims without any form of a struggle? One theory was that he had pulled hard on their legs forcing them out of the bath. This would have submerged the victim's head, causing the rapid inhalation of water and subsequent drowning.

On trying to prove this theory with a willing female friend, Inspector Arthur Neil almost had disastrous results. His friend lay in the bathtub wearing just a swimsuit and, when Neil pulled sharply on her legs, her head slipped under the water before she had any time to protest. To his horror when he held up her arms he discovered they were limp and he had nearly drowned her in trying to get to the truth.

Throughout the trial Smith was prone to noisy outbursts, calling one witness a 'lunatic'. Another time he shouted at the judge, 'I am no murderer, though I may be a bit peculiar'.

It only took the jury thirty-five minutes to find George Smith guilty and on July 1, 1915, was sentenced to hang.

A FITTING END

George Smith was hanged on Friday 13, 1915, at Maidstone prison by hangman John Ellis. A huge crowd gathered to witness the event and, in a state of near collapse, Smith was carried across the prison yard to be held up on the scaffold.

He was certainly a pathetic figure at the end, but there was little sympathy for him, especially from his three surviving wives. After the execution, his body was formally identified, and then tossed into a pit of quicklime – a fitting end to the serial bigamist and murderer.

Whether he committed his acts through a hatred for women, or whether it was purely for monetary gain, no-one will ever really know.

The Cannibal Killer

Jeffrey Dahmer's obsession with death started early in his childhood. From a very early age he would take dead animals and remove their skin. Next he would use chemicals to remove the flesh just leaving the skeleton. By the time he was fourteen he fantasized about killing men and having sex with their corpses.

Jeffrey was born in Bath, Ohio on May 21, 1960, to Lionel and Joyce Dahmer. He was a normal, healthy child who was adored by his doting parents. As a toddler he was happy and playful, loving all the normal things like soft toys, wooden blocks, etc. He also had a pet dog named Frisky, who he absolutely adored. Apart from some normal childhood illnesses, Jeffrey developed into a normal little boy. So you can see from this profile that Jeffrey Dahmer was not the subject of neglect and abuse during his formative years.

The first time his parents noticed anything unusual about Jeffrey was when he was four years old. His father had swept out the remains of some small animals from underneath their house that had been killed by civets. Lionel noticed that as he gathered up the tiny animal bones, Jeff seemed

231

oddly excited by the noise they made. He dug his small hands deep into the pile of bones. His father found it hard to dismiss it as simply a childish fascination, but instead somehow felt there was something more macabre about his behaviour.

At the age of six he required a regular operation for a hernia. For some inexplicable reason Jeffrey never seemed to fully recover from this surgery, and grew more and more inward, sitting on his own for long periods of time, with his face oddly motionless. By the time he reached first grade he had developed many fears and a complete lack of self-confidence. He seemed to need the reassurance of familiar people and places and the happy-go-lucky little toddler had now been replaced by a deeply shy, distant, almost uncommunicative little boy.

His father blamed it on the fact that they had moved from Iowa to Ohio. Lionel, as a child had also suffered from being shy and introvert, but as an adult had managed to overcome these problems. He felt that Jeffrey would get over them with time, but little did he know that his problems went far deeper.

In April of 1967 the family moved once again. Jeff seemed to adapt much better after this move and formed a close friendship with a boy named Lee. He certainly was much happier at his new school and had formed a bond with one of his teachers. As a present, he took a bowl of tadpoles into school for his new teacher. However, when he found out that the teacher had given the tadpoles to his friend Lee, Jeff sneaked into the garage where Lee now kept them and killed all the tadpoles with motor oil.

Over time his posture changed from loose-limbed, relaxed boy into a strangely rigid and tense figure. Once again he grew intensely shy and found it very difficult to interact with his fellow pupils. At home he would stay more and more in his room on his own, and was constantly lethargic. He had one friend but they drifted apart when he was fifteen. It was around this time that Jeff would go around with plastic bags gathering up the remains of animals for his own personal cemetery. He seemed to have a morbid fascination with dead creatures.

All the while Jeff became more isolated and uncommunicative from his family and indeed the rest of the human race. He certainly could never be classed as a rebellious child, in fact it was the opposite he never argued with his parents because nothing really seemed to bother him. By the time he was sixteen, Jeffrey had become an alcoholic. His fellow classmates described him as an unusual boy who always seemed to be trying to get attention. When he was eighteen his parents got a divorce and he went to live with his father and stepmother, Shari.

FANTASIES FULFILLED

Although it was apparent that Jeffrey Dahmer had fantasies about killing men and having sex with their corpses at a very early age, he didn't actually do anything about it until June 1978.

Jeffrey had just graduated from high school when he picked up a hitchhiker by the name of Stephen Hicks. They had sex, drank some beer, but then Stephen wanted to leave. Dahmer appeared to get upset at the thought of Stephen leaving and hit him around the head with a barbell and killed him. He needed to dispose of the body and so he cut it up and put it into plastic rubbish bags, burying them in the woods just behind his house.

In 1978 his father and Shari convinced him he should try going to college. They drove him to Ohio State University, but he remained drunk for the whole of the first semester and that was the end of his college years. His parents, who were now totally frustrated with his behaviour, said that he either had to get a job or enrol in the army. He joined the army at the end of 1978 and was stationed in Germany, although after a couple of years he was discharged for perpetual drinking.

During his college and army years Jeff seemed to have kept his gruesome fantasies under control. However, on returning home he went out and dug up the body of Stephen Hicks, pounded the decomposing corpse with a sledgehammer and then scattered the remains in the woods.

Jeffrey was arrested in October 1981 for drunken and disorderly conduct, and it was then that his father felt it would be better if he went to live with his grandmother in Wisconsin. It wasn't long before he discovered the city's gay bars and this was where he picked up twenty-four-year-old Steven Toumi, who was to become his next victim. The two of them had been drinking heavily in one of the popular gay bar when they left to spend the night in a hotel room. Dahmer was so drunk that he was not aware that he had killed Toumi until he woke up to find Steven dead with blood on his mouth. He went out and bought a large suitcase and then stuffed the body inside. He returned to his grandmother's house and took the body down to the basement. It was then that the really sordid and dark side of his nature came to the fore. He first had sex with the corpse, masturbated on it, and finally dismembered it and threw it in the garbage. For some reason this second murder seemed to open the floodgates and started Jeff on his killing spree.

The way Dahmer worked was to pick up young homosexual or bisexual men in the many gay bars around the city. He would either offer them money to pose for photographs or invite them back to his place to have a drink and watch videos. Having no idea that this was a wicked trap his victims would willingly accompany Jeffrey to the basement where they would fall into a drugged sleep following one or two spiked drinks. Then Dahmer would start to fulfill his fantasies. He either stabbed or strangled his victim to death before dismembering their bodies with a hacksaw.

As if that was not sick enough, Dahmer would retain certain parts of the dismembered bodies as a trophy, for example the heads and genitalia. But, perhaps the most nauseating aspect of his heinous acts was that he froze the biceps and other muscles which he would eat later on. The remainder of the corpse would be boiled down using chemicals and acids and then poured away down the drain.

Dahmer carried also carried out his own kind

sick medical experiments. He would perform lobotomies on some of his hapless victims. He claimed later on that most of his victims died immediately, except one that is. He apparently drilled a hole into the man's skull and poured acid into it. Dahmer said he behaved like a zombie for several days before he actually died. Dahmer was obviously an extremely sick man and was known to dabble in the occult.

While all these sordid activities were going on, Dahmer's grandmother was totally unaware of what horrific things were taking place in her basement. She was, however, fully aware of all the noise and drunkenness of Jeff and his male friends, and eventually she asked him to move out.

And so it was on, September 25, 1988, Jeffrey Dahmer moved into his own apartment on North 24th Street in Milwaukee. However, the very next day he was make his first big mistake.

DAHMER'S ARREST

On September 25, 1988, Jeffrey Dahmer offered a thirteen-year-old Laotian boy $50 to pose for some photographs. When he got the boy back to his apartment, he drugged him, fondled him, but on this occasion did not become violent or indeed have sexual intercourse with him. By an amazing coincidence the boy turned out to be the older brother of Konerak Sinthasomphone, the boy Dahmer would kill in May of 1991.

Dahmer let the young boy go, but when he arrived back home his parents realised that there was something amiss with their child and took him straight away to hospital. The doctors confirmed that their son had been drugged and the police were given the details of what had occurred. They arrested Dahmer while he was working at his job at a chocolate factory. He was arrested for sexual exploitation of a minor and also second-degree sexual assault. He pleaded guilty to the charges, although he did claim that he thought the boy was much older than thirteen.

While Dahmer was waiting for his case to come to trial he met a black homosexual named Anthony Sears, at a gay bar. As usual he enticed him back to his apartment and carried out all his normal fetishes.

Dahmer went to court on May 23, 1989. The assistant District Attorney, Gale Shelton suggested to the judge that he should have a prison sentence of at least five years, but three psychologists had previously examined him and suggested it would be more beneficial for him to be hospitalized to receive intense psychological treatment.

A magnificent performance by Dahmer stating that it was all a nightmare and admitting that he did need help, convinced the judge and he put Jeff on probation for five years. He was ordered to spend one year in a house of correction which allowed him to go to work during the day but had to return to the jail at night time. After having served ten months the judge granted Dahmer an early release, despite the fact that he had received a pleading letter from Dahmer's father that he should not be released until he had finished his treatment.

On May 14, 1990, Dahmer moved into his own apartment in Milwaukee, and this was when his killing spree really started.

MAY 27, 1991

In the early hours of the morning of May 27, three police officers were called out to a rundown area of Milwaukee by a couple of black teenage girls. They reported to the policemen that they had come across a young Asian boy who was running about the streets completely naked and rambling incoherently. The two girls were Sandra Smith and her cousin Nicole Childress. They said that although they were unable to get the boy to explain exactly what had happened to him, they were both convinced that he was genuinely terrified. They told of a tall white man who had followed the boy out onto the street and that he was trying very hard to convince the lad to come back into his apartment.

For some reason, when the police arrived at the scene they seemed to pay more attention to the story the white man gave them than the evidence of the two black girls. The man told the police officers that the nineteen-year-old boy was his lover, and the boy was upset simply because they had had a lover's tiff. He had run out on the streets because he was crying and upset by the argument. The police did not seem to doubt his story and accompanied the young Asian lad back to the man's apartment, leaving them to sort out their differences. The two girls protested strongly, totally convinced that the situation was far more serious than the white man had led the police to believe.

It was a costly mistake for the police for when the whole matter became public six weeks later, it proved to Milwaukee's black community that the city's white establishment, the police in particular, were racist.

A KILLER IS LEFT TO KILL AGAIN

The tall white man was Jeffrey Dahmer – a depraved and psychopathic killer, a cannibal and a necrophile – the teenager was Konerak Sintha-somphone. Although Dahmer had said that his 'lover' was eighteen, Konerak was in fact only fourteen years old. He was the thirteenth of Dahmer's seventeen victims, the majority of whom were either black, Asian or Hispanic.

As soon as Dahmer got Konerak back inside his apartment he strangled him, and then abused his body and proceeded to dismember it. As was his normal modus operandi, he retained some parts of the body to eat and others as bizarre trophies. Had the police bothered to investigate the case a little further when they were called out that night, they would have discovered that the tall white man was in fact a convicted child molester who was currently on probation.

Because of their mistake, Konerak and four other young males were all to die before Dahmer was finally apprehended.

Whether Dahmer was in fact rascist or not is unsure, but he probably chose mainly black victims because he lived in a mainly black area of Milwaukee, or perhaps he had a certain sexual fetish.

THE GRUESOME DISCOVERY

Two police officers were driving around the streets of Milwaukee on July 22, 1991. At around midnight the two officers noticed a short, wiry black man stumbling along with a handcuff dangling from one of his wrists. The man was thirty-two-year-old Tracy Edwards. The police pulled alongside the man and asked him what he was doing. He started to pour out a fantastic story about a strange man inviting back to his house and then after a couple of drinks had become very sleepy. This 'weirdo' then put on the handcuffs, threatened Tracy with a knife as they watched a film on video. Although Edwards was still feeling very woozy he managed to punch his assailant, and escaped from the apartment still wearing the handcuffs.

The police were curious, although they felt that it had all the trademarks of some sort of homosexual encounter. They asked the man to lead them back to the apartment as they felt they ought to check out the man he had mentioned.

When they arrived at apartment 213 on North 25th Street, the door was opened by a nice-looking, tall blond man. The man was Jeffrey Dahmer. He appeared very calm and rational and tried to wriggle his way out of the situation by saying that he had just lost his job at the chocolate factory, and that he had lost his temper after becoming drunk. He offered to get the officers the key to the handcuffs from his bedroom. Edwards immediately told the policemen that the knife he had been attacked with was also in the bedroom, and one of the policemen decided to accompany Dahmer into the room. The first thing the policeman noticed were numerous Polaroid photos of dismembered human bodies and of skulls in the refrigerator. Shocked by what he saw it took the officer several minutes to compose himself and call to his colleague to put handcuffs on Dahmer and place him under arrest. However, the calm, rational man suddenly turned on them and fought hard to try and prevent them from handcuffing him.

Having subdued Dahmer the officer, feeling increasingly worried about what he had seen in the bedroom, walked into the kitchen area and noticed that the refrigerator was the same as the one in the pictures. He pulled open the refrigerator door, and even though he was an experienced officer who had seen many gory cases, he screamed out loud at what he saw. On the shelf, staring back at him, lay a human head. Tracy Edwards stared at the head in horror, realising that Dahmer's threats to 'cut out your heart and eat it' would probably have come true had he not managed to escape.

While Dahmer was taken down to the police station for questioning, a thorough search was made of apartment number 213 in Oxford Apartments. What the search revealed was just one horror after another . . .

Apart from the freshly severed head they had found in the refrigerator, there were three more human heads in the freezer compartment, wrapped neatly in plastic bags which were tied up with plastic twist-ties. They also discovered several pairs of hands in the freezer and a quantity of unidentifiable human meat. Neatly concealed in the back of a cupboard was a severed penis in a stockpot, and in the bedroom cupboard were two skulls that had been boiled to remove the flesh and then painted grey. Also in the same cupboard the police discovered containers of ethyl alcohol, chloroform, formaldehyde and a number of glass jars containing preserved male genitalia.

The stench of death and decomposing flesh was hanging in the air and neighbours that had congregated outside the front door admitted that there were several clues which should have alerted them to the fact that they were living next to a psychopath.

Among the polaroid photographs taken by Dahmer at varying stages of his victims' deaths, was one that showed a man's head, with the flesh still on it, lying in a sink. Another one showed a man who had been cut open from the neck right down to his groin, the cut being so clear that it actually showed the pelvic bone.

With the help of pathologists and forensic scientists and the gentle but persistent questioning of Dahmer, the Milwaukee police gradually uncovered the horrifying fact that this mild-mannered man who worked in a chocolate factory had in fact killed sixteen people.

THE TRIAL AND RETRIBUTION

Jeffrey Dahmer admitted a plea of guilty but

242

insane on July 13, 1992. The security surrounding his trial was quite unique as he needed to be protected from the wrath of his victims' families. They employed sniffer dogs to sweep the courtroom for explosives and everyone who entered the room had to be searched thoroughly with a metal detector. Finally an eight-foot-high barrier was constructed out of bullet-proof glass and steel, designed to isolate Dahmer from the people in the gallery.

The jury deliberated for five hours before reaching a verdict that he was guilty but sane and he was sentenced to serve fifteen life sentences – totalling 957 years in prison.

Dahmer was sent to Columbia Correctional Institute in Wisconsin to serve out his sentence. He adjusted well to prison life, although initially he did not join his fellow inmates for fear of an attempt on his life. As it was he was attacked on July 3, 1994, by a Cuban he had never seen before, while he was attending a service at the prison chapel. In fact, Dahmer was a model prisoner and soon convinced the prison authorities to allow him more contact with the other inmates. He was allowed to eat with his fellow prisoners and was also allocated some janitorial work in the main prison. To do this work he was paired up with two very dangerous men – Jessie Anderson, a white man who had murdered his wife, and a black man named Christopher Scarver, a schizophrenic who thought he was the son of God and who had committed first-degree murder. So you can imagine how Scarver saw Jeff Dahmer, someone who had victimized so many black men; it was a lethal concoction.

On the morning of November 28, 1994, the three men had been left on their own to get on with their work. The guards returned only twenty minutes later to find Dahmer's head crushed and Anderson's fatally wounded body lying close by. Jeffrey Dahmer was pronounced dead at 9.11 a.m.

WHY DID IT HAPPEN?

Apart from his parents' doomed marriage and eventual divorce, Dahmer had been brought up in a fairly normal and happy environment, so his sick mind cannot be attributed to childhood abuse, bad parenting, or indeed any injury to the head. So what did turn Jeffrey Dahmer into a serial killer, a necrophilliac, a cannibal and a psychopath? Although many people have tried to come up with various theories, no-one can ever really be sure.

The factor that makes Dahmer different from the normal serial killer is that they normally stop once their victim is dead. Dahmer, on the other hand, seemed to get his kicks after his victims had died . . . satisfying his extraordinary sexual cravings on something over which he had total control.

At the request of his mother, Jeffrey's brain was preserved in formaldehyde so that it could be used in future studies in an effort to get some insight into why he behaved the way he did. His father, on the other hand, took the matter to court in an attempt to honour his son's request for cremation. On December 12, 1995, more than a year after his death, Columbia County Circuit Judge Daniel

George took the side of Jeff's father and ordered that the brain be destroyed.

Six months later Circuit Judge Daniel George ordered the city of Milwaukee to release Jeffrey Dahmer's personal belongings to a lawyer named Robert Steurer. Steurer was representing the families of some of his victims and he planned to auction the 'tools of the trade' – hammers, drill bits, hatchets, saws and his world-famous refrigerator – to settle claims filed against the city by the victim's families.

On May 29, 1996, the matter was settled when the city of Milwaukee raised more than $400,000 to buy Dahmer's gruesome collection. Terrified that someone might actually buy the items and erect a Jeffrey Dahmer museum, on June 28, 1996, the items were finally incinerated. This marked the end of Jeff's necrophilic legacy and hopefully laid to rest his grisly ghosts.

Vampire Killer of Sacramento

Richard Trenton Chase enjoyed harming, mutilating and killing small animals. He had an obsession with blood and was also an incessant fire starter. His case is still used today by the FBI as a perfect example for getting inside the mind of a disorganized killer.

Richard Trenton Case was born on May 23, 1950, and even as a small child loved to torment animals and start fires. He was obviously a very disturbed person right from the very beginning. He had a sister who was four years younger than him, and grew up in an unhappy, strict and extremely angry household, where he was frequently beaten.

By the time he became an adult, Richard was showing signs of mental instability and hypochondria, which became further exaggerated by his dependency on drugs. He had an intense fear that his body was going to disintegrate and thought that the only way of preventing this was by drinking blood. His fear became so pronounced that on one occasion he rushed into the emergency room of his local hospital claiming that his pulmonary artery had been stolen, that his bones were protruding out of his neck and that his stomach was backwards. To feed his obsession he would kill small animals, put their blood into a blender and drink it. On another occasion he was admitted to hospital suffering from a severe case of blood poisoning which he had bought on himself by drinking the blood of a rabbit that he had killed.

Eventually he was committed to a mental institution as a schizophrenic who was suffering from somatic delusions. He was put on medication which appeared to have very little effect, indicating that maybe it was his early drug abuse that had turned him into a psychotic. He escaped briefly in 1976, returning to his mother's house. He was returned to the hospital but ended up at a place called Beverley Manor, which was a facility for mental patients, and it was here that he earned the nickname 'Dracula'. He often spoke about killing animals and drinking their blood, and one day the doctors discovered two dead birds and blood all around Chase's mouth.

By 1978 the doctors at Beverley Manor felt that the medication they had been administering was finally starting to take effect, and he was released back into the community convinced that his paranoid schizophrenia was now under control. Unfortunately, once he was released, he did not take his medication regularly and so all his old problems returned. Voices in his head told him that his blood was turning to power and that his mother was being paid by the Nazis to poison him. These voices also told him how to treat his illness and that was to drink more blood.

Chase moved into an apartment and began to catch and torture cats, dogs and rabbits so that he could drink their blood. He even resorted to stealing neighbourhood pets, and on one occasion even called a family whose dog had gone missing to tell them exactly what he had done. It was around this time that he bought guns and started to experiment with them.

Although he was still on the medication provided by the hospital, he was allowed to live quite freely unsupervised. His mother, now believing he was free from his psychotic problems, weaned Richard off his medication. This was despite the fact that one day Richard paid his mother a visit, and when she opened the door to her horror she found her son holding a dead cat. He threw the cat to the ground, ripped its lifeless body apart, and then proceeded to smear the blood all over his face and neck. His mother failed to do anything about it and didn't even report it to the authorities.

That same year, on August 3, police discovered Chase's car stuck in some sand near Pyramid Lake in Nevada. There was a pile of clothes on the front seat along with a couple of rifles. There were blood smears on the inside of the car along with a plastic bucket containing a liver. Suspicious that there had been a murder, the police searched the area and eventually spotted Chase through their binoculars. He was running around totally naked with his body covered in blood. When he saw the police he tried to run away, but they caught up with him and he said that the blood had just seeped out of him. The liver in the bucket was one that had been removed from a cow.

A KILLER OF HUMANS

Richard Chase was inspired by reports on 'The Hillside Strangler' which was the name the media gave to a series of rape, torture, abduction and murder crimes that had taken place not far from where Chase lived. Chase decided to move onto bigger and better things.

Chase started to kill humans on December 29, 1977, when he shot fifty-one-year-old Ambrose Griffin in the back from his moving car. Other attempted shootings were reported in the area, but these attacks were merely a warm-up of what was to come.

On January 11, 1978, one of Chase's neighbours, Dawn Larson, had a strange encounter with him. She had previously seen him take three animals into his apartment and was a little curious as to why she had never seen them again. Possibly he had kept them hidden away because it was against the rules to keep animals in the apartment building. On this occasion Chase asked her for a cigarette but, even though she gave him one, he prevented her from walking away until she had given him the remainder of the packet.

About two weeks later a lady named Jeanne Layton saw an unkempt young man with fairly long hair walking towards her. She watched as he tried to open patio door, but on finding it locked tried to open one of the windows. When he discovered that this was also locked he went and knocked on her front door. She decided to confront him and opened the door only to find that the man showed no emotion whatsoever as he looked her up and down. Saying nothing, he turned away, first pausing to light a cigarette, and then walked off through her back garden.

A little further down the street Barbara and Robert Edwards were bringing their groceries into the house when they heard a noise coming from inside. They heard a window slam at the back of the house and to their surprise were confronted by a dishevelled looking man coming round the corner. Mr Edwards tried to stop him, but the man ran away down the street. Edwards gave chase but lost sight of him after the intruder had jumped a neighbour's fence.

The Edwards' called the police and when they arrived they found the house in a total shambles. They assumed the motive was theft of valuables, but discovered to their disgust that the burglar had not only urinated in a drawer containing clean laundry but had also defecated on the child's bed.

Chase was once asked by the FBI how he chose which victim to kill. He responded by saying that he went from house to house until he found one that was unlocked, because if the door was locked it meant that you weren't welcome.

Unfortunately, for Teresa Wallin, he found her door unlocked. Teresa was twenty-two years old and three months pregnant. Teresa ran into Chase as she was taking out the garbage. When she saw the man with the gun, she dropped the rubbish bag, and put her hands up as if to protect herself. Chase shot her three times, once in the palm of the hand, one through the top part of her skull and another in her temple after she had fallen to the ground. But this was not the end of his bloodlust. His next move was to drag her body into the bedroom. He then went into the kitchen to get a knife and also removed an empty yoghurt carton from the rubbish bag that Teresa had dropped. At last Chase had a human victim at his mercy. He proceeded to slice off her left nipple, and cut her open from the neck to her groin pulling out many of her internal organs. Then he stabbed her many times in the chest area and left the yoghurt container in the bathroom, from which he had drunk his victim's blood.

Two days later a puppy was found killed and mutilated not too far from where Teresa Wallin had been so brutally murdered.

It wasn't long before Chase struck again, in fact only four days. This time his victims were Evelyn Miroth, her six-year-old son Jason, her twenty-two-year-old nephew David Ferreira, and a family friend by the name of Danny Meredith. The bodies were discovered when a friend of Jason's called round to the house to see if he could come out to play. When no-one answered the door even though she was certain she had seen someone inside, the child alerted the neighbours. The neighbours were concerned that something had happened, but didn't expect to find such a gruesome scene when they opened the door. Jason Miroth and Danny Meredith had been shot exactly where Chase had come across them, but Evelyn Miroth had been shot in the head, sliced open with her intestines removed, stabbed in the anus, eyes and neck, and had also been sodomized. There were also signs once again that he had drunk her blood, from a container that was found at the scene. But what was even more horrifying was the fact that they could not find the body of Evelyn's son, Jason, although blood was discovered in the child's playpen. Apparently, Chase had stolen Meredith's car and taken the body of the baby back to his home where he continued with his mutilations and blood-drinking until his cravings were satisfied. The child's decapitated body was discovered a couple of months later in a vacant car park.

AN END TO THE KILLING

Thankfully that was to be the end of Richard Chase's horrifying spate of killing. The day after the murders the police were inundated with calls from people who said they had seen a suspicious looking man hanging round. The FBI developed a composite sketch and profile of the man they thought they were looking for. They felt that this was a psychotic, disorganized killer who had clearly not planned any of his murders. He did little, if anything, to destroy the evidence and possibly walked around in broad daylight with blood still on his clothes. The fact that the killings had been within the same area, pointed to the fact that maybe the assailant didn't have a car and lived in the close vicinity. They knew that he was very likely to kill again and the FBI had to act quickly.

Luckily witnesses came forward to say that a man named Richard Chase had an uncanny resemblance to the composite sketch issued by the police. They also had another clue from a gun, a .22-calibre semi-automatic handgun, that had been sold in December 1977 and registered to a Richard Chase. The police immediately ran a background check on Chase and discovered that he had a history of mental illness, a concealed weapons charge, and a series of minor drug busts.

When the police arrived at Chase's apartment they knocked on the door, but he would not let them in. The police pretended to leave and waited round the corner to see if he would come out. This is exactly what happened and Chase came out of his apartment carrying a box under his arm. The detectives immediately pounced on him and managed to apprehend him but not without Chase putting up quite a considerable fight.

The first thing they noticed about the dishevelled man was the fact that both his clothes and shoes were covered in blood. Also he was carrying a .22 handgun and in his back pocket they found a wallet which belonged to Dan Meredith and a pair of latex gloves. Inside the box he was carrying were a collection of blood-stained rags and pieces of paper. Chase was immediately taken to the station for questioning, where he admitted to killing several animals, but refused point-blank to talk about any of the murders.

While Chase was being questioned back at the police station, other detectives were searching his apartment for clues as to the disappearance of the baby, David. What they did discovered at Chase's home sickened the detectives right to the pit of their stomachs. The first thing they noticed as they entered the front door was the putrid smell and the fact that nearly everything within the apartment was covered with blood. In the kitchen they found human body parts in the refrigerator, several small pieces of bone, and a food blender that was badly stained and smelt of decomposing flesh. There were also three pet collars, but no sign of any pets.

THE TRIAL

The FBI now had all the evidence they needed to prosecute Richard Chase, who entered a plea of not guilty by reason of insanity. The trial had to be moved one hundred and twenty miles to a new venue in Santa Clara County, San Jose, because of the intense hatred that was being directed at Chase by the residents of Sacramento.

Chase was examined by at least a dozen psychiatrists. He admitted to them that he was disturbed about what he had done, but he needed the blood for therapeutic reasons, but at no time did he ever admit that he was compelled to do it.

The entire trial stretched across a period of four months during which time they called upon nearly one hundred witnesses, and gave 250 exhibits as evidence. Chase took the stand in his own defence, he had lost an incredible amount of weight, his eyes were sunken, his face was expressionless and he looked as though he barely had the strength to stand. He described in detail about how he had been mistreated throughout his life and that he barely remembers any of the killings. He admitted to drinking the blood from his victims because he said it was 'his medicine'. He felt that his problems all stemmed from the fact that he was unable to have sex with girls as a teenager and finally admitted to the court that he was sorry for what he had done.

Although his defence pleaded with the judge to be lenient in this case as they felt their client was a legally insane and had never really received the correct treatment. However, the prosecution disagreed and described his as a sexual sadist who knew exactly what he was doing at the time of the murders.

The jury took five hours to come up with their verdict and on May 8, 1978, found Chase guilty of six counts of first-degree murder. They also considered that he was legally sane and he was sentenced to death in the gas chamber at San Quentin. Chase, however, never did get to go to the gas chamber, as he overdosed on a prescribed medication and died on December 26, 1980.

VAMPIRE OR NOT?

Even though Richard Chase was dubbed 'Vampire Killer of Sacramento', he did not hide from the sun, nor did he sleep in a coffin during the day, change into a bat, or indeed have mesmerizing powers that were inescapable by human prey. He did not flinch from the glare of a cross, start to melt from the touch of holy water, nor did he wither away when exposed to fresh garlic. On the contrary, this vampire-like offender murdered his victims and then drank their blood with little or no remorse. This vampire was human.

Andrei Chikatilo

Andrei Chikatilo is Russia's, and possibly the world's worst serial killer. He is responsible for the murders of at least 53 people, most of them young boys and girls under the age of ten, his motive – sexual gratification. His rampage started in 1978 and ended in 1990, but only because he was captured.

Andrei Romanovich Chikatilo was born on October 16, 1936 in Yablochnoye, a village in the heart of rural Ukraine. The Soviet Union, and the Ukraine in particular, suffered a period of great upheaval during the 1930s. His family suffered greatly during Stalin's enforced collectivization and were subjected to extreme poverty and hunger.

In 1931 Andrei's older brother, Stefan, went missing and it is alleged that he was murdered and cannibalized by neighbours during the famine which claimed millions of Russian lives. Whether this story was true or not, Andrei's mother constantly warned him not to stray from the back yard or he might be eaten as well. This must have played on his mind as a young child and the death of his brother certainly had a terrible psychological effect on the young Andrei.

Times were hard, especially during the Nazi

occupation and it wasn't unusual for children to see bodies blown up in the streets. Andrei later admitted that although it was all very frightening, at the time he found it quite exciting as well. A lot of his childhood was spent on his own in a sort of fantasy world, for which he received a lot of mockery from the other children in the neighbourhood. He started to become angry which soon developed into a deeper rage. In his fantasies he used to envisage scenes of torture which gave him great pleasure, and this was to become a big part of his killings later in his life.

Although times were hard during the war, things were even worse when it was over. His father, Roman, had been captured by the Germans and held in a prisoner of war camp until 1945. When he returned home he was a broken man which was only exacerbated by the fact that he was accused of treachery for 'allowing himself to be caught' in the first place. Andrei, who by this time was a true Communist, condemned his father's betrayal of the homeland, but he was still teased and ridiculed about it by his fellow schoolfriends.

Andrei was always being picked on at school for being effeminate and desperately shy. Even though he was desperately shortsighted, Andrei refused to wear his spectacles to school for fear of being further ridiculed. Finally, Andrei would go to any lengths to cover up a very embarrassing problem even into his teenage years, and that was that he was a bedwetter. So the scene is now set for a very troubled child to grow into an even more confused adult.

HIS LOVE OF VIOLENCE

His first sexual experience as a youth was when he fumbled with a ten-year-old friend of his sisters, and during the ensuing struggle he ejaculated. That struggle and ultimate sexual satisfaction remained implanted in his brain as much as his fantasies about torture.

Andrei was now starting to realise that violence was more of a turn-on for him than the sexual act itself. After leaving school, he failed the entrance exam to get into Moscow University and decided to join the army. He got a job as a telephone engineer in the town of Rodionovo-Nesvatayevsky, near Rostov and in 1963 his sister moved in with him. She noticed he wasn't really interested in girls and introduced him to a local girl called Fayina and before long they were married.

Fayina was soon to realise that her husband was painfully shy and was not at all interested in conventional sex, but amazingly they did manage to conceive two children, Lyudmila and Yuri. In 1971 Chikatilo took a correspondence course and obtained degrees in Engineering, Russian and Marxism-Leninism. With these new qualifications, Andrei was able to obtain a job as a school teacher.

Even as a teacher he was desperately shy and was unable to keep his pupils under control. But what he did realise that he loved to be around the company of young girls and boys, and before long he began to commit indecent sexual acts on them.

When the complaints started coming in he was forced to resign his job, but as the matter was never reported he was able to get a job at another school. His abuse started up again and on one occasion was actually caught trying to perform oral sex with a sleeping boy. He was severely beaten by a group of older boys who had discovered his disgusting act, and from that moment on he always carried a knife.

Again the incident was not reported, instead it was just covered up and denied, which allowed this pervert to change into a killer. The sexual acts he had been committing had made him feel powerful, but to achieve complete satisfaction he knew he needed to get violent.

In 1978 Chikatilo moved to the town of Shakhty where he took a job at a mining school. On December 22, 1978, Andrei claimed his first victim – nine-year-old Lena Zakotnova. He started talking with the young girl while she was waiting for a tram and, luring her with the promise of some American chewing gum, he tricked her into going back to his house. Once behind closed doors, this polite, shy, meek man turned into a complete monster. He jumped on top of the petrified little girl, and as she screamed for her life, he covered her mouth and started to tear at her clothes. He rubbed his genitals against her body but for some reason was unable to obtain an erection. This caused him to get really angry and he forced his finger inside the helpless little victim, causing her to bleed. As soon as he saw the blood trickle out, Andrei achieved a satisfying orgasm, the strongest and most pleasurable one he had ever experienced. It was from that precise moment that he realised that fondling and rape was not what he needed, he needed to see his victim's blood. Now in a complete sexual frenzy he took out his pocket knife and plunged it into the girl's stomach. Seeing the child in agony only enhanced Chikatilo's excitement and he tore open her chest cavity using his hands to get at the blood and organs. Finally he ended her life by squeezing the girl's throat until every last breath was out of her.

His grotesque act over, Chikatilo began to realise the seriousness of his crime. The body lying in front of him was a mutilated mess and the bloody torso was barely recognizable as that of a small girl. He managed to regain his composure and covered the little girl's corpse with the remains of her clothes and carried her body to the nearby Grushevka River.

The body was discovered two days later. A witness, Svetana Gurenkova, told the police that she had seen Lena with a tall, thin, middle-aged man who had been wearing glasses and a dark coat. They made an artist's impression of the man and when it was shown to the Principal of the local mining school, he noticed the similarity to one of his teachers, Chikatilo. When the police arrived at Andrei's house they noticed some specks of blood on the front steps and Chikatilo was taken in for questioning but was later released, because his wife gave him an alibi. Instead the police turned their attentions to a man named Aleksandr Kravchenko, who had a previous conviction for rape. But Kravchenko was far too young to fit the description of the man seen with Lena, nor had he ever worn glasses. He was questioned mercilessly and the police eventually forced a confession out of the innocent man. He was charged for the murder and sentenced to death in 1984. It wasn't until a few years later when Chikatilo confessed, that the authorities realised that they had executed the wrong man.

THE SECOND VICTIM

In 1981 Chikatilo was forced to resign his post at the mining school due to the fact that there had been numerous reports regarding his inappropriate behaviour with the students. This time he took a job as a supply clerk at the Rostovnerud factory in Shakhty.

It had been almost three years since Andrei had killed his last victim – but now his frustrations had built up again and he was ready to kill once more. On the evening of September 3, 1981, Andrei Chikatilo was wandering around the streets seeking out his next victim. Seventeen-year-old Larisa Tkanchenko caught his eye while she was sitting waiting for a bus. The not-so-innocent girl accepted the man's invitation to go for a walk, and while they headed to a quiet area the couple chatted as if they were old friends.

However, once in a secluded spot, the man turned into a depraved, manic beast and stripped Larisa of all her clothes, punching her, strangling her and piling dirt into her mouth to muffle her screams. As her life ebbed away Chikatilo ejaculated over her body and bit off one of her nipples in his excitement. He then dumped her body in the River Don where it was discovered the very next day.

The murder of Larisa had temporarily satisfied Chikatilo's obsession with torture and he did not attack again until June of the following year. This time the victim was thirteen-year-old Lyubov Biryuk and his method of attack followed the same pattern as before. Most of the wounds were to the girl's breasts and genitals, but what differed about this attack was the fact that she had been stabbed in both eye sockets.

It was now that the killing would start in earnest and over the period of the next nine years, numerous corpses would be discovered in wooded or secluded areas. A team, headed by Major Mikhail Fetisov, was sent to Rostov to take control of the investigations. They concentrated their investigations around the area of Shakhty, and their main priority was to interview the mentally disturbed and any known sexual criminals that might fit the profile they had built up of the killer. The police spread their search wider and wider until eventually over 150,000 people had been questioned, but all to no avail. In 1984 alone another fifteen murders took place, and the police posted additional patrols at bus and train stations, as it appeared this was where the killer picked up most of his victims.

THEIR FIRST BREAK

Then the police got their first break. Inspector Aleksandr Zanosovsky spotted a middle-aged man wearing glasses acting suspiciously at Rostov bus station. He seemed to be paying particular attention to young girls. The inspector approached the man and asked him to produce his papers. The man produced some documents which identified him as Andrei Chikatilo, a freelance employee of the Department of Internal Affairs, which was a wing of the KGB. He was allowed to go on his way, but a couple of weeks later Kanosovsky spotted the man again acting suspiciously. This time, instead of approaching him, he watched him for several hours as he caught one bus after another, just riding around the district. Chikatilo did not seem to have any particular destination, but he did seem to concentrate his efforts on chatting up young girls. After several rejections, Chikatilo eventually found a young girl, who was drunk, who was prepared to put her head in his lap and let him fondle her. The Inspector seized the moment and went over to Chikatilo, who started to sweat profusely. Kanosovsky asked him to open his briefcase, and inside he discovered a jar of lubricant, a length of rope and a long-bladed knife. He was taken back to the police station and when they looked up his records they discovered that he was already under investigation for a minor theft from the factory where he worked. This was sufficient for the police to keep him in custody, and while they held him they checked to see if he could be the 'Rostov Ripper' as he had been so aptly named by the media.

Unfortunately Chikatilo's blood group did not match that found at the crime scenes. Also the police made the mistake of returning the suitcase to Andrei who swiftly disposed of their contents. With no evidence the police could only charge Andrei with the theft and although he was charged with one years imprisonment, he was freed in December 1984 after serving only three months.

After his release Chikatilo found new work in Novocherkassk as a travelling buyer for a locomotive company, and managed to maintain a low profile. Whether his prison sentence had any initial effect on him is hard to say, but he did not kill again until August 1985, when he murdered two women in separate incidents. His killings then stopped until May 1987 when he murdered a thirteen-year-old boy in Revka up in the Ural mountains.

OUT OF CONTROL

From then on his killing spree seemed to spiral out of control. In 1988 he killed a further eight people and, in 1990, which was to be his last year of freedom, he killed another nine, most of whom were young boys. By now Issa Kostoyev, the director of the Central Department for Violent Crime, had taken over the investigations, and he started going over all the evidence very carefully. When the body of sixteen-year-old Vadim Tishchenko was discovered on November 3, 1990, Kostoyev decided to put out night patrols who were equipped with night vision goggles.

However, even with all the extra police on patrol, they were unable to prevent Chikatilo from killing his final victim, twenty-two-year-old Svetlana Korostik, on November 6 at Donleskhoz Station. This time he cut off parts of the girl's body and ate them at the scene before finally covering the body with leaves and branches and walking back to the station. A plain clothes officer at the station noticed Chikatilo perspiring heavily and that he had spots of blood on his face. He checked his papers, but unaware that there had been another murder, had no real reason to apprehend the man and Andrei was allowed to go on his way.

After the discovery of Svetlana's body, Kostoyev decided to look further into the report of the incident. When his research showed that Chikatilo was recorded as having been in the vicinity at the time of many of the murders, Kostoyev decided to use a team of undercover agents to follow him.

On November 20, 1990, Chikatilo left work so that he could get treatment for a broken finger which, unbeknown to the doctors, had been bitten by one of his victims. Following the treatment he picked up his briefcase and went on the hunt for young boys. The first boy he approached was called away by his mother and a little frustrated at having his plans foiled, carried on further down the street to look for another victim. This time, however, he was approached by three men who identified themselves as policemen, who subsequently arrested him. Once again a search of the briefcase revealed that it contained a jar of lubricant, a length of rope and a knife. When they searched his home they found a further twenty-three knives, a hammer and a pair of shoes that matched a footprint that had been found at one of the murder scenes. Andrei himself was searched and there was a cut on his finger, and his genitals had abrasions on them.

A leading Russian psychologist, Dr Bukhanovsky was called in to interview Andrei. He eventually confessed to all his crimes and told the doctor that he got sexual gratification from murder, torture and mutilation, and even confessed to cannibalism on some occasions. Chikatilo admitted to at least 53 murders but also led police to some undiscovered victims.

THE TRIAL IN A CAGE

The trial started on April 14, 1992, and to protect him from his victims' relatives, Chikatilo was placed in a large iron cage where he was allowed to either sit or stand. During the trial Andrei spent a lot of his time ranting and raving and acting outlandishly. It is not clear whether this was all an act to try and persuade the judge that he was totally insane, or whether his mental condition had actually deteriorated to that extent. At one point he pulled down his trousers, waved his penis at the public gallery insisting that he was not a homosexual and shouting: 'Look at this useless thing, what do you think I could do with that?' He was removed from the courtroom.

The trial carried on into August 1992. Chikatilo was given a final opportunity to stand up and speak for himself, but on this occasion he remained silent. It took the judge two whole months to reach a verdict and, on October 14, six months after the trial began, he pronounced Andrei Chikatilo guilty of five counts of molestation and 52 counts of murder. On hearing the sentence, Andrei started shouting incoherently, spitting at the judge and demanding that he see his corpses. Despite his outlandish behaviour Chikatilo was pronounced legally sane and was sentenced to die by execution.

A last-minute appeal for clemency was rejected by President Boris Yeltsin and on February 15, 1994, Chikatilo was taken to a special soundproof room and was executed with a pistol shot to the back of his head. Unlike the pain and suffering he subjected on his victims, Andrei Chikatilo died quickly and mercifully.

Who Was 'Jack the Ripper'?

In 1888 a mysterious monster stalked the streets of London's East End killing women. The killer was never caught and, for this reason, there are many many theories on his personality and his motives.

Between the months of August and November, 1888, the Whitechapel area of East London was plagued with a series of horrific murders, which to this day remain unsolved. The assailant, originally known as 'Leather Apron', stalked the dimly-lit, fog-ridden streets of the East End of London with a single, gruesome ambition . . . to murder in the most foul way. Why was this mysterious figure that was shrouded in a cape, armed with a long knife and black Gladstone bag, never apprehended. That will always remain an unanswered question and that is probably why the name of 'Jack the Ripper' is still so famous this century as it was in 1888.

The 'Ripper' as we will call him in this story, seemed to confine his attacks on poor women, who were forced to rely on prostitution as their only means of income. All his attacks occurred after dark and, with the exception of his last victim, they all lived in close proximity to the East End of London.

In Victorian England the East End of London was somewhat of an outcast from the main city. It was occupied by around 900,000 people and the streets were filthy, covered in rubbish and the liquid sewage gave the area an awful stench. Most of the inhabitants of the East End lived in deplorable conditions. They were either working for a pittance of a wage, did not work at all, or ended up as criminals in an effort to just survive. Prostitution was one of the only reliable means by which a single woman or widow could maintain themselves and it was estimated that around 1888 there were as many as 1,200 prostitutes in the Whitechapel district alone.

The squalid tenements, narrow, darkened alleys and streets of this area of London, was the perfect place for the Whitechapel murderer to carry out his gruesome crimes.

THE VICTIMS

Mary Ann Nichols, was forty-two years old and was the daughter of a locksmith. Polly, as she became known, was married to William Nichols, a printer's machinist and they had five children. Her marriage broke up due to her heavy drinking, and Polly was now living off her meagre earnings that she received from being a prostitute. She did not manage to overcome her drinking problem, but from time to time she did try and get her life in some sort of order. Although she was a sad, piteous woman, she was liked by everyone that knew her.

It was in the early hours of Friday, August 31,

1888, that Charles Cross came across the body of a woman lying on her back, with her skirts lifted up above her waist. He called over a fellow passer-by to assist him, assuming that the woman was merely a drunk who had fallen asleep, or maybe she had been the victim of an attack. However, as they tried to help the woman they suddenly realised that she had in fact been murdered, and that the awful wounds to her neck had almost decapitated her. To try and retain a modicum of dignity they pulled the woman's skirt down and then went off in the search of a policeman.

Shortly after the two men left, Police Constable Neill, came across the body of a woman lying on the footpath. On stooping down to help her up, assuming that she was in a drunken sleep, he noticed with horror that her throat had been cut almost from ear to ear. He called back to his station and asked that they send out a doctor to Buck's Row. Doctor Llewellyn inspected the body and pronounced that the poor woman was dead and proceeded to carry out a brief examination in the place where she lay. He discovered that, apart from the severe gash across her throat, she had also received terrible stab wounds to her abdomen. When the police ambulance arrived, her body was removed and taken back to the mortuary for further examination.

It was at the mortuary that they truly realised the horror of the crime that had been committed. The police realised that it was going to be difficult to obtain identification of the victim, as the only possessions she had on her was a comb, a broken mirror and a handkerchief. The clothing was inexpensive and well-worn and bore no identifying marks other than the Lambeth Workhouse on her petticoats. She was around five feet two inches tall, with brown-grey hair, brown eyes and several of her front teeth were missing.

As the news spread around Whitechapel they learned that the woman affectionately known as 'Polly' was in fact Mary Ann Nichols, who lived in a lodging house at 18 Thawl Street. She was identified first by a woman from the workhouse, and the next day by both her father and her husband.

Whoever had viciously murdered Polly Nichols had left no clues whatsoever at the scene of the crime. None of the other residents in the neighbourhood had seen or heard anything unusual, and no-one had been seen running away from the body. The people of Whitechapel had already been warned that there had been several other attacks in the area and they, particularly the prostitutes, were becoming rather wary. Several weeks before the murder of Polly, on Monday, August 6, thirty-nine-year-old Martha Tabram, also a prostitute, had been found murdered in George Yard. She had been stabbed thirty-nine times on her body, neck and private parts with what they thought was possibly a knife or a dagger.

The attacks were not linked to the murder of Polly Nicholls as the nature of the wounds inflicted on these people were quite different and the motive was probably robbery, but there were similarities in the Tabram case.

271

The attacks and two murders had left the East End of London in a state of shock and there was now a lot of pressure on the police to apprehend the assailant. There were many theories being banded around, but the main three were: (1) that it was a gang of thieves, (2) that it was a gang extorting money from prostitutes and they were penalizing the women for not paying and, finally (3) that a maniac was on the loose. Considering how poor the the victims were, the first two theories were considered to be not very plausible.

While the police were busy trying to prove their theories a story surfaced in the press about a bizarre character named 'Leather Apron'. He was claimed by The Star to be a Jewish slipper maker who was going around beating up prostitutes who would not pay him money. However, with all the publicity and the threat of mob violence, the 'Leather Apron' went into hiding.

ANNIE CHAPMAN

Annie Chapman or 'Dark Annie' as she was affectionately known, met her demise on the foggy night of September 8, 1888. She was a pathetic woman, who was homeless and wandered around the streets of the East end earnestly searching for clients to earn her enough money to buy food, drink and shelter for the night. She was very undernourished and was suffering from a terminal lung and brain disease. It was the death of her husband, John Chapman, that had left poor Annie penniless. She had had three children with John, one of whom had died from meningitis and another was a cripple. Annie suffered from severe depression and alcoholism and just before 2 a.m. she was turned out of her lodging house to earn some money to pay for her bed. Later that same morning, her body was discovered in the backyard of 29 Hanbury Street in Spitalfields.

The Spitalfields Market opened at 5 a.m. and the surrounding streets were busy with people and commercial vehicles. Annie's body was found by an elderly man named John Davis. He saw that her skirts had been pulled up above her waist and went immediately to get help.

The amazing thing about this case it that the killer took the risk and committed his crime in daylight. Amazingly though, even though the streets were crowded, no-one had seen or heard anything suspicious, and again no-one was spotted running away from the crime with blood on his clothes or carrying a weapon. There was also a tap in the backyard where the body was found, and yet the murderer had not bothered to stop and wash the weapon or his hands clean of any blood.

Annie did not appear to have put up any fight and there were a few clues near the body that might help in the apprehension of this ruthless killer. Items that Annie had had in her pocket – a small piece of cloth, a pocket comb and a small-tooth comb – were all found near her body and appeared to arranged in some sort of order. There was also an envelope near her head containing two pills and on the back was written the words *Sussex Regiment*, and a postmark that said London, Aug.

23m 1888. Finally, a leather apron was found along with some other rubbish in the backyard.

However, the investigation turned out to be just as frustrating as that of the Nichols and Tabram case. The physical clues found at the scene – the leather apron, a nailbox and a piece of steel – turned out to be owned by one of the residents of 29 Hanbury Street, Mrs. Richardson's son. The envelope was widely sold at a local post office and a man at the lodging house said he saw Annie pick it up off the floor to put her pills in when her pillbox broke. Several witnesses came forward to say that they had seen a man in the backyard of Hanbury Street but could not give any real detail. The main witness though, Mrs. Elizabeth Long, did see a man talking with Annie at around 5.30 a.m. but unfortunately the man had his back to her. She did her best to describe what she saw. But these witnesses gave the police a further problem because the coroner had estimated that Annie Chapman had died no later than 4.30 that Saturday morning, and yet all the evidence pointed to the fact that she died around 5.30.

The recent murders now left the normally busy streets of Whitechapel quiet and virtually deserted by night. The local population were angry with the police for not coming up with any results, and their anger was further fuelled by the rumours and stories that were appearing in the papers. However in a week or so the normal seedy nightlife of Whitechapel was virtually back to normal, as there were just too many people who depended on prostitution in order to just survive.

BORN TO BE KILLERS

ELIZABETH STRIDE AND ANOTHER

Elizabeth Stride was born in 1843 in Sweden, and probably came to England as a domestic worker. She moved to London in 1866 and married a carpenter named John Thomas Stride. Stride was a survivor of the Thames River tragedy, but he had died later in the poorhouse. They allegedly kept a coffee shop prior to the breakdown of their marriage in 1882. Elizabeth was known locally as 'Long Liz' and over the years she had eight convictions for drunken behaviour. She lived with a labourer named Michael Kidney for three years before her death, and although she may occasionally have prostituted herself, she mainly earned a living by either doing cleaning or sewing work.

Elizabeth's body was discovered by a Russian Jew by the name of Louis Diemschutz on Sunday, September 30, 1888 in the yard outside the International Working Men's Education Club where Louis lived with his wife. As he pulled in Dutfield Yard he saw something lying on the ground near the wall of the Club. He struck a match and realised that it was the body of a woman. He rushed into the club and got one of the young members to come out and help him. When the two men took a closer look at the body and saw a pool of blood beneath her, they screamed and then ran to fetch the police. She had the similar injuries to the other murders, whereby her throat had been cut virtually from ear to ear and she had multiple knife wounds to the body.

Meanwhile, the police were dealing with yet

another murder in Mitre Square. The square at 1.30 a.m. was quiet and deserted, and Police Constable Edward Watkins was making his routine patrol of the area. However, when he shone his torch into a corner of the square he made a horrible discovery. He found the body of a woman lying on her back with her skirt pushed up above her waist. Her throat had been cut, and her stomach had been ripped out to reveal her bowels. When the police arrived on the scene the body was still relatively warm and realising that the crime had only been committed a short while before, started a thorough search of the area in the hope that the killer was still about.

There was no money on the body and, once again, no evidence of any struggle. Somehow the murderer had managed to lure his victim silently into the square, carve her up and completely vanish in a very short period of time.

During the search of the square, Constable Alfred Long discovered a piece of apron covered in blood lying in the entrance to a building. Just above where the apron was found, written on an archway in white chalk was the message:

The Juwes are The men That
Will not be Blamed
For nothing

The piece of apron came from the murdered woman in Mitre Square and the police believed that the writing was the work of the killer. It is quite bewildering how the attacker could possibly have killed two women in such a short space of time without causing any suspicion, especially as the area was already on a careful watch for anyone that looked remotely suspicious.

The victim was quite easily identified as Catherine Eddowes, the daughter of a tin plate worker, as she had some pawn tickets in her pockets when she was found. When the police gave out that information John Kelly, the man with whom she had been living for the past seven years, came forward and was able to identify the body.

Catherine, or Kate as she was better known, was born in 1842. Her parents died when she was very young and at the age of sixteen she met Thomas Conway, who she went to live with as his common-law wife. They lived together for twenty years and had three children. However, due to Kate's excessive drinking, and Conways physical abuse, the relationship ended in 1880. Although Kate's friends were adamant that she was not a prostitute, there is some evidence that possibly when under the influence of alcohol she did sell her body on the streets.

Although the police did not seem to be getting any closer to catching the murderer, one important witness did emerge from the investigations. A man called Joseph Lawende, who had been in the Imperial Club with two friends on the night in question, saw a couple talking at around 1.35 a.m. at Church Passage which was close to Mitre Square. He described the man as being fairly young, of medium height, a small, light-coloured moustache and wearing a dark jacket, and deerstalker hat. He did not manage to see the woman's face but was able to identify the clothes that Kate was wearing. It was only nine minutes after this sighting that Kate Eddowes was murdered.

Again panic rose on the streets of Whitechapel, especially after they discovered there had been two murders on the same night. Once again everyone stayed off the streets after dark and many of the prostitutes laid low in various shelters or stayed with family or friends. Police visited all the common lodging houses and interviewed over 2,000 of the inhabitants. They also had handbills printed and distributed in the neighbourhood, requesting people to come forward with any information they might possible have. The police questioned many people in professions where they would be proficient in the use of a knife and even tried using a dog to follow a single scent, but none of their efforts came to fruition.

MARY JANE KELLY

There hadn't been an attack for over a month and once again the streets settled down to normality. Mary Jane Kelly was born in Limerick and had lived in Wales for a while. When she was twenty-one she came to London to work in a brothel. She was very popular as she was both young and attractive, and would probably have suited the prestigious West End clients as opposed to those of the grim streets of the East End.

In 1887 she met Joe Barnett who was a respectable market porter and, although they lived together, never really settled in one place. On occasion they would drink away their rent money and consequently get evicted. Following an argument, Joe left and Mary had to return to prostitution to earn her crust.

It was Friday, November 9, 1888, and the day of the Lord Mayor's Show. Mary's landlord was a man called John McCarthy, and on the day of the Show he sent his assistant round to 13 Miller's Court to collect some rent from Mary. He knocked on the door, but as he got no answer, he put his hand inside the broken window and pulled back the curtains. He wasn't quite sure what he had seen lying on the bed, so he went and got McCarthy for a second opinion. When McCarthy looked through the window, he was so sickened by what he saw he sent his assistant to go and fetch the police.

Bowyer soon returned with a Constable and the broke into the house by forcing the door. Once their eyes had become accustomed to the dim light they were totally horrified by their discovery. Mary's body was lying sprawled on the bed and it had been unbelievably mutilated. She died from having her throat cut, and the rest of the horrific injuries were inflicted after her death. The whole surface of her abdomen and thighs had been removed, her breasts had been cut off, and there were several jagged wounds to the arms. The face had been mutilated beyond recognition. The contents of her abdomen were found in different places and the police were astounded at the ferocity of this murder.

THE RIPPER LETTERS

Following the spate of attacks the police, the press, and individuals who were involved with the investigations, received literally hundreds of letters – presumably from the killer himself. The name 'Jack the Ripper' came about because it was the name the writer used when he sent a letter to the boss of the Central News Office on September 25, 1888.

Dear Boss

I keep on hearing the police have caught me but they wont fix me just yet. I have laughed when they look so clever and talk about being on the right track. That joke about Leather Apron gave me real fits. I am down on whores and I shant quit ripping them till I do get buckled. Grand work the last job was. I gave the lady no time to squeal. How can they catch me now. I love my work and want to start again. You will soon hear of me with my funny little games. I saved some proper red stuff in a ginger beer bottle over the last job to write with but it went thick like glue and I cant use it. Red ink is fit enough I hope ha.ha. The next job I do I shall clip the lady's ears off and send to the Police officers just for jolly wouldn't you. Keep this letter back till I do a bit more work then give it out straight. My knife's so nice and sharp I want to get to work right away if I get a chance.

Yours truly
Jack the Ripper

Don't mind me giving the trade name.
(from 'The Times' 1888)

The editor considered that the letter was a hoax and didn't bother to forward it on to the police for a couple of days. It was the night of Liz Stride and Kate Eddowes murder when it finally arrived in the hands of the police. On the Monday morning following the two murders, the news agency received yet another letter in exactly the same handwriting. The police circulated the letters and placed copies outside every police station in the hope that someone would recognize the writing. This had no effect other than to encourage a few cranks to write a few hoax letters.

THE MAIN SUSPECTS

Only a few clues were ever unearthed by the very bewildered police force. Never before had detectives experienced the apparently motiveless, brutality of the world's first serial killer. Pressurized by an angry public and indeed Queen Victoria herself, the police arrested several suspects on extremely flimsy evidence. Most of these suspects, who were merely scapegoats, were committed to mental institutions in an effort to rid the streets of the 'mysterious monster'. It appeared no-one was above suspicion – Sir Charles Warren, the Chief of the Metropolitan Police – was himself suspected of being involved in a cover up. The prime suspects who are still to this day eligible to be dubbed 'Jack the Ripper' are as follows:

Francis Thompson, 1894

In the book entitled *Jack the Ripper* by Stephen Knight, the British poet, Francis Thompson, is considered to be the culprit of the evil East End murders. Knight explains that Thompson had a violent childhood, flunked his medical training, had a growing fascination with murder, and eventually ended up as a vagrant due his dependence on drugs. Thompson apparently had a secret affair with a prostitute and its tragic ending reduced him to a frenzied delirium. Knight reveals the sordid events surrounding the murders and its sinister parallels to Thompson.

John Pizer

John Pizer was a Jewish shoemaker, who unfortunately fulfilled the public's view of the murderer's profile. The profile being that of a butcher, a slaughterman or a craftsman, in fact anyone who had access to a 5-inch blade knife and a leather apron. Pizer was known to have an intense dislike for prostitutes, and added to that he had a previous conviction for stabbing which immediately went against him. He aptly fitted a description that had been distributed of a short man with a dark beard and moustache who was thought to have a foreign accent. The press portrayed Pizer as a man with a 'cruel sardonic look', but when he provided a solid alibi the press were forced by the libel courts to make a compensation payment. Once more this left the already frustrated Police Force fumbling in the dark.

After the death of Annie Chapman and the subsequent pathology reports, the Coroner suggested that the murdered might possibly have an anatomical knowledge of dissection. This then forced the police to turn their attentions towards members of the medical profession. Based upon this assumption three major suspects came to the fore . . .

Thomas Neil Cream

Thomas Cream was an American doctor who had already been arrested in connection with the poisoning of prostitutes. He also wrote to the police on numerous occasions giving false names and false accusations regarding a number of crimes. Cream was eventually hanged for the murder of the Lambeth prostitutes in 1892 and his departing words were: 'I am Jack the Rip. . .' just as the rope snapped tightly round his neck. There were many clues that pointed to Cream as being the Ripper. For example, an American had been making enquiries as to the availability of certain organs at medical schools in and around the Whitechapel district. Added to this, the letter received by the police just prior to the double killings of Liz Stride and Kate Eddowes which contained many 'Americanisms' he was certainly a prime candidate. Unfortunately, though, Cream was actually in prison at the time of the last murders attributed to Jack the Ripper.

Michael Ostrogg

Michael Ostrogg was a Russian doctor was questioned by the London police, but was unable to reliably account for his whereabouts. Ostrogg was a confidence trickster who was known by various names – Dr. Grant and also a former surgeon in the Russian navy. He was in and out of police custody for different theft and fraud offences, and was clearly a complete rogue. He became a high profile suspect when it was stated in the Police Gazette to 'pay special attention to this dangerous man', after he failed to report to the police on charges of suspicion.

Alexander Pedachenko

Another Russian doctor, Alexander Pedachenko was very tenuously linked to the Ripper murders when it was suggested that the name 'Ostrogg' was one of the aliases used by him. He was considered to be a Russian lunatic with distinct criminal tendencies. Added to this, Pedachenko had trained as a barber's surgeon and had also joined the staff of the local Maternity Hospital. The *Ochrana*, the Russian Secret Police Gazette, described him as 'the greatest and boldest of all Russian criminal lunatics'. *Ochrana* also associated Pedachenko with the Ripper in an effort to discredit the Metropolitan Police, and this act of propaganda appears to have been successful as Sir Charles Warren subsequently resigned from the Police Force. Pedachenko was then smuggled back to Moscow where he was immediately sent to a lunatic asylum for the murder of a woman in St

Petersburg. Pedachenko died in the asylum but it seems he was merely a suspect of convenience for a short period of time.

Prince Albert Victor – The Duke of Clarence

The theory that a royal conspiracy was behind the Whitechapel murders is probably the most popular one. This appealing theory unfolds like this:

Prince Albert was believed to have made several night-time trips to the East End of London to indulge in homosexual practices in a brothel in Cleveland Street. He is also supposedly to have learned the techniques of disembowelling on his many deer hunting excursions. He was also alleged to have had syphilis of the brain, which would have made him mad enough to commit the murders.

Another story goes is that Albert had an affair with a shop girl named Annie Crook who he kept in an apartment in Whitechapel. Annie, who was a Catholic, became pregnant with his child and, in one version of the story, married Albert secretly. A Catholic girl of low social standing was definitely a no-no for a future king and when the news got back to his grandmother, Queen Victoria, she insisted that the problem be resolved. The job was left to her physician, Sir William Gull. Doctor Gull supposedly had Annie taken away to a lunatic asylum where he savaged both her memory and her intellect, leaving her institutionalized for the remainder of her life. The key victim to link royalty with the murders was Mary Kelly. She was evidently the nursemaid to the prince and his wife around this time. As the story goes Mary and her friends Polly Nichols, Annie Chapman and Elizabeth Stride all knew about the affair between Annie Crook and the prince but, due to the fact that they were unable to keep the matter a secret, were consider a major threat to the Crown. Once again Doctor Gull was summoned to help alleviate the problem. He was asked to permanently silence these troublesome whores, and to cleverly disguise their disappearance, Gull devised the persona of Jack the Ripper. He was to pick up the women in the Royal carriage, slaughter them inside the carriage and then dispose of the body. This would of course explain the lack of noise and blood at the scene of the murders.

The Royal theories are mainly based on conjecture and have only really come to light in recent years. Would the Crown really have resorted to the murder of five unfortunate women in order to protect themselves? Of course we shall never know because there is no evidence to support this theory.

Aaron Kosminski

The chalk writing on the archway using the word 'Juwes' led the police to another suspect, Aaron Kosminski. The Commissioner of the Metropolitan Police, Sir Charles Warren, had ordered the removal of the writing so as to avoid an uprising from the already agitated Jewish community, especially since the false arrest of Pizer was still fresh in their minds. However, despite this, another Jew, Aaron Kosminski became a prime suspect. Aaron was a hairdresser and had lived in Whitechapel since 1882. He was a man who had an extreme hatred of women, especially prostitutes, and he was definitely the most insane of all the police suspects. He was described as having strong homicidal tendencies and a history of related crimes. Following the night of the double killings, George Lusk, who was leader of the Whitechapel Vigilance Committee, received a letter. This letter told Lusk that the writer had fried and eaten half a kidney which had been removed from the body of Kate Eddowes. The uneaten half of the kidney accompanied the letter in a box, and the organ was found to be human and belonged to a woman in her forties who was suffering from Brights disease – as did Kate Eddowes. However, because the style of writing did not match the first 'Jack the Ripper' letter, it was concluded to be the writings of a crazed lunatic. Clearly the man who wrote the letter was deranged and Kosminski became a prime suspect. He was repeatedly identified by one of the witnesses even though Kosminski was not a medium build but a slender one. It was never proved that Kosminski was the perpetrator of these ghastly crimes, but he was removed from society in 1890 and placed in an infirmary for the insane. For the last 25 years of Kosminski's life he was put in Colney Hatch Asylum where he degenerated to the point where he could no longer answer any questions. He died in 1919 of gangrene of the leg and was medically described as both demented and incoherent.

Montague John Druitt
Our last suspect is Montague John Druitt. He was

a gentleman, a successful college teacher, a keen cricketer and came from a 'good family'. Druitt didn't become a suspect in the Ripper case until the year 1959. Case notes written by Sir Melville Macnaghten, described Druitt as 'sexually insane' and it was suggested that even his own family suspected him of being the Whitechapel murderer. Druitt's personal circumstances also link him with the murders. He was an extremely intelligent man who had studied medicine for a time before switching profession to become a barrister. As a barrister he would have known that you would need to distance yourself as far as possible from the scene of the crime, if his case were to be defended with any success. Druitt was discovered playing cricket in Dorset after the murders of Mary Nichols and Annie Chapman, but his actual whereabouts on the nights concerned still remain unresolved. The main reason that Druitt became a suspect is that he feared he would go insane like his mother. Druitt wrote a suicide note saying that he felt like he was going to be like Mother and the best thing for him to do was to die. His body was found drowned in the River Thames on December 31, 1888. His pockets were full of stones and the suicide note was discovered on his body. Druitt's suicide came almost one month after the last Ripper murder and two days after he had been dismissed from his teaching job. His death still remains a mystery, as does his connection with the Ripper case. But what is certain is that the police closed their files after Druitt's death and indeed there were never any more dreadful murders

A police investigator is seen here carrying a box of human remains which were excavated from the backyard of 25 Cromwell Street. A female police officer stands guard at the entrance to the property of accused serial killer Fred West. Over a period of about twenty years Fred and his wife, Rosemary, abducted, tortured, raped and murdered an unknown number of girls, many of whom lay buried in the garden until the police dug them up. (Getty Images)

MURDER

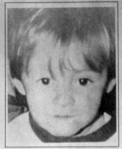

JAMES BULGER

If you have *any* information call the Police on

051-777 2655

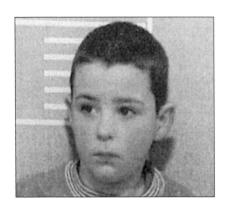

*Robert Thompson (above) and Jon Venables (below)
- both age eleven - were accused of killing two-year-
old James Bulger (opposite) in Liverpool, in 1993.
Although this unspeakable crime was committed
when they were only children themselves, how can
be we sure as young men, they they will not re-
offend. Their release certainly provoked outrage in
some quarters, while others saw their rehabilitation
as a mark of success. The photo on the opposite page
shows the image from the security camera at the
shopping mall, with Thompson and Venables leading
the innocent James to his death.* (Getty Images)

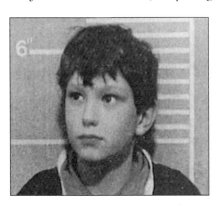

Did Lizzie Borden really kill her father and her stepmother Abby Durfee Gray (right)? She certainly had a good side and a bad side to her character, and perhaps it was the bad side that came out on that fateful day. Above is the exterior view of the house where the Lizzie Borden axe murders took place. (Getty Images)

Above: Lizzie Borden on the right, with her sister Emma.

Few names conjure up such mystery as that of 'Jack the Ripper'. Between the months of August and November 1888 an unknown killer stalked the foggy streets of Whitechapel with a single, brutal ambition . . . MURDER. Under the cover of darkness he lurked in the shadows waiting for his prey – the women of the street – in London town. Above is a London street where one of the murders took place. (Getty Images)

Ed Gein's crimes were so bad that they inspired the movies Silence of the Lambs, Texas Chainsaw Massacre *and* Pscyho. *Below is a picture of Gein's kitchen where the police first started the gruesome task of searching his house.* (Getty Images)

Her name was Mary Bell, and she was a beast in the form of an eleven-year-old girl. A wickedly intelligent, manipulative, cold little girl with dazzling blue eyes and dark, short hair who killed without remorse. Above is a Staffordshire police photograph of Mary Bell after she had escaped from Moor Court Open Prison. (Popperfoto)

carried out by the Ripper. Was this pure coincidence or was Montague John Druitt really 'Jack the Ripper'? Case closed.

SO WHO WAS JACK THE RIPPER?

The mystery still continues more than one hundred years later and I am sure this case will never be really solved. Doctors, members of the Royal Family, aristocrats, black magicians, writers, painters, slaughtermen, coachmen and policemen have all been suspected and accused of being the most famous killer of all times. Even a diary supposedly written by 'Jack the Ripper' has turned up, but as to its authenticity, no-one really can be certain. If only the foggy, dismal streets of the East End of London could tell their story we would actually know the truth but as they can't all we can do is conjecture.

The Boston Strangler

Although no-one has officially been on trial for the spate of vicious murders in Boston from the period of June 1962 to January 1964, it has always been believed to be the work of a man called Albert DeSalvo. The most famous name he became known as was The Boston Strangler, but over the years he was also dubbed The Mad Strangler, The Phantom Strangler, The Measuring Man and The Green Man.

Albert DeSalvo was born on September 3, 1931. His father, Frank DeSalvo, was a labourer and plumber and was married to Charlotte. The family lived in Chelsea, which was a poor, working-class area of Boston. Albert's childhood was not a happy one due to the fact that his father was an alcoholic who physically abused his wife and six children. At the age of seven he witnessed his father knocking out his mother's teeth and then, one by one, bending her fingers back until they snapped. As if this was not bad enough, his father sold Albert and two of his sisters as slaves to a Maine farmer for the sum of only nine dollars, but they managed to escape a few months later. The family were exceptionally poor and in order to survive Frank DeSalvo taught his children to steal, either by shoplifting.

robbery or breaking and entering. Albert could remember times in his childhood when his father
brought home prostitutes and had sex in front of
his own children. Albert, desperate to bring some
money into the home to help his family, resorted to
selling his body for sex to homosexuals in the local
community. His first sexual experience was when
he wasabout ten and this undoubtedly played a
great part in his unusual sexual appetite which
eventually drove him to kill.

Albert's father finally left the family in 1939
and his parents were eventually divorced in 1944.
In November 1943 Albert was arrested on charges
of assault, battery and the robbery of $2.85. In
December he was sent to the Lyman Reform
School for boys. On October 26, 1944, he was
paroled and went to work as a delivery boy for a
flower shop. However, his good behaviour did not
last for long and by August 1946 he was back in
the Lyman Reform School for stealing a car.
During his teenage years, Albert was already
showing signs of a perverse personality that is the
signature of a serial killer. He liked to capture dogs
and cats in milk crates and watch as the animals
tried to kill each other. While the animals were
fighting he liked to shoot arrows through the box
and watch them die.

Charlotte remarried in August 1945 to Paul
Kinosian and they had one daughter. Paul, unfortunately, was just like Albert's real father, he had
the same sadistic temper and loved to take it out
on his stepchildren. So this wretched start to his
life, being the product of an insanely brutal up-

bringing, gave the young DeSalvo an early taste for violence.

Albert left school in 1948 and enlisted in the army. He was posted to occupied Germany for five years and while he was in Frankfurt met a middle-class catholic girl called Irmgard and they were later married. Albert bought Irmgard with him back to the USA in 1954, where he was posted to Fort Dix in New Jersey. In January 1955, DeSalvo was charged with molesting a nine-year-old girl, but as the family declined to press charges, Albert was released from the army with an honourable discharge. Around the same time as the attack, Albert was experiencing sexual difficulties with his wife, forcing her to have intercourse with him at least five or six times a day. Matters went from bad to worse after the birth of their first child and, being short of cash, Albert decided to resume his life of crime. He was arrested twice of breaking and entering, but on both occasions received only a suspended sentence.

Due to his wife's constant rejections, Albert started his career as the 'Measuring Man'. The idea came from a television show where a photographer auditioned women who wanted to become models, by taking their measurements. Posing as a talent scout for a modelling agency, DeSalvo preyed on young female students. They would either allow him to take their measurements with their clothes on or fully naked, and he often got the opportunity to fondle her intimately in the process. Some of the students complained to the police but most, hoping to actually be signed up as models, didn't take it any further. The police, noting that there was never any violence connected to the assaults, put the case right to the bottom of their list.

In 1960, despite their sexual problems, Albert and Irmgard had a son who they called Michael. On March 17, 1960, the Cambridge police arrested DeSalvo on suspicion of burglary and, while being questioned, he swiftly confessed to his role as the 'Measuring Man. He was charged with assault, battery, lewd conduct and attempted breaking and entering, but was only actually convicted of the last charge. He was sentenced to two years in prison but was paroled after eleven months.

Possibly due to his period of incarceration, DeSalvo was now driven by sexual frustration to take a much more aggressive role. This time dubbed the 'Green Man' because of his green work clothes, DeSalvo started a two-year reign of sexual assaults that claimed victims in Massachusetts, Connecticut, New Hampshire and Rhode Island. It was later estimated that he had raped at least 300 women, but the real number claimed by Albert was probably closer to 2,000. He once bragged to having seduced six women in one day, spread over four different towns.

THE STRANGLINGS START

While the Police in New England were looking for the man responsible for the Green Man assaults, homicide detectives in Boston had a more serious case on their hands.

Fifty-five-year-old Ann Slesers lived in an apartment at 77 Gainsborough Street in Boston. On Thursday, June 14, 1962, Ann's son Juris, was visiting his mother at her apartment. When he knocked on the door and received no answer, he automatically presumed that his mother couldn't hear him and so he waited another thirty minutes dawdling up and down the street, and then tried again. When he still received no answer he became suspicious and decided to break down the door. At first he couldn't find his mother but noticed that the drawers in her bedroom had been left open. As he entered the bathroom he discovered the body of his mother who was wearing a blue housecoat which had been left open at the front. She was naked from the shoulders down, and the blue cord from her housecoat had been tied round her neck in the form of a bow. Juris Slesers immediately called the police and the homicide division arrived around 8 p.m.

After inspection, the police concluded that an intruder had entered the apartment in an attempt to carry out a robbery, but upon coming across the old lady had felt a necessity to strangle her. Although there was no evidence of rape, her body had been sexually molested. Even though robbery was suspected as the main motive (due to the fact that the drawers in her bedroom had been ransacked), nothing appeared to have been taken as a valuable gold watch and other items had not been taken. There was no visible sign of a break-in, but her son told the police that there was no way his shy mother would open the door to a stranger, especially if she was only wearing a housecoat and did not have her dentures in. The police questioned over sixty people but could not produce any leads in this rather bizarre case.

Two weeks later, on June 30, 1962, the strangled body of sixty-eight-year-old Nina Nichols was discovered in her apartment. Like Mrs Slesers before her, she had been strangled with two of her nylon stockings, which again were tied in a bow around her neck. Her housecoat had been pulled up to her waist exposing her naked body, and there was evidence that she had been sexually molested. Just like the previous case, there was no visible sign of entry and, although the house had been rummaged through with items scattered all over the place, nothing of value appeared to have been removed.

With two virtually identical murders in the space of only two weeks, the Boston Police Commissioner decided to hold a conference of his department heads on Monday, July 2, 1962. Before the conference drew to a conclusion, the police received the news that there had been a third strangling.

This time the victim was sixty-five-year-old Helen Blake. It had all the markings of the other murders in that she had been strangled with a nylon stocking, but this time there was a bra looped through it. The bra straps had been tied in the form of a bow around her chin and once again there was no visible sign of a forced break in. When an autopsy was carried out on the body they discovered that Helen Blake had actually died on the same day as Nina Nichols, June 30.

The police were now aware that they had a serial killer on their hands who had an obsession with strangulation. They set up an emergency 24-hour hot-line and there was a lot of pressure put on the police to solve the case as quickly as possible.

The next murder was on August 21, 1962, seventy-five-year-old Ida Irga, who was found strangled in her apartment in Boston's West End. Again this had all the signature marks of the other murders with the exception of one thing – the body had been placed in a weird sexual position. This was to become the hallmark in DeSalvo's future signature.

The women of Boston were now living in fear, scared to even be in their own homes. They put iron bars on their windows, added additional locks and put other security devices in their homes. Some women bought weapons while others resorted to getting guard dogs. With all the extra security, media hysteria and additional police patrols, it is hard to believe that the Boston Strangler was able to go about unheeded taking more and more victims.

On August 30, 1962, the strangled body of sixty-seven-year-old Jane Sullivan, was found in her apartment in Dorchester. Once again the autopsy showed that Jane had been killed just one day after Ida Irga.

The killer seemed to break his pattern when he murdered twenty-year-old black, Sophie Clark, on December 5, 1962. Another change was seen with twenty-three-year-old Patricia Bissette, who was strangled on her bed and then covered with a blanket up to her chin, instead of the usual bow around the neck. When twenty-three-year-old Beverly Samans was killed on May 6, 1963, the killer used a knife for the very first time. He stabbed his victim twenty-two times before tying the traditional nylon stocking around her neck. His normal pattern seemed to be restored in the murder of fifty-eight-year-old Evelyn Corbin, who was strangled and violated by an 'unnatural' assault, but the killer returned to young victims with the strangling of twenty-three-year-old Joanne Graff, on November 23. This time the assailant left teeth marks in the breast of his victim. The final victim, nineteen-year-old Mary Sullivan was discovered on January 4, 1964. She had been strangled with a scarf and there was the shaft of a broomstick protruding from her vagina.

POLICE INVESTIGATIONS

Two weeks after the murder of Mary Sullivan, Assistant Attorney General John S. Bottomley took over the Boston Strangler case. The first thing he did was to gather up all the information from the various police departments involved in the investigation and combine it all together. This resulted in a case report that consisted of 37,500 pages and the information was then filed onto a computer.

Even with all this information there was only one real witness to the Stranglers identity. On

February 18, 1963, a twenty-nine-year-old German waitress opened the door to her apartment to a man who said he had come to fix a gas leak. The lady was still feeling the effects of a sleeping pill she had taken the night before, but decided she would let the man in anyway. As soon as she turned to walk away from him, the man leaped on her and attempted to strangle her. As they struggled on the floor she managed to bite into his hand, he let go and she screamed as loud as she could, alerting several people in close proximity. The man panicked and ran away. The petrified woman was unable to give a very accurate description of her attacker.

The police had now been on the case for over nineteen months and still seemed to be a long way off from solving the murders. Realising that regular methods were not giving results, they decided to enlist the help of an international psychic investigator by the name of Peter Hurkos. He had had numerous successes around the world, helping to solve as many as twenty-seven murders in seventeen different countries. Hurkos arrived in Boston in January 1964, and didn't waste any time in helping to solve the case.

Hurkos used his psychic powers to give the police mental images of the crime scenes and a description of the possible killer. He would sometimes go into a trance-like state in which he would actually talk to the victims. The things he talked about in his trance were details that were only known to the police, so when he gave an accurate description of the attacker, the police followed it up. The man the police suspected was brought in for questioning but, although he fitted Hurkos' description in every way, there were just too many points that could not fit the man to the crimes, and he had to be released. Unable to give the police any further help Hurkos left the country.

Now really desperate to solve the case, the police offered a reward of ten thousand dollars for information leading to an arrest. In March 1965 they did manage to catch their man.

THE ARREST

For nine months after the murder of Mary Sullivan, Albert DeSalvo carried out some three hundred sexual assaults on women, spanning from Connecticut, Massachusetts, New Hampshire and Rhode Island. He did not murder any of these victims, and one of them managed to identify him as the Green Man from police records. On November 6, 1964, DeSalvo was finally arrested. He was sent to Bridgewater State Hospital for observation, then on December 10 Albert was returned to jail in Cambridge. While in prison he showed disturbed behaviour and signs of suicidal tendencies. As his mental state further deteriorated he was returned to Bridgewater in February 1965, where he awaited trial for his offences under the name of the Green Man.

While at Bridgewater DeSalvo started to confess to the stranglings. His cellmate was a thirty-three-year-old violent criminal named George Nassar. They became friends and before long DeSalvo started bragging to Nassar about how he sexually dominated women, and eventually confessed to killing thirteen women as the Boston Strangler. Nassar contacted his lawyer, Lee Bailey, and told him that DeSalvo was now ready to talk to him. At first Bailey was reluctant to interview DeSalvo, but eventually agreed. Bailey first telephoned Detective Lieutenant Donovan saying that he needed to ask a man, who was claiming to be the Strangler, some questions. He needed to find out certain things in order to ascertain whether the man was actually telling the truth.

On the day of the interview, Bailey used a tape recorder as he asked DeSalvo about the murders. Albert went into great detail of how he had killed the women and even drew sketches of their apartments, and gave details of the big floppy bows he tied around their necks. In his confession Albert even told Bailey about two victims that had never linked with the Boston stranglings. One was eighty-five-year-old Mary Mullen, who had been found dead on June 28, 1962. Although the post mortem showed that Mary had died from a heart attack, DeSalvo claimed that the cause was shock when he invaded her apartment. The second victim was Mrs Brown, aged sixty-nine, who had been stabbed and beaten in her own home, but there was no sign of the stranglers 'knot'.

Bailey was totally convinced that this man was indeed the Boston Strangler and contacted Detective Donovan handing over the tape containing details of the interview. Donovan then contacted the Attorney General's office and the police were now convinced they had their man. Although it seemed like an open-and-shut case, there was still the problem of no solid evidence. There were no fingerprints at any of the scenes of the crimes and they had no witnesses, other than the German waitress, who was unable to positively identify her attacker.

UNSATISFACTORY CONCLUSION

The case against DeSalvo fell apart when the police could not supply any real evidence proving that he was the man that had committed all the stranglings. These could have just been the ramblings of an insane man. However, DeSalvo did still face trial for the Green Man crimes, for which they had plenty of evidence. Realising that he was never going to be released from prison, Albert wanted to be judged insane so that he could be committed to a mental institution and consequently receive psychiatric help. But DeSalvo's new lawyer, Lee Bailey, was facing a difficult case in trying to prove that DeSalvo was insane at the time of the Green Man assaults.

At a pre-hearing on June 30, 1966, Albert DeSalvo was pronounced competent to be able to stand trial and was remanded without bail to Bridge-water Hospital.

The trial started six months later on January 9, 1967, at the Middlesex County Superior Court. There were ten counts of indecent assault and armed robbery, for which he pleaded not guilty to reasons of insanity. Despite psychiatrists testifying to DeSalvo's mental sickness, the jury still found him guilty on all charges and he was sentenced to a life sentence to be carried out at Bridgewater Hospital. Bridgewater was far more a prison than a hospital and in an attempt to get people to take notice of his cry for psychiatric help, DeSalvo, along with two other prisoners, escaped on February 24, 1967. Boston went into complete panic, but shortly after the escape DeSalvo calmly walked into a clothes shop and telephoned his lawyer to give himself up.

Now DeSalvo was committed to a maximum security prison in Massachusetts, still not receiving the psychiatric help he so desperately wanted. Six years later, on November 25, 1973, he was found dead in his cell. He had been stabbed in the heart as a result of, or so the authorities would have us believe, a prison fight. His killer was never brought to justice.

To this day, DeSalvo's killer has never been found and, at the request of his family, his body was exhumed in the year 2000. It was hoped that it would give more evidence as to who actually killed him, but even more than that, that it would show some evidence that he was not in fact the Boston Strangler.

Although everything points to the fact that Albert DeSalvo was indeed the Boston Strangler, no-one can ever be really certain. There are beliefs that DeSalvo's cellmate, George Nassar, may have been the killer and gave Albert all the details of his crimes. Others believe that DeSalvo, who was already facing many years in jail for the Green

Man offences, made up his confession in the hope that it would lead to a book or a film deal which could take care of his wife and children.

As to the reason why DeSalvo supposedly committed these heinous crimes, when questioned on the subject he said . . .

> 'I'm a sick person. I know that. How could a normal guy do what I did? . . . It was like another guy was inside me.'

> 'Society right from the very beginning started to make me an animal . . . that's why I started all that killing.'

> 'I never knew where I was going, I never knew what I was doing . . . that's why you never nailed me . . . you never knew.'

(quotes taken from the 'Serial Killer Archive')

Martin Bryant

It would be very difficult to have not heard anything about Martin Bryant, as his case has been in the media worldwide. He is a twenty-eight-year-old wanna-be surfer with a history of mental problems, who went on the rampage at the historical Port Arthur site in Tasmania in 1996.

Carleen Bryant always felt that her son, Martin, was a little strange, and she made this known to many of her family and friends. She was mainly concerned about his temperament and eventually Martin's father, Maurice, took early retirement from his job as a dockworker so that he could look after his son.

From the moment he started school his erratic behaviour made him an outcast from the rest of the class, but it wasn't until he started primary school that they discovered he had an IQ that was well below average. He was placed in a special needs class where his teacher noticed that he was in a little world of his own, even more so than the several deaf children that were also in his year. Strangely, Martin seemed perfectly content in his fantasy world and was far happier when he didn't have to interact with any of the other children.

The older Martin got, the more apparent his odd detachment became, he not only distanced himself from the rest of the human race, but he also showed no sign of emotion when confronted with a traumatic or sometimes dangerous situation. This became very evident when his father theoretically committed suicide by drowning himself in the dam on the family property. When the police asked Martin to help them look for the body, instead of showing the normal signs of concern he seemed to be enjoying himself immensely.

As a young child Martin was frequently being bullied because of his strange behaviour. However, as he grew older his behaviour became even more cruel and bizarre. Neighbours reported that he was often throwing rocks at their children, cutting down trees, untying their boats from the jetties and destroying fruit trees in their orchards.

When Martin left school there was no need for him to look for a job as he was entitled to a pension due to his below average IQ assessment. But some time later, possibly bored with nothing to do, he took a job working for a woman named Helen Harvey, which was to influence him for the rest of his life. Helen was a rich, middle-aged, eccentric heiress and she employed Martin to work as a handyman. Martin and Helen formed a very close bond, and not only did she lavish him with affection she also lavished him with material objects. She was well known in the area for being eccentric and in one particular car she was alleged to have bought a different car for every month, but never actually drove any of them. Before long, Martin moved into her mansion not far from his parent's home. Helen loved animals and her home was full of dogs, cats and birds living in every part of the house. Once the living conditions became so squalid that an RSPCA animal welfare officer forced Harvey to clean up her property as it did not comply with health and safety regulations. After the cleaning up operation, no less than seven skips were filled with rubbish from inside the house alone.

Harvey decided to move to the country and, along with Martin, went to live in a small rural town of Copping. Martin's behaviour by this time was becoming more and more erratic, and the neighbours started to complain that he was prowling around their properties late at night. He became obsessed with firearms and was constantly seen showing off with his guns and taking pot shots at anyone who stopped at an apple stand near their front gate. It was obvious, despite his somewhat uncontrollable behaviour, that Martin spent some of his happiest years with Helen. Unfortunately this happiness was not to last and it all came to a tragic end when Harvey was killed in a car accident.

Martin had now lost his father and his close friend, both of whom had influenced him greatly, and now he was a loner who was left to do exactly as he pleased. When Helen died Martin inherited her estate and he now owned a mansion and cash in the excess of $500,000. After Helen Harvey was buried Martin moved back to the mansion in Hobart but soon became restless. He had plenty of money to spend and before long he discovered the joys of travelling. He made thirty trips within a three-year period, and throughout his travels he never really made any real friends. Martin had no confidence with women and seemed unable to form any sort of relationship, so he resorted to hiring prostitutes. Many who visited his house refused to go back because they found him and the whole atmosphere totally macabre.

In the months before the massacre, Martin visited Port Arthur on many occasions. He bought a new sports bag, and the shopkeeper said he remembered him because he measured several of his bags before actually buying one. Although many of the psychologists that were involved with the case believed that Martin Bryant's acts on that date were totally on impulse, the fact that he bought the sports bag and visited the site a few times beforehand, all point to the fact that it was most probably a cold, calculated act.

THE MASSACRE

Sunday, April 28, 1996 at Port Arthur, Tasmania, was a warm and sunny day, and the historical site had attracted a good crowd of people. The site was famous for being one of Australia's most brutal penal settlements, and had become a very popular tourist attraction. By 1.00 p.m. there were over five hundred visitors looking around the site, visiting the many shops and cafés. The lunchtime rush had died down at the Broad Arrow café, but there were still around sixty people finishing off their meals.

The young man with blond hair sat down at a table and ordered his food without drawing any attention to himself. He sat on the front balcony and, apart from commenting on the lack of wasps and number of Japanese tourists, just sat eating his lunch without further conversation. When he had finished eating he picked up his sports bag and went back inside the café. He went to the back of the room and placed his sports bag, along with a video camera, on top of one of the tables. For a while he just stared around at the people inside, and then, before anyone realised what he was doing, he unzipped the bag and produced a semi-automatic rifle. His first victim was an Asian man, Moh Yee Ng, who he shot in the neck, killing him instantly. Then he pointed his gun at the man's companion, and shot her through the back of the head. When he had methodically shot at everyone inside the café either killing them or leaving them bleeding from their wounds, he went outside and continued the fusillade.

People were running and screaming everywhere. Ignoring what was going on around him, the gunman walked towards a tour bus that was parked nearby, and shot the driver and three passengers. Several of the passengers who had been waiting to get on board the bus dived underneath it for cover, but the gunman had seen them and he calmly crouched down and shot them where they lay. Then he walked back to his car, a yellow Volvo sedan which had a surfboard attached to the roof and proceeded to drive three hundred yards down the road to where a woman and her two children were walking. He murdered the woman, the child she was carrying, and chased after the five-year-old toddler and killed her as well. Next he drove up to the entrance gate where a gold coloured BMW was parked. The gunman opened fire on the three occupants and killed them instantly. Next he dragged the bodies from the BMW and transferred his firearms into the car and drove away.

A little distance down the road he saw a couple sitting in a Toyota and stopped beside them. As soon as the woman saw the man was carrying a gun she froze. He ordered the man out of the car and ignoring his pleas not to kill him, made him climb into the boot of the BMW car. Slamming down the lid of the boot he turned and fired two shots in succession into the front of the Toyota, killing the young woman instantly. With the man still inside the boot of his car, the gunman drove to a small bed-and-breakfast called Seascape Cottage. By the time he had left the site of the old colonial ruins, 32 tourists lay dead and 18 others were wounded; 20 were killed in the café, and another 12 on the roads surrounding the historic ruins. It was at the Seascape Cottage that the final part of this deadly story starts to unfold.

Martin apparently already knew the owners of the Seascape guesthouse. At this point in the story it is uncertain whether he killed them then, or before he started his massacre at Port Arthur. After shooting a few more people in their cars who were either passing by or driving up to the guesthouse, the gunman walked back to his car and drove up to the front of Seascape Cottage. He then removed the guns from the car and let the man out from the boot of the trunk. He then took the man inside the house and handcuffed him to a stair rail.

The gunman then went back outside, poured petrol on to the BMW and then set fire to it.

Now holed up inside Seascape Cottage, Bryant was surrounded by over 200 police officers. The siege lasted for twelve hours, during which time an Australian journalist managed to speak to Bryant on the phone. What he told her was quite horrifying: 'I can't speak now, I'm having too much fun. I want to have a shower and if you ring me back again I will shoot the hostage.' Later that night he did in fact kill the poor man that had been bundled into the boot of his car.

The next morning, which was Monday, April 29, the police were waiting outside the cottage trying to decide what course of action to take next. Soon they saw some smoke billowing out from the house, and shortly afterwards Martin Bryant ran out with his clothes on fire and surrendered. He was taken to the Royal Hobart Hospital where he was treated for second-degree burns and had to have several skin grafts. Once his wounds had healed sufficiently he was removed to Risdon Prison Hospital.

THE CONSEQUENCES

Following the fateful day at Port Arthur, while Martin Bryant was recovering in the hospital under heavy guard, the families and friends of the victims were trying to come to terms with what had happened. After the police had completed a reconstruction of the events, which had all happened in a space of around eight minutes, they recorded the official death toll as:

11 Tasmanians
12 Victorians
1 South Australian
4 from New South Wales
4 from Great Britain
2 Malaysians
1 from South-East Asia

Of the injured:
15 Australians
1 Canadian
1 American

When the case eventually came to trial Martin Bryant pleaded guilty, and stood sentence for crimes in respect of:

- the murder of no less than 35 people;
- of 20 attempts to murder others;
- of the infliction of grievous bodily harm on yet three more; and
- of the infliction of wounds upon a further eight people

In addition he was sentenced for:

- four counts of aggravated assault;
- one count of unlawful setting fire to property, namely a motor vehicle which he seized at gunpoint from its rightful occupants, all of whom he murdered;
- and for the arson of a building known as 'Sea-

scape', the owners of which he had likewise murdered the previous day.

Martin Bryant was subsequently sentenced to life imprisonment and was not eligible for parole. During his incarceration at Hobart's Risdon prison Bryant is known to have made at least four suicide attempts. He was found bleeding after trying to cut his femoral artery in the groin region and several smaller cuts to his inner arms with a razor blade. He had also taken an overdose of sedatives which were supplied to him by another prisoner, tried to strangle himself with bandages and finally attempted to choke himself by swallowing a rolled-up tube of toothpaste.

PSYCHIATRIC ASSESSMENT

Martin Bryant was assessed as being a person with a schizoid personality disorder. The normal signs of this condition are that the person concerned is usually pale, exceptionally quiet and appears rather strange to others. Their head is very often tilted to one side so that it gives the appearance of someone who is being continually hung by a noose. Their life is usually full of trauma and most often has experienced a strange, string of fantasies and failures. They normally show little or no emotion to events and have difficulty in forming a relationship with another person. The overpowering part of their nature is that they have no emotion and consequently have little capacity for pleasure. Martin Bryant is a classic schizoid personality type – but is not paranoid or schizo-phrenic. In fact, no-one really knew what to make of Martin Bryant. Most people who did know him described him as a loving, gentle and kind person, while others described him as having strange, steely cold blue eyes.

Basically, in summing up, Martin Bryant was set loose in the world with plenty of money but with nothing to do and nowhere to go. He was excep-tionally lonely and once said that if he could have a girlfriend his life would be complete. He did actually have a relationship with a girl for two months just before the shootings, Jenetta Hoani. She claimed that he was obsessed with bestiality, violent videos and owned over 200 teddy bears, most of which were in his bedroom. She claimed his best friend was his pet pig with whom he shared his bed.

Martin showed very little emotion about anything, in fact the only thing that really excited or indeed interested him were all his guns. Martin Bryant did not seem to be angry at any one person in particular, he was just angry at life. He was angry at all the people for what he had become – on the one hand a child who had never grown up and on the other an adult who had tried to inte-grate but with no success.

Charles Whitman

*In a period of ninety-six minutes, sniper
Charles Whitman killed sixteen people and
wounded thirty from the observation deck
of the University of Texas Tower.*

Charles Joseph Whitman was born on June 24, 1941, in Lake Worth, Florida. He was the oldest of three sons of Margaret and Charles A. Whitman, Jr. On the surface the family appeared to be a happy one, but the lovely home with all its amenities and swimming pool, were just a mere façade. All the luxuries did nothing to alleviate the trouble within the Whitman household. His father was a disciplinarian with a violent temper. He not only beat his wife, he was known to use belts or his fists to make sure they didn't disobey him.

At school Charles was an above-average student, became an Eagle Scout at twelve, and graduated from High School in 1959. In June of that year, just before his eighteenth birthday his relationship with his father got rather out of hand. Charlie had been out drinking with some friends and arrived home drunk. His father beat him severely and threw him into the swimming pool, which nearly caused Charlie to drown. A few days later, fed up with the treatment he received at home, Charlie decided to enlist in the United States Marine Corps. He was stationed for a year and a half at Guantánamo Bay, Cuba. He worked very hard at being a good Marine, always followed orders and studied hard for his exams. He excelled at his shooting and earned himself a Sharpshooter's Badge for his excellence at rapid fire from long distance. It was important for Charlie to be the best Marine after all the years of belittling he had received at home from his father. He passed a test to enter officer training and was sent to a preparatory school in Bainbridge, Maryland, and then to the University of Texas in September 1961, to major in engineering. While he was at the university he met Kathy Leissner, a student from a small Texas town of Needville. They were married on August 17, 1962. Unfortunately because of low grades he was ordered back to duty as an enlisted man in the Marine Corps on February 12, 1963. He was sent to North Carolina, where he eventually found himself having to face a court martial for gambling, usury and unauthorized possession of a non-military pistol. He was sentenced to thirty days confinement and ninety days hard labour. Charlie was released in December 1964, was honourably discharged from the Marines and returned to the University of Texas to continue his studies in engineering.

While at the University, Charlie worked part-time as a scoutmaster and in the spring of 1966, his mother left his father and moved to Austin to be near her eldest son.

THE HEADACHES BEGIN

In 1966 Charles Whitman started to have severe headaches and sought medical and psychiatric advice at the University health centre. He was prescribed Excedrin for the headaches, but he failed to return to the health centre for further assistance as instructed.

At around 12.00 a.m. on August 1, 1966, Whitman killed his mother in her apartment by strangling her from behind with a rubber hose, and then hit her in the back of the head. He left a note on the body. A few minutes before 3.00 a.m. Whitman also killed his wife, Kathy, as she slept, this time by stabbing her five times in the chest with a hunting knife. Again a note was left beside her body, below is an excerpt of what it said:

> '*I don't quite understand what it is that compels me to type this letter. Perhaps it is to leave some vague reason for the actions I have recently performed. I don't really understand myself these days . . . I have been a victim of many unusual and irrational thoughts . . . It was after much thought that I decided to kill my wife, Kathy, tonight after I pick her up from work at the telephone company. I love her dearly, and she has been as fine a wife to me as any man could ever hope to have . . . Similar reasons provoked me to take my mother's life also. I don't think the poor woman has ever enjoyed life as she is entitled to . . .*'

Later the same morning he placed the following items in a green footlocker and left for the University tower at around 11.30 a.m.:

Transistor radio, notebook, a full water jug, a full plastic gas jug, sales slips from Davis hardware, batteries, lengths of cotton and nylon rope, compass, pen, rifle scabbard, hatchet, machete with scabbard, hammer, ammunition box with gun cleaning equipment, alarm clock, cigarette lighter, canteen, binoculars, hunting knife and whetstone, large Randall knife, large pocket knife, pipe wrench, eye glasses, matches, 12 assorted cans of food and a jar of honey, two cans of Sego, can of charcoal starter, flashlight, earplugs, white adhesive tape, steel bar, green army rubber duffel bag, green extension cord, lengths of clothesline wire and yellow electric wire, grey gloves, deer bag, bread, sweet rolls, Spam, peanuts, sandwiches, a box of raisins, deodorant and toilet paper, but NO medication which he was supposed to be taking on a regular basis.

In addition the guns he took with him were a .357 Magnum Smith & Wesson revolver, a Galesi-Brescia pistol, a .35 Remington, sawn-off Sears 12-gauge shotgun, a 6mm Remington bolt-action rifle with telescope, and a .30 calibre M-1 Carbine, along with 700 rounds of ammunition.

On entering the University building Whitman clubbed the receptionist to death, killed two and wounded two other people who were coming up the stairs from the twenty-seventh floor and then ascended to the observation tower which was at an elevation of 231 feet. Whitman then opened fire on people who were crossing the campus and on nearby streets, killing ten more people and wounding thirty-one (one of whom died a week later). Police arrived at the scene and immediately returned fire whilst other officers worked their way up to the tower. At 1.24 p.m. two police officers along with a deputized private citizen burst onto the observation deck and killed Whitman.

The horror, which had lasted a total of ninety-six minutes, was finally over. It was a massacre which not only shocked Austin but the rest of the nation. A nation which hadn't even had time to recover from the brutal slayings of nine young nurses in Chicago the previous week.

WHY?

When the police searched Whitman's house they found a letter written by him asking the authorities to carry out an autopsy on his brain, to discover any visible physical disorder. In fact, a small tumour was discovered just above his brain stem. Could it be that this tumour attributed to Whitman's rage and outrageous behaviour? Not, in the opinion of the neurosurgeon and medical experts. Could it have been the amphetamines that Whitman was taking due to the violent headaches? Maybe it was just that he wanted to get back at his father and all the violence he had suffered in his childhood.

The observation deck remained open for several years following the shootings, and the University spent $5000 repairing bullet holes in 1967. Due to a spate of suicides which were connected to the massacre in 1966, the University of Texas Regents declared the deck permanently closed in 1976, and so it remained for over twenty years.

Peter Manuel

What was it that stimulated Peter Manuel's abhorrent appetite for human suffering? He killed entire families while they were asleep, even lingering after the crime to gloat.

Peter Manuel was born in the United States in 1927. Both his parents were Scottish and they returned to their native country in 1932. He took to crime early in his life and spent days in and out of approved schools and Borstal for a string of petty crimes.

As Peter grew up he was seen as a loner who had an obsession with the dark. His petty crimes grew more sinister as his need for sexual gratification came out first in assault and rape, and then peaked with the killings of several families. He lived with his parents in Birkenshaw, and this was to become the centre of his killing territory.

THE BAKER

William Watt was a master-baker who lived in Burnside, and the proud owner of a string of bakery shops. He was happy as he left work because he was planning to have a fishing holiday around Loch Lomond. On the afternoon of September 9, 1956, he packed his suitcase, put his fishing gear and black Labrador bitch into the car and kissed his wife farewell. He was a little worried about leaving his wife, Marion, because she had been suffering from a heart complaint for some while. She had recently undergone an operation and was still not back to full strength, so he promised to phone her when he arrived at his destination. While he was away the couple had arranged for Marion's sister to be staying at the house, and their sixteen-year-old daughter, Vivienne, would also be at home.

As promised, when William arrived at the hotel he immediately phoned his wife to tell her he had arrived safely, and to check that everything was well with her. Indeed, everything was fine and she told him not to worry and to enjoy his fishing trip. He said he would, but he would keep in touch by telephone.

On the evening of September 16, Marion Watt and her sister were chatting in the lounge while Vivienne and a friend where giggling in the kitchen. By midnight the house was quiet and the three occupants were all asleep.

The Watts had a daily help named Helen Collinson, who arrived at the house around 8.45 the following morning. She was surprised to find the bungalow still locked and the curtains closed. She wandered around the house knocking on the windows and calling out her employer's name. When she arrived at the front door she knew that something was wrong, and thought that the house had probably been burgled. The door had glass panels and one, just above the lock, had been smashed. She went to the house next door to fetch help, which was where Vivienne's young friend Deanne lived. Mrs. Collinson, accompanied by Deanne and her mother, returned to the bungalow and stood outside discussing what to do next. The next person on the scene was the postman. Having heard the women's story he said they should investigate further, and put his hand through the broken glass and turned the lock from the inside. Mrs. Collinson went in before him and went into the first room on the left. Seconds later she appeared, gasping, ashen and she had to clutch the door jamb for support. The rest of the group looked at her in horror as she told them, 'They are – they are covered with blood!'

The postman immediately rushed past her and went into the room. What he discovered was a bed, dark with blood and in it were two women who had both been shot in the head. Even to a layman it was very obvious they had been shot at close range. Meanwhile, Mrs. Collinson, who was recovering from the initial shock, felt concern for Vivienne and went into the other bedroom. She could see from the door that the scene was the same, the bed was covered in blood and Vivienne was just lying there. As she started to approach the inert body, the form gave out the most terrifying noise which was heard by the other two, who subsequently rushed into the room. The agonising noise, in fact, came from Vivienne in her last fight for life.

A PRIME SUSPECT

The police arrived at the bungalow by 11.00 a.m.

and quickly ascertained that the three women had been shot at close range by a .38 revolver. Initially, they thought the deaths were the result of a bungled burglary, but as there was no evidence of anything having been taken, they realised that this was not the main motive.

Then the police were notified of a break-in at another bungalow in the same street the same night. An officer was sent to the house to investigate and when he returned had some important information. He told his superior officer that there were certain aspects about newly-discovered burglary, that clearly pointed to the handiwork of a local villain who was known to the police. The suspect's name was New York-born Peter Thomas Anthony Manuel. He was a known sex offender with previous convictions for indecent assault, rape, and burglary and was currently on bail on charges of an attempted break-in at a colliery canteen.

The police didn't waste any time going round to the house where Peter lived with his parents, and searched it. Unfortunately they found nothing in their search which would incriminate Manuel in the burglaries. While the police were searching, Manuel sat quietly smirking. He was a well-built man, with dark eyes and oily hair. He had an extreme hatred of the police and considered himself as something of an amateur lawyer who was able to outwit any authority. He refused point-blank to account for his movements on the night of the murders or to answer any of their questions. Very frustrated, feeling they had got their man, the police left.

A NEW SUSPECT

Several weeks later following his trial for previous convictions, Peter Manuel was serving an eighteen month prison sentence for the break-in at the colliery. By now the investigations into the Watt's murders had taken a new and dramatic turn. The police now suspected Mr. Watt himself, and for a number of curious reasons. The police had contacted the ferrymaster on the river Clyde, who claimed that he had ferried Mr. Watt and his dog across the river in the early hours of the day of the murder. From this the police had convinced themselves that he had slipped out of his hotel room at Lochgilphead soon after midnight on September 16, driven the ninety miles home, broken in and murdered his wife, daughter and sister-in-law. Then they made the assumption that he had driven all the way back to Lochgilphead in time to eat a large breakfast, pretending that he had had a good night's sleep. It was on this theory, and this alone, that William Watt was held in Glasgow's Barlinnie prison, the same prison where Peter Manuel was currently serving his sentence.

A CONCOCTED STORY

While Peter Manuel was in Barlinnie prison he wrote a letter to the lawyer acting for Mr. Watts. He told him he had vital evidence regarding the murders and that he would like to meet up with him. The lawyer, Lawrence Dowdall, agreed to keep the appointment, during which Manuel proceeded to tell him a lengthy, if not concocted, story. He told the lawyer that the man in question gave him very precise details about the inside the the Watt's house, but Manuel refused to give a name. The lawyer said that he was very surprised that anyone would give such unimportant information as regards to the inside of the house, and suggested that Manuel was in fact there himself. This he denied categorically.

Meanwhile, on December 3, William Watt was released from prison, and having been incarcerated for sixty-seven gruelling days, came out a broken man. Not only had he been accused of killing his beloved family, but he also had to come to the terms that he was now on his own. He tried to resume to a normal life, ignoring the gossip and rumours that were going on around him.

Exactly one year after his release, William Watt met up with Peter Manuel, who had by now completed his term in prison. Manuel had asked Mr. Dowdall if he would fix up the meeting, and for some inexplicable reason told the same detailed story to Mr. Watt as he had already recounted to the lawyer. Once again, as he went into the details of the Watt household, William shouted: 'Now look, you know far too much about the house not to have been there!' Manuel vehemently denied this allegation.

Directly after the interview with Watt, Manuel left Scotland and travelled to Newcastle-upon-Tyne for a short trip. It was December 7, 1957 and around 4.30 in the morning when Peter Manuel arrived at the city's railway station and hailed a taxi. The taxi was driven by Sydney Dunn and he recalled later that it was a very dark night, and the streets were empty because of the stormy weather.

The next day a Police Constable was cycling along a lonely moorland road when he came across an abandoned car. On inspection it appeared that the car had blood on the steering wheel but there was no sign or either a driver or passenger. The policeman immediately summoned assistance and they searched the area around the car. It wasn't long before they discovered the body of Sydney Dunn about 140 yards from where the car was parked. He had been shot and his throat had been slashed, and his wallet containing five pounds in notes was found lying near his body.

On December 28, seventeen-year-old Isabelle Cooke left her home in Glasgow on her way to meet her boyfriend. They had arranged to meet at the bus stop and then go on to a dance in nearby Uddingston. The boyfriend waited but she never turned up. When her father realised that his daughter had not returned home that night, he reported to the police that he feared she was missing. The police began a search of the area and discovered various items of clothing – panties, an underslip, a cosmetics bag and a raincoat – all scattered around the vicinity. As the items were discovered they were shown to a distraught Mr. and Mrs. Cooke who immediately identified them as belonging to their daughter. Unfortunately there was no sign of Isabelle.

The dance that Isabelle and her boyfriend were heading for was held at a bungalow in Uddingston.

The house was owned by Peter Smart who lived there with his wife, Doris, and their ten-year-old son, Michael. The Smarts had decided rather than join in all the festivities of Hogmanay, they would drive seventy miles to Ancrum to the home of Mrs. Smart's parents. The custom at Hogmanay is for neighbours to call on one another to wish them good luck for the newly-arrived year. At 1.30 a.m. some neighbours called at the Smart house and noticed that the lights were out. They knew they were making an early start New Year's Day so they just assumed they had gone to bed. Nobody paid any attention to the lack of activity at the Smart's house over the next few days as they knew they were going away. However, one neighbour noticed that strange things were happening at the house – one minute the curtains would be open, the next closed. Gradually there was a sense of unease in the adjoining homes, which was only heightened when two local residents, Mr. and Mrs. John McMunn woke to find a leering face peering around their bedroom door on January 4.

With great courage and presence of mind, Mr. McMunn cried out asking who it was and asking his wife where the gun was. Immediately Mrs. McMunn answered, 'Here it is', at which the intruder fled.

When Mr. Smart failed to return to work on January 6 the authorities were notified. His car was found abandoned on a Glasgow street, and the police then went to make a search of the bungalow. They forced the back door and made a careful inspection of every room in the house. The first room they went into was the main bedroom as they noticed that the curtains were still drawn, even though it was broad daylight. He was sickened by the sight of Mr. and Mrs. Smart laying dead beneath blood-soaked sheets, they had both been shot. Fearful of what he might find in the other bedroom, the officer was right when his worst fears were confirmed. They found the young Michael lying beneath his covers also the victim of shooting.

Panic was now starting to spread around the suburbs of Glasgow, and people became fearful that they might become the next victim of these apparently senseless killings. The police were baffled by the crimes because there seemed to be no discernible motive, but information started to filter back that would help them in their search for the ruthless killer.

Once again their attention was drawn to the normally hard-up Peter Manuel, who had been seen by locals spending money quite freely in a bar near his home. They managed to recover some of the notes he used and luckily for the police they proved to be part of a newly-printed batch. The bank had a record of the serial numbers and one particular group had been paid to Mr. Smart when he cashed a cheque for money to spend on their forthcoming holiday.

READY TO TELL ALL

The police did not waste any time in apprehending Manuel and placing him in an identification line-up. Witnesses from the bar were able to point him out as being the man who had handed over the crisp new bank notes. At last they had Peter Manuel backed into a corner.

He was arrested on January 13, 1958 and for his own sordid reasons, this time he was ready to tell the whole sordid story. Not only did he admit to the killing of the Smart family but he also told them of many others that had been killed in and around the area of his home town. He seemed to be bragging about his horrendous actions and gave them details of exactly how he had killed his victims. Detail by detail he gave the gory details and about the death of Isabelle Cooke he said:

> 'I met the girl walking . . . When we got near the dog track she started to scream. I tore off her clothes and tied something round her neck and choked her. I then carried her up a lane into a field and dug a hole with a shovel. While I was digging a man passed along the lane on a bike. So I carried her again over a path beside a brick works into another field. I dug a hole next to a part of a field that was ploughed and put her into it.'

After the admissions, even though the murder took place after dark, Manuel was able to take the police directly to the burial place. As they walked across the ploughed field the police officers noticed the lack of any sensitivity in Manuel's manner. Suddenly he stopped and said, 'This is it. This is the place. In fact, I think I am standing on her right now.' The police started to dig, and to their shock and horror he was exactly right.

Peter Manuel had confessed to killing eight people, but at his trial he was only found guilty of murdering seven. He was acquitted of the murder of a seventeen-year-old girl named Anne Knieland, who he had named earlier, due to the lack of the corroboration of his statement by Scottish law. He was also not charged with the murder of the taxi driver, Sydney Dunn, as it was outside the jurisdiction of Scotland. However, there is no doubt that this evil and sick man did commit the crime. Although the police could not prove it, it is considered that Manuel was in fact responsible for the death of no less than fifteen people. Peter Manuel was sentenced to death and was hanged at Barlinnie prison on July 11, 1958.

THE SICK MIND

No one can really know what possibly stimulated Manuel's loathsome appetite for inflicting so much suffering on a fellow human being. The most likely reason is that he somehow achieved a dark, possibly sexual satisfaction from killing completely defenceless victims. The mysterious movements of the curtains at the Smart house certainly indicate that this man had such a perverted mind the he returned to the bungalow several times just to gloat over the sight of what he had done. Another indication of how sick this man was, is that he talked in such precise details about his crimes, in fact, he 'talked' his ways to the gallows.

Peter Manuel can probably best be described as a 'thrill killer' – someone who kills for the pure pleasure of killing. They enjoy the sport of killing and relish in the misery that it creates, not only for the victim but for everyone connected to the victim and even the shock that it generates for the wider community.

There is usually no particular victim 'profile', the satisfaction simply comes from the killing itself. There is no set pattern, the victim could just as easily be a man, woman, a child or even an animal, the fact that they are responsible for killing *something* is in itself enough. To these sick people the ritualistic torture, mutilation and sadism are important elements of killing, without it there is simply no 'thrill'.

George Chapman

George Chapman, otherwise known as
Severin Antoniovich Klosowski was dubbed
'The Borough Poisoner'. Klosowski was one
of the suspects in the case of Jack the Ripper
because he arrived in London shortly before
the murders began, and they stopped after he
went to America. He had also studied medicine
and surgery in Russia, so he had experiences
with human bodies . . .

Severin Antoniovich Klosowski was born in the Polish village of Nargornak on December 14, 1865. His mother was Emile and his father, Antonio, was a carpenter who apprenticed Severin to a senior surgeon named Moshko Rappaport. Severin studied to be a surgeon from December 1880 until October 1885, after which time he finished his studying at the hospital of Praga in Warsaw. Records are uncertain as to whether he actually qualified as a junior surgeon, or indeed when he exactly moved to England. The most likely date appears to be around spring of 1887.

Once in England he started a career as a hairdresser's assistant, working for a man named Abraham Radin. He stayed in this job for around five months and then started running a barber shop at 126 Cable Street, in the East End of London. It is most likely that this is where he resided during the times of the Ripper murders. In the year 1890, Severin took a similar job in a barber shop on the corner of Whitechapel High Street and George Yard. This is also significant in the Ripper case because Martha Tabram, who was murdered in August 1888, was found in the George Yard buildings, only a few yards from the barber shop.

Severin soon proved that he was a competent barber and gradually moved up from assistant to proprietor of the shop around October 1889. Then he met and married Lucy Baderski in a German Roman Catholic ceremony. He had only met her five weeks before in a Polish Club in Clerkenwell. This was a big mistake for Klosowski, who was already legally married to his first wife whom he had left back in Poland. Somehow, she found out about his bigamous marriage and moved to England in an effort to force Lucy to leave. It appears the three of them cohabited for some time, that is until his first wife had had enough and left. Severin and Baderski had a son, Wladyslaw or Wohystaw, and the family never seemed to live in any one place for very long. Again the dates are a little difficult to prove, but around 1891 they emigrated to New Jersey. It could possibly have been due to the death of their son from pneumonia which prompted their move from London.

Once in New Jersey Klosowski found work once again in a barber's shop, but by this time the couple were arguing constantly and he ended up attacking Lucy with a knife. Lucy was pregnant at the time, and understandably was very perturbed by the assault, so she returned to live in London in February of 1892. She lived with her sister at 26 Scarborough Street in Whitechapel and their second child, Cecilia, was born on May 15. Klosowski returned to London in June that year and the couple were reunited for a short while, before finally ending the relationship.

In 1893 Klosowski met a woman named Annie Chapman in a hairdresser's shop in South Tottenham. May I add at this point it was not the same Annie Chapman that was murdered by the Ripper. They became romantically involved and lived together for around a year, that is until Severin started to roam once more. Annie was upset and walked out on Severin even though she was expecting his baby. When Severin eventually found out from Annie about their baby he offered her no support whatsoever. They had no more contact whatsoever, but he did keep one thing from their relationship – her surname. He decided to call himself George Chapman in the hope that he could escape the tangled web of his previous love affairs. But as George Chapman he was no less of a philanderer than Severin Klosowski.

In 1895 Chapman became an assistant in William Wenzel's barber shop in Leytonstone, and he resided at a lodging house in Forest Road. He soon became friends with an alcoholic called Mary Spink. Mary was down on her luck, she had been deserted by her husband who had also taken her son with him. The relationship developed and they had a mock wedding ceremony at which time Mary signed over the proceeds of a £500 legacy over to Chapman. They leased a barber's shop in a poor section of Hastings. However, the venture soon turned sour so they moved their location to a more profitable site. They became famous for their 'musical shaves' whereby Mary would play the piano whilst her husband would service the customers. Business thrived for a while and soon they had sufficient funds for Chapman to buy himself a boat, which he named 'Mosquito'. However the success in their business venture did not reflect on their personal relationship and Mary became the subject of brutal beatings. Mary was often heard by the neighbours crying out in the middle of the night. They also witnessed that she had bruises and cuts on her face on many an occasion, and at least once noticed that she had bruise marks around her throat.

On April 3, 1897, Chapman purchased a one ounce dose of tartar-emetic from a pharmacy in the High Street. Tartar-emetic is a white powder which dissolves in water. It contains a substance called antimony which is a colourless, odourless and almost tasteless poison, the effects of which were little known in the late nineteenth century. If the powder were to be taken in large doses it is likely that it would make the person sick and therefore reject it from their system. On the other hand, if it were to be administered in small, regular doses it would induce a slow, gradual and extremely painful death. One interesting side-effect of the poison, however, is that it would preserve the body of the deceased for many years after their death. Soon the business at the barber shop declined rapidly and Chapman resorted to becoming a manager at the Prince of Wales public house in Bartholomew Square. It was while he was working at the pub that Mary started suffering from severe stomach pains and nausea. They called in Dr. Rodgers but he could find no cure, and it was her husband who sat religiously by her bedside. She finally died on Christmas Day, with the cause of death being recorded as phthisis, better known as consumption. Mary had been nursed by two ladies Elizabeth Waymark and Martha Doubleday during her sickness, who later remarked on the condition of Mary's body, which they said was just a mere skeleton. Doubleday also commented on Chapman's behaviour after the death of his wife. She said he just stood beside the body and cried 'Polly, Polly, speak!' Then he went into the next room and cried, and then went downstairs to open the pub as normal.

His grieving, however, did not last for long. Chapman hired a former restaurant manageress called Bessie Taylor to work at the pub. He didn't waste any time in getting to know her personally and soon a romance blossomed. Once again there was a fake marriage and once again he started to abuse his new 'wife'. Bessie started to suffer from the same symptoms as Mary – violent stomach cramps and nausea. She had an operation but it did nothing to improve her rapidly failing health. By now Chapman had left the Prince of Wales pub

BORN TO BE KILLERS

and was working in another pub called The Grapes in Bishops Stortford.

His next career move was to lease the Monument Tavern in Borough, and all the while Bessie's condition was deteriorating. Bessie died on what should have been a romantic occasion for her, Valentine's Day, 1901. The cause of death was recorded as 'exhaustion from vomiting and diarrhoea'.

Bessie had a good friend by the name of Mrs. Painter who visited her almost every day throughout her illness. She was the constant butt of Chapman's sick jokes and on more than one occasion would answer 'Your friend is dead', when she enquired after her health. However, when she visited on the 15th and asked how her friend was, Chapman simply replied that she was much the same, but much to Mrs. Painter's indignation she later learned that she had actually died on the previous day. Around the time of his wife's death Chapman attempted arson on the Monument Tavern as it was about to lose its lease.

The next 'Mrs. Chapman' was a woman named Maud Marsh. She had been hired as a barmaid in the Monument Tavern in August 1901. Again, another bogus marriage which survived barely a year before Chapman turned his attention to Florence Rayner. He pleaded with Florence to leave for America with him, but she flatly refused saying that he already had a wife downstairs. To this he snapped his fingers and said it wouldn't take much for her not to be Mrs. Chapman any more. Just like his other two victims, Maud became the victim of his vicious beatings. Just like her predecessors she started to have strange symptoms.

POST MORTEM REVEALS ALL

Maud's mother noticed how keen Chapman was to administer her daughter's medicine, and out of concern called in another doctor for a second opinion. Chapman panicked and administered an extremely strong dose of the poison. Maud only survived one more day and died on October 22, 1902. The doctor was very suspicious and would not issue a death certificate until a post mortem had been carried out. When they examined the body they found traces of arsenic and 7.24 grains of antimony in Maud's stomach, bowels, liver, kidneys and brain. Chapman's days as a wife poisoner were now over.

Chapman was arrested on October 25, at which time they discovered that Severin Klosowski and George Chapman were one in the same person. They exhumed the bodies of his two previous wives and discovered both had large amounts of metallic antimony in them, and what was even more remarkable was the fact that they were remarkably well preserved.

Chapman was charged with the murders of Maud Marsh, Mary Spink and Bessie Taylor. He was only charged with Maud's murder, even though evidence was submitted for the other two. On March 20, 1903, the jury took just eleven minutes to find him guilty.

After he was put in prison Chapman became

exceptionally quiet, restless and irritable, and continued to protest his innocence. When his appeal was turned down he was put on suicide watch. Chapman was finally hanged at Wandsworth prison on April 7, 1903.

WAS HE JACK THE RIPPER?

George Chapman was on the high suspect list of the Ripper case. There were many similarities that sparked off the suspicion. First on the list was the time he arrived in England and the time he left, which seemed to coincide with the time span of the Ripper murders. Second, he was known to have studied as a surgeon in Russia, and the first murders were definitely committed by someone with a medical knowledge. Moreover, his crimes of poison were certainly carried out with someone with more than a little knowledge of medicine.

The Ripper was known to be a man who had freedom to roam the streets at night, and Lucy Baderski even admitted that her husband was in the habit of staying out until the very early hours of the morning. Added to this we know that he was capable of extreme violence and even murder, albeit that it was a different method. So the question still remains that although the man was a misogynist, a man with a very high sexual appetite, a good medical knowledge, and a foreign appearance that fits the description of certain witnesses, could he turn from a savage mutilator into a calculated poisoner just seven years later?

Graham Frederick Young

*Graham Young was a smartly dressed and
intelligent child – or so it appeared on
the outside! He killed three people who
he poisoned by administering doses of thallium
in cups of tea, he so kindly made for them at work.*

Graham Frederick Young was born on September 7, 1947 in Neasdon, a suburb of Greater London. His mother died the year he was born and he was raised by an aunt and uncle until his father remarried in 1950. He had a sister who was eight years older than him, and although she remembered him as a bright child, she admitted he always like to be on his own. As he grew older his intelligence was certainly above average, and he achieved exceptionally high marks for both English and chemistry whilst at school. As a child Graham was obsessed with anything to do with the Nazis, and Adolf Hitler was his hero. He was also intrigued with black magic and potions, and loved anything to do with chemistry. What did go unnoticed though was the fact that he became very interested in the effects of several kinds of poison,

340

and over the years this would become a complete obsession.

In his teenage years his obsession with the Nazis grew even stronger and he learned all he could about their movement and their leader. He later said that he envied Hitler because of the power he had over other people and he was determined to reach the same status. Ironically, it was his growing knowledge of poisons that would help him achieve this empowerment.

In 1961, instead of spending money on the normal things that teenage boys buy, Young would purchase small doses of antimonium and digitalis. This was to be the year that he slowly started to poison members of his family. He didn't give them lethal doses that would kill them instantly, but it was enough to make them feel nauseous. When asked why he was buying the toxic substances, he told his family that he needed them for experiments he was doing at school in his chemistry lessons. With that as an excuse he was able to accumulate huge amounts of poison, it was estimated that he had enough to kill at least three hundred people.

It appeared that in his sick mind Graham was using members of his family as a sort of laboratory experiment. He later admitted that he was experimenting with poison so that he could measure the time between the dosage administered and the first sign of discomfort in the victim. On occasion he would forget which portion of food he had poisoned and would himself suffer from vomiting and stomach cramps. Another tactic he used to put himself above suspicion, was to administer small doses of the poison to himself. Sometimes he would use his best friend to test out his poisonous concoctions, which would result in the same severe debilitating symptoms.

After a while the diseases that the Young family were haunted with, were starting to cause some concern. Graham's aunt Winnie was well aware of his peculiar obsessions and she didn't really trust him. The family arranged for him to see a psychiatrist, and in a roundabout way Graham told the doctor that he had control over his family's health. The doctor subsequently warned the police of his suspicions and on May 23, 1961, a couple of police officers called round to the house and found Graham at home. Being a bright lad he realised it was futile to lie and so he confessed to what he had been doing, but what he omitted to tell them was that he had given his grandmother a lethal dose.

Graham Young was arrested and held in custody, where he tried to commit suicide by hanging himself. When asked why he wanted to kill himself, he told the psychiatrist that he felt helpless because he didn't possess any poison. When his case went to trial in 1962, although he admitted to poisoning his family, he still omitted to say anything about what he done to his grandmother. It was too late anyway to carry out a post mortem on her body – she had already been cremated.

Medical experts suggested that Young be placed in a psychiatric institution, and the judge committed him to fifteen years in Broadmoor secure psychiatric hospital. During his years spent in

Broadmoor, Young spent much of his time studying medical books and, indeed, any other book that could teach him anything about his beloved chemicals and poisons. Nine years later, when he professed to have been cured, he was an expert in the subject he loved so much. He was released from Broadmoor in February 1971 and allegedly told a nurse when leaving, that he intended to kill one person for every year that he had been detained.

On his release, Young was sent to a government training centre where he befriended and then poisoned, although this time not fatally, thirty-four-year-old Trevor Sparkes. Not long after his training he took a job as a shopkeeper in Bovingdon, Hertfordshire. His supervisor was not informed of his past record and the very day before he started his new post, he bought some antimonium and thallium. Graham had only been working at the shop for a very short time when there was an unusual spate of sickness sweeping through the other workers. The bug was nicknamed the 'Bovingdon Bug'. Many fell victim to the bug, including the storeroom manager, Bob Egle, who eventually died from the fatal dose of poison that Young had been secretly slipping into his tea. The death of Bob Egle came as a terrible shock to his work colleagues, and Young appeared to be particularly upset. Several weeks later, Bob Egle's successor, Ron Hewitt, also fell ill. He decided that the safest thing was to quit his job and thereby saved his own life. The number of employees that were showing the same symptoms continually grew – up to seventy of them suffered from vomiting and diarrhoea. Many were admitted to hospital because their symptoms were so severe, but luckily there were no more deaths. The cause of the mysterious bug still remained a mystery. Many of the victims became sick after drinking a cup of tea or coffee, but they did not seem to think that there was any connection between the drinks and the illness. They all just assumed that there was some sort of highly-infectious virus going round which they had all succumbed to.

Several months later this mystery 'virus' infected the distribution manager, Fred Biggs. He was hit particularly hard and in an effort to get to the bottom of strange bug, he was taken to the National Hospital for Nervous Diseases in London. However, they were unable to save him and he died as well. After the second death the authorities decided that this mysterious virus needed further investigation. Young asked one of the investigators whether he had considered the possibility of a large-scale thallium poisoning.

Some of Young's work colleagues were starting to get suspicious and wondered whether he really was as innocent as he made out. Young had already bragged about his hobby – studying the effects of toxic products – and so his colleagues reported him to the chief. He immediately told the police of their suspicions, and they started to check to see whether Graham Young did in fact have any criminal past. When they delved into his files they couldn't believe what they found and Young was immediately arrested. Following the arrest the police searched him and found a lethal dose of thallium in his pocket.

His apartment was searched and they found antimonium, thallium and aconitine, but what was even more incriminating was the discovery of his diary, which showed him to be a cold and calculating murderer. In the diary he had described in a scientific way the amount of toxin he had administered to his victims, the effects it had, and whether he would allow them to live or let them suffer an excruciating death.

When Young was questioned about his diary, he said they had nothing to do with reality and that he was planning to write a novel, but later he did confess.

Young's case went to trial at St. Albans Crown Court in July 1972 and lasted for ten days. He pleaded not guilty to the charges, still claiming that his notes were for a novel that he was writing. He was found guilty and was convicted to life imprisonment. While he was in the dock he told his warders that if he was found guilty he would break his neck on the dock rail, however, when the verdict was ready out he did not carry out his threat. His life sentence ended on August 1, 1990, at Parkhurst prison, where he died of a heart attack at the age of forty-two.

THE MOTIVE

It appears the only motive Graham Young had for the murders was that it gave him the power he yearned over other people's lives. It was possible that he didn't see his victims as human beings, but thought of them more as laboratory experiments. When he was finally charged with the murders and several more attempts of murder, he pretentiously reacted that he could have killed them all, but that he chose to let some of them stay alive!

Thomas Wainewright

*By the age of thirty Thomas Wainewright was an
extremely popular and successful gentleman in the
literary and artistic circles of London society.
By the age of forty he was working on a chain
gang in a Tasmanian penal colony alongside
thieves and murderers. Wainewright went from
being a poet and a painter . . . to a poisoner!*

Born in Chiswick, West London, Thomas
Wainewright, who was orphaned at an early
age was adopted by his grandfather, Ralph
Griffiths. They lived at Linden House, Turnham
Green. His grandfather was the founder and editor
of London's first literary magazine *The Monthly
Review*, and the young Wainewright soon found
himself in the midst of London's high society and
the Romantic revolution. It was a world of
dandies, dilettantes, poets and artists, and with his
artistic temperament and incredible wit, Wainewright was in his element.

Thomas attended art school where he showed a
talent as a draughtsman, but even at this early
stage of his life he was already showing signs of
being a little maladjusted. He joined the forces for
a little while, but was forced to leave because of his

love for whisky, and the fact that he had become a hypochondriac. He was now living at 48 Great Marlborough Street and he had turned his hand to painting, and even managed to have a few exhibitions. It was around this time that he discovered that he had a talent as an art critic and through his contacts he met many celebrities, including Wordsworth and William Blake. However, his glamorous lifestyle was starting to get expensive and within a few years he found himself in financial difficulties. Wainewright made his living by selling paintings and the occasional dodgy art deal, which gave him an income of around £175 a year, but it was certainly not enough to support his extravagant lifestyle.

In 1821 he married, shy and extremely poor Frances Ward. By 1822, Wainewright had turned his artistic talents to forgery, counterfeiting his signature on documents which allowed him immediate access to some of his inheritance which was being held for him in a trust fund. In 1824, again using his skills as a forger, he managed to get his hands on the full amount of his legacy, £5,250. However, due to his already accumulating debts, this money did not last long and he resorted to borrowing money from loan sharks and friends, and once again ended up in arrears.

THE DEATH OF HELEN ABERCROMBIE

In 1828, Wainewright and his wife Frances, convinced their bachelor uncle, George Edward Griffiths, to let them come and live with him at

Linden House. Linden House was a huge property and stood in two acres of ground off Chiswick High Road (the site today of Linden Gardens). Within one year of them moving to Linden House, Griffiths died suddenly, and his estate – now considerably reduced in value – was passed to Wainewright, who was by this time in debt up to his ears. His next move was to invite his mother-in-law and his wife's two half-sisters, Helen and Madeleine, to make their home at Linden House. In 1930 he took out a hefty life insurance with Palladium and Eagle offices, on the life of Helen, which only covered a short period of between two to three years. When Wainewright tried to increase the sum of the insurance to £5,000, his mother-in-law, Mrs. Abercrombie, objected. Conveniently for Wainewright, she died very suddenly in great pain from a mystery illness. Without his mother-in-law's objections, Wainewright was able to increase the insurance on Helen's life to £20,000.

Then, suddenly, Helen was taken ill with a strange illness, and died in extreme pain on December 21, 1930, at the age of only twenty-one. The symptoms of her brief illness were described by her nurse as being identical to those of her mother and George Griffiths.

The most widely accepted story of the death of Helen Abercrombie is that she was poisoned with antimony, causing her to be taken ill with symptoms of extreme stomach pains and vomiting. However, at the same time, the Wainewright's served a particularly indigestible meal, and this provided an alternative explanation for her sudden sickness. After a couple of days and a visit from a doctor, Helen was fed with a jelly that had been laced with strychnine. The bitter taste of the strychnine would have been masked by the sweet jelly, and she may well have been told that the powder was a part of the remedy. A powder named 'black draught' was used regularly in the nineteenth century as a laxative, so there is no reason to think that Helen would have had any suspicions. Unfortunately, due to her already weakened state, Helen died almost immediately.

The convulsions were characteristic with strychnine poisoning, which would have been readily available from any apothecary. Also, it has been reported that Wainewright had several books on poisons in his library.

Helen was a normal, healthy, young woman until, that is, the life insurance policies were fully taken out. However, the insurance company was suspicious about the nature of Helen's death and refused to pay out for the life insurance. Wainewright immediately borrowed £1,000 and instructed a solicitor to sue the insurance company, but his reputation by now had taken a serious blow and there were widespread suspicions about the three deaths in his family. He decided it would be a good idea to lie low for a while, and fled in the spring of 1831 to Boulogne. His career during the next five years is a little uncertain, but he was known to have spent some considerable time in prison at Paris. Also, and probably of no surprise by this time, that a man that he shared lodgings with died suddenly in great pain from a mysterious illness, Wainewright inheriting £3,000 as his only beneficiary.

In June 1837 Wainewright returned to England. Shortly after his arrival in London he was arrested in a Covent Garden Hotel by Forrester, the Bow Street runner, using a warrant obtained against him by the Bank of England for a forgery which he had committed in 1826. His previous attempt at trying to sue the insurance company had failed, and Wainewright was now known by the nickname of 'Wainewright the Poisoner'.

He was tried at the Old Bailey on July 6. He was found guilty of forgery and was sentenced to transportation to Van Dieman's land (Tasmania) for the rest of his life. While he was awaiting transportation in Newgate prison, he apparently confessed to the murder of Helen Abercrombie, stating that it was her 'thick ankles' that had offended him. Also, while in Newgate, it is reported that an actor and author by the name of Charles Dickens was sitting chatting with some friends. He spotted Wainewright and was heard to shout, 'By God it's Wainewright', and the party of literary companions were horrified to find one of their number amongst the scum of London.

Unlike many others, Wainewright actually survived the transportation. Initially he worked as a hospital orderly and and it was said that he painted a number of pastel and watercolour portraits while he was a convict at Hobart Town. He painted portraits of many of the local dignitaries and their families, and these pictures are considered to be his most accomplished work as an artist.

Thomas Wainewright died in hospital at Hobart in the year 1852 aged fifty-eight.

THE PSYCHOLOGY

It is very difficult to form any sort of realistic picture of the psychology of someone like Wainewright. It appears that the most important thing in his life was to try and retain the status of a gentleman at whatever cost. Perhaps it is this rather tragic display of dignity that provides us with a little insight into the mind of Thomas Wainewright. Throughout his life it appears that his social position, whether it was in the prestigious circles of London society or in a prison cell, was something in which he put the utmost significance. While he was in Newgate prison it is reputed that he said:

> 'I will tell you one thing in which I have succeeded to the last. I have been determined through my life to hold the position of a gentleman. I have always done so. I do so still. It is the custom of this place that each of the inmates of a cell shall take his morning's turn of sweeping it out. I occupy a cell with a bricklayer and a sweep, but they never offer me the broom!'

(Wilde, 1927)

Indeed, it was his strive to maintain his social standing that drove him to forge, defraud, and quite possibly murder. While all his crimes seem to

352

have been precipitated by extreme financial difficulties, the truth of the matter is that it was his love of extravagance that forced him to be in this position time and time again. He was a victim of his own pride, and perhaps it is a little easier to understand when you study the type of world in which he lived.

Where There's a Will...

*This story shows the cases of two deadly doctors
who killed their patients for monetary gains.
The first case we will study is that Dr. John Bodkin
Adams and the second Dr. Harold Shipman.*

At first glance there are many similarities between the case of Dr. John Bodkin Adams and
Dr. Harold Shipman, who both preyed on their
elderly patients in order to extort money from
them. For that reason I am writing about the two
'doctors of death' in one case history, and we will
start with Dr. Adams.

DR. JOHN BODKIN ADAMS

John Adams was a bachelor and teetotaller, with a
lust for money and high-living. He had a passion
for cars and at one time owned three Rolls Royces.
His friends and neighbours often wondered how
he managed to finance such a lavish lifestyle. He
was short and plump in stature – just 5ft 5in tall
and weighed almost 18 stone. He was bald, with a
rather pink, podgy face, small eyes and wore horn-
rimmed spectacles. He had a rather daunting
habit of rolling his eyes upwards, leaving only the

whites showing. He was a master of the bedside manner and completely charmed his ageing women patients. He was Irish and was a member of the Plymouth Brethren, who are small groups of Christians with a deep and rich history. Adams' practice was in Eastbourne in the South of England, and although his medical knowledge was limited, he was extremely popular with his patients. As well as administering to their medical needs – at half a guinea a visit for his wealthier clients – he would also stroke their hands, comb their hair and, on occasion, even caress their breasts. In addition to this he offered comfort in the form of his faith by kneeling in prayer before entering a patient's room.

On the night of Sunday 22, 1956, the East-bourne coroner was woken by a curious phone call from Dr. Adams. He was after a favour from the coroner and wondered if he would be prepared to arrange a private post mortem for one of his patients. The coroner refused his request, stating that he was not prepared to deviate from his normal practice. He asked Adams when his patient actually died, to which the doctor replied, 'The patient is not dead yet'. The coroner was so shocked by the response that he sat bolt upright in his bed.

The next day his patient did die. She was fifty-five-year-old Gertrude Hullett, who was a second-time widow. Her second husband was the rich, retired Lloyd's underwriter, Jack Hullett. Gertrude Hullett was better known as 'Bobbie' and was also called the 'Grande Dame' of Holywell Mount. She had a vivacious personality and was known to mix with the theatrical set, including the actress Marie Lohr.

The reason Adams had made the strange phone call in the middle of the night, was because his junior partner was suspicious of the senior doctor's diagnosis of Hullett's illness, and he had insisted on a post mortem. The younger doctor suspected that there was more to the sudden demise of Mrs. Hullett than Adams had admitted, feeling sure that the patient was dying from an overdose of drugs. It was not only Adams' partner who was suspicious. The English comedian Leslie Henson even took to calling the Chief Constable of the Eastbourne police to express his concern. He was disturbed by the way Dr. Adams had kept Mrs. Hullett heavily sedated for the four months since her husband had died. He said he had gradually seen her turning into a drug addict, and he felt that although she was going down hill mentally, that it was in fact the pills that were making her mad.

The police carried out some discreet enquiries and found out that just before Mrs. Hullett fell into a fatal coma, she had given her doctor a cheque for £1,000. Three days before that she had made a will leaving her beloved Rolls-Royce to Bodkin Adams. The staff at her Holywell mansion confirmed their boss's doped state, and one commented that she even staggered down the stairs most mornings as though she were under the influence of alcohol.

To the outside world, the doctor was already

rich. He certainly had no need for another Rolls-Royce, for he already had one and several other cars besides. But the police chief was well aware of the gossip that was buzzing around the town. Gossip that linked the doctor's reckless use of addictive drugs to his rich haul of legacies. Laughingly he was accused of doing his round with a bottle of morphine in one pocket and a blank will form in the other.

The considerable age and relative insignificance of his supposed victims had kept the rumours to a minimum, that is until the death of Bobbie Hullett. This was a completely different story. She was not a frail and solitary pensioner, but a very popular, middle-aged socialite with many connections in the show business world. Bobbie Hullett's body was the subject of three separate post mortems, and the last one was carried out by a famous Home Office pathologist, Dr. Francis Camps, who specialised in capital crime cases.

The world in large learned the name of Dr. Bodkin Adams on Thursday, July 26, 1956, when he made headline news. Apart from the death of Mrs. Hullett, the demise of three other women, two widows and a spinster, were under investigation. In later issues of the newspapers the headlines read: 'Six Women In Murder Riddle' and the case became of major significance when Detective Superintendent Herbert Hannam of Scotland Yard arrived in Eastbourne to head the investigation.

After much delving, the Hullett inquiry came back with the verdict that her death was the result of suicide from an overdose of sleeping tablets. Dr.

Bodkin Adams was severely reprimanded for the careless treatment of his patient.

Publicity about the doctor reached a frenzy in the following weeks, with exaggerated reports in the press hinting at his involvement in the death of at least four hundred widows. The local police along with their fellow colleague from the Yard decided to delve deeper into the professional life of Dr. Bodkin Adams. They probed into all the files where elderly patients of the doctor had died, and went to question their relatives. Unfortunately in many of the cases the relatives were already dead, or too old to remember anything with any clarity. Besides that most of the bodies had been cremated or had decomposed beyond the point of being any use for research purposes. Most of the deaths had been recorded by the doctor as the result of cerebral thrombosis or haemorrhage, and their investigations also revealed that most of these patients had been prescribed narcotic drugs.

The picture that emerged of Dr. Adams was far from pleasant. It appeared he was a selfish, avaricious physician of very dubious morality and an insatiable legacy hunter. Statements that the police collected from both solicitors and bank managers proved that Dr. Adams had been persistent in forcing patients to alter their wills in his favour, even to the point of guiding a dying hand. There was evidence of forgery and extortion, and one old lady even remembered driving the doctor from her home when she overheard him whispering to her dying husband, 'Leave your estate to me, and I'll look after your wife'.

After much thorough and painstaking research, the police discovered 132 wills amounting to £45,000, that had been bequested to the doctor. This was an immense amount of money at that time. They uncovered cases where the bodies had been cremated, but nothing was mentioned on the cremation form itself about the doctor being a beneficiary under his patient's will. This omission meant that there was no necessity for a post mortem. When they studied the death certificates it raised even further questions as to the diagnostic capability of this so-called doctor, since an unusually high number were reported to have died of cerebral haemorrhage or cerebral thrombosis.

There were so many cases of sudden decline following the change in a will, that relatives suddenly started to draw the attention of the Yard to other cases. One prime example was that of eighty-five-year-old Julia Bradnum. Her niece told the police that her aunt had come to see her all rosy-cheeked and even walked part of the way. Three days later she was dead, leaving the doctor as sole executor of her new will – with assets of around £4,000. When they heard of the enquiries into the deaths in the town they approached the police and made official statements.

Other witnesses came forward with solid testimonies. In the case of a widow named Annabella Kilgour, who died in 1950, a nurse came forward to say that she had been astonished by the high quantity of drugs that the doctor had injected into her before she fell into a fatal coma. She actually said to the doctor, 'Do you realise, doctor, that you have killed her?'

Another case that was brought to the attention of the Yard was that of Hilda and Clara Neil-Miller. They were genteel, spinster sisters who had died in 1953 and 1954 respectively. Hilda had left everything to her sister who in turn left most of her estate to Dr. Adams. A guest who had been visiting the rest home where Clara died remembered that she had been concerned about the amount of time the doctor spent in Clara's bedroom. He had remained in the room for around forty-five minutes, and she can remember being concerned because it seemed just too quiet. She said she opened the door and was horrified to see that the bedclothes had been pulled back and Clara's nightdress had been folded across her body right up to her neck. It was a bitterly cold night and all the windows in the room had been flung open. The room was exceptionally cold and that was just how the doctor had left her.

So much had come out in their investigations that the Yard made a thorough dossier of their findings and submitted it to the Director of Public Prosecutions. It has been said that it was around 23cm thick.

Superintendent Hannam confided to a reporter that he was quite confident that Adams was a mass-murderer. 'He has certainly killed fourteen people. If we had arrived on the scene years ago, I think I could have said he killed more.' Hannam was positive that he could establish a homicidal pattern – making his victims dependent on drugs, influencing them to change their wills, then easing them out of life with an overdose. However although it all appeared to be clear cut it was going to be difficult to prove.

Hannam decided that his best course of action was to break Adams down gradually by a constant series of interviews. Throughout all the questioning Adams always portrayed himself as the caring family doctor, and often referred to the deceased as 'his very dear patient'. All the while their were whispers and rumours spreading throughout the town and he became the subject of speculation and stares everywhere he went.

At 8.30 p.m. on Saturday, November 24, 1956, Hannam returned with a search warrant under the Dangerous Drugs Act. The doctor was wearing a dinner jacket and was on the point of leaving to chair a YMCA prize-giving ceremony. Hannam asked Adams if he could inspect the register for restricted drugs, which all doctors are required to keep. Adams replied that he didn't know what he was talking about. He said he didn't keep a register and then added that he very seldom used such drugs. Then Hannam produced a list of restricted drugs that Adams had prescribed for his patient, Mrs. Morrell. Although the woman had been dead for six years, the ledger from the chemist showed the massive doses of both morphine and heroin that had been administered to her.

When asked why he had given his patient such a high dose of toxic drugs, Adams replied: 'Poor soul she was in terrible agony . . . Do you think it was too much?'

While his surgery was being searched, Adams sat slumped in his office chair, sobbing with his head in his hands. Then one of the police officers noticed that he was trying to slip something into one of his pockets. It turned out to be two bottles of morphine solution. The doctor was immediately arrested and taken to Eastbourne police station, and read thirteen minor charges.

THE TRIAL

The case was brought before Eastbourne magistrates on Monday morning, November 26. The doctor was granted bail and made to surrender his passport. Back in the police station, Adams said that he was worried that there might be other charges. Hannam told him that they were continuing their inquiries into the death of some of his rich patients, and in particular Mrs Morrell.

In the meantime Hannam, and an officer from Eastbourne, were summoned to the House of Commons. The Attorney General briefly quizzed his medical advisers on the effects of heroin and then told Hannam to go straight back to Eastbourne and arrest the doctor for the murder of Mrs. Edith Morrell.

Adams seemed both stunned and confused at the time of his arrest and did not seem to think that he could possibly be charged with murder. He was taken back to the police station cell where he was stripped and searched. The next day he was taken to the little court room at the town hall, which was packed with people to hear the remand proceedings. The charge of failing to keep a drugs register was tagged on to that of murder, and the doctor was quickly hustled away.

Eastbourne's most notorious doctor was now housed in Brixton Prison in London. The trial itself began on March 18, 1957. At this trial devastating new evidence was introduced by the defence which fundamentally changed the whole nature of the case. The defence played a trump card when they produced medical records from Cheshire, which showed that it was not Dr. Adams who first introduced Mrs. Morrell to morphine, but another doctor after she had suffered a stroke in the year 1948.

The trial was to last for seventeen days, which was a record at that time, and saw numerous witnesses who were prepared to testify against Dr. Adams. Medical experts called by the Crown gave evidence that could further discredit the reputation of the doctor. It became a constant battle between the defence and the prosecution. The jury was sent out on April 3 to consider their verdict. They returned forty-four minutes later and delivered the verdict that he was 'not guilty'. Any further charges against the doctor were subsequently dropped. The doctor, who was wearing a blue somewhat crumpled suit, stood up, bowed stiffly, took a deep breath, and said to the Judge 'Thank you'. They were the first words he had spoken since his plea of innocence.

The doctor later pleaded guilty at Lewes Assizes to fourteen charges of professional misconduct and was fined a total of £2,400. Five months after the trial his licence was taken away which gave him the right to possess or supply dangerous drugs. In November he was brought before the Disciplinary Medical Council and his name was struck off the medical record.

REFUSING TO GIVE UP

The doctor refused to be humbled by the proceedings and, even though he had been stripped of his qualifications, continued to treat some of his loyal patients. What is even more astounding is the fact that he still continued to receive legacies. Adams gradually eased himself back into public life. In 1961, following several unsuccessful applications, Adams was restored to the medical register.

With renewed courage he now turned on to his accusers and filed a libel suit against the press which had so badly slandered his name. A settlement was reached in which thirteen newspapers agreed to pay an undisclosed, but substantial, amount of money for the excessive zeal with which they had publicized the case in the pre-trial phase.

The doctor spent the last twenty-two years of his life practising medicine in the town of Eastbourne, in fact from the same practice. On June 30, 1984, Bodkin Adams, now aged eighty-four, slipped at a hotel in Battle and fractured his hip. He died four days later.

He left an estate worth £402,970 and sums of between £500 and £5,000 were left to relatives and friends, including twenty women who had stood by him at the time of his trial.

DOCTOR HAROLD SHIPMAN

To endeavour to understand some of the motives behind Doctor Harold Shipman's murders, it is worth taking a look at his childhood years. He was the middle one of three children, and affectionately known as Freddy by his adoring mother. He was definitely her favourite, and she did tend to over-protect him. At school he was rather a mediocre student who found it very difficult to make friends. His mother, Vera, always wanted to choose his friends for him and indeed tried to organize his personal life.

Freddy was devoted to his mother and was completely devastated when he discovered that she was suffering from lung cancer. He would rush home from school each day to make her a cup of tea, sit by her bedside and chat to her as she lay there in terrible pain. As a young boy, Freddy must have been amazed by the morphine administered to his mother by their family doctor, which gave his mother instant relief from her terrible suffering. As Freddy was at such an impressionable age, perhaps he decided then that he would like to use this magic potion to help other people who were suffering. His mother died in June 1963, when Freddy was seventeen.

When he was nineteen Shipman started at Leeds University medical school. He struggled academically, but eventually managed to obtain a degree and got his first job as a hospital intern. Although Shipman had never really had any girlfriends, he eventually found companionship in a girl named Primrose. She was three years his junior, and her background was very similar to that of Harold's. Her mother had also restricted her friendships and tried to control her activities. Primrose, having never been very popular with the opposite sex, was delighted to have finally found a boyfriend. They married when Primrose was only seventeen and five months pregnant. It certainly could not be classed as a shotgun wedding, and there was no doubt that they had a deep and mutual affection for one another. Shipman settled down with his new wife and by 1974 he was a father of two. He took up his first role as a General Practitioner in the small Yorkshire town of Todmorden. In this North England setting, Shipman seemed change drastically he became an outgoing, respected member of the community. He fitted in well but did not suffer fools gladly, and was sometimes known to have angry outbursts with his staff if they made mistakes.

At home Primrose was a good mother and wife and everything seemed set for a rosy life for the Shipman family. But then in 1975, disaster struck, which was to change their destiny forever.

SUSPICIOUS SIGNS

It was the receptionist at the practice, Marjorie Walker, that noticed the first signs. There were some strange entries in the Drugs Ledger of a local pharmacist. It seemed that large quantities of pethidine – a morphine-like painkiller – had been ordered by the young doctor Shipman.

She brought the matter to the attention of the senior GP, Dr John Dacre, who investigated the matter. He found that Shipman had been ordering the drug for many of his patients, but it soon became apparent that they had never been prescribed or, indeed, had any need for pethidine. It was also around this time that Shipman, now aged twenty-nine, started to have blackouts. He told the rest of the staff that they were due to epilepsy and that he had it under control.

Dr Dacre confronted Shipman, who openly confessed that he had been injecting himself with the pethidine. He begged the doctor for another chance, but then his mood changed and he became angry. He stormed out of the surgery and threatened to resign. This was just a threat, he never did resign, but he was eventually forced out of the practice and ended up in a drug rehabilitation centre.

Shipman was prosecuted and was fined £600 for forgery and prescription fraud, but, ironically, he was allowed to continue practising as a GP.

By 1977, apparently cured of his addiction to pethidine, Shipman was offered a job at the Donneybrook Medical Centre in Hyde, a suburb of Manchester. He was completely open with his new colleagues and told them all about his past. He said, 'All I can ask you to do is to trust me on that issue and to watch me'. Before long he had earned the trust and respect of both his work colleagues and his new patients. He was conscientious, hardworking, and had a wonderful manner with his patients. It was now apparent that Shipman had managed to put all his problems behind him and was ready to make a new start. But what wasn't apparent was that over the next twenty years as a GP he was able to kill quite freely.

AN ESTIMATE OF 236 MURDERS

It has been estimated by the Department of Health that Harold Shipman managed to kill at least 236 of his patients between the years 1974 and 1998. It seems amazing that a doctor that had many more patients dying than any of his colleagues, could have gone unnoticed for so long.

Kathleen Grundy can probably be considered as Shipman's last victim, but what he didn't realise at the time was that he had made a fateful mistake. If it hadn't been for Mrs. Grundy's daughter, Angela Woodruff, Shipman would probably have been free to go on killing for many more years.

When Kathleen Grundy died at the age of eighty-one her daughter could easily have just thought of it as sad but inevitable. But, Mrs. Grundy, who was the former Mayor of Hyde, was healthy and energetic right up until her death on June 24, 1998, and so it came as somewhat of a shock. She was discovered by some friends who called on her when she failed to turn up at the Age Concern Club. She was just lying on her sofa at home and the last person to have seen her alive was Shipman, who had allegedly gone round to take some regular blood samples.

Shipman told Mrs. Woodruff that there would be no need for a post mortem as he had seen her mother shortly before she died. Angela, who was deeply distressed by her mother's death, accepted his words, and her mother was buried in the local cemetery.

What did cause concern to Angela, though, was the fact that her mother had made a new will which left a total of £386,000 to none other than her family doctor. Apparently Shipman had forged Mrs. Grundy's signature on her new will. Angela Woodruff was a solicitor, and was immediately alarmed as her mother had already made a will back in 1986, and this was lodged at her own law firm. When she discovered that a new will had been made without her being informed, she was of course very suspicious of foul play. She went to the police with her suspicions, and although Shipman was a respected doctor in the community, Detective Superintendent Bernard Postles agreed that it needed investigating.

When the will was studied it was obvious from the cheap nature and typing on the document, that the will had been drawn up by someone other than Kathleen Grundy. The further the investigating team delved into Shipman's past history, the more and more information came to the fore regarding the doctor's callous behaviour towards many of his patients. Postles ordered that they exhume the body of Kathleen Grundy so that it could be forensically examined.

Shipman himself was affronted by the investigations and continued to deny that he had done anything wrong. But gradually they were building more and more evidence against him. The police discovered at his house an old Brother typewriter which matched the type used on the counterfeit will. Realising, at once, that he was in a tight spot, Shipman made up a ridiculous story that he had loaned the typewriter to Mrs. Grundy. As news of the investigation became public knowledge, other doctors and various undertakers came with their suspicions regarding the high death rate among Shipman's patients. The police went through all the death certificates in the doctor's book and made a list of fifteen that they considered needed further investigation. Out of the fifteen victims on the list, nine had been buried and the other six cremated. More exhumations were ordered and gradually their research revealed Shipman's method of working.

His modus operandi was to kill his victims, the majority of whom were quite elderly, with an injection of morphine. He would then return to his office to tamper with their medical reports on his computer, exaggerating about their exact state of health. In the case of Kathleen Grundy he had even backdated several entries to suggest that she had become addicted to morphine. He was able to stockpile large quantities of the drug because he would exaggerate the quantities required for his 'terminally ill' patients. He would always advise the relatives of the deceased to have the body cremated, and so as to not to alert too much suspicion on himself, he would rotate the signing of the cremation certificates among other doctors in the area. Obviously Shipman was unaware of modern technology, as he was quite shocked when he discovered that they were able to examine his computer hard drive and find out exactly when he had made any particular one entry. This piece of information alone, proved to be damning evidence when the case when to trial.

THE TRIAL

As a result of all the enquiries, the Manchester police arrested Harold Shipman on suspicion of murdering Mrs. Grundy. The Hyde doctor was tried at Preston Court in 1999. Shipman's barrister, Nicola Davies, had several aborted tries to have the trial halted. First she stated that there had been inaccurate and misleading coverage in the press. This didn't work. Then she sought to have the case of Mrs. Grundy separated from the other murders, because this one alone had an obvious motive. This didn't work. She also sought to persuade the judge to exclude the evidence about stockpiling morphine from the jury. This also failed.

Witness after witness – many of them relatives of the victims – took the stand and painted a picture of a callous and deceitful man who turned out to be a compulsive liar. Even though his defence did everything they could to portray him as a happily married man, a caring family doctor, a true professional, nothing they could say could break down the mountain of evidence that had built up against Shipman.

On January 31, 2000, the jury returned with a unanimous verdict. He was found guilty on all fifteen counts of murder and of forging Mrs. Grundy's will. The judge handed out fifteen life sentences and told Shipman that he would be recommending to the home secretary that he never be released.

Since his sentencing, Harold Shipman has been in solitary confinement in the Frankland prison, near Durham. He is visited frequently by his wife, Primrose, and their four children. Primrose still adores her husband and has remained totally loyal to him, even though she must know more about his other victims as she has been working at the medical practice for quite a while. Neither Primrose or Shipman himself were prepared to co-operate with the ongoing investigation, and at no time has Shipman ever shown any remorse for what he had done.

AN ENQUIRY

The conviction of Harold Shipman for the murder of fifteen of his patients inevitably raised questions as to how it happened, could it happen again, or indeed how it could have been prevented. After all, there was not an entirely dissimilar case fifty years ago, in which Dr. Bodkin Adams was suspected of killing several of his patients. In response to these questions, the government decided to set up a public inquiry.

The inquiry has been given the task of looking at what went wrong in the Shipman case so that they can come up with recommendations about changes that need to be made. The need for changes in the way deaths were examined. As the system stood at the time of the Shipman trial, it was obviously inadequate and needed to be brought up to the standards of the twenty-first century. At present coroners are not involved and post mortems are not compulsory, if the deceased has recently been seen by a doctor or has been in hospital. If the body is to be cremated then the form must be countersigned by another doctor. However, Dr. Norman Beenstock, a former GP who practiced in Hyde and who countersigned eighteen cremation forms for Shipman, said doctors rarely ask questions of one another. He said, 'I was reliant on what Dr. Shipman told me and I would have trusted a fellow GP to have been honest and open with me'.

The official results of the inquiry were released on July 20, 2002. The report announced that Shipman may have killed as many as 260 patients, but is only positive of 215, the other 45 have just been labelled as 'suspicious'.

MOTIVES

At their trials Dr. Bodkin Adams and Dr. Harold Shipman both reacted very differently. Adams projected himself as a bumbling, inoffensive old duffer, utterly devoid of any malice, and a dependable and Christian family doctor. By way of contrast Shipman portrayed himself as a solitary, rather insular character, inscrutable and somewhat dour, with no obvious endearing or humane qualities.

Dr. Adam's patients were all extremely elderly, and either seriously or terminally ill. Shipman's, on the other hand, all appeared to be in good health and ranged from middle age upwards. The verdict on why Dr. Adams so-called 'murdered' his victims was that they felt any doctor in his situation was 'entitled to all that was proper and necessary to relieve paint and suffering even if the measures he took might incidentally shorten the life by hours or perhaps even longer. The doctor who decided whether or not to administer the drug could not do his job if he were thinking in terms or hours or months of life'. It was considered that in the case of Dr. Adams, that the treatment he gave his patients was only designed to promote comfort. For some reason the fact that he obtained a vast amount of money in legacies from his patients somehow seems to have been overlooked in this summing up.

Shipman, conversely, is portrayed far more as a monstrous serial killer. When he was examined by psychiatrists they discovered that he seemed to be obsessed by having control over his patients' lives. It appeared to give him some sort of a sexual thrill. As to why the majority of his patients were older women, this probably stems back to his childhood when he saw his mother dying from lung cancer. Perhaps these women reminded him of his mother and he couldn't bear the fact they were still alive and healthy. Shipman thought of himself as untouchable and even mocked the police and anyone who tried to ascertain the motives for his killings.

Meanwhile, Hyde will take a long time to recover from the repercussions of this wicked doctor. The town had already been rocked by the forces of evil in the 1960s, for it was the hometown of the Moors Murderers, who are still the most hated murderers in England.

Harold Shipman hanged himself in his cell on Tuesday, January 13, 2004, at Wakefield prison. It is believed he took his own life because he was unable to face up to the prospect of an appeal court appearance at which his guilt would undoubtedly be re-affirmed and his life sentence upheld.

Although the scale of his crimes might be unique, Harold Shipman is certainly not the only doctor to have hit the headlines over the years. Back in the 1850s Dr. William Palmer of Rugeley, managed to poison a dozen of his relatives and patients. Jack the Ripper, whose murders were so anatomically perfect, could also have been a doctor. Finally, the name of Dr. Hawley Harvey Crippen will always be famous for the murder of his wife in 1910.

The Ultimate 'Psycho'

Ed Gein is seen as one of the most weird and bizarre killers of the twentieth century. His crimes inspired the movies 'Psycho', 'The Texas Chainsaw Massacre' and 'Silence of the Lambs'.

Ed Gein was born in 1906 into the small, farming community of Plainfield, Wisconsin. The area was heavily wooded and had many isolated smallholdings and farms. His father was a heavy drinker and his mother was totally domineering, and much of his childhood was spent in solitude. His brother, Henry, was rather a weak and ineffectual character, and his mother taught the boys that sexual acts were a sin even from an early age. When their father died in 1940, the two brothers took over the running of the farm. Even as adults their mother still ruled their lives, insisting that they remain bachelors and instilled in them that women would only break up the family unit and eventually betray the love the boys gave them.

It was a hard life with the two boys doing all the work. The farm itself was not profitable and things went from bad to worse when Henry died from fighting a fire in one of their barns. Shortly after his brother's death, Ed's mother suffered a stroke which left her totally helpless. Ed managed to nurse her for a year, but then she had another stroke and died in 1945. Ed was now thirty-nine years old and was on his own for the first time in his life.

Ed was still emotionally enslaved to the woman who had ruled him for the whole of his life. In his solitude, Gein began to lose any sense of reality. He started to read medical dictionaries and books on anatomy and, for the first time in his life, developed an interest in women. He loved pulp horror books and pornographic magazines, and became obsessed with the atrocities committed during World War II. For reasons only known to himself, he developed a sick fascination in the medical experiments that were performed on Jews in the concentration camps.

Meanwhile, the large, rambling farmhouse became a complete shambles. Thanks to a government subsidy, Gein was able to give up his work on the farm and to earn extra cash he started doing odd jobs for the residents of Plainfield. While his neighbours thought he was a little strange, he was regarded as no more than a harmless eccentric, and they even entrusted him to the job of babysitting. His behaviour at home became more and more weird and he sealed off every single room in the farmhouse, with the exception of his bedroom and the kitchen. He was still haunted by the ghost of his dead mother, and her bedroom remained locked and completely undisturbed, in fact exactly as it had been before she died.

The first real sign of Gein's impending insanity was when he took to exhuming decomposing female corpses, under the cover of night, from remote church graveyards. He enlisted the help of another very weird man named Gus and together they opened their first grave less than a dozen feet away from where Ed's mother was buried.

Ed would store his grisly booty in a shed attached to the side of his farmhouse. Here, he would dissect the bodies retaining parts such as the head, sex organs, liver, heart and intestines. Next he would strip the skin from the body and either drape it over a tailor's dummy or wear it himself in some weird ritual dance. A practice, apparently, that gave him a great deal of gratification. Over the next ten years Ed continued to rob the graves of the dead. He would check the newspapers for any fresh bodies and always visited the graveyards when it was a full moon. Sometimes he would take the entire female corpse and on other occasions just the parts he wanted. His experiments on the corpses became more and more bizarre. He would construct objects out of the skin and bones and would store some of the organs he had removed in the fridge to eat later. He committed acts of necrophilia and on one occasion even dug up his own mother's corpse.

Gein was particularly fascinated by the removed parts of female genitalia which he would fondle and play with. Although Gus was aware that Ed was carrying out bizarre experiments, what his friend failed to tell him was that he had a growing desire to become a woman himself. Although he fantasized about having an operation to change him into a woman, the closest he ever got was by wearing a complete bodysuit with mask and breasts intact, made entirely of human skin.

His friend Gus was taken away to a mental asylum which meant that Ed was once more totally on his own. He was already considered to be a very eccentric recluse, which meant that none of his neighbours bothered with him or his very decaying property.

MOVING ON TO MURDER

Gein's complete obsession with the female body eventually led him into seeking out fresher samples – so he turned to murder. His first victim was fifty-one-year-old Mary Hogan. Mary was a divorcee who ran Hogan's Tavern at Pine Grove about six miles from her home. It was a very cold afternoon on December 8, 1954, and she was on her own in the tavern when she was approached by the strange man. Ed shot her in the head with his .32 calibre revolver, put her body in the back of his pick-up truck and then took her back to his shed.

The police were alerted when a customer called by the tavern to find the place deserted and a large bloodstain on the floor. There was a used cartridge on the floor, and the stains ran out of the back door, into the parking lot, and stopped beside tyre tracks, that looked like those of a pick-up truck. It was easy to assess that Mary had been shot and her body had been driven away. The police were unable to find any clues as to her disappearance, but a few weeks later a local sawmill owner was talking to Ed about the disappearance of Mary, when Gein replied, 'She isn't missing. She's at the farm right now'. The sawmill owner, who knew that Ed was very strange, didn't even bother to take any notice of his response.

Although there were probably other victims in the following year, nothing is really certain until November 16, 1957. Bernice Worden was a woman in her late fifties who ran the local hardware store. On finding Bernice on her own in the shop, Ed Gein took a .22 rifle down from a display shelf in the shop, inserted his own bullet into the gun, and then shot and killed Mrs. Worden. Next he locked the store and and took her body home with him in the back of the store's truck. Gein also took the cash register containing $41 in cash, not because he wanted to commit robbery, but because he wanted to see how it worked. He genuinely intended to return the cash register later.

Mrs. Worden's son, Frank, served as the Deputy Sheriff in Plainfield, and was often known to help his mother out in the shop. On this particular Saturday morning he had gone deer hunting, so it wasn't until later in the day that he returned to the shop to discover the door locked and the lights still on. When he went inside he immediately noticed the blood on the floor and that the cash register was missing. A local garage attendant told Frank that the had seen the store truck driving away at around 9.30 that morning. Frank immediately alerted the Sheriff, Art Schley, and told him what he had found. They went through the record of sales made that morning and discovered that one of the purchases had been for antifreeze. At that moment Frank remembered that Gein had stopped by the previous evening at around closing time and told him that he would be back in the morning to buy some antifreeze. Ed had also made a point of asking Frank whether or not he intended to go hunting the next morning. Ed also remembered that Frank had been in and out of the stores on several occasions during the past week, which was quite unusual. It would appear that since the cash register was missing, they assumed that Gein had planned a robbery once the coast was clear.

Frank, the Sheriff and Captain Lloyd Schoephoester set off for the farmhouse which was seven miles down the road, the place the local children called the haunted house.

When they arrived at the house it was dark and Ed Gein was nowhere to be found. So, acting merely on an assumption, they drove to a store in West Plainfield where they knew Ed normally bought his groceries. Their hunch paid off and sure enough Gein was there as he had just had dinner with the proprietor and his wife.

Gein was about to climb into his truck when the Sheriff stopped and asked him to get into the police car for questioning. Ed immediately told the Sheriff that he thought someone was trying to frame him for the murder of Bernice Worden. The Sheriff knew at that point they needed to take him into custody for not once had he mentioned anything about Mrs. Worden being missing or indeed anything about a murder. After taking Ed down to the Sheriff's office, the Sheriff and the Captain along with some fellow officers, returned to the farmhouse. The doors were locked, but the door to the shed at the side of the house wasn't and it opened quite easily when the Sheriff pushed it with his foot. It was very dark by now and since the farmhouse did not have any electricity, the Sheriff had to use a torch. As he shone it around the shed his eye caught something hanging from a crossbeam in the roof. It was a naked corpse with the legs wide apart, and a long slit running right the way down the front of the body. The head and throat were missing, along with the genitals and the anus. Bernice Worden had been disembowelled just like a deer after hunting.

Horrified by what they had found, the officers then moved their search to the house. Once again the house was dark so they used lanterns, oil lamps and torches to carry out their inspection. The place was filthy and looked as though it had not been cleaned for years. There were piles of rubbish everywhere and they discovered that most of the doors had been nailed up. The rooms that were open were full of books, old papers, magazines, utensils, tin cans, cartons and a lot of other things that could only be described as junk. But what else the police officers found in that house was far more nauseating – the work of an extremely sick mind. They discovered two shin bones, four human noses, a can covered with human skin to convert it into a tom-tom, a bowl made from the inverted half of a human skull, nine 'death masks; from the well preserved skin

382

from the faces of women', a belt fashioned from carved-off nipples, ten female heads with the tops removed from above the eyebrows, bracelets made from human skin, a purse made with a handle of human skin, a sheath for a knife made from human skin, a pair of leggings made from human skin, four chairs with the seats replaced by strips of human skin, a shoe box containing nine salted vulvas (one of which was his mother's which was painted silver), a hanging human head, a lamp-shade covered with human skin, a shirt made of human skin, a number of shrunken heads, two skulls for Gein's bedposts, a pair of human lips hanging from a string, Ed's full woman bodysuit constructed from human skin and complete with mask and breasts, Bernice's heart in a pan on the cooker, and finally the refrigerator was stacked with human organs.

The scattered remains of an estimated fifteen women's bodies were found at the farmhouse, but Gein could not remember how many murders he had actually committed. It is also rumoured that Gein used to take gifts of fresh venison round to his neighbours, and yet it is well known that he never shot a deer in his life.

Gein was committed to a mental institution and stayed there for ten years before he was judged to be sane enough to stand trial. Gein was found to be criminally insane in December 1956 and was committed to Wisconsin's Central State Hospital. He died at the Mendota Mental Health Institute in 1984, at the age of seventy-seven. He was a model prisoner who was also polite, gentle and discreet and his death was natural from respiratory and heart failure.

THE MOTIVE

Gein was subjected to numerous psychological examinations at the Central State Hospital, where they proved without doubt that he was completely insane. The reasons for his actions were quite obvious – his mother. He had both loved and hated his mother, and that is why he always killed older women. He would never admit to being either a cannibal or necrophiliac, but did own up to robbing graves. The case created a sensation purely because of the atrocity of his crimes. After Gein was arrested thousands of people flocked to the farm at Plainfield to get a closer look at the scene of such horrendous crimes. Eventually the entire place was burned down by the citizens of Plainfield as they regarded it as a place of evil.

ALWAYS REMEMBERED

The heinous activities of Ed Gein certainly attracted the media. An early film which was based on Gein's character was *Psycho*, portrayed originally in a novel by Robert Bloch and made into a film by Alfred Hitchcock. The connection here was the overpowering mother and the horror content of the film, which made it one of the first of a kind. When Bloch wrote the original book he got most of his ideas from the life of Ed Gein.

The Texas Chainsaw Massacre was another

movie lightly based on Ed Gein. The story is about a group of teenagers who stumble across a house of horrors when they are out travelling. The people who live in the house are a family of weird homicidal cannibals who like to rob graves and construct furniture out of the human remains. The man who plays the leading role likes chasing people while wielding a chainsaw, he was known as 'Leatherface'. His fetish was to wear a human face mask when he was chasing after his victims.

One final film which was also influenced by the true life story of Ed Gein is *Silence of the Lambs*. It is about an FBI agent who is trying to track down a serial killer and employs the help of an intelligent cannibal named Hannibal Lector. The killer she is trying to track is known as 'Buffalo Bill', a man who likes to kill women, make clothes out of their skin, and dress up in them because of his desire to be a woman. All very familiar when you have just read the case of Eddie Gein.

The 'Real' Dracula

*Believe it or not there was a real Dracula,
not just a figment of Bram Stoker's imagination.
He was a prince and as legend suggests
was actually born in Transylvania.*

For this story we are delving back into the archives of the fifteenth century. The true prince of darkness was Prince Vlad III, better known these days as 'Vlad the Impaler'.

Vladislav Basarab was born in the town of Sighisoara, in the Tîrnava Mare valley, Transylvania, in the year 1431. He was the second son of the prince of Wallachia, and he had a elder brother named Mircea, and a younger one named Radu the Handsome. His mother was either a Moldavian princess or a Transylvanian noble, and it is said that she educated the young Vladislav.

The country of Wallachia was a principality, which meant that it was ruled by a prince, rather than a king. The throne was not necessarily handed down from father to son, the new ruler had to be elected by the country's boyars, or land-owning nobles. This caused fighting among the family members even resulting in assassinations.

Vladislav's father, nicknamed Vlad Dracul, was

hungry for the throne and did not wish to remain in the post of governor for ever. During his years spent in Transylvania he managed to gather supporters for his plan to seize the throne of Wallachia from its current ruler – a Danesti prince by the name of Alexandru I. In late1436 or 1437 Vlad Dracul killed Alexandru and became Prince Vlad II. The young Vladislav was educated at court and received training that was appropriate for knighthood.

At a young age, probably around eleven, Vladislav, along with his younger brother Radu, were taken captive by the Turks. The two brothers were valuable hostages, being sons of a local prince, and they were taken to Istanbul to be imprisoned by the Sultan Mehemet. Vlad Dracul tried unsuccessfully to bargain for their release, but this bargaining was seen as treason by the King of Hungary and he hired assassins to kill Dracul and his eldest son Mercea.

Back in Istanbul, Sultan Mehemet tried to indoctrinate the two young captives into Islam, hoping to make allies of them. He hoped to use their claim to the Wallachian throne to his advantage later on. Radu, who was a handsome lad who attracted the attention of the future sultan, converted quickly, and was subsequently released from prison. Vlad, on the other hand, was far more stubborn, and a bitter hatred and rivalry developed between the two brothers as a result of this. It has also been suggested that Vlad's sadistic tendencies started as a result of his years spent as captive under the Sultan.

Radu, on his release in 1448, chose to remain in Turkey. Vlad, who finally seemed to have been subdued by the Sultan, decided to return to Wallachia only to find that his father had been assassinated, and his older brother Mircea buried alive. The Sultan had already taken control of Wallachia and appointed Vlad as the new prince, but his first period of rule in 1448 was short-lived. He did not want to rule his country on behalf of the Sultan, and so after a few months he fled the country, going north to Moldavia, where he stayed with his cousin and close friend Steven.

Vlad spent the next few years plotting his return to power. He knew the only way to become the true prince of Wallachia, was to oust the Turks. To do this he enlisted the help of John Hunyadi – the very man who had murdered his father and brother. However, so eager was he to regain control of the throne, Vlad was prepared to put that aside and they plotted their revenge on their common enemy, the Sultan.

When Vlad had fled from Wallachia, the Sultan had appointed his younger brother Radu as the prince. Hunyadi agreed to back Vlad with his military forces and together they were successful in driving out Radu. Vlad then retook the Wallachian throne, beginning his second and most notorious reign.

VLAD THE IMPALER

Vlad's immediate priority when he regained his throne in 1946 was to consolidate his position in

Wallachia. Vlad Dracolya was neither a good or a charitable prince. He was determined to break the power that the nobles, who preferred to support the puppet (or weak) leaders who would protect their interests. Vlad took to repeatedly raiding certain towns that came under his domain, and he murdered a great number of people during these assaults. For some unknown reason, the towns he selected for his raids seemed to be ones who had a largely German ancestry, and as a result most of the information you can find out about Vlad is from the pamphlets printed by the Germans on their newly-invented printing press.

One of his earliest actions as the reinstalled ruler of Wallachian was to punish the nobles of Tirgoviste whom he held responsible for the deaths of his father and brother. The story goes that he invited 500 boyars to a banquet and whilst they were eating he asked the nobles how many princes had ruled during their lifetimes. They said that they had lived through many reigns, admitting that it was their fault due to their years of plotting. After they had finished their meal, Vlad ordered his soldiers to surround them. The older nobles were impaled and the remainder were forced them to march fifty miles up the Arges River to Poenari. Here they were forced to build his mountain fortress labouring for many months under very difficult conditions. Those who actually survived the ordeal were subsequently impaled to death.

Impalement was a particularly sadistic form of execution, as the victims would suffer excruciating pain for many hours, and sometimes, days until they succumbed to death. While impalement was Vlad's favourite form of punishment he did like to employ other methods such as boiling, quartering, decapitation or burying alive.

While it is impossible to be one hundred percent certain that all the stories about Vlad are true, there are certainly many accounts of his life that seem to verify his cruelty. Here are some of the stories that led to his reputation:

Two ambassadors arrived from the Sultan to give a message to Vlad. When they entered into his throne room he ordered them to remove their turbans. It was considered to be very rude if you did not remove your headgear in the presence of a prince. The Turks, however, took exception to this and refused to comply. They felt that as the Sultan and Vlad were already arch enemies, it wouldn't really matter if they insulted him, and also to them the turbans were sacred they represented their Muslim religion. What they didn't realise was that by refusing Vlad's request they had made a very grave mistake. Vlad, who was incensed by the refusal to comply with his orders, told his guards to seize them and said that if they weren't prepared to remove their turbans then they should have them nailed to their heads. Vlad watched in utter delight as the Turks writhed and screamed in pain as large nails were driven into their skulls.

Vlad did not have a very pleasant way of dealing with the sick or the poor people under his domain, for he had no respect for such weakness. He only wanted people that could help him achieve his political, economic and military objectives. He started to notice that the number of poor, vagrants, beggars and cripples had become very numerous in his land. He issued an invitation to all the poor and sick in Wallachia to come to Târgoviste for a great feast, saying that no-one should go hungry under his rule. When they arrived in the city the poor, cripples, beggars alike, were all ushered into a great banqueting hall where a fabulous feast was spread out for them. Vlad's guests ate and drank late into the night, at which time the prince appeared on the scene. 'What else do you desire? Do you want to be without cares, lacking nothing in his world?' asked the prince. Needless to say they all agreed thinking that their ruler was going to do something about their pitiful situation. However, to the contrary, Vlad ordered that the banquet hall be boarded up and set on fire. Not one of the guests managed to escape the fire and Vlad justified his actions by saying 'in order that they represent no further burden to others so that no-one will be poor in my realm'.

Vlad was so adverse to evil that should he find out that anyone had stolen, lied or committed some injustice, the culprit would be immediately impaled. It didn't matter whether he was a nobleman, a priest, a monk, or just a common man, they could not escape the punishment of death. He created a very severe moral code by which the citizens of Wallachia had to live, and needless to say there was very little crime during his reign.

As an example of how well his laws worked, Vlad placed a gold cup in the middle of a public square. Anyone who was thirsty was permitted to drink from the cup, but no-one was allowed to take it outside of the square. No one ever did.

A visiting merchant once left his money outside all night believing it to be safe because of the strict laws in the town. However, in the morning he discovered his coins had been stolen. He immediately reported it to the prince who put out a proclamation that the money must be returned or the city would be destroyed. Vlad himself had secretly taken the money and he returned it to the merchant with one extra coin. When the merchant counted the money the next morning he found that all the coins had been returned, but he had in fact one extra. He told Vlad about this, to which he replied that the thief had been caught and would be impaled. He also added that if the merchant had not mentioned the extra coin, then he too would have been executed.

The incident that perhaps he will be best remembered for and did the most damage to his reputation, took place in the town of Brasov. The merchants of Brasov refused to pay their taxes in spite of repeated threats from Vlad. Angered by their disloyalty, Vlad led an assault on Brasov in 1459 and burned down the entire place, impaling many of the captives on a place called Timpa Hill. This scene has been immortalized in a rather gruesome woodcut which appeared as a frontispiece in a pamphlet that was printed in Nuremberg in 1499.

By 1462, the end of the period of his second reign, Vlad the Impaler had killed between 40,000 and 100,000 people, and possibly more. Despite all this and his strict laws, Vlad's subjects still

BORN TO BE KILLERS

respected him for fighting the Turks and for being a strong ruler.

OVERTHROWN

During Vlad's second reign, Wallachia had been, for the most part, free from any form of invasion. However, a new Sultan, Suiliman II, had come to power and once again the Ottoman empire turned its greedy eyes towards Wallachia. Vlad was informed by his spies of the overpowering strength of the invading Turks. He knew that his army was not strong enough to survive an open battle, and so he undertook a very desperate mission.

Waiting for the cover of dark, Vlad and a few of his elite army, stole into the Turkish camp in the hopes of catching the Sultan offguard and killing him. Vlad thought that the Turks might lose heart if they lost their leader, and retreat. Vlad's venture was almost successful, the Sultan was wounded, although not fatally, and the prince's entire army managed to escape without any casualties.

However, this assault on the Sultan did not stop the Turks from attacking. Vlad immediately retreated to his castle at Târgoviste and got ready to flee. His wife, believing that it would be impossible to escape the enormous Turkish army, committed suicide by leaping off a cliff into a river, which subsequently became called *Princes River*. Vlad suffered another tragedy when he was escaping through the forest on horseback with his servants. One of the servants who had been given the job of carrying Vlad's infant son, dropped the baby. The pursuing Turks were too close by now for Vlad and his party to stop, and so they had to leave the child behind. Vlad was devastated, in one day he had lost his wife, his beloved son, and his home.

In search of help Vlad went to King Mathias of Hungary, but his reputation had finally caught up with him and some of the people that Vlad had persecuted had managed to reach the king first. They told the king that Vlad was an ally of the Turkish army and that he was coming to him as a spy. When Vlad arrived he was seized and he was imprisoned in a tower.

When the Turks arrived at Târgoviste they were greeted by a horrifying scene, the impaled heads of thousands of their spies. Before Vlad had fled he had also burned his own villages and poisoned the wells, so that the invading Turks would not have access to any food or water. The Turks took what was left of the ruins of the city but, after only a few days, the Black Plague broke out amongst the soldiers and they were forced to retreat.

Meanwhile, Vlad who had been imprisoned for several months, had caught the eye of the King's sister, Ilona. She used her influence on her brother and talked him into allowing Vlad to go free. Vlad, who was partially pardoned, married Ilona, and was given a large home within the city. He lived there for several years with his new wife, and she provided him with another son.

Once the King totally trusted Vlad he allowed him to leave the city, and he returned to Wallachia to claim the throne for the third time. He built up a new capital called Bucharesti (now called

Bucharest, and the modern-day capital of Romania). Not long after retaking the throne, a peasant came to Vlad with a young boy clutching his hand. He told the prince that he had found him as a baby in the forest many years ago on the night of the Turkish attack. Vlad was to his delight reunited with his long lost son, and he greatly rewarded the peasant.

THE DEATH OF DRACULA

Vlad the Impaler died in battle, over the age of fifty, when he was fighting near Bucharest in December 1476. It is rumoured that he either died at the hands of a Turkish assassin posing as a servant, or that he was accidentally killed on the battlefield by his own men because he had disguised himself as a Turk to confuse the enemy. The Sultan, delighted to have at last defeated his quarry, displayed Dracula's head on a pike in Constantinople just to prove that he was actually dead. He was eventually buried at the island monastery of Snagov, but excavations in 1931 failed to turn up any sign of his body! Some will remember him as a cruel fiend, while others will remember him as a fierce defender of his kingdom. However he is portrayed he was certainly a cruel, sadistic and ruthless murderer.

The Witch Doctor

In the year 1989 in Mexico, sixty people went missing. One person came to the fore in the ensuing investigations and that was a leader of a bloodthirsty band of sadistic drug-runners. He was young and handsome, bisexual, and a self-proclaimed psychic and cultist.

Our last story in the section delves into the mysterious world of black magic and cult worship. The success of a cult relies on the charismatic appeal of their leader to attract and control the number of their followers. For many reasons, one of them probably being fear, the cult members tend to follow their leader's every order without question or hesitation. This might have something to do with the threat of death that accompanies a hint of anything but total obedience.

ADOLFO DE JESUS CONSTANZO

Adolfo Constanzo was born in Miami on November 1, 1962, the son of a teenage Cuban immigrant. His father died when he was very young and he moved with his mother to Puerto Rico, where she married for the second time. Adolfo was baptized

396

in the Catholic faith, and served the church as an altar boy. When he was ten, the family returned to Miami. A year after the move Adolfo's stepfather died, which left his mother well provided for and he was now totally in her care.

They lived in an area called Little Havana and it wasn't long before the neighbours started to notice that there was something peculiar about Aurora Constanzo and her son. Some people thought she was witch and anyone that got on the wrong side of her would find a headless chicken or goat on their front doorsteps the following morning. Adolfo was introduced into the santeria cult when he was about nine years old. It is a cult that believes the life and power of the gods reside in stones secured beneath an altar. Animal sacrifice and spirit-possession are also elements of Santeria. Adolfo would have regular trips to Puerto Rico for instruction in voodoo, and in the year 1976 he was apprenticed to a practitioner of palo mayombe. Palo mayombe combines aspects of traditional African Kongo religion with Catholicism and Spiritism. Adolfo's occult godfather had made a lot of money from working with local drug dealers and the young Adolfo was greatly influenced by his powerful beliefs.

Much to his mother's delight, Adolfo started displaying psychic powers and predicting the future. He began to foretell events with frightening accuracy and even predicted the shooting of President Ronald Reagan in 1981. Adolfo took to petty crime and was subsequently arrested in 1981 on two charges of shoplifting, one involving the theft of a chainsaw. When he was released he declared that he would become a man of evil and worship his own devil. It was also around this time that he started showing bisexual inclinations, with a strong preference for male lovers.

In 1983 this handsome young devil-worshipper was assigned a modelling job in Mexico, were he spent his free time reading tarot cards and telling peoples' fortunes. It was while he was in Mexico that he gathered his first followers. His disciples at this time included Martin Quintana, a homosexual psychic Jorge Montes, and Omar Orea who had been obsessed with the cult since the age of fifteen. In1984 Adolfo moved permanently to Mexico and Quintana and Orea became his lovers. They shared an apartment in a strange *mènage à trois*. It wasn't long before he had quite a following as his reputation spread throughout the city. Constanza soon realized that he could make money from his spells and offered ritual cleansings to those who felt they have been cursed. He also started making money out of sacrificial animals charging:

roosters	$6
goats	$30
boa constrictors	$450
zebras	$1,100
African lion cubs	$3,100

True to the lessons given to him by his mentor, Constanzo went out of his way to be accepted by wealthy drug dealers. One of the services he offered them was to make them invisible to police and bulletproof to their enemies by casting spells. It was all hocus-pocus of course, but they were taken in and were prepared to pay good money to this charming young man. According to one of the ledgers that Constanzo kept, one drug dealer in Mexico City paid him as much as $40,000 for his magical services over a period of three years. Constanzo knew it was important to stay in with these drug barons because not only could he earn a lot of money, but get on the wrong side of the gun-toting crooks and he could end up dead. As his medicinal rituals grew he realised that he needed more powerful ingredients. It was around mid-1985 that Adolfo and three of his disciples decided to rob a Mexico City graveyard for human bones to start his own *nganga*. A nganga is a cauldron of blood employed by the practitioners of palo mayombe.

The mystery surrounding Adolfo Constanzo was enough to lure a real cross-section of society. But what was even more amazing was the power he seemed to have over law enforcement officers, for some reason they saw him as God. Indeed, in his own right, Adolfo was a minor god and everyone seemed to worship him.

THE DRUG BARONS

In 1986 Adolfo was introduced to the drug-dealing Caldaza family by Florentino Ventura. At the time they were one of Mexico's most dominant narcotic cartels. Once more Constanzo won them over using his charm, his mumbo-jumbo and prophesies, profiting immensely from his acquaintance with the gang. By early 1987 he was able to buy himself an apartment in Mexico City, and also a fleet of luxury cars. If he was not working for the Caldazas he would carry out his own scams, once posing as a DEA agent to rip off a cocaine dealer in Guadalajara. His sold his rewards through his police contacts for the amazing sum of $100,000.

No words can really explain just how powerful this man had become. It is not really certain at what time he started taking human sacrifices. There is no final tally of his victims, but there are twenty-three ritualist killings that have been recorded. Many men that defied Constanza ended up losing their life.

In 1987, believing that he was the one responsible for the Constanza family's success, he demanded to be made a full partner in their syndicate. His request was curly refused, and on the outside it appeared that Constanzo had taken the rejection in his stride.

On April 30, Guillermo Calzada and six members of his household vanished under very peculiar circumstances. When they were reported missing on May 1, the police noticed melted candles and other evidence of some strange religious ceremony at the office of the syndicate. After many days of searching the area, the police eventually fished out mutilated human remains from the Zumpango River. Seven corpses were recovered in total all bearing the marks of sadistic torture. Fingers, toes and ears removed, hearts and sexual organs excised, part of the spine ripped from one body and a brain from another two. The body parts, as was later discovered, went to feed his nganga cauldron to build strength for future ceremonies.

In July 1987 one of his disciples, Salvador Garcia introduced Constanzo to another drug family. This one was led by two brothers Elio and Ovidio Hernandez. In the same month Constanzo was to have another important introduction, this time to twenty-two-year-old Sara Aldrete, a college student in Brownsville, Texas, who was born in Mexico. Like everyone else he met, Adolfo charmed Sara, who at the time was having a relationship with a drug dealer named Gilberto Sosa. However, she soon ended up in bed with Adolfo and he quickly put a stop to her previous lover by making a phone call and telling him of her infidelity.

Constanzo moved his headquarters to a plot of desert called Rancho Santa Elena, around twenty miles out of Matamoros. Now totally infatuated by Adolfo Sara entered his world of black magic. She became his high priestess and between the two of them they frightened their adoring disciples into organizing complicated and gruesome rituals. They chanted what he told them was an ancient African dialect while he blew marijuana into their faces.

After the move to Rancho Santa Elena his ritual killings seemed to increase. On May 28, 1988, a drug dealer by the name of Hector de la Fuente and farmer Moises Castille were shot, but this did not seem to satisfy the bloodthirsty leader. He ordered his disciples to dismember a transvestite by the name of Ramon Esquivel, and his mutilated remains were left on a street corner for all to see. Constanzo saw himself as invincible, especially as he had narrowly escaped being caught following a drug raid on a house in June 1988. During the raid they had seized many items of occult paraphernalia and it what turned out to be the city's largest-ever shipment of cocaine.

On August 12, Ovidio Hernandez and his two-year-old son were kidnapped by rival drug dealers, and his family turned to Constanzo for help. That night there was another human sacrifice at their headquarters in Rancho Santa Elena, but this time the hostages were released unharmed. Constanza was becoming more and more intoxicating to his followers and he barely noticed when Florentino Ventura committed suicide on September 17, shooting his wife, a friend and himself in a burst of gunfire.

In November 1988, Constanzo sacrificed one of his own followers, Jorge Gomez, who was accused of using cocaine, which was a direct violation of the cult's ban on any form of drug use. In December of the same year Constanzo managed to cement his relationship with the Hernandez family, by the initiation of Ovido Hernandez as a fully-fledged cult member.

HIS DOWNFALL

Constanzo's power just grew and grew and he carried out human sacrifice after human sacrifice. However, Adolfo started to become dissatisfied with the normal peasant, transvestite or small-time pusher who could disappear without causing too many waves, and he ordered his disciples to search the streets for an Anglo for his next ritual killing. They returned with twenty-one-year-old Mark Kilroy. Mark was a popular pre-med student from Texas and his disappearance marked the beginning of the end for Adolfo Constanzo and his 'family'.

Mark's family and friends soon noticed that he had gone missing and they soon started a massive investigation into his disappearance. By late March 1989, Mexican authorities were conducting one of their regular anti-drug campaigns, erecting road blocks and sweeping the district for unsuspecting drug smugglers. On April 1, an ex-policeman turned gangster, Victor Sauceda, was sacrificed at the ranch. Constanzo claimed that the spiritual messages he received from this sacrifice were strong and this instigated the smuggling of a half-ton of marijuana across the border.

On April 9, Serfain Hernandez, who had just returned from a meeting with Constanzo, failed to stop at one of the road blocks set up by the Mexican police. The police followed in hot pursuit, but Hernandez who totally believed in the el padrinos philosophy that he was invisible, didn't take any notice. In fact, he appeared totally shocked when he was apprehended at his final destination of Matamoros. Thinking the was totally invincible, Hernandez became arrogant inviting the police to shoot him, convinced that the bullets would just bounce off his invisible protection. The police arrested him along with another cult member, David Martinez, and took the pair back to Rancho Santa Elena. They carried out a search and discovered drugs and firearms, and also two other family members Elio Hernandez and Sergio Martinez. They took all four back to police headquarters and started to interrogate them throughout the evening. They all talked freely and told of black magic, torture and human sacrifice with some sort of perverse pride.

The following morning the police knew they needed to do a far more thorough search of the Ranch. This time they discovered the foul-smelling shed where Constanzo kept his nganga. It made the officers wretch when they saw that it was full of blood, spiders, scorpions, a dead cat, a turtle shell, bones, deer antlers and worse of all a human brain. The four captives, who were still talking quite freely about the activities of the cult, directed the police to Constanzo's private cemetery. The police started to excavate the site and discovered the remains of fifteen mutilated corpses.

Now the hunt for Adolfo Constanzo was well and truly on, and the police raided his luxury home at Atizapan, which was just outside Mexico city. On April 17 they came across a stash of gay pornographic literature and a concealed ritual chamber. The news of the evil goings-on at Rancho Santa Elena had reached international headlines and sightings of Constanzo were reported as far away as Chicago. He was actually hiding out in Mexico City in a small apartment, with his girlfriend Sara Aldrete and three other disciples. Sara was starting to panic that she would soon be killed and she threw a note out of window asking for help and giving the precise address of their hideout. Although it was picked up by a passer-by, he unfortunately kept the information to himself thinking that it was nothing more than a sick joke. However, on May 6, the police were called out by neighbours in the apartment block who were complaining of a loud and vulgar argument that had broken out in one of the flats. When the patrolmen arrived on the scene, Constanzo immediately opened fire, and the ensuing gunfight lasted for approximately forty-five minutes. Miraculously, only one of the policemen was injured.

Constanzo, realizing that it was going to be impossible to escape, handed his gun to one of the other cult members, Alvaro de Leon Valdez (a professional hitman nicknamed El Duby) and ordered him to kill himself and Martin Quintana. At first Valdez refused, but Constanzo struck him in the face and told him he would boil in hell if he didn't carry out his instructions. Scared by his threats Valdez stood in front of the two men and shot them down.

Constanzo and Quintana were already dead by the time the police stormed into the apartment. They arrested the remaining two, Sara Aldrete and El Duby. As a result of the raid and subsequent questioning, fourteen cult members were indicted on various charges, including multiple murder and narcotics violations.

In August 1990 El Duby was convicted of

killing Constanzo and Quintana and was given a thirty-year prison sentence. Cultists Juan Fragosa and Jorge Montes were both convicted in the Ramon Esquivel murder and were sentenced to thirty-five years each. Omar Orea, who was convicted in the same case, actually died of AIDS before he could be sentenced. Finally Sara Aldrete was acquitted of Constanzo's murder but sentenced to a six-year prison term for her part in associating with known criminals. In 1994, when she was just about to come to the end of her prison sentence, she was tried again for multiple murder charges and received a further conviction of sixty years.

IS IT ALL OVER?

How can we be certain that the death of their leader, Adolfo de Jesus Constanzo, will be the end of the sadistic, ritualistic cult. There still remains a very gruesome list of cult-related crimes in Mexico, that have remained unsolved.

Sara Aldrete told reports that she didn't think the religion would end with the arrest of some of the members, because there were an awful lot of people who were members of the cult. Apparently a temple has been uncovered in Monterrey that isn't even related to Constanzo's cult. So it looks like the sick ritual killings may well continue. Between the years 1987 and 1989, police in Mexico City recorded seventy-four unsolved ritual murders, fourteen of them involving infant victims. Constanzo's cult is suspected in at least sixteen of those cases, all involving children or teenagers, but authorities lack sufficient evidence to press any further charges.

Although the authorities would like to say that Constanzo was responsible for all of the unsolved killings, the fact is that they can never prove it, and of course with his death a lot of the evidence has died with him. Of course if he didn't carry out those sacrifices, it means someone else did, which is even more scary because they are still out there and free to kill at their will.

PART 3

WOMEN
WHO KILL

Can Women be as Cold-Blooded as Men?

'Everyone starts out totally dependent on a woman. The idea that she could turn out to be your enemy is terribly frightening.'
Lord Astor, *a British philanthropist*

ALTHOUGH violent crimes are generally carried out by men, this doesn't mean that a woman cannot be just as cold-blooded or dangerous. There are many incidents in life where a woman has shown more daring and fearlessness than perhaps Mr. Smith who lives down the road. But it is a common view generally held by most, and also of crime researcher Patricia Pearson who states: 'Violence is still universally considered to be the province of the male'. Women, especially for men, still hold the image of someone who is vulnerable, soft and gentle – in fact the weaker sex. It is not surprising therefore, that based on the number of murderers who have been caught, it is still the men who greatly outnumber the women. However, when it comes to the death of children, women outnumber the men and, when it involves the killing of other family members, the numbers are about equal. There are many different motives that have been used by women who have committed a murder, for example:

– Monetary gain,
– Ridding themselves of a burden
– Revenge
– Dislike
– Pressure from a gang
– Seeking power
– Following orders
– Delusions
– Pleasure
– Self-defence
– Acting out from a long history of abuse
– Sexual compulsion
– Team chemistry
– Psychopathy
– Misplaced mercy
– Rivalry

These cold-blooded murderers, whether male or female, share three common denominators of which one is the ability to portray a normal 'persona' – which is essential if they are to blend into the everyday crowd. Also these individuals are not classed as insane, but psychopaths, and so they know the difference between right and wrong. Thirdly, being psychopaths they have no conscience or remorse after their crime.

With all this taken into account, there are also some very noticeable differences in behaviour between male and female serial killers:

– While the length of time a woman's killing spree may range, on average, from six to eight years, a man's is shorter, varying from several months to several years.

– Women tend to choose a method that is not easily detectable and less aggressive, such as poison or asphyxiation, whereas men tend to be more physical and often commit a stabbing, battering, strangulation or shooting.

– Victims of women are quite often intimately close, such as family members or someone who is dependent on their care, while it is usually strangers that are often stalked by men.

– When victims are killed by a woman, the motive is often for profit, revenge or control, but for a man, over half of the murders committed are sexually driven.

Following the liberation of women in the 1970s, there seems to have been a noticeable increase in violent crime by women, although, generally not as brutal and torturous as men. However, one should not forget the deadly result of such abhorrent and atrocious motives. Amongst all violent offenders, it may be the psychopathic woman, being the most criminally versatile, who is most likely to repeat an offence – but this is still a much understudied subject. The most common age that the crimes of these wicked women are committed varies – even grandmothers have been found guilty – but it seems to be generally around the age of thirty. The longest length of time a killing period has lasted without the culprit being caught is thirty-four years.

WOMEN SERIAL KILLERS

At one time serial killings performed by women could have been put into two main groups. These being 'Black Widows' and 'Angels of Death'. More recently, however, the list of groups has broadened to eight different categories.

– *Black Widows* – usually starting their evil career after the age of twenty-five, this manipulative woman will kill their partner/s for monetary gain, usually committing this crime more than once and capable of killing children if needs be. The typical cycle is about six to eight victims over a ten to fifteen-year period. The preferred weapon of choice is generally poison.

– *Angels of Death* – often beginning their criminal career at around twenty-one years old, seeks victims who are usually already on some form of medication, the elderly, or those who are in hospital. The victim is usually dependent on the killer and the method of death is hard to trace, such as a lethal injection of a chemical or a pillow used to suffocate the prey. A typical cycle is around eight victims over a one to two-year period, although if the offender is mobile the number of victims can be much higher.

– *Sexual Predators* – this crime, as the name suggests, is very rare. Whether being driven by the hatred of men, revenge or theft, the predator would be driven by sexual fantasy. These female predators are often middle-aged or in their thirties and usually have killed at least six victims before finally being caught. Their criminal career spans to around three years.

– *Revenge Killers* – love, hate and jealousy being the most frequent motive, this crime is as infrequent as the sexual predator. Usually younger, around the mid-twenties to early thirties, these killers strike with a vengeance being strongly driven by obsession. Repeat offenders are rare, and when apprehended, show great remorse.

– *Profit killers* – here the woman kills for others, usually to gain money. They are hired as 'hit women', for example, to kill the cheating husband of a jealous wife, or a business competitor. Generally dispassionate about the murders they have committed and driven by greed, they may claim up to as many as twenty-five victims. These cold-blooded females are considered to be the most intelligent, resourceful and careful of all the serial killers.

– *Team Killers* – this comes in three different categories, male/female, female/female and family. Team killings account for about one third of all female serial killings. Most common of these three teams are the male/female kind, with the crime normally being sexually driven. The female partner here is usually in her early twenties, whereas in the all-female team the members are generally older. Each of these three teams have an average victim count of between nine and fifteen, using a variety of killing methods including knives and guns.

– *Killers whose sanity is in question* – although women serial killers represent a small number, in general the insanity defence strategy is rarely successful. For example 'angel of death' offenders are most capable of launching a successful insanity defence, especially if the psychological disorder is Munchausen syndrome by proxy, a common symptom among this killer group.

– *Killers whose motives defy explanation* – these women are motiveless killers, therefore neither they, nor the authorities, can find any explanation of why they committed their crime.

– *Unsolved Crimes* – these are crimes, like the names suggest, where a women may have been suspected, but there is no proof or motive and these cases remain unsolved.

These nine groups can be further categorized into murderers who act alone or those who work alongside others:

– *Acting Alone* – killers of this type are often mature, careful, deliberate, socially adept and highly organised. They usually attack victims in their home or specific place of work. These crimes are commonly committed using a specific weapon like poison, lethal injection or suffocations. The type of killers that fall into this group are:

> Black Widow
> Angel of Death
> Sexual Predator
> Revenge
> Profit or Crime

– *Acting in Partnership* – the killers in this group generally tend to be younger, more aggressive and vicious in their attack, more disorganised, and their crime is not normally carefully planned. Also they tend to attack victims in diverse locations and have a tendency to use guns, knives or torture. Killers that fall into this group include:

> Team Killer
> Question of Sanity
> Unexplained
> Unsolved

THE BLACK WIDOW

Appropriately named after the eight-legged spider with a fast, lethal and venomous bite, these killers are still around today.

An example of one such fiendish woman is Mary

415

Ann Cotton who was born in northern England in 1822. This evil woman, over the course of twenty years, poisoned many of her children, husbands and people that she either became very familiar with or worked alongside, with arsenic. Cotton was devoted to the church and by the age of nineteen was married and pregnant with her first child. This child was not to live for long, dying from a violent bout of 'gastric fever'. This was the first of many who suffered the same grisly demise.

Her killing spree lasted for nearly twenty years, and it was not until March 1873 that Mary Ann Cotton was finally brought to justice and hanged for murder.

In the late 1800s very little was known about psychopaths and less still of the female kind.

Not all 'Black Widows' are as melodramatic as Mary Ann Cotton, and many never get caught. These women kill mainly for money and often kill their own children as well. Other motives include anger and bewilderment, made worse by being under the influence of drink or drugs. It is believed that up to twenty per cent of babies that die each year from SIDS, or cot death, may have actually been victims at their own mothers' hands – this is, of course, particularly difficult to prove.

Exclude the movie-made impression that 'Black Widows' were models of complete physical beauty, for which reason the victims were drawn to them. In reality most of these cunning women were rather plain and ordinary, but using the right body language and female charm, were able to entice and captivate the attentions of their prey until they had total trust and most importantly, access to their finances. Once she had managed to get her hands on what she wanted – his money – this seductive killer would then dispense with the victim giving herself full control over her victim's estate. After a period of time the 'widow' would change her identity and personality and perhaps move to a new area where she would not be recognised, a new victim would be found and the performance would start all over again.

MOTHERS WHO KILL THEIR OWN CHILDREN

One crime that is more common among women than one would suspect is the mother taking the life of her own flesh and blood – her child. Unfortunately society's belief that every woman is born a natural 'mother' is not always the case, and some may need to be watched closer than others. Why would any mother want to harm her own newborn baby? It is difficult to comprehend that a woman who carries a new life around in her womb for nine months, would be able to take this life away as soon as it starts to breathe on it's own. But this is a difficult crime to prosecute as murder. There have been many incidents where young mothers hide themselves away, give birth on their own and then kill and dump the newborn in a dustbin, pretending the event had never happened.

Women, however, have been guilty of killing their children for centuries, the motives once being the lack of money to feed or clothe them, or provide any sort of place for them live. It may be that there was no husband or father present and so to prevent herself from being a social outcast, would remove any possible evidence of motherhood. Another factor was that there was not the choice of reliable contraception that is around today, and a woman may have had as many as ten babies in as many years.

Today things are a little different, people are not so heavily victimized if they have a child out of wedlock and the social system now provides better facilities for these women. However this type of barbaric crime still occurs. The reason for most infanticides has now changed and women tend to kill their young so that they can enjoy a less restricted lifestyle. However, horrifying this may sound, these crimes are actually premeditated and well thought out.

This is a most immoral act, killing a completely dependent being who is totally unable to defend itself. Certainly for this reason, it is much easier to kill a young baby than an older child. In the case of Melissa Drexler from New Jersey, who at the age of eighteen, gave birth in a toilet, strangled her newborn, and disposed of the body in a dustbin. After this event, Drexler danced the night away at her senior prom. Being sentenced to fifteen years in prison for aggravated manslaughter, Drexler spent only thirty-seven months behind bars before she was released. There are many similar cases to this one, involving older children as well as young babies.

More often than not, these women who kill their offspring are given sympathy and offered help or a course of treatment. But who is to say that some mothers are just not as naturally nurturing in motherhood as society says they should be. Pleading temporary insanity, being a battered wife, being a victim of abuse or having severe P.M.S. have all been used as grounds for the horrific and murderous behaviour of these women.

When the word killer is uttered, people tend to forget about women and focus more on the men who lurk in shadows and are more directly violent.

CASE
HISTORIES

Susan Smith

While parked on the gravel boat ramp,
Smith considered what she was going to do while
Michael aged three and Alex just fourteen months
slept in the back of the car.

Susan Leigh was born in the city of Union, South Carolina, on September 26, 1971. Her parents Harry and Linda, were both still young when she was born, and maybe as a result of their inexperience and maturity Susan experienced an unhappy and difficult childhood. Her father was a violent man with a drinking problem, who repeatedly accused Susan's mother of being unfaithful. Susan had two brothers, Michael and Scotty, Michael was her older half-brother, the result of a previous relationship.

The disturbing homelife had repercussions on all three children, especially Michael, who tried unsuccessfully to hang himself. During Susan's childhood, Michael was treated on many occasions at residential treatment facilities. At her own school Susan was described as an 'unusual and sad' child. When Susan was only six years old, her parents finally got divorced and her father, being totally devastated, started to drink far more heavily. Five weeks after the divorce was made final, on January 15, 1978, Harry Vaughan, aged thirty-seven, committed suicide by shooting himself. This loss left a huge gap in Susan's life as she worshipped her father. After his death she kept two treasured possessions, her father's coin collection and a tape recording of his voice.

Her mother, on the other hand, only waited two weeks after the divorce was finalized before getting married again, this time to a man named Beverly Russell. Russell was a businessman, a South Carolina State Republican executive committee man and a member of the advisory board of the Christian Coalition, and the owner of an appliance store in downtown Union. Susan moved, along with the rest of her family, into Russell's exclusive three bedroom house in the Mount Vernon Estates part of Union.

Susan changed completely after her mother remarried and she started to excel at school, even joining extra maths and Spanish classes. At secondary school she was named president of the Junior Civitan Club. She also joined the Red Cross club, worked with the elderly, and joined in other volunteer work within the community. She was even voted as the 'friendliest female' at Union High School, and Susan was remembered by her classmates as 'down to earth' and cheerful'. All this was a very different image than she had projected through her primary school days. Her private life, however, was not so happy. Still being very insecure, she craved male attention, especially that of her stepfather and she competed with her mother for his affections.

One evening, shortly before her sixteenth

birthday, Susan was sent to sleep downstairs in the sitting room as one of her stepsisters was staying in her room. While her stepfather sat on the end of the settee, Susan decided to snuggle up to him. Totally unaware of the effect that her behaviour was having on her stepfather, she proceeded to fall asleep. Stimulated by this, her stepfather started to run his hand over her body from her shoulders to her breasts, then placed Susan's hand on his genitals. Susan who had become aware of what was happening, decided the safest thing to do was to pretend that she was still asleep and hence ignored his gropings.

However, later she filed a complaint against Russell, which was investigated by the South Carolina Department of Social Services and the Union County Sheriff's office. It was recommended that the family attended counselling sessions, and Susan, her mother, and stepfather made about four or five visits. However, Russell still continued to molest Susan on occasion even after they had completed their counselling session.

Susan's first job was as a cashier at the Winn-Dixie supermarket, where she was soon promoted to the markets' book-keeper. While working here she started dating an older, married man and she fell pregnant but the pregnancy was terminated. During this time Susan was also having a relationship with another co-worker. After the abortion, the married man found out that she had been seeing someone else and ended the relationship. Susan became very depressed over the breakup and she tried to kill herself with an overdose. When she was admitted to Spartanburg Medical Centre in November 1988 to recover, it was found that she had tried to commit suicide before, when she was only thirteen. After a month of recovery, Susan returned to her job at Winn-Dixie.

Just before she tried to take her own life, Susan had become friendly with one of the store clerks at work, David Smith. They had become friends at Union High School, where they both attended and when Susan returned to work, David finished with his long-term girlfriend, Christy Jennings, in the hope of starting a relationship with Susan.

David Smith was very pleasant and had very strong work ethics. He started to date Susan in the summer of 1990, then in January 1991 Susan found herself pregnant again. As both David and Susan were against having an abortion they decided to get married. Giving up her idea of attending college, Susan saw marriage as a place of stability and safety.

In many ways the two were very similar, as they were both needy and found comfort in each other. But problems arose because they were from completely different backgrounds, Susan being brought up in the city and David in the country. Because David had no college education and was from a different economic background Susan's mother and stepfather were far from pleased, and even more so when they heard of the impending marriage and pregnancy.

Shortly before Susan and David were due to be married, Danny, who was David's younger brother died from complications relating to Crohn's disease. Susan was adamant she wouldn't postpone the wedding for the simple reason she didn't want people to see that she was pregnant on her special day. So at the wedding, David's parents were still dealing with the loss of their other son.

After the wedding, Susan refused to move to the simple country house that David had found, it was not good enough for her as she had much higher expectations. In the end she moved in with David at his great-grandmother's house. About three months after they were married, on a visit to her inlaws, Susan found David's father on the floor of his home. He had attempted to kill himself with an overdose of pills. Apparently, David's parents' marriage was falling apart, partly due to the death of their son and the attempted suicide. Because of this, David's mother, Barbara, left and moved away to South Carolina. David's father, however, recovered and continued to live in Putnam after being hospitalised and treated for depression. This is where he met his second wife.

Susan continued working at Winn-Dixie until she went into labour and Michael Danny Smith was born on October 10, 1991. After the birth of their son, Susan went part-time at work and enrolled at the University of South Carolina in Union, attending several college courses. With all the responsibilities of a young child, college and work, a lot of tension developed between the couple which put a great amount of stress on their marriage. These tensions were made worse by the fact that David did not get on with Linda, Susan's mother. Linda was accused, by David, of giving unwelcome advice and opinions on how he and Susan should conduct their marriage and bring up their child. Added stress came from the fact that both still worked at Winn-Dixie where David was now Susan's boss and gradually things were going from bad to worse.

In November 1992 Susan became pregnant again and they tried hard to reconcile their differences. They had tried separation on several occasions, but, with the financial assistance of Susan's mother and stepfather, David and Susan tried to patch things up and bought a small ranch-style house in Toney Road, Union.

This second pregnancy was not as easy as the first for Susan, who complained of being 'fat and ugly'. Things did not improve at home for very long as Susan was miserable and unhappy. David started to feel excluded from Susan's life and so looked elsewhere for friendship. He started to see fellow employee at Winn-Dixie, Tiffany Moss. Susan became increasingly jealous and would visit him at work, screaming at him while he was talking to women in the store. After a difficult second birth, Alexander Tyler Smith was born on August 5, 1993, by caesarian section. Although they both were devoted parents, three weeks after the birth of their second child, David moved out.

HER INFATUATION

When Susan had fully recovered from the birth of Alex, deciding that she could not work at the same place as her husband and his mistress, she found a job at Conso Products. Here she worked as a bookkeeper and in the course of time became the assistant to the executive secretary for the president and CEO of Conso, J. Carey Findlay.

Findlay, was an accountant from North Carolina, who lived in Union. With a group of investors he bought Conso in 1986, then bought out his partners in 1988. Conso became the first publically owned corporation in Union and by the end of 1993 had factories in Canada, Mexico and Great Britain. Susan enjoyed the expensive surroundings that Conso provided, and also loved her work and the responsibility that came with it. She also enjoyed working at Conso for another reason – Tom Findlay – who was one of three sons of J. Carey Findlay. Being young, rich and available, Tom was popular with most of the young women in Union. After graduating from Auburn University, he was in charge of the graphic arts department at Conso, and responsible for designing and producing company brochures.

Susan now had many new friends, and she also started to see Tom Findlay, attending many lunch dates and parties with him. Then, a few months into 1994, Susan and David tried one last attempt to save their marriage. David stopped seeing his girlfriend Tiffany and Susan finished with Tom. However, this did not last for long and by the end of July 1994 Susan asked David for a divorce. He, on the other hand, had wanted the marriage to work as he felt that their two sons needed both their mother and father together. Finally, David moved out in August and rented a two bedroomed place a couple of miles away. In this apartment he provided facilities so that he could have his two boys, Michael and Alex, to stay.

By September both Susan and David were on friendly terms and Susan was once again seeing Tom. At this time Susan was sexually involved with three men, her stepfather Beverly Russell, Tom Findlay and her estranged husband, David. When Susan felt that she had a stable future with Tom Findlay, she filed for a divorce from David on the grounds of adultery.

Findlay, however, had other ideas about the relationship he shared with Susan. He liked her but found her too needy and possessive. He was honest enough to admit to her that he didn't want to raise a family and in October Susan received a letter from Tom, ending their relationship. In this letter, Tom had expressed how proud he was that Susan was trying to improve herself by attending college and how he thought she was a great person but also how he thought that they were not well suited for each other. He also wrote how her behaviour was inappropriate and that she would have to behave like a nice girl if she was to catch a nice man like himself. Not to be seen fondling and kissing other married men like at a recent hot tub party he had thrown. As well as this, their backgrounds were too dissimilar and he did not want the added responsibility of caring for another man's two small children.

Susan grew depressed at managing the two young children on her own as well as her college work and she also suffered anxiety when she was on her own in the evening. In an attempt to restore her relationship, she visited Tom at his home and used the story of her sexual relationship with her stepfather to try and gain his sympathy, but this did not gain the right reaction, only one of shock.

It was the morning of October 25, 1994. Susan fed and dressed her two small boys and took them to their day care as usual, before going to work. At lunch time she joined a group of friends from work, which included Tom, at a restaurant in Buffalo. Susan appeared very quiet while the rest of the crowd talked and laughed happily. During lunch Susan asked her supervisor if she could leave work early and when they asked why, Susan explained that she was in love with someone who didn't love her in return. When questioned further as to whom this person was, she replied 'Tom Findlay, but it can never be, because of my children'.

Instead of going home as she has requested, Susan stayed at work. Then at about 2.30 in the afternoon Susan called Tom into his office and asked him if he could meet her to talk. She also mentioned that David was threatening to expose some information about her in the divorce proceedings. When Tom asked what this had to do with him, she replied that he was going to accuse her of cheating the IRS and of having an affair with Tom's father. After hearing this, Tom stated that their intimate relationship would have to end forever, although they could remain friends. Later that afternoon, around 4.30, Susan pursued Tom once again in order to return to him a sweatshirt that she had once borrowed, but he told her to hang onto it.

After work, once Susan had collected her two boys from the care they attended during the day, she drove on to Hickory Nuts, the only bar in Union. Before she got there she bumped into Sue Brown, Conso's marketing manager, at the bar's car park. Instead of going in, Susan persuaded Sue to go back to work with her so that she could apologise to Tom for the fictional story she had concocted about her sleeping with his father. She had wanted to see his reaction, but when they got there Tom was not at all happy to see Susan. Sue was left waiting in the car to watch over the two children. When Susan got back to the car she appeared upset and spoke of 'just ending it'. Sue was dropped back at the Hickory Nuts bar and then Susan drove on home with the children. The time was approximately 6.00 p.m.

Later on at Hickory Nuts, where Tom also joined Sue Brown and other friends for dinner, there was a phone call for Sue. The waiter brought the phone over to the table and Sue found Susan on the other end of the line calling to see if Tom had been asking about her. Sue replied discreetly that he had not, ended the call promptly, and handed the telephone back to the waiter, going back to her meal.

DESPERATE MEASURES

A more stable woman would have recovered from the rejection, but Susan's life had not been stable right from the beginning. Now Susan started plotting in her head ways of getting her attractive boyfriend back. She could have given her children to their father to look after, for he certainly adored them. However, she knew that would have gone against what society expects, and she was always desperately seeking approval. To the outside world she was a devoted mother. So she came up with another, far more dramatic, solution.

At home, Susan dressed her two boys at around 8.00 p.m., put them into the car, strapped them in their car seats and began driving around Union. She had never felt so lonely and sad and it was all due to Tom's rejection. While she drove along highway 49 she became overwhelmed by a consuming desire to commit suicide. She thought of driving to her mother's house so she could look after the children, but she felt so bad that she did not think even her mother would be able to help the way she felt.

In the end, Susan drove off the highway and onto a road which led to John D. Long Lake. Horrific thoughts entered her mind, and she decided that rather than leave her children motherless and alone, they would be better off with their mother and God. The plan was that they would all die together. By putting the car into neutral and then letting it roll down the boat ramp was to be the solution, but Susan could not do it. After rolling a little way she pulled the handbrake on and stopped the car. This happened three times. She got out of the car and looked around, it was very dark, no-one was about, just blackness.

While standing outside of the car, overwhelmed with loneliness, grief and pain, Susan reached into the car and released the brake. The two boys, Michael who had celebrated his third birthday only a few weeks before, and Alex, just fourteen months old, were asleep and still securely strapped in child safety seats at the back of the car. The car rolled down the gravelled boat ramp and into John D. Long Lake.

Susan watched as the car floated into the lake, filled up with water and then finally sunk. It was all over in minutes. Susan had not wanted her sons to suffer and she had planned to take her own life as well but in the end she could not do it.

Once the car and her children has disappeared, Susan ran to a nearby house. She was in a state of great distress and screamed that she had been attacked at the traffic lights by a black man. This man had proceeded to steal her car and the two sleeping children within it.

Nine days later, after many intensive and lengthy interrogations Susan was confronted by Sheriff Wells in a small room in the Baptist Church. He told Susan that she was lying and finally Susan broke down and admitted that her plan was that the three of them were supposed to have all died together, she loved her sons very much.

In a study of missing, exploited and murdered children in the United States during the 1990s, it found that mothers who murdered their children did so in a clear and noticeably womb-like manner, some submerged in water and others wrapped in plastic, and all the bodies of the victims were found to be within ten miles of the family home.

A more stable woman than Susan Smith would have found alternative ways to end their feeling of isolation that didn't involve the killing of their young. But these infant killers tend to fit into a borderline psychological category. They haven't received enough love and attention during their own childhood and so become desperate to latch their attentions onto someone else. They usually have a huge desire to have children themselves in an effort to give them the love that they so lacked. These type of women tend to overdramatize a situation and consequently act on impulse. They can superficially look like loving, caring mothers, but in truth they seem to save most of their feeling for themselves, even if only in self-pity. Just like a doll, they tire of the child that is in effect in the way of progress, and the baby becomes ultimately expendable, especially if a new man comes into their life.

Perhaps in an effort to lessen the figures of infanticide, society should stop romanticizing about motherhood and give out the message instead that perhaps having babies is not right for every individual. Many women cry for help after they have a baby, saying that they are unable to cope, perhaps we need to start listening.

Genene Anne Jones

*Accused of two murders and charges of injury
to six other children, her own two children
were cared for by her adoptive mother
– this was a woman who declared that she'd
wanted children all her life.*

Genene Anne Jones was born on July 13, 1950,
but was immediately given up for adoption to
Dick and Gladys Jones. This couple lived in a four-
bedroomed, two-storey mansion just outside of
San Antonio. They also adopted three other
children, two older and one younger than Genene.
Dick Jones worked in the entertainment business
being an entrepreneur and professional gambler
and, although a generous man, his lifestyle would
have repercussions on the rest of the family. Jones
also tried his hand at running a restaurant but this
did not do well and so he sought after other work.

When Genene was ten years old her father was
arrested for burglary, but the charges were later
dropped as it turned out to be a practical joke.
Dick then opened a bill-board business and took
Genene around in the truck with him. This was
one of the happiest times in her life as she felt
involved, while the rest of the time she felt ignored

434

and that her parents did not like her much – the 'black sheep' of the family.

Not popular at school, Genene was accused of lying, manipulating and being aggressive. Then at the age of sixteen, Travis, her youngest brother and closest companion, accidentally killed himself after a pipe bomb he was building accidentally blew up in his face. He had only been fourteen years old and Genene, who was sixteen at the time, cried and fainted during the funeral. During the following months her father became quite ill and a year later died of cancer. Genene was devastated and it is possible her sadistic nature stemmed from these two close deaths in her family.

Even though she still attended school, Genene thought it best to get married as soon as she could to fill the void in her life. Although she was described as short and overweight, once graduated, she married James Harvey Delany Jr. He was also overweight, a high school dropout, whose only interest seemed to be hot rods. After seven months James joined the Navy, and as soon as he had gone, Genene started to sleep around. She had an insatiable appetite for sex and with her husband away at sea she needed to fulfil her desires. She also started to spread rumours around that she had been abused as a child.

Genene was still dependent on her mother, Gladys, for money, and she convinced her daughter that she should think about getting a career and earning herself some money. Genene enrolled into beauty school and when James returned from the Navy, she fell pregnant and they had their first child. Four years later Genene left him and filed for divorce, stating in the papers that he had been violent with her during their marriage.

A little while later Genene suffered another loss – her older brother died from cancer. She decided to change jobs after being concerned that the hair dyes she was using in the beauty salon could possibly cause cancer. She also found herself pregnant for a second time and was worried that she would now have two children to care for.

Genene had already worked in a hospital beauty salon and found the idea of becoming a nurse most appealing. She started her training and left her children with Gladys to take care of. Genene was in awe of the doctors, she loved to be around them as she saw them as both powerful and mysterious. After just one year of training she had become a licenced vocational nurse, and was good at it, but also started an obsession with diagnosing people.

Her first job at San Antonio's Methodist Hospital lasted only eight months before she was fired. This was partly due to the fact that she tried to make decisions in areas where she had no authority and partly because she had made rude demands of a patient who had subsequently issued a complaint. Although she did not find any problems in getting another job, this did not last for very long either. Eventually she was employed by Bexar Medical Center Hospital to work in the intensive care section of their pediatric unit.

The first child that Genene had contact with had a fatal intestinal condition. When the child died shortly after surgery Genene became hysterical. She sat staring at the lifeless body even though she hardly new him, and the other nurses became disturbed by her strange behaviour.

Genene would skip important lessons on how to handle certain drugs, in favour of spending a long time on the ward with certain patients. She thoroughly enjoyed the feeling of being needed. Because of the missed lessons she made eight separate nursing errors in her first year. While insisting that 'she' wanted to do what was 'best for the child', Genene would go against certain orders. Lucky for her that she was liked by the head nurse, Pat Belko, for there was certainly enough evidence to have her dismissed. This gave Genene Jones the feeling that she was invincible and had certain powers. But she used this power in the wrong way, and before long her bossy manner forced new nurses to transfer to other departments.

Genene gradually became more arrogant, bossy and loud-mouthed, bragging constantly about her sexual conquests. She was not very popular with her fellow workers, and upset them on many an occasion by predicting which baby she felt was going to die next.

A NEW DOCTOR

James Robotham was hired as the medical director of the pediatric intensive care unit. He was prepared to take far more responsibility for his own patients, which meant that he gradually filtered out the nurses he no longer needed. He also said that they all had to be accountable to him, which did not go down well with the rest of the nurses, that is except Genene. She seemed to thrive on the fact that she could now bring more problems to someone's attention which would ultimately mean more attention for herself. Another way Genene tried to gain sympathy and attention was to keep attending outpatients with minor complaints. Although she was never officially diagnosed with any one specific problem, it is said that she visited there as many times as thirty in just under two years. It is possible that she was suffering from a form of Munchausen Syndrome – a complaint whereby someone with factitious disorders will feign, exaggerate, or actually self-induce illnesses. Their aim is to assume the status of 'patient' and thereby to win attention that they feel unable to obtain in any other way.

In 1981 Genene Jones asked if she could be put in charge of the terminally ill patients. This meant that she could be nearest to the patients who would ultimately die. For some perverse reason she seemed to thrive on some form of excitement when a child failed to survive some emergency treatment. While she prepared the body she could be heard singing and talking to the corpse, and was always the one that wanted to take it down to the morgue.

The drugs on the ward were kept in an unlocked cabinet and were freely available. No one seemed at all concerned about this – at least not until later on. No one had ever followed up why Genene had been dismissed from her last hospital job and consequently she was placed in a position of authority. Her speciality was to place intravenous tubes into veins and her thirst for knowledge on handling drugs impressed her superiors.

UNNECESSARY DEATH

Over a two-week period on the intensive care unit seven children died from problems that should have been easily cured. The need for resuscitation seemed constant, but apparently it was only when Genene was around. Those in the most critical condition came under her care and there was no doubt that she loved the excitement that an emergency situation brought about. It all seemed to happen on her shift – one child had three seizures in a row one particular night.

One day she jokingly said, 'They're going to start thinking I'm the Death Nurse', and in fact she was very close to the truth. They had started calling her on-duty hours the Death Shift, purely based on the numbers of resuscitations and deaths that seemed to occur while she was there. Rumours started spreading around the ward that she was actually doing something to these children to speed up their deaths, but her old friend Pat Belko wouldn't hear any of it, and just said they were jealous because she was such a compassionate nurse.

Then one night a six-month-old baby called Jose Antonio Flores came into the ward with a common childhood ailment – fever, vomiting and diarrhoea. However, while he was under Genene's care he suddenly developed unexplained seizures and went into cardiac arrest. The doctors fought for almost an hour to save his life and at last the worst was over. However, they noticed he was bleeding badly and that his blood wouldn't clot. Soon the problem seemed to subside, that is until Genene's shift the following day. Once again Jose started having seizures and bleeding profusely. They were unable to save him this time and Jose's father was told about the death of his son. On hearing the devastating news, Mr. Flores suffered a heart attack and had to be taken to the emergency room. Genene meanwhile was allowing Jose's older brother to carry the baby's body down to the morgue. Suddenly, and without any apparent reason, she grabbed the body from the boy and started to run down the corridor towards the morgue. Members of the family ran after her, but not knowing the complicated corridor system they lost her. When the baby's blood was tested it indicated an overdose of a drug called heparin, which is an anticoagulant – no one had ordered it and for once her superiors became suspicious.

A short while later a three-month-old boy named Albert Garza was being treated by two resident physicians, when they discovered he had been given an overdose of heparin. They confronted Genene who became angry and stormed out of the room, luckily this time the child survived. They decided that they would tighten up the control on the use of heparin by nurses, and also made them make far more accurate records so that these could be checked regularly. They were determined that if someone was trying to harm the children in their unit they would soon find out who it was.

Genene's health started to deteriorate around this time. She refused drugs to help her condition, complained continually, and yet the doctors could find no evidence of any ailment. Once more it seems as though Genene was trying to get the attention she craved for. Her previous ally, Dr. Robotham, now started to lose his patience with his nurse. He put his suspicions to the hospital administration who were rather reluctant to start any form of internal investigation. They felt it would do the hospital no good to bring the matter to the attention of the public. So Robotham, himself, continued to watch the shift that Genene was on very carefully.

The use of heparin was now very carefully monitored on his ward, but all of a sudden another drug showed up when the test the blood of eleven-month-old Joshua Sawyer, who had recently died. He had been brought in suffering from the effects of smoke inhalation and had suffered a cardiac arrest. The doctors ordered that he be given dilantin, but he remained in a coma. Doctors were surprised that he was not responding to the drug, while Genene told his parents that it would be kinder if they allowed him to die. All of a sudden Joshua had two violent heart attacks and died. When they tested his blood it was clear that someone in the hospital had blundered, for there was a toxic amount of dilantin in his body.

As soon as Genene became aware that her previous allies were started to get suspicious of her actions, she turned to blackmail. She said that she had kept precise records of every child that had died and she knew exactly who had administered the drugs. Robotham immediately requested that she should be fired, but unfortunately no one listened to him. Neither did they listen to a nurse who kept reporting that supplies of toxic drugs were going missing.

Several more incidents happened on the ward over the next couple of weeks which just added to the suspicions that Genene Jones was actually killing the children under her care. A doctor also found a manual amongst Genene's possessions that gave precise details of how to inject heparin subcutaneously without leaving a mark on the skin. Once more the hospital administration refused to take any action.

When another child died suspiciously after undergoing open-heart surgery, more doctors complained and finally a committee was formed to look into the problem. A series of internal inquiries were held but they did not come up with any positive recommendations, so a panel of experts was called in from hospitals in the USA and Canada to look into the unusual number of deaths on the pediatric ward. This panel interviewed all of Bexar's staff and seemed quite shocked when one of Genene's colleagues bluntly accused her of the infants' deaths. The panel failed to reach any firm conclusions after their investigation other than to suggest that they replace the LVNs with RNs on the unit, which meant that Genene would be transferred away from the babies. As a result of this Genene resigned and the administrators felt relieved that she was no longer their problem.

THE PROBLEM IS TRANSFERRED

Although the problem was solved at Bexar County Hospital it was by no means the end of Genene's killing spree. In 1982, Dr. Kathleen Holland opened a pediatrics clinic in Kerville, Texas. She hired a licensed vocational nurse by the name of Genene Jones. Within months of her starting work a number of children began to experience problems with their breathing. As all the children eventually recovered no particular significance was placed on the matter and least of all on Genene Jones.

However, when fourteen-month-old Chelsea McClellan was brought to the hospital for a regular mumps and measles injection, it was Jones who gave the first injection. This resulted in the child having an immediate seizure and she was taken to San Antonio for emergency treatment. On the way the McClellan baby went into cardiac arrest and lost its fight for life. Back at Kerville a bottle of succinylcholine, which is a powerful muscle relaxant had gone missing, and then suddenly Genene found it. The missing bottle had been filled with a saline solution which meant that someone had been using this dangerous drug under suspicious circumstances. As there had been many other babies that had suffered strange seizures under Genene's care, Holland decided to dismiss her.

HEALTH AUTHORITY INVESTIGATES

By now the health authorities had become very perturbed about the number of deaths at both the hospitals and Genene Jones was suspended from further nursing pending a grand jury investigation. The press leaked reports that they were investigating as many as forty-two baby deaths. The grand jury finally returned indictments against Jones and she was officially charged with murder following the discovery of the drug succinylcholine in Chelsea McClellan's body.

At her trial during January and February 1984, Genene Jones was found guilty and sentenced to ninety-nine years imprisonment. She was also tried a second time for another charge of administering an overdose of the blood-thinning drug heparin to another baby, and this time she was given a concurrent term of sixty years. The two sentences totalled one hundred and fifty-nine years, but with the possibility of parole.

Jones came up for parole after serving only ten years of her sentence, but relatives of Chelsea McClellan successfully fought to keep her behind bars, where she will remain until at least 2009, when once again she will be eligible for parole.

WHY DID SHE KILL?

Although we are unlikely to ever really know why Genene Jones killed so many babies that were entrusted to her care, the most probable answer is that she liked the excitement and the attention that it brought her. She definitely took pleasure in creating life and death dramas in which she could play an influential role, so indicating that there was a power motive. It was certain that she was suffering from Munchausen Syndrome by Proxy, which means that she was getting the attention from doctors by making someone else sick. This is a form of abuse in which children are the usual victims.

Another symptom of Munchausen is that the sufferer will complain of factitious disorders, feign, exaggerate or actually self-induce illnesses. Their aim is to assume the status of 'patient' and thereby to win attention, nurturance and lenience that they feel unable to obtain in any other way. These are certainly all symptoms that Genene Jones showed on numerous occasions.

Nurse Beverley Allitt

The nurse who murders is always held in particular dread because they prey on someone who is at their most vulnerable and in whom they put their trust. Beverley Allitt is probably Britain's most famous female hospital killer. She pretended to adore the children under her care but in truth she was totally indifferent to their suffering.

Beverley Gail Allitt was born on October 4, 1968 in Corby Glen, Lincolnshire. She was the second of four children born to Richard and Lillian Allitt and had a normal, happy family life. However, as a child Beverley would always seem to be suffering from some sort of illness, and would often appear wearing bandages or plasters on wounds that she would not allow anyone to examine. She suffered from an erratic temperament and would often become aggressive towards others. She would feign numerous illnesses that would be serious enough to send her to hospital, until eventually doctors realised that there was nothing wrong with her and told her parents that the child was wasting their time.

When Beverley was sixteen she showed an interest in caring for children and enrolled on a nursing course in Grantham. In 1988, when she

446

had completed the course, she began her training at Grantham and Kesteven Hospital as a trainee nurse. When her two years training was up, Beverley successfully passed her examinations, but her attendance records showed that she had missed a total of one hundred and twenty-six days through illness. One of the sisters in the ward was concerned with the amount of time she had had off and suggested that Allitt should be offered some psychiatric help. However, none was ever offered.

Allitt was turned down for the first nursing job she applied for because they felt she had a lack of basic knowledge. She was required to work an additional ten weeks before she could be registered as a nurse, and this time would be spent on Ward 4 at Grantham Hospital.

Beverley took to nursing enthusiastically and she was determined to show the hospital just how competent she was. On February 21, 1991, the mother of seven-week-old Liam Taylor brought him in to the hospital suffering from congested lungs. He was diagnosed as having Bronchiolitis and it was suggested he spend a couple of days in Ward 4 after which time he should be well enough to go home. Liam was given an oxygen mask to help with his breathing, and immediately he started to look a lot better. His parents, Chris and Joanne, felt much happier, and it was suggested by a staff nurse that they go home and get some rest while nurse Allitt fed Liam.

It was less than two hours later that Chris and Joanne returned to the hospital, to be told that Liam had taken a turn for the worse. Nurse Allitt told them how Liam had suddenly violently vomited while she was feeding him, and had also produced yellow faeces. Liam was lying motionless in his cot and the parents immediately began to panic. A consultant was called in to examine the baby and he diagnosed that Liam had pneumonia on his lung and that the next twenty-four hours would be critical in their young infant's life.

Chris and Joanne stayed with their son throughout the twenty-four hour ordeal. At times he would seem to improve, smiling and giggling at his parents, and the next moment his muscles would contract in pain. Just before midnight Liam went into another respiratory crisis but again he pulled through and his parents were told to go and rest. Allitt reassured the parents and said that she would watch over their child carefully. As soon as she was left alone with the baby things soon went from bad to worse. She sent two nurses out of the room to fetch some things that she needed, and one they returned they saw Allitt standing over Liam whose face was now totally ashen. Then some red blotches appeared on his face and Allitt yelled out for the crash team. They fought hard to save him and in the end Liam Taylor was only alive because of the life-support machine that was helping him breathe. He had undoubtedly suffered brain damage due to the cardiac arrest, and his parents had to make the difficult decision of allowing him to die.

As they turned off the life support machine Beverley Allitt watched emotionless, and then left for home. She returned to work that afternoon as if nothing had happened – joyous in the knowledge that she had committed murder and had got away with it.

MORE DEATHS

Within the next two months she attacked nine children and murdered four and all the while to the suffering parents she appeared to be the angel of mercy. How could it be that someone so caring on the outside could be so demented on the inside?

Two weeks after Liam Taylor died, eleven-year-old Timothy Hardwick was brought into the hospital. Tim had suffered all his life, he had Cerebral Palsy from birth, was virtually blind and had very little control over his limbs. Despite all of this he still had the ability to be happy. On March 5, Tim suffered from an epileptic fit while he was at his special needs school, and the decision was made to take the boy to Newark Hospital. After receiving a treatment of Valium, Tim's body relaxed and he fell into a deep sleep. The doctors advised that Tim be allowed to stay in hospital for observation and he was left in the care of nurse Allitt. He arrived in Ward 4 at around 3.15 p.m. but by 5.00 p.m. Allitt sought help from a fellow nurse because she felt that Tim was uncomfortable. The two nurses turned Tim on his side and for a while he seemed to improve. Nurse Allitt raised the alarm forty-five minutes later because Tim had suddenly stopped breathing. When the crash team arrive his face was ashen, his lips were blue and there was no visible sign of a pulse. They tried to save his life but unfortunately it was too late and at 6.15 p.m. Tim lost his fight for life. The nursing team were totally baffled as there was no obvious reason for his sudden and unexpected death. Even an autopsy failed to provide an obvious cause for death and it was put down to the fact that he suffered from epilepsy.

Five days later Kayley Desmond entered Ward 4 at only fifteen weeks old. She was under-nourished, dehydrated and suffering from a chest infection. Once again Allitt tended to her and she appeared to be making very good progress. Kayley's mother, Maggie, was asleep in a chair next to her daughter's bed when Allitt called for a fellow nurse, Lynn Vowles, to come and help modify some of the medical equipment. Being careful not to wake Maggie, Lynn adjusted a drip monitor when she noticed that Kayley did not look right and that her face was exceptionally pale. She bent over and realised immediately that the child was not breathing. Lynn told Allitt to call the crash team while she carried out mouth to mouth resuscitation. They managed to revive Kayley and they were satisfied that the worst was over, putting the relapse down to a complication connected with a chest infection.

Nurse Allitt was given strict instructions to stay by her side and watch over the child, but at 4.00 p.m. the crash team were once again called into the ward to revive Kayley. She was given an injection of Aminophyline along with a heart massage and after a few minutes her pulse returned and her breathing returned to normal. Physicians were puzzled by her condition and so gave her a thorough examination. They discovered an odd puncture hole just under her armpit and near it was an air bubble. They put it down to an accidental injection, and there was no further investigation. They decided to transfer the tiny patient to Queens Medical Centre in Nottingham where she recovered fully without suffering any further attacks. The doctors there were surprised at the speed of her recovery due to the severity of her attacks, after a couple of days she seemed to be completely back to normal.

After the stress of the mystery illness of Kayley, Ward 4 were gradually returning to normal. Allitt, who was obviously upset by the lost opportunity, didn't wait long and struck again and again, in fact a total of three times over the next four days.

With three deaths and nine suspicious incidents in a period of two months, Doctor Nelson Porter, had to admit that something was wrong on Ward 4. He requested that security cameras were placed to monitor people who went in and out of the ward, but a fellow doctor, Dr. Nanayakkara felt there was no reason for concern, and his request was ignored. While the two doctors discussed the need for extra security, Claire Peck was being admitted to the ward.

Claire was only fifteen months old and had been in and out of hospital due to breathing difficulties. The doctors attending to Claire decided it would be advisable to put a tube down her throat to help her breathe more easily and she was taken off to the treatment room to prepare her for the treatment. While waiting for the team to arrive Claire was left in the capable hands of one of the attending nurses. In the few moments they were left alone Claire started to turn blue, and she stopped breathing. A nurse returning to the treatment room immediately noticed the child's condition and that the nurse was just standing watching her. She immediately put an oxygen mask over her face and slapped her backside to start her breathing again. A doctor was called and she was given an injection of Aminophyline and after twenty minutes she was breathing normally.

The doctor went off to inform Claire's parents of the incident, when minutes later nurse Allitt rushed out of the treatment room saying that Claire's had stopped breathing again. The doctor rushed back to the child, but it was too late her heart and lungs had already stopped working. They tried very hard to revive the child but in the end it was hopeless and they had to pronounce her as officially dead. The doctor concerned, Dr, Porter, could not believe that the child had died and took blood samples to try and ascertain the cause. He also took all the intravenous drips that had been used in her treatment and sent them to the laboratory for testing, this time he wanted an answer.

A science officer at the hospital laboratory, Alan Willis, informed the doctor that his results showed a very high level of potassium in the blood, in fact it was so high it was off the scale. The hospital decided it was essential that they started an investigation into the mysterious deaths that had been happening recently, but it still took more than two weeks before the police were actually called in.

The body of Claire was exhumed and further tests showed that the body contained traces of the drug lignocaine – a substance used in cardiac arrest, but never in the case of a baby. The Superintendent in charge of the case, Stuart Clifton, believed that he had a killer on his hands and he started to examine more carefully some of the other baffling cases. The results of their tests showed an unusually high dose of insulin, and he also learned that it was nurse Allitt who had reported the key missing to the refrigerator that contained the insulin. He checked all the records, talked with the parents of the victims, and interviewed all the staff that worked in Ward 4. He installed security cameras and even made a point of learning more about the psychological illness of Munchausen by Proxy Syndrome.

Detectives carefully studied the nursing log and found several pages missing, which added up to twenty-five separate suspicious events. They needed to find something they all had in common and it wasn't long before they found it – nurse Beverley Allitt was on duty on every single occasion. Within three weeks of the investigation, they arrested her.

During her time on police bail, Allitt admitted herself to hospital. She was suffering from urinary infection which required that she be fitted with a catheter. However, the catheter broke quite mysteriously which meant she had to have a longer stay in hospital. The nurses on the ward noticed that, although she seemed quite well during the day, at night time she would complain of feeling unwell, of having a temperature and that her breasts were very painful. It was suspected that she was injecting her own breasts with water, which would cause her to have a higher than normal temperature and painful breasts.

Allitt denied that she had any part in the attacks at the hospital, and that her total aim was to care for the patients. She was certainly very nervous when she was being interviewed and when they searched her home they found parts of the missing nurses' log.

By July 1991 the police felt that their case was sufficiently strong to charge Allitt with murder and in November of that year she was formally charged.

The trial opened on February 15, 1993 at Nottingham Crown Court. Beverley Allitt was painfully thin when she appeared in court, having lost five stone in weight as a result of anorexia. While she had been waiting for the trial she had been held in Rampton Psychiatric Hospital as it was obvious that she had a serious personality disorder. It was while she was there that she returned to an old childhood habit of hurting herself by scalding and eating pieces of broken glass. The trial itself lasted for almost two months, and for that period of time Allitt was actually too ill to attend the hearing. On May 11, 1993, the jury returned their verdict and she was subsequently charged to thirteen life sentences, four on charges of murder and nine for causing grievous bodily harm. Beverley Allitt eventually confessed in October 1993 that she had committed three of the murders and was responsible for six other attacks.

A VERY SICK GIRL

Although Beverley Allitt's physical condition improved her mental health remained frail. She has been diagnosed as suffering from both Munchausen Syndrome and Munchausen by Proxy Syndrome. These conditions are both serious medical conditions that can be confused with hypochondria, and is very often an overlooked or even minimized condition. With hypochondria a patient will believe they are suffering the physical symptoms of illnesses and will frequent doctors' surgeries truly believing they are ill. Munchausen Syndrome, however, is when the patient knows that she or he is not really ill but seeks medical help in order to gain attention, attention that they feel they cannot receive in any other way. In certain cases of Munchausen Syndrome, the sufferer will even inflict harm upon themself in order to make the sickness real enough that medical attention is really required.

Munchausen Syndrome by Proxy, however, is a far more dangerous form of hypochondria, whereby the afflicted person purposely inflicts harm on another person – usually their own child – once again to gain attention from the medical profession. Many children have been severely deformed, and indeed killed, because of this disorder.

The normal cause of Munchausen is severe

abuse or neglect in the childhood of the sufferer. A victim might find themselves in hospital at some point, possibly for the removal of tonsils or appendix, and they find that they received better care and attention there and they did in their own home. In certain people this can release a trigger, ad the sufferer will fall into a pattern where they crave medical attention and will do whatever possible to get admitted back into hospital.

People who suffer from Munchausen by Proxy are very complex and far harder to treat. They are not only attention-seeking, but they are usually apathetic towards the person upon whom they are inflicting the pain. These people are very often isolated and find it hard to form any sort of stable, loving relationship.

Beverley Allitt was indeed a very sick person who should have received psychiatric help at a very young age. However, although it didn't go unnoticed, she never received the help she needed until she actually was arrested.

Kristen Gilbert

Kristen Gilbert worked on Ward C of the Veteran's Affairs Medical Center in Northampton, Massachusetts. When she was on duty it seemed that just too many patients were dying from cardiac arrest.

Kristen Gilbert was born in Fall River and is the oldest of two daughters of Richard and Claudia Strickland. Her friends remembered that she liked to brag that she was related to the famous Lizzie Borden, another Fall River resident who was accused of hacking her father and step-mother to death with a hatchet.

Richard Strickland worked in the electronics business and during Kristen's childhood they moved house on occasions. When she reached eighth grade she transferred from a school outside of Fall River to the Groton-Dunstable Regional School District. She was a bright and popular teenager and she had a talent for both maths and science. She was a superior student who achieved both advanced and honours level courses. In Groton the Stricklands lived on Boston Road, which was a neighbourhood that had large, rambling and isolated houses. Kristen used to babysit for the couple who lived next door, the Moores. They had two young children, and they remembered her as an unremarkable teenager who

457

sometimes talked about her boyfriend.

There is evidence that Kristen had a few boyfriends, one being a boy named John Elsbree who had escorted her to the school prom. He says that she was always smart and friendly, and his relationship with her was based far more on friendship than romance.

Another boyfriend, who wished to remain un-named, remembered Kristen as being an intelligent manipulator, who could work things in her favour and was mentally unstable. When their relation-ship finished, this boyfriend received many phone calls that consisted of heavy breathing and then the caller hung up.

Kristen dated another boy from 1983 to 1985, again someone who didn't want to be named, and he described his relationship with her as very strange. He told investigators that he once found a suicide note from Kristen saying that she had eaten broken glass, but he found her in her room completely unharmed. He also also received haras-sing phone calls which ended with the caller hang-ing up abruptly. When the relationship ended, the boy stated that he bumped into Gilbert by chance and she ripped her fingernails through his cheek for no apparent reason.

Kristen's serious emotional problems seems to have started after she was transferred to Bridge-water State College in her senior year. No one is really sure why Kristen chose to finish her studies more than fifty miles from her home. She appears to have received good grades during her first semester, but their were concerns about her behavioural problems during her second semester. She failed two courses but somehow managed to earn enough credits to graduate.

Kristen had always shown an interest in biology ever since high school, and she subsequently went on to study at Mount Wachusett Community College and Greenfield Community College, where she obtained an associates degree in nursing.

She met Glenn Gilbert in 1985 at Hampton Beach, and they married in 1988. They moved from Greenfield to Florence and started to raise a family. For a while Kristen worked at the Baystate Medical Center in Springfield before moving on to the Veteran's Affairs Medical Center in Massachusetts. She was a popular employee and fellow workmate Carole Osman still has high praise for her today, both as a person and a nurse. She also said that she was a good mother, and was always very caring and attentive to her patients.

HER WORLD FELL APART

It seemed that Kristen's life was in balance until she started to have a relationship with a security officer at the hospital, named James Perrault. James was a possessive lover and told Kristen that she either had to leave her husband and children or the relationship is over. Although Glenn Gilbert was desperate to try and save the marriage, Kristen moved out in December of 1995, giving her husband custody of their two children.

Back at the hospital, Kristen was assigned to work on Ward C. Ward C was a twenty-six bed acute care ward for veterans who were suffering from chronic illnesses. In the autumn of 1995, other nurses who were working on the ward noticed a marked increase in the number of deaths and medical emergencies that seemed to be occurring. Her co-workers seemed to think that Kristen was normal enough but were very suspicious when four patients died and three others had mysterious near-fatal heart failure, while they were all under her care.

On February 17, 1996, shortly after three nurses reported their suspicions to the hospital, Kristen left the hospital due to a shoulder injury. Soon after this an investigation was opened.

To look into the matter of the deaths, the investigators had the bodies exhumed. It was just as the nurses had feared, when the bodies were examined it showed that there were high levels of epinephrine in the tissues. They checked the patients' records and it showed that the drug had not been prescribed and should therefore have not been present in their bodies.

As part of their investigations Gilbert was photographed and handwriting samples were taken from her. She was very upset that she was being treated as one of the suspects and made her feelings known to the investigators. She went to see her former husband, Glenn, saying that he didn't need to answer any questions, but when she learned that he had already co-operated with the authorities, she became upset and very angry. She then disparaged him to several people by belittling him and calling him names. Gilbert also expressed anger and resentment against any of her fellow co-workers who were assisting in the enquiries, and became even more irate when they refused to talk to a private investigator that she had employed.

Kristen talked quite freely with her boyfriend, Perrault, about how her colleagues 'had it in for her' and that 'she wanted everybody here to see what they had done to ruin her life'.

In June of 1996 Perrault tried to end the relationship, but Kristen told a friend of her that if he did dump her she would probably start stalking him. He tried again in August 1996 to break off the relationship, but once again Kristen became angry and tried to blame the break-up on the investigation that was being carried out against her.

In September, of the same year, Perrault told Kristen of an interview that had been arranged in Springfield with the United States Attorney's Office. Gilbert became very upset and begged her boyfriend not to attend. When Perrault made it clear to her that he would do exactly as he wished, she got in her car and drove off in a violent temper. When Perrault returned to his car after the interview, he found that the air had been let out of one of his front tyres.

Over the next few days Perrault's car had eggs thrown at it, the windscreen had been sprayed with paint, there were scratches on the exterior of the car, probably made by keys, and the front number plates had been damaged.

Starting in mid-September Perrault received a number of strange phone calls. When he picked up the phone no-one spoke, but there was the sound of heavy breathing and then the caller would hang up. At first Perrault unsuccessfully tried to trace the calls, but after contacting NYNEX they managed to trace seven of the phone calls to Gilbert's telephone number.

Then on September 26 the Veteran's Affairs Medical Center received an anonymous phone call claiming that there were three bombs in Building One that were about to go off. Gilbert purchased a toy called a 'Talkgirl Jr.' along with some batteries, which the police managed to trace because she had paid with her VISA credit card. The toy was a hand-held voice changer that records a sentence which can be played back at a higher or lower speed than the original recording. Words that are recorded by a woman and played back at a lower speed make them sound like those of a man.

In January 1998 Kristen was convicted with trying to divert the investigation by making hoax phone calls and was sentenced to fifteen months imprisonment.

The police received so many bogus phone calls regarding Gilbert that they eventually resorted to installing a telephone trace device. A friend of Kristen's told the police that on one occasion she found her in a confused state reading a Hemlock Book on how to help terminally ill patients commit suicide. When Gilbert's apartment was searched in October of that year they found a book entitled *Final Exit*, which again discusses suicide issues, and a suicide letter dated September 22, 1996.

It read, '. . . over the last few months I have changed. I was a fairly likeable, independent

462

woman that ended up a weak, dependent, unlikeable person who can't make it through two hours, never mind a whole day, without crying. I've become completely unpredictable, impulsive and self-destructive – I really don't like this person. . .'

Throughout the summer of 1996 Kristen Gilbert was admitted to Holyoke Hospital, Cooley Dickinson Hospital, Baystate Medical Center and Arbour Hospital for periods ranging from one to about ten days. Gilbert's lawyers requested that she be examined by a psychiatrist and his report stated that she was suffering from an adjustment disorder which was brought on by emotional stress. The factors contributing to her distress were – the recent death of her grandfather, custody issues relating to her divorce, problems with her boyfriend and finally the trauma of a murder investigation.

THE FINAL SENTENCE

Kristen Gilbert was tried and convicted of three first-degree murder charges and one second-degree murder count. She was also convicted of attempting to kill two other patients, who luckily survived.

The same jury had to reconvene at a later date to consider whether the thirty-three-year-old woman should be executed or sentenced to life imprisonment. Since the crimes had been committed on Federal territory, the punishment could easily have been execution, especially as the prosecutor portrayed her as being a cruel and heartless woman who preyed on dependent and highly vulnerable victims.

When the sentence was eventually read out Gilbert hung her head and wept quietly, she was to spend the rest of her life behind bars.

Why did Kristen Gilbert inject her patients with overdoses of epinephrine or adrenaline, sending their hearts racing totally out of control? To gain the attention she was so desperate for, especially from her lover, James Perrault. She loved the thrill of medical emergencies and she knew by provoking these emergencies she could respond and attract the attention of Perrault, who worked there as a hospital guard. On one occasion, during an emergency procedure, she was seen to be flirting with Perrault and pressing her body suggestively against him.

Throughout her hearings Kristen was painted as volatile, out-of-control and needing repeated psychiatric care. The attorney called the murders barbaric and morally repugnant, and described some of the victims' suffering. One was burned by defibrillators, he told the court, while the son of another victim testified that his father sat up in bed and cried, 'I don't want to die!' Kristen Gilbert did indeed have a very sick mind and even though she survived the sentence of death, hopefully she will be tucked away behind bars with no chance of parole.

Marie Noe

*Over a period of eighteen years, Marie Noe would
give birth to ten children, but only one of these
would ever see its first birthday.*

Marie Noe was at one time considered the un-
luckiest mother alive. Marie had one child
after another, ten in total, and every single one of
them died. For each death there was an investigation and for eight of them the verdict was the same
– SIDS, or sudden infant death syndrome.

THE BABIES

The first baby to be born was Richard Allen Noe.
He was born on March 7, 1949 and weighed 7 lb
11 oz. He died one month later. Marie told the
police that she had left her baby sleeping peacefully, but when her husband returned home from
work he found Richard dead in his crib. No autopsy was performed, and death was attributed to
congenital heart failure.

The second baby was born on September 8,
1950, Elizabeth Mary. She lived for five months.
Marie told the police that she found the baby in
her crib vomiting milk and blood. This time an
autopsy was performed, but it is not evident
whether she was actually examined internally. The

cause of death was given as bronchopneumonia.

Baby number three, Jacqueline, was born on April 23, 1952. She only survived twenty-one days. Once more Marie told the investigators that she had found her baby in her crib blue in the face and lying in vomit. An autopsy was performed and the coroner ruled that she had choked on her own vomit.

Arthur Junior, was born on April 23, 1955. When he was twelve days old Marie Noe took him to hospital saying that he was having problems trying to breathe. He was found to be a healthy baby and discharged. The very next day he was dead. Cause of death ruled as bronchopneumonia.

On February 24, 1958, Constance was born. Once again Marie took her baby to the hospital saying that she was having breathing difficulties. She was discharged as healthy, and was found dead in her crib two days later by the father. Cause of death – undetermined.

Baby Letitia was delivered stillborn at thirty-nine weeks on August 25, 1959.

Baby number seven was Mary Lee, born on June 19, 1962. After she was born the baby was kept in hospital for one month under observation. Once she was at home, Marie called the doctor out on repeated occasions saying that the child 'was getting on her nerves' with constant crying. Mary Lee died on January 4, 1963, Marie saying that she found the child turning blue. She was already three months pregnant with her next baby at the time. Cause of death – undetermined.

Theresa was born prematurely in June 1963, but only survived for six hours.

Catherine Ellen was born on December 3, 1964 and kept in hospital for three months for observation. Marie complained of difficulty in feeding her and a nurse overheard her say, 'You better take this or I'll kill you!' when she was feeding her at the hospital. In August 1965, Marie reported that she had found the baby with a dry-cleaning bag over her head, but luckily she was not seriously injured. She was hospitalized on two other occasions when Marie reported that the baby had stopped breathing, but was released both times and told that she was healthy. She was found dead in her crib on February 25, 1966, a short three months after her first birthday. Cause of death – undetermined. Sadly, this was the baby that survived the longest.

Arthur Joseph was born on July 28, 1967. Once more Arthur was hospitalized for two months for observation. Marie took him to hospital again when she reported that he had turned blue and again, just five weeks later, when the mother reported that she had found a cat lying on his face. Arthur was found dead in his crib in January 1968. Cause of death – undetermined.

After the birth of Little Arty, as he was called, Marie Noe received a hysterectomy due to medical reasons, so that was the end of spell of short-lived births. All of her babies were dead within months of their birth and yet the results of the autopsies were inconclusive. There was no evidence of any form of violence or foul play, but of course it is possible for an adult to smother a defenceless child without leaving any mark.

HOW COULD IT HAVE HAPPENED?

So between the years 1949 and 1968, Marie and Arthur Noe had ten babies, and none of them survived. Two undeniably died from natural causes, but what about the others? Mrs. Noe was certainly at home alone with the children when she claimed they died in the sleep. I suppose the local police and doctors all presumed that it wasn't possible for a woman to kill her own children.

Of course there were many people who suspected Marie Noe of having killed her own babies, but forensic testing was not as up-to-date as the current methods, and there was no substantial proof to charge either Mr. or Mrs. Noe. They were both questioned at the time and given polygraph tests, which they both passed. The police were powerless and they had to let them go.

However, it was not the police who broke the story, it was a book on SIDS that was entitled *The Death of Innocents*, which profiled the Noe case. It caught the attention of a reporter named Stephen Fried who worked for the *Philadelphia Magazine*, and he began his own investigations into the deaths. In January 1988, Fried took his findings to the police homicide unit and the head of the special investigations squad became so intrigued that he decided to re-open the long-closed case.

The police brought Marie Noe in for questioning but not until forty years later, in April 1998. Under repeated questioning she eventually cracked and admitted to murdering her own children. She told the police that she had used pillows to kill at least three of her children, but when asked why, she could give no reason. 'All I can figure is that I'm ungodly sick,' she told the detectives.

So it was in 1999 that seventy-year-old Marie Noe stood up in court and confessed to killing eight of her ten infant children by smothering them to death.

At her bail hearing in August 1999, the district attorney called her 'as much a mass murderer as Ted Bundy', but this still didn't stop the judge from feeling sorry for the old lady and he allowed a plea bargain between the prosecutor and the defence attorney. Marie Noe was given twenty years probation with the first five years spent in home confinement monitored by an ankle bracelet and psychiatric analysis. She has a compulsory meeting once a month with a court-appointed psychiatrist to try and figure out her motive for the murders.

Whether this is justice for what she has done is down to the individual to decide, but one thing I would like to add is that this so-called sweet old lady did not shed a single tear throughout any of the court hearings, or indeed the interviews. Noe did admit to the psychiatrists that she would like to confront her responsibility for the deaths of her children. She also said she wanted to co-operate with medical science to explore why this type of tragedy occurs. She also said she would like to assist doctors who are helping mothers who may be prone to infanticide.

I think what this case really points out though is

society's unwillingness to believe that mothers are
truly capable of killing of their own babies.

Elizabeth Bathory

*Here is the story of the most bloodthirsty
vampiress of all time. She slaughtered six hundred
innocent women so that she could improve
her complexion and maintain her failing
grasp on youth . . .*

Erzsébet (Elizabeth) Bathory was born in
Hungary in 1560, around a hundred years
after the death of Vlad the Impaler. Her parents,
George and Ann Bathory belonged to one of the
oldest and possibly richest families in Hungary.
Her cousin was the then Prime Minister of the
country, while her uncle Stephan later became
King of Poland. However, besides her rich and
famous relatives, there was one very strange side
to the family. One of her uncles was known to be a
devil-worshipper, while other members of the
family were mentally insane and perverted.

Elizabeth was raised as royalty and was a fit
and active child. She was described as quite beautiful with delicate features, a slender build and she
was quite tall for her age. However, her personality
did match her beautiful image. She considered her
most redeeming feature to be her glorious, creamy-
white complexion and she was very vindictive to

anyone who did not agree with her and pay her compliments.

At the age of fifteen, Elizabeth was 'married off' to twenty-six-year-old Count Ferencz Nasdasdy. The marriage was purely for political gain, and the Count added her surname to his, so that she did not lose her royal name. After the marriage, Elizabeth became the lady of the Castle of Czejthe, the Count's home, which was situated deep in the mountains of Carpathia (now central Romania), an area known as Transylvania. The castle was surrounded by a village of simple peasants and rolling agricultural landscape, with a background of the snowy-topped Carpathians.

Her husband, the Count, was a brave and daring soldier and spent a lot of time away from his castle fighting. He later earned a reputation as the 'Black Hero of Hungary. The castle was typical of its day, a cold, gloomy and damp place and life was too boring for a very active, bright teenager. While her husband was away, an old maid by the name of Dorothea Szentes, nicknamed Dorka, introduced her to the occult. Elizabeth started to invite people back to the castle – people that believed in rather peculiar and sinister arts. Among them were those who proclaimed to be witches, sorcerers, seers, wizards, alchemists and other devil-worshippers. She was thrilled by their stories and they taught her their sinister crafts in intimate detail. Elizabeth was fascinated when Dorka starting talking about inflicting pain on people, and, with Dorka as her assistant, Elizabeth began the task of disciplining her female servants.

Her husband used a horrid device of torture on prisoners that he captured, and this was a clever articulated claw-like pincer which was made of hardened silver. These pincers were attached to a stout whip which would tear and tip at the flesh of the victim to such a degree that even the Count, who was known to be a cruel man, abandoned the apparatus in disgust in the cellar of his castle.

Elizabeth discovered the apparatus in the cellar and made the underground room into a torture chamber. Soon she turned the Castle Czejthe into a pure place of evil. She always managed to find some sort of excuse to punish her poor servant girls. She would take them down to her chamber, strip them naked and then using her husband's heinous silver claws, would indulge herself in the pleasures of flagellation. Another favourite pastime of hers was to stick pins in various sensitive parts on the victim's body, such as under the fingernails. The more shrill the victim's screams became and the more blood that flowed, the more exquisite and orgasmic her amusement became. She always like to whip her subjects on the front so that she could watch with glee as their faces contorted in agonizing pain.

THE DEATH OF THE COUNT

In the year 1600 Count Ferencz died and this is when Elizabeth's real period of terror began. Elizabeth started to dream about taking a lover, but when she looked in the mirror at her once beautiful face, she saw that her once 'angelic' complexion had long since faded. She had now reached the age of forty-three. After her husband's death, the first thing she did was to send her hated mother-in-law away from the Castle. She wanted peace to pursue the activities that gave her most pleasure, but the ultimate experience was still to come.

Maintaining her youth and vitality became her total driving force. She was driven by vanity, sexual desire, and the fact that if she lost her youth she would have nothing. Her mood became darker and darker as the days went by and then one day it happened. A young chambermaid accidentally pulled Elizabeth's hair one day while she was grooming it. The Countess was infuriated and slapped the girl's face so hard that blood spurted from her nose and splashed onto Elizabeth's hand. Elizabeth noticed that where the servant's blood had touched her skin, it had taken on a new fresh, youthful appearance. Immediately she called her two faithful servants, Ujvary and Dorka to undress the hapless girl and, holding her arms over a large vat, they proceeded to cut her arteries. When the young girl was dead, drained of all her blood, Elizabeth removed her own clothes and stepped into the vat. She now knew that she had found the secret of eternal youth and she would be beautiful and strong once more.

Over the period of ten years, Elizabeth's trusted helpers provided her with young, beautiful virgins from the neighbouring villages, luring them with the promise of a job at the castle. The young girls would be mutilated and then killed and Elizabeth would then bathe luxuriously in their blood. If the victim was especially pretty, the countess would drink their blood believing that she would gain some sort of inner beauty.

After a few years Elizabeth began to realise that the blood of simple peasant girls was having very little effect on the quality of her complexion. She knew she needed better quality blood and she turned her attention to the virgin daughters of the aristocracy. In the early 17th century in Transylvania it was the tradition of the aristocracy to have their daughters educated into the appropriate social graces and etiquettes and Elizabeth saw her chance. She established an academy in the castle and offered to take twenty-five girls at a time to finish their education. But what the parents didn't realise was quite how finished their education would be.

Assisted by her faithful servant Dorka these poor students were tortured and bled just as the poor peasant girls before them. However, Elizabeth was now becoming careless and, unlike the peasant girls from the village, girls of noble birth were not so easy to make disappear. During one particular frenzy of lust and excitement, four of the girls' bodies were thrown from the walls of the castle. They realised their error too late, for the villagers had already collected the bodies and the girls had been identified. The rumours spread far and wide about the horrors that took place at Castle Czejthe, and the news soon reached the ears of the Hungarian Emperor. The Emperor ordered Elizabeth's own cousin, Count Cuyorgy Thurzo, who was the Governor of the province, to go and raid the castle. On December 30, 1610, a band of soldiers led by Thurzo, raided the castle under the cover of night. They could not believe what they found and were horrified by the horrendous sights. As they entered the main hall a girl was lying dead on the floor, completely drained of blood. Another girl, who had had her body pierced, was still alive and writhing in pain. When they went down into the dungeon they found several girls in prison cells, some of whom had already been tortured, while below the castle they found the bodies of around fifty dead girls.

The extent of the horror was passed back to the Emperor, Matthias II, who immediately ordered that the Countess be placed on public trial. However, her aristocratic status did not allow her to be arrested and so, due to the fear of her slipping out of their hands, parliament passed a new Act to reverse this privileged status. Elizabeth was brought before a formal hearing in 1610.

During the trial, which took place in 1611, a register was found in the castle which contained the names of around 650 victims. A complete transcript was made of the trial and it can still be viewed today in Hungary. Throughout the hearing Elizabeth admitted to nothing. Dorka and Elizabeth's other three accomplices were burned alive but the Countess, due to the reason of her noble birth, could not be executed.

Elizabeth Bathory did however receive her due punishment. She was sentenced to spend the remainder of his life imprisoned in her own castle. Stonemasons were sent to the castle to wall up the windows and doors to the bedchamber with the Countess still inside. Here she would spend her last days with only a small opening left for food to be passed through to her.

In the year 1614, four years after she was walled into her castle, one of the Countess's gaolers found her food untouched. After peeking through the small aperture he found Elizabeth lying face down on the floor. The 'Blood Countess' or 'Female Dracula' was finally dead at the age of fifty-four.

POSTSCRIPT

Throughout the whole trial Elizabeth Bathory was never heard to utter even a single word of remorse or regret. One thing that was discovered about the Countess, though, that could possibly have attributed to her horrific behaviour, is that she suffered from very violent seizures when she was around four or five years old. They were not attributed to epilepsy but were more likely to have been some other kind of neurological disorder.

There are some connections between the Bathory family and the Dracula family. Prince Steven Bathory had helped Dracula regain his throne in 1476 and also a Dracula fief, Castle Fagaras, became a Bathory possession during Elizabeth's life. Another connection was that both families had a dragon design on their family crests.

Lizzie Borden

Lizzie Borden took an axe
And gave her mother forty whacks
When she saw what she had done
She gave her father forty-one

It is a rhyme that many of us learned when we were at school but do you really know anything about the real Lizzie Borden?

Lizzie Borden was born on July 19, 1860 in an area of Massachusetts called Fall River. Her father, Andrew, at the age of seventy was one of the richest men in Fall River, but had a reputation for being thrifty. He was a white-haired man with rather a stern image. For the first two years of her life Lizzie had a happy, normal childhood, but then a series of life-altering events started to happen.

Lizzie's mother, Sarah, suffered from a uterine congestion and died in March 1863. Andrew was then left on his own to bring up little Lizzie and her older sister, Emma. Two years after the death of his wife, Andrew remarried. Abby Durfee was a short, heavy-set and exceptionally shy woman. Gossip was rife around Fall River that he had only taken Abby as his wife to provide himself with a housekeeper and babysitter, but it does appear that he did genuinely care for her.

However, the relationship between Abby and

the prosecution called witnesses to testify that Andrew was about to make a new will leaving half of his estate to Abby and the remainder to his two daughters. Lizzie had also been seen trying to buy 10 cents worth of prussic acid from a local drugstore, with the possible assumption that had she been allowed to buy it she could have used it to poison her parents.

The defence only took two days to present their case, calling on witnesses to testify that they had seen a strange man in the vicinity of the Bordon's house. They also used Lizzie's sister, Emma, to confirm that there really was no motive.

On June 20, 1893, Lizzie was found not guilty on all three counts, but she would remain guilty in the eyes of the public for ever. Five weeks after the trial Emma, and the spurned Lizzie, bought a house in a fashionable area of Fall River. Lizzie decided to change her name and became known as Lizbeth, the name she used for the rest of her life.

Eight years later Lizzie met an actress named Nance O'Neill. She soon moved into their house and Lizzie started to throw wild parties for her new friends from the theatre. Emma, who was offended by her sister's new lifestyle, moved out and the two girls never spoke again.

Lizzie Borden died on June 1, 1927 after a long illness resulting from surgery to her gall bladder. Emma died nine days later from a fall down some stairs. They were both buried in the family plot next to their father, stepmother and a third sister who had died early in childhood.

The case remains unsolved to this day.

Velma Barfield

Velma Barfield made headline news when she became the first person to be executed in America since 1962 and the first since the reintroduction of the death penalty in 1976.

Born on October 23, 1932, in Carolina, Margie Velma Barfield was the oldest girl and second of a large family of nine children. Her father, Murphy Bullard was a farmer, while her mother Lillie stayed at home and looked after the children.

The family were extremely poor and lived in an unpainted wooden house which had no electricity or running water. The conditions were extremely cramped and when the Great Depression got worse, Murphy found that farming did not give him enough income to support his ever-growing family. He managed to find work in a sawmill as a logger which was owned by a man named Clarence Bunch, and it was through him that the family managed to move into a small house which was closer to town. It was here that the couple's third child was born.

Murphy Bullard was a dominating man who liked to drink and was known for his temper. Lillie on the other hand was submissive and always felt as though she had to tread carefully in her own home to avoid the backlash of her husband's anger. It was always Murphy who disciplined the children and he often handed out beatings as a punishment for insubordination.

When Velma was seven years old, in 1939, she started school, and at first she thoroughly enjoyed it. She was an intelligent child and managed to achieve good grades and received much praise from her teachers. School was also a blessed relief from the overcrowded home in which she lived and also the fear of her father's strap against her backside.

However, it wasn't long before Velma started to stand out from the rest of her schoolmates. She wasn't able to wear the same pretty clothes that the other girls did, and she was often teased for her shabby appearance and her rather plain lunch boxes. Velma started to hide away from the other children, too embarrassed to eat her lunch in front of them. Next she took to stealing change out of her father's pockets so that she could buy some sweets from a shop which was just across the road from her school. Her stealing became more serious when she was discovered to have stolen $80 from an elderly neighbour, for which she received a very severe beating. This appeared to have taught her a lesson as there is no record of any more stealing when she was a young child.

As she grew older, Velma was assigned more and more chores at home to assist her father with the farm and also her mother with her siblings. She resented the amount of work that her parents made her do, and in her heart she felt they didn't really love her they just looked at her as their slave.

Velma's life was not always bad though for their father could also be loving and organized many games for them to play. Sometimes he would arrange a baseball game, or perhaps take them swimming to the local pond. She got on really well with her father most of the time – and some might say perhaps too well. Sadly, as she started to develop into a young lady her father allegedly entered her bedroom and raped her.

When Velma started attending high school she no longer achieved the good grades she achieved in elementary school, but she did have one love, and that was basketball. She joined the school team and loved to play at every opportunity. Then her mother told her that she would have to give up playing because she needed her help at home. Lillie had recently given birth to twins and she was finding the housework too much to handle on her own. Once again Velma felt as though she were the underdog and just being used.

While Velma was at high school she met a boy named Thomas Burke and they developed a mutual crush on one another. She asked her father if she might be allowed to meet Thomas outside of school, but he was adamant that there would be no dating until she was sixteen. Her sixteenth birthday came and went and still her father would not allow his daughter to go out on a date. He placed restrictions on his daughter and told her that she had to be home by 10 p.m. and must always have someone with her, although she was angry with his rules she went along with it because she didn't want to be on the receiving end of his temper.

Thomas proposed to Velma when she was seventeen which caused a dreadful argument with her father. Eventually Murphy Bullard broke down and cried, something which Velma had never experienced before as he was so traditionally masculine and not one to show his feelings.

Velma and Thomas left school shortly after they got married. Thomas took several jobs, in a cotton mill, as a farm labourer and then driving a delivery truck. Velma did work for a while in a drug store but Thomas didn't like her working and so she left.

On December 15, 1951, Velma had her first child, Ronald Thomas. His sister, Kim, was born on September 3, 1953. Velma was a loving mother and became very involved in her children's upbringing. When they started school she was always around prepared to take part in any activity, in fact she became known as the woman who could always be relied upon to give a helping hand. As the family were a little short of cash, Velma took another job, this time with the approval of her husband. She took a night-shift job at a textile factory. Thomas also became a delivery driver for Pepsi-Cola and eventually the couple had enough money to move a more comfortable house in Parkton.

For many years they were a happy and devoted family. In 1963, Velma had to undergo a hysterectomy due to medical complications. The couple were not distraught as they were happy with the family they already had, but for some reason the surgery had a drastic effect on Velma. She became exceptionally nervous, was often depressed and started to snap at the slightest thing. She felt cheated that she could no longer bear children, and that for some reason made her less of a woman. Apart from the mental problems she also suffered physical problems including very severe back pain.

Thomas Burke decided he wanted to join the Christian organization, the Jaycees, and went to their weekly meetings leaving his wife sitting at home minding the children. She hated the fact that he was away from home, and hated even more the fact that he had started drinking. Velma was a firm teetotaller and became very upset when she discovered that Thomas was meeting up with his male friends for a few beers.

In 1965, Thomas had a car accident which rendered him unconscious. He suffered from concussion which left him with with severe headaches. Velma was convinced that the accident has been caused because he had been drinking, and this became almost a daily issue. The children became disturbed by all the constant shouting and verbal abuse that they threw at each other, and became frightened that it would end in violence.

Thomas was not prepared to let his wife try and control his life and he continued to drink. In 1967, he was arrested for drunken driving and as a result lost his licence and his job with Pepsi-Cola. This brought an air of depression over the entire household, so much so that the children did not want to bring their friends back to the house for fear of them hearing their parents fighting. The constant tension at home was taking its toll on Velma and she began to drastically lose weight. One day Ronnie came home from school to find his mother lying unconscious on the kitchen floor. He was able to rouse her but insisted that she paid a visit to the hospital to have a check up. The doctors, on seeing the poor state of health that she was in, suggested that she remained in the hospital for a week. She was given vitamins and sedatives, and given a prescription before she left for a mild tranquillizer, librium.

Velma began to like the feeling she got when she took the tranquillizers and starting to take more than she had been prescribed. She also visited another doctor and got him to prescribe valium, and from then on she would accumulate a stockpile of tranquillizers from various different physicians. She still worried constantly about her husband's constant drinking, while the children and Thomas fretted about her overuse of prescribed medicines. She became drowsy and a little incoherent, almost as if she too was suffering from too much alcohol.

In the year 1969 their house caught fire and the only person at home at the time was Thomas. Both the children were at school and Velma said she was coming back from the laundromat when she found the house in flames. Thomas Burke was taken to hospital but later died of smoke inhalation. When Velma was told about her husband's death at the hospital she was completely devastated to the point of collapse.

HUSBAND NUMBER TWO

Not long after Thomas's death Velma started to date a man named Jennings Barfield. Barfield had taken early retirement due to ill health and he suffered from diabetes, emphysema and heart disease. He was a widow and lost his wife around the time Velma had lost her husband, so they were probably brought together through grief.

The romance developed and they were married on August 23, 1970 and after the wedding Velma moved into the small house in Fayetteville, that Barfield shared with his teenage daughter, nancy. It wasn't long before the honeymoon period was over and the marriage was having problems. Jennings was very worried about his wife addiction to the prescription drugs, and on one occasion had to take her to hospital in a semi-conscious state. The doctor on duty said that she had over-dosed on the drugs and the couple decided to separate for a trial period. For a while Velma seemed to be under control but then she slipped back to her old ways and had to be readmitted to hospital with another overdose. The couple decided at this point that the marriage was really over and thought that divorce would be the best thing for both of them.

However, it never actually got that far because Jennings died on March 21, 1971, with what they presumed was a heart attack. Once again Velma was on her own and she was not coping very well. She would spend much of her time in bed dosing herself up with more and more pills in the hope that they would alleviate her pain and loneliness. To add to her utter despair, Velma's son, Ronnie, enlisted in the military. She hated being separated from her beloved son. Disaster struck again in the form of a fire, and again Velma's house was destroyed. Velma was devastated and couldn't understand why it kept happening to her, and again, along with her daughter, she moved back in with Murphy and Lillie Bullard.

Velma got more and more depressed and she was unable to hold down a job for any length of time due to her dependence on drugs. The final straw was when Murphy Bullard died of lung cancer at the age of sixty-one. This was when she reached rock bottom and decided that life was no longer worth living. As if losing her son to the army was not bad enough, Ronnie then broke the news to his mother that he planned to get married. Velma did not take the news well and it took Ronnie a lot of persuading that his love for a wife would not take away his love for his mother.

In March 1972 Velma was arrested for forging a prescription to which she pleaded guilty. She escaped with a suspended sentence and a fine. Then she got the news she had been waiting for for so long – her son was being discharged from the army. During his absence the relationship between Velma and her mother had deteriorated and they now had constant arguments. Lillie was disturbed about her daughter's over-use of drugs and Velma was not prepared to take any orders from her mother, so when Ronnie returned the atmosphere was rather taut. In the summer of 1974 Lillie became ill with dreadful stomach cramps and vomiting. Her condition deteriorated so much that Velma had to drive her mother to the hospital, but the doctors were unable to diagnose the cause of the sudden sickness. After a few days she recovered and Velma brought her back home.

Things went well for a while and they enjoyed a nice family Christmas without any traumas. However, Lillie was troubled by a letter that she had received from a finance company telling her that the repayments were overdue on her car. She told her son that she owned the car outright and that she didn't have any finance to pay on it. Her son said it was probably just someone that had got their paperwork in a mess and that she was not to worry about it.

A couple of days later Lillie became really sick again, the same symptoms as before but this time she was vomiting blood. Velma immediately phoned her brother who was appalled to see the condition his mother was in. Velma rode in the back of the ambulance with her mother, but sadly she died two hours after arriving at hospital.

In 1975 Velma had another brush with the law and this time she served three months of a six month prison sentence for forging cheques. When she was released from prison Velma decided to take work as a carer for sick, elderly people. In 1976 she went to live with Montgomery and Dollie Edwards. Montgomery was ninety-four years old and bedridden. He had lost both his legs and his eye sight to diabetes and he was unable to do anything for himself. His wife, eighty-four-year-old Dollie, was in better shape than her husband but was recovering from cancer and had had to have a colostomy. For a while all went well and Velma seemed to have settled into a nice routine. However, tensions soon started to surface and Dollie didn't consider that Velma was pulling her weight. Velma accused her of being too fussy and their rows got more frequent and more heated as time went by.

Montgomery died in January 1977, but although the two ladies were still arguing, Velma stayed on and took care of Dollie. Saturday, February 26, and Dollie was not feeling at all well. She had violent stomach cramps, vomiting and diarrhoea and she told her stepson that she thought she might have flu. Preston, her stepson, came to visit her the next night and was horrified to find her so pale and weak and told Velma that he felt she should be in hospital. They called an ambulance and after receiving treatment in the outpatients department, she was sent back home. The next day she got even worse and had to return to hospital and by Tuesday evening she was dead.

Once more Velma was without a home and a livelihood and she took another job looking after a frail old couple, eighty-year-old farmer John Henry Lee and his seventy-six-year-old wife, Record. The position suited Velma as she had freedom to go to church services and once again she had a nice house to live in. Once more problems started to surface due to Record's constant talking which got on Velma's nerves. Also the elderly couple were prone to arguing and Velma

493

did not like to be around when they had their fights. There was one incident when the police were called because Record had discovered a cheque that she knew she hadn't endorsed. The case came to nothing and then on April 27, John Henry became sick. Once again he suffered from severe pain in his stomach, vomiting and diarrhoea. His condition became so serious that he had to be rushed to hospital, but the medics were mystified by his sudden illness. After four days he returned home but throughout the rest of the month he continued to be sick. The family felt they were very lucky to have Velma looking after their elderly parents and thought she was a sweet and caring lady.

John Henry took a turn for the worse and was taken back to hospital, a very sick and dehydrated man. He died on June 4.

By 1970 Velma was in another relationship with a widower by the name of Stuart Taylor. Stuart was a farmer and considered himself very lucky to have the now forty-six-year-old Velma as his girlfriend. Velma's children were a little shocked that she had moved in with a man out of wedlock, but Stuart had discovered that she had a criminal record for forgery and that he did not want to take her for his legal wife. Stuart was not a very religious man but he was quite happy that Velma was a devoutly pious Christian and went along with her to some of her meetings. It was at one of these Christian meetings that Stuart started to feel unwell. He was wracked with pain and he was suffering from nausea and diarrhoea. Back at home his condition deteriorated and Velma phoned his daughter to tell her that he she was worried about him. Velma also went to see one of her boyfriend's best friends, Sonny Johnson, and told him how worried she was, so much so that he came over and visited his friend. He found Stuart in a very weak state and was asked by his friend to look after his pigs until he had recovered from the flu. Stuart got worse and worse until eventually Velma drove him to the hospital. The physician at the hospital described the condition gastritis, gave him some medicine, and then sent him home.

Stuart never recovered and was rushed back to the hospital, where he died about an hour later. In the waiting room were Stuart's children along with Velma, his caring girlfriend who had nursed him through this dreadful illness. The doctor said he was puzzled by the man's sudden illness and suggested they perform an autopsy. They turned to Velma to see what she thought and she replied, 'If you don't do it, you'll always wonder'.

THE WARNING

Ronnie felt sad for his mother because he felt that anyone she got close to in her life seems to die. Meanwhile a detective from the Lumberton Police Station had received a strange telephone call. It was from a woman who was crying and difficult to understand, but what he could make out was that she was trying to warn them of something. The words he could decipher sounded like: 'Murder! . .

. I know who did it! You've got to stop her! You've got to stop her!' The policeman just thought it was a crank but suggested that she call again when he was at the police station. As he suspected no-one called and he just got on with his daily duties. Then the phone rang, it was the same voice but this time she was a lot clearer and coherent. The caller admitted that she had no proof but that she knew two people had been murdered by Velma Barfield, one was her boyfriend Stuart Thomas and the other her very own mother. When the policeman asked her how she knew this, she replied: 'Because, Velma is my sister.'

The policeman was totally baffled by the call but decided to phone the local hospital to see if anyone had died over the weekend. When the answer came back, yes a man named Stuart Taylor, he knew he had to take the matter further. He asked how the man had died, but the hospital said they had not had the results of the tests carried out at the autopsy back. When the results eventually came through it revealed that Stuart Taylor had died from arsenic poisoning. The authorities then decided to take a look at the death certificates of several other people who had been close to Velma who had subsequently died. They discovered with rather peculiar regularity that the cause of death was given as 'gastroenteritis'. The police were now certain that they were not just dealing with a single murder, but a serial poisoner.

Velma Barfield was arrested and subsequently confessed to the murder of Stuart Taylor and several others. Her son was totally dumbstruck and couldn't believe that the caring, loving woman that had looked after him as a child, was now a cold-blooded killer.

LIFE ON DEATH ROW

When her case came to trial, Velma's defence was a plea of insanity. At the hearing she showed no signs of remorse or caring for her victims. She told the court that she had mishandled money from her victims, not meaning to kill them, but just to make them ill so that she could nurse them back to health whilst looking for another job. Throughout the trial she was cold and callous.

Some of the physicians who had been treating Stuart testified that they had also treated Velma and prescribed medications for her. Their testimony showed that she was on drugs that could have badly impaired her judgment and were addictive.

Velma took the stand in her own defence. Her attorney thought it would be a good idea to let her explain her own confused thinking to the jury. She did well on direct examination, saying that she had given her boyfriend poison to make him sick but did not intend to kill him. She also admitted to extensive use of various medications, of combining a wide variety of drugs, and that she was totally dependent on them. She also admitted forging cheques because she was addicted to drugs and could not pay for them out of her own limited resources.

The jury were not impressed by the evidence

provided by the defence and they came back with a verdict of guilty of first-degree murder. Then it found the "aggravating circumstances" to recommend the death penalty. Judge McKinnon then said that due to the 'aggravating circumstances' her punishment would be execution.

While on death row at Raleigh, Velma managed to come off the drugs she had been addicted to for so many years. She expressed remorse for the years that the drugs had blurred her judgement and destroyed her moral reasoning. She was, however, unable to explain exactly why she had killed.

She became a 'born again' Christian and during the six years she was on death row took to counselling other female inmates. There were many appeals to try and save her life, but these were all declined. Gradually Velma began to accept her fate and told her attorney to drop all appeals and that she wanted to 'die with dignity'. She believed that when she was finally executed it would be her 'gateway to heaven'.

Velma Barfield, a serial killer, was executed by lethal injection and pronounced dead at 2.15 a.m. on November 2, 1984.

CONCLUSION

So can we say without doubt that Velma Barfield was a monster and a serial killer with no remorse for her deeds? Or, was she just a poor demented soul whose brain had been so completely bewildered by drugs that all she could think about was how to get the money to finance her addiction?

Probably the answer is somewhere between the two.

Only two women, Rosanna Phillips in 1943 and Bessie May Smith a year later, have ever been executed in North Carolina. There are currently four more women waiting on death row there.

Mary Ann Cotton

Mary Ann Cotton is regarded as Britain's greatest female mass murderer. She murdered four husbands, a lover and several children.

Mary Ann Robson was born in October 1832 in the small English village of Low Moorsley, County Durham. Mary's parents were both under twenty when they were married, and her father hardly earned enough money to support his family as a miner. Mary herself had rather an unhappy childhood, being a shy girl who found it very difficult to make friends. When she was only eight the family moved home, and, along with her brother Robert, had to start at a new school. Mary found this really hard due to her shyness, and to make it even worse her father was killed in a mining accident shortly after the move. Mary was only fourteen at the time and lived with her mother for a further two years. Life in Victorian times was never easy unless you had a good income, but it must have been especially hard for a widow and two young children. The shadow of the workhouse and the separation from her mother must have had a lasting impact on the young Mary, and it is around this time that she started to suffer from nightmares. Mary's mother eventually remarried in an effort to remain out of the workhouse and probably to put a roof over her family's head. Mary did not like her new stepfather but she did like the fact that he had a good salary and they could afford things that they had never had before.

When she reached the age of sixteen, deciding that she no longer wanted to put up with the harsh discipline inflicted by her stepfather, Mary took up an apprenticeship as a dressmaker.

At the age of twenty Mary married William Mowbray at St. Andrew's Church in Newcastle-upon-Tyne. William was a timekeeper whose work took him to various faraway towns. After a couple of years in Newcastle-upon-Tyne the couple moved south to Cornwall where Mowbray took up a job as a nanny. William already had four children by a previous marriage and Mary produced another five. By the time they had returned to County Durham just five years later, four sons had died in infancy, victims of gastric fever – or so it was believed. The fifth child, this time a girl, succumbed to the same sickness and died a short while later.

Next the family moved to Sunderland where two more children were to die, as did William Mowbray himself. He died quite suddenly from an unexpected bout of diarrhoea, having only just taken out a sizeable life insurance. He had insured himself and all his children with the Prudential, and as a result, Mary Ann collected the sum of £35. No-one seemed suspicious about all the family deaths and this was probably due to the fact they moved around and the deaths happened in different areas. Also infant mortality in the nineteenth century was commonplace and it would not be unusual for a child to die of gastric fever.

Mary moved on again and made a fresh start at Seaham with another new husband, George Ward. She took a job as a nurse at Sunderland Infirmary which is where she met George who was one of the patients. It wasn't long before George died prematurely of gastric fever at the age of thirty-three and Mary Ann helped herself to another insurance payout.

Mary did not remain on her own for very long before she took up a new responsibility as housekeeper to a man named John Robinson, a shipyard foreman, and his five children. Mary quickly became pregnant by John and six months later they were married. But somehow tragedy seemed to follow Mary around because three of John's children had died, as well as Mary Ann's remaining child by her first husband. She had two children by John Robinson, one of whom died at birth, and she suggested to her husband that it might be a good idea to take out a life insurance. However, he told her that he thought her motives were sinister as he already suspected that she had been poisoning the children. Not only that he told her he was fed up with her running up huge debts and Mary, fed up with being castigated, helped herself to his savings and fled. She left behind one child, who had luckily survived her murderous ways.

She went to stay with her mother for a while, who died very suddenly shortly after Mary's arrival, and her daughter inherited all her furniture.

In 1870 Mary was introduced to a man named Frederick Cotton by his sister, Margaret. Some months later Mary was again pregnant, and she married Frederick at St. Andrew's Church, Newcastle. This marriage was bigamous as John Robinson was still alive at the time and their marriage had not been annulled. She now bore the name which was to become notorious – Mary Ann Cotton. However, shortly afterwards Margaret Cotton, Frederick's sister, went down with gastric fever and died shortly before her brother's wedding. Luckily for Margaret she had left her savings to Frederick and his new wife. Next door neighbours of the Cottons owned some pigs, and mysteriously one by one they began to die. The farmers were suspicious of Mary and started to accuse her of foul play and made their life very uncomfortable in the village of Walbottle. Frederick, Mary, two children from Cotton's earlier marriage and the new baby thought it wise to leave the area and moved to West Auckland.

Resettled in the new home and hoping that life would be a lot more peaceful, tragedy struck again. Frederick died on September 19, 1971. The Cotton's had also taken a lodger named Joseph Nattrass who had unwisely become Mary's lover and even more unwisely made a will in her favour. Unfortunately for Joseph, Mary was asked to take care of a Mr. Quick-Manning who was suffering

503

from smallpox. Mr. Quick-Manning was a real gentleman and worked as an excise officer, who lived in a house in Brookfield Cottage, which was far superior to anything Mary had been used to. This was a real climb up the social ladder for Mary. They became lovers and over a period of three weeks Mary Ann disposed of Frederick Cotton's eldest ten-year-old-son, her own baby, Robert, and, of course, Joseph Nattrass.

This only left little Charles Edward, Frederick's remaining seven-year-old son who had actually managed to survive the mystery illness. By now Mary was pregnant again by Mr. Quick-Manning but this gentleman, while he didn't mind sharing his bed with Mary, had no intention of allowing her to live in his house. Mary stayed in her own lowly home and took in lodgers to help pay the bills. It was not easy for Mary had very little money, a small allowance for Charles Edward, and a paltry amount left to her by her lover Nattrass. She could barely look after herself let alone look after a child that didn't even belong to her.

Thomas Riley, who was the overseer of the village, called on Mary and asked her if she would be prepared to take care of another smallpox patient. She told him she was unable to do that as she had to look after Charles Edward, and asked if it was possible for the boy to be put in the work-house. He told her that it was only possible if she went as well, and she told him quite curtly that it was out of the question and no place for a woman like her to be. Charles Edward never saw his eighth birthday, he died on July 12, 1872.

Riley was very suspicious about the death of the child, especially as he had seen him healthy a few days before. He went to the police station and told Sergeant Tom Hutchinson of the Bishop Auckland police of his suspicions. The attending doctor, Dr. Killburn, refused to issue a death certificate until he had made further examinations, but even after all this time it was only down to sheer chance that the truth actually emerged.

True to form, Mary went off to the Prudential to collect the insurance money on the death of her stepson, a princely £4 10s. However, they would not hand over the money because they said that with no death certificate the claim was not valid. Mary downtrodden returned home.

The coroner ordered a post mortem on the body of Charles Edward, which was carried out the following day by Dr. Kilburn, amazingly on a table in Mary Ann's house. The inquest was held on the same day in the pub next door, but without the time and proper equipment the doctor was unable to ascertain the true nature of the boy's death and the verdict was that he died from 'natural causes'. Mary heaved a sigh of relief, she had got away with it again.

Dr. Kilburn, however, was still not satisfied with the outcome and decided to take some of the organs home with him for further research. He removed the stomach and some other organs and placed them into a closet. The next day he poured the contents of the stomach into a jar and then buried the remainder of the organs in the garden. Then he tested the stomach contents by using the

Reinsch test, which was a method of tracing arsenic. He must have been totally dumbstruck when the results proved to be 'positive'. He immediately reported to Superintendent Henderson and at last the game was up for Mary Ann Cotton.

She was arrested and then it came to light that she had sent her stepson to the local chemist to buy some arsenic and soft soap. The chemist had refused to sell the items to such a young boy and so a woman called Mrs. Dodds had purchased them for him. This was not an unusual purchase at the time because arsenic and soap were often used to rub down bedposts to kill or deter bed bugs.

During the trial the evidence of Dr. Kilburn was not holding up as he had disgraced himself by burying the boy's organs in his own garden, not really the practice of a respectable doctor. But a more eminent doctor, Dr. Scattergood of Leeds, confirmed that there had been more than half a grain of arsenic in the stomach contents and that it undoubtedly caused the death of Charles Edward.

Mary Ann was duly charged with murder to which she replied, 'I am as innocent as the child unborn'. With Mary locked away some of her victims' bodies were exhumed, and all were found to have traces of arsenic in their stomachs. She was charged with four murders – her stepson, Charles Edward, Joseph Nattrass, Frederick Cotton (whose body they could not find) and Robert Robson Cotton. Mary continued to deny the charges and said that they had most probably swallowed arsenic by accident – a very lame

506

excuse. Whether or not the trial was truly fair is a matter of opinion and right up to the end Mary continued to proclaim her innocence. But the jury thought otherwise and they found her guilty.

She was sentenced to death and put in prison to await her fate. While there waiting for the end of her life she produced a new life, her very last child, a little girl, named Margaret Edith Quick-Manning Cotton.

On March 24, 1873, at 8 a.m. Mary Ann Cotton was led across the yard at Durham County Gaol with two women warders on either side. Mary walked a little unsteadily but with determination, holding her head high and praying. There were about fifty people present, most of them press, to watch the execution, with around another two hundred outside the prison gates. Those that were present saw a frail woman wearing a black dress who met her maker at the end of a swinging rope.

Just before she died she said, 'Heaven is my home', but with all the callous murders she had committed I should think it is more likely to be Hell.

Her name will always be immortalized in the rhyme that children chanted in the streets after her death:

Mary Ann Cotton
She's dead and she's rotten
She lies in her hed
With her eyes wide oppen
Sing, sing, oh, what can I sing?
Mary Ann Cotton is tied up wi' string
Where, where? Up in the air
Sellin' black puddens a penny a pair

Florida's 'Black Widow'

*Our final case study in the section looks at the
story of Judias Buenoano who was the first
women to get the electric chair in America
since Rhonda Belle Martin in 1957. She may
have given the impression of a successful business
woman but she was also a charming seductress.
With each man she bewitched she became richer
as she benefitted from their agonizing deaths.*

Like so many of the other criminals discussed in
this book, Judias (Judi) Buenoano had a very
difficult childhood. She was born Judias Welty, in
Quanah, Texas, on April 4, 1943. Judi was the
daughter of a travelling farm worker, but she took
her mother's name. She described her mother, also
named Judias, as a member of a non-existent
Mesquite Apache tribe, but in truth Judi hardly
knew her, for she died of tuberculosis when her
daughter was barely four years old. The family
became parted after her death and Judi, along
with her baby brother Robert, went to live with
their grandparents, while the two older children
were put up for adoption. For Judi life became a
long uphill struggle from that moment.

Her father remarried and Judi and Robert were

sent back to live with him and his new wife in Roswell, New Mexico. Judi was very miserable as she soon found herself to be the target of abuse from both her father and her stepmother. She was beaten, starved, burned with cigarettes and forced to work exceptionally long hours around the house. This was hardly a healthy environment for a growing adolescent. By the age of fourteen, the anger which had built up inside Judi, exploded. She attacked two of her stepbrothers with hot oil and flew at her parents with her fists and her feet, and in fact any object that she could get hold of. This outburst cost Judi sixty days in jail where she was confined with adult prostitutes and criminals. When she was released the Judge asked her if she was now ready to go back home, but rather than be subjected to the constant abuse she received there, she opted for a reform school. She went to Foothills High School in Albuquerque, a girl's reformatory, and stayed there until her graduation in 1959. She despised her family and vowed that she would have nothing further to do with them, including her brother Robert.

HER LIFE OF CRIME

In the year 1960 Judi returned to Roswell where she worked as a nursing assistant, assuming the name of Anna Schultz. On March 30, 1961, she gave birth to an illegitimate son, Michael, but would never admit to who the father was. Rumours spread like wildfire that the father was in fact a pilot from the local air force base, but she refused to confirm or deny the allegations. On January 21, 1962, she married another air force officer, James Goodyear, who adopted Michael as his own. Four years later on January 16, 1966, Judi gave birth to their first child, James Jr. A year later they had a daughter, Kimberley, by which time they had moved home to Orlando, Florida.

Judi opened her first business in 1968, the Conway Acres Child Care Center in Orlando, with the aid of her husband's finances. He was named as co-owner despite the fact that he was still serving with the Air Force. James was sent to do a tour of duty in Vietnam and barely three months after his return was admitted to the U.S. Naval Hospital in Orlando suffering from a mysterious illness. He never recovered and died on September 15, 1971. Judi waited for a discreet five days before she cashed in his three life insurance policies. Before the year was out Judi suffered a fire at her home, for which she received a further $90,000 from the insurance company. She felt she had had some rotten luck of late, but at least she had been well compensated.

Judi wasted no time in finding herself a new lover, Bobby Joe Morris, and she moved into his home in Pensacola in 1972. She was happy for a while but her new life was being ruined by her son Michael, who was being very disruptive at school and was of below-average intelligence. Although Michael was refused treatment at the military hospital due to his father's death, Judi managed to get an evaluation carried out at the state hospital in 1974, and for a while he was put into a foster care home while he received psychiatric treatment.

Bobby Morris invited Judi and her family, including Michael, to move with him to Trinidad, Colorado, in 1977. She stayed behind for a while, but before she left Pensacola she was once more the victim of a house fire which brought another hefty insurance payout. She waited until she had got the money, went and collected Michael from foster care, and then moved west with her family. She settled into life in Trinidad and now used the name of Judias Morris. Soon after she moved to Colorado, Bobby became sick and was admitted to hospital on January 4, 1978. Once again the illness was a mystery to the doctors and he was released into the care of Judi. Two days after arriving home Bobby collapsed again and was returned to the hospital, where he died on January 21. The cause of his death was put down to cardiac arrest and metabolic acidosis.

Before his body was barely cold Judi had cashed in three life polices on Morris giving her a nice healthy balance in her bank account. However, Bobby Joe's family were suspicious that their son had been murdered and felt that he was not the only victim. In 1974, Judi and Bobby had been visiting Bobby's hometown of Brewton in Alabama, where a man had been discovered dead in his motel room. The police had received an anonymous phone call from a pay phone which led them to the body. The man had been shot in the chest with a .22-calibre gun and his throat had been slashed.

After the news of the murder hit the headlines, Bobby Joe's parents overheard a conversation between their son and Judi in which she said, 'The son of a bitch shouldn't have come up here in the first place. He knew if he came up here he was gonna die'. Bobby Joe admitted to his part in the murder when he was in a delirious state on his deathbed. However, the police were unable to come up with any fingerprints from inside the motel room, no bullet was ever recovered from the corpse, and consequently had no firm suspects.

Judi changed her name legally on May 3, 1978, to Buenoano, which is the Spanish equivalent of Goodyear, in an apparent tribute to her late husband and her Apache mother. Within a month the family had returned to Pensacola and set up home in Whisper Pine Drive.

Judi's son Michael, now Buenoano, had continued to do badly at school and in 1979 joined the Army. After he had completed his basic training he was assigned to a post at Fort Benning in Georgia. Before leaving for Georgia he visited his mother in Florida, this turned out to be a very big mistake. By the time he reached Fort Benning he was already showing signs of being poisoned. Army physicians found seven times the normal level of arsenic in Michael's body and said there was little they could do to stop the deterioration and he ended up wearing heavy metal leg braces and he was unable to use his hands. Unable to walk and do very little for himself he was discharged from the military hospital in the care of his 'loving' mother.

On May 13, 1980, Michael was out canoeing with his mother and younger brother, James, on

the East River near Milton. Sadly the canoe cap-
sized and although James and Judi were able to get
out from underneath the overturned boat,
Michael, weighed down by the heavy braces, didn't
stand a chance. The police accepted Judi's account
of what happened, but the military police were far
more suspicious. Judi had received $20,000 from
Michael's military life insurance, but the Sheriff's
office started taking a keen interest when they discovered that there were an additional two civilian
policies that had been taken out on his life.
Experts studied the handwriting on the policies
and it was suggested that the applications could
possibly have been forged.

In the meantime, Judi carried on bravely after
the loss of her eldest son, and proceeded to open a
beauty salon in Gulf Breeze. Shortly after she
opened the salon she started to date a Pensacola
businessman called John Gentry II. To gain further
credit with the wealthy businessman, Judi fabricated various bogus qualifications and that she had
worked as a senior nurse at a West Florida
Hospital. Of course the whole thing was nonsense,
but John Gentry was taken in. He indulged her in
the lifestyle she so craved, giving her expensive
gifts, taking her on Caribbean cruises and drinking champagne. She persuaded John that they
should take out life insurance polices on each
other in October 1982. Judi later raised the
amount of coverage on John's policy from $50,000
to $500,000 without his knowledge, paying the
additional premium out of her own pocket. She
also persuaded him to start taking vitamin pills for

his health, but these made him feel nauseous and dizzy. When he complained to Judi how he felt she told him to protect himself and double the dose. John felt so bad at one time he was hospitalized for a period of twelve days, but he soon noticed that his symptoms disappeared when he stopped taking the vitamins. Even with this realization, he was not suspicious of his girlfriend and saw no reason to end the relationship.

On June 25, 1983, Judi told John that she was pregnant and he went out to get some champagne so that they could celebrate. However, when he turned the ignition key his car exploded which left him with severe injuries. Fighting for his life he was rushed to hospital where trauma surgeons managed to pull him round. Four days later he was well enough to be questioned by the police, which led them to start examining Judi's past with minute detail. Many inconsistencies came up about what Judi had told John and what was actually true and as if to confirm his suspicions he discovered that she had been sterilized in 1975 and so even her pregnancy was a lie. Then the detectives learned that Judi had been telling her friends about John's terminal illness since November 1982, and that she had booked a luxury cruise for herself and her children – not however Gentry!

John now realised that the Judi he thought he knew and the real Judi were not the same person, and he supplied the police with some of the vitamin pills that she had made him take. When these tablets were analysed it revealed that they contained paraformaldehyde – a poison with no medical uses. At this stage, however, the Florida state attorney felt there was not sufficient evidence to charge her with attempted murder, and so the matter was held over. The investigation continued, though, and on July 27, Federal agents searched Judi's home in Gulf Breeze and found wire and tape in her bedroom that matched the car bomb in Gentry's car. In James' room they found marijuana and a sawn-off shotgun and he was subsequently jailed with possession of drugs and an illegal weapon. Judi was arrested at her beauty salon on charges of attempted murder. Later the police also traced the source of the dynamite and were able to link it to Judi through long-distance telephone calls made from her home. Judi was released on bail on the attempted murder charge, but was re-arrested on January 11, 1984, when she was indicted with first-degree murder in the death of her son, Michael. There was an additional charge for grand theft and insurance fraud. On hearing the charges she staged a fit of convulsions and was taken to Santa Rosa Hospital under police guard.

The bodies of both Bobby Joe Morris and James Goodyear were exhumed, and both were found with traces of arsenic in their bodies.

THE CONVICTION

Judi was tried separately for each murder and for the attempted murder. She was sentenced to life imprisonment without parole for the first twenty-five years on June 6, 1984 for the murder of Michael. Surprisingly, she was acquitted on the charge of attempted murder but was found guilty of first-degree murder of her first husband, James Goodyear. The jury took ten-and-a-half hours to reach a verdict, and she was finally sentenced to death by electrocution on November 26, 1985.

It is estimated that she managed to collect around $240,000 in insurance money from the deaths of her husband, son and boyfriend.

TIME ON DEATH ROW

Judi spent thirteen years at the Broward Correctional Center at Pembroke Pines in Florida. She continued to appeal and had three death warrants handed down over those years. It is a harsh regime whereby they are confined to the cell for most of the time except when they are handcuffed to be taken to the exercise yard or for a shower. They are allowed visitors every weekend from 9 a.m. through to 3 p.m. Judi spent her time here writing letters, crocheting blankets and baby clothes, and teaching the Bible to other inmates. She was always described as a gentle and mothering figure.

Judias Buenoano was finally executed on March 30, 1998 with no explanation as to why she committed the crimes other than greed.

PART 4

COUPLES
WHO KILL

Torturous
Teams

As if a single murderer is not bad enough, when two people decide to join forces, then you double the evil.

Murders committed by people working in teams are just as horrific as those committed by killers who work on their own — or perhaps even worse. It is just as much of a risk to accept a ride offered by a couple as it is to hop into a car driven by a single male. We all like to think that women are nurturing and motherly, in fact, when they participate in criminal activities their influence often heightens the cruelty and sadism.

Put in simple terms, couples or groups that kill are more often than not found to have perverted tendencies as individuals, but it is only when they come together that their combined personality becomes a lethal concoction. The French have an expression for this – *folie a deux* – which indicates a delusion shared by two emotionally-linked persons.

Team killers generally share some common characteristics, for example, they are usually Caucasian, have partial or complete high school education, generally around their mid-twenties, and more often than not are blue-collar workers. There are normally two offenders working together, with a male/male ratio of around one third. Around fifteen percent of serial murders are committed by teams, and more often than not the victims are strangers.

Sometimes one of the accomplices acts as the team leader or dominant partner sending the other one out to do what he wants, and on occasion he will participate himself. Sometimes the couple are related or married, and other times they're strangers who just happen to spark off the right chemistry. When females are involved, it is generally the male who masterminds the homicides, that is unless the female is the dominant one, such as in a mother-son team. There is always one person who maintains psychological control.

As mentioned earlier the killer team will generally target strangers, that is, someone with whom they have had no prior contact. They tend to like the hands-on method of killing – strangulation or suffocation – and will often retain trophies or souvenirs from the victims, such as a video-recording or their actions, or personal items taken from the victim. They normally display extreme cruelty towards their victims, loving to torture or even dismember. In contrast to a serial killer acting alone, team killers are unique in that they share, or appear to share 'two minds with one single psyche' (Brady, 2001).

Another possible explanation is that males as a general rule are socialized to externalize their feelings of anger and/or rage through acts of aggression. In the case of male/female team serial murderers, however, it appears that the right of entitlement is transferred and traditional gender roles become somewhat distorted. In other words, the female offender participates in the traditional [male] acts of aggression. Particularly, married female and male team serial killers and where sexual acts of aggression are involved.

Generally you will find the opinion of the public is that they are not surprised by the male part of the killing teams, but when it comes to the woman they tend to make excuses, seeing her as the victim of her male partner. In truth, both the male and female have usually come from equally abusive backgrounds and are similarly full of both fear and hatred.

Why these people team up to kill is not a question I shall attempt to answer, but whatever the reason the result is totally sickening.

The Lonely Heart Killers

This is about a desperately lonely, overweight woman, who falls in love with a man who murders women for money. The story is intertwined with voodoo magic, kinky sexual activities and was to become one of the most sensational cases of the 1940s.

PLAYER NUMBER ONE

Martha Jule Seabrook was born in 1920 in the town of Milton in northwest Florida. As a young child, like many serial killers before her, she was abused by her mother. She was regularly beaten and verbally taunted, and to make matters worse when she was only nine years old she developed a glandular problem which made her exceptionally fat. She was raped by her brother when she was still quite young, but when she told her mother what had happened she was severely beaten and told not to tell lies. Even as she grew into her teenage years she was always the subject of jokes and ridicule which made her withdraw into herself. She became almost reclusive and withdrawn and had virtually no friends.

Undoubtedly this bad start to life had a lot to do

521

with her longing for a life of romance and her eventual appetite for bizarre sexual acts. It certainly would have been the root of her increasingly callous view of her fellow human beings.

Martha was a highly intelligent girl and eventually gained top nursing qualifications. However, her weight (250 pounds) kept her from being accepted by the hospital boards and she ended up taking a job working for a mortician in a local funeral home. The job was ideal for her as she was a loner who found it difficult to interact with others, and so she may well have found solace working with bodies that could no longer criticize or ridicule her overweight body.

In 1942, Martha was desperate to improve her lifestyle and she moved to California, where she worked as a nurse at an Army hospital. In the evening she would spend her time hanging round the city's bars and picking up soldiers who were on leave. She would frequently have sex with these soldiers and one of these liaisons ended up in pregnancy. When she told the soldier about the baby he attempted suicide by jumping into a nearby bay. Realizing that a man would rather die than actually marry her, Martha returned to Florida very depressed and all alone.

Back in Milton she needed to explain how she had got pregnant and so she devised a story that she had married a Navy officer and that her husband would soon be back from the Pacific to join her. Sadly she bought her own wedding ring and wore it proudly round the town. She even went as far as having a telegram sent to her home informing her that her husband had been killed in action and feigned hysterics when she read the news. The town mourned with her and the story even appeared in the local news. Eventually in the spring of 1944, the baby was born, a daughter, Willa Dean.

Several months after the birth of her baby, Martha met a Pensacola bus driver named Alfred Beck and once again she fell pregnant. Alfred, probably feeling guilty about the baby, reluctantly married her in late 1944. However, within six months they were divorced and Martha found herself on her own again. She now had two children, no income, and fell into the world of romance novels and afternoon movies. In early 1946 she took a job at the Pensacola Hospital for children, and she threw herself into the job to make up for the lack of any form of social life.

As a result of a practical joke by a co-worker, Martha ended up putting an advert in the 'Lonely Hearts' column of a newspaper and waited eagerly for the replies to come.

PLAYER NUMBER TWO

Raymond Fernandez was six years older than Martha, and was born on the island of Hawaii on December 17, 1914. His parents were both Spanish and were more than a little disappointed at their son's frail and sickly appearance. His father criticized everything he did and took very little interest in his education. He was beaten regularly and forced to do manual work that he really wasn't strong enough to handle. From the age of three Raymond was raised in Bridgeport, Connecticut until 1932, when he decided to move to Spain to work on his uncle's farm. When he was only twenty he married a local girl named, Encarnacion Robles, and gradually Raymond blossomed into a handsome, confident, well-built young man. He had a very calm and gentle manner and was very popular in the village where they lived.

During World War II Raymond served briefly with the British Intelligence Service. Although little is known of his war activities it is said he carried out his difficult and sometimes dangerous duties with distinction. In late 1945, when the war was over, Raymond decided to return to America to find work and then send for his wife and son to join him. He managed to get a passage on a ship headed for the Dutch West Indies, but while on board he was to suffer a severe head injury which would affect him for the rest of his life. An open steel hatch fell directly on top of his skull causing a severe indentation and could possible have damaged his brain in an irreversible way. When the ship docked he was transferred to hospital, where he remained until March 1946.

When he was released from hospital, it was obvious that the previously kind, calm man had undergone a personality change. Raymond became distant, moody and was quick to lose his temper – in short he was a changed man. He served a short prison sentence for stealing a large quantity of clothes and other items from a ship's store room and it was while in prison that he be-friended his cellmate, a Haitian man. This man introduced Raymond to the practices of voodoo and soon he was totally involved in the world of black magic. He believed that he had a secret power over women, that his sexual powers were now at a peak and he took to wearing a wig to cover his scar

After his release from prison Raymond moved to Brooklyn to live with his sister. She was initially upset by his appearance, because the once hand-some young man was now practically bald with a large scar plainly visible on the top of his head. For most of the time Raymond locked himself away in his bedroom and complained of severe headaches. He started writing letters to 'Lonely Hearts' ads where, through the mail, he managed to seduce gullible females who were looking for a man. Once he had gained their trust he stole money, jewellery, or whatever he could get his hands on, and then he would become invisible. Most of his victims were too embarrassed to report it to the police and so Raymond realized he had found a way of earning money without having to work.

THE LETTER

Martha checked her mailbox everyday to see if she had any answers to her advert, but each day she was disappointed. That is until just before Christ-mas in 1947, when she received her first and only reply. The letter was from a man named Raymond Fernandez who lived in New York City. He told her that he was a respectable businessman who made his money importing and exporting goods. Longing for a life of romance she read with relish the words: '. . . here in this apartment much too large for a bachelor but I hope someday to share it with a wife.' It was just too much for the love-struck Martha and she cherished every single word in that letter. She wrote back and for two weeks they corresponded, she was concerned what he would think when he eventually met this overweight young woman, but what she didn't realize was that he didn't actually care what his women looked like as his only interest was their assets.

After several letters being exchanged Raymond asked Martha for a lock of her hair so that he could perform his voodoo ritual. He believed that this would make Martha succumb to his sexual charms. Martha was thrilled that someone should care enough that they should want a lock of her hair, and she dreamt of her lover taking her away from her life of drudge.

They eventually met on December 28, 1947, in Pensacola, Florida. Although initially Raymond may have been shocked at her size, he showed no signs of any disapproval. Martha was thrilled when she saw him and couldn't believe that she could have a date with such a handsome man. She took him back to her home, introduced him to her children, gave him a nice meal and then put the children to bed. Raymond quickly made his move and for once in her life Martha achieved sexual fulfilment.

They spent the next day and night together and

Martha swore undying love to her newfound man friend. Martha tried to convince him to stay with her but Raymond told her that it was essential he return to New York. To keep her happy he told her that he would send some money so that she could join him and Martha misread this as some kind of proposal.

Once back at home she told all her friends that she was about to get married again. Then she received a letter from Raymond saying that she had totally misinterpreted his feelings and that he would not be coming back to see her. She was totally devastated and attempted to take her own life. On hearing this Fernandez weakened and allowed Martha to come and visit him in New York. She stayed for two blissful weeks and then returned to her job in Florida. For some reason, on her return, she was fired without being given any explanation. Realising how much she missed Raymond, she packed her bags, dressed her two children, said goodbye to her friends and boarded the next bus to New York.

When Raymond saw them standing at his door on the morning of January 18, 1948, he realized that this could be a major obstacle in his career of theft and deception. Soon he realized that he liked the mothering nature of Martha and felt comfortable with her around pampering his every whim. But the children were a different matter and he insisted that they had to go. Martha reluctantly decided that if that was the price to pay to keep her beloved Raymond, then she would give up her own children. On January 25 she dropped them

off at the Salvation Army and abandoned them
without a second thought.

So here we have a very dangerous combination
of two people with already insecure characters,
who together became totally lethal. Posing as
brother and sister they managed to gain the confidence of their victims.

THE LONELY HEARTS CLUB

Now they were totally on their own with no children to get in the way, Raymond showed Martha
all his lonely hearts letters. He told her everything
about how he befriended and robbed women,
about his wife in Spain and several other wives as
well. Although Martha was initially upset she
knew it was too late to turn back and told him that
it was her duty to help him.

They chose their next victim, Miss Esther Henne
from the many photographs and then made
arrangements to travel to Pennsylvania. Martha
posed as Raymond's sister-in-law and within one
week Raymond and Miss Henne were married. She
later reported to the police that for the first few
days he was the model husband, but after that the
insults started when she wouldn't sign over her
insurance policies and teacher's pension fund.
Things went from bad to worse and eventually the
new Mrs. Fernandez left the apartment without
her car and several hundred dollars which he had
already embezzled out of her.

Several other women followed in quick succession but things went steeply downhill when they

met up with Myrtle Young from Arkansas. She agreed after some persuasion to marry Robert and the ceremony took place on August 14, 1948 in Cook County, Illinois. This time Martha posed as his sister and did everything she could to prevent the marriage from being consummated. She even resorted to sleeping with Myrtle herself until the poor woman complained so much she was given a heavy dose of drugs which rendered her unconscious. With Martha's help, they carried her onto a bus and sent her back to Little Rock, Arkansas, where she came from. Before they dumped her the couple had robbed the poor woman of four thousand dollars. Myrtle Young died the very next day in a Little Rock hospital.

Back in New York, with their money gradually dwindling away, Martha and Robert were once more scouring the lonely hearts adverts for possible victims. They located Janet Fey, a sixty-six-year-old widow who lived in Albany, New York. Raymond wrote her a letter and their little game started all over again.

Robert gradually gained her trust, despite the fact that Janet Fey's friends had warned her of the dangers, until eventually she agreed they could meet. Martha and Robert arrived in downtown Albany on December 30, 1948, and checked into a hotel as Mr. and Mrs. Fernandez. The following day Fernandez arrived at Janet Fey's door with a bouquet of flowers. They met several times over the next few days and Martha often accompanied them on their dates, being introduced as his sister. Soon Raymond proposed marriage, to which Janet readily accepted and they made plans to move to an apartment on Long Island. Janet, urged by Raymond, cleared out her bank accounts and she collected over $6,000 in cash and cheques. On January 4, 1949, Raymond, Martha and Janet left Albany and drove to Long Island.

Once at Long Island the real problems started. They spent a nice evening having a meal and talking but then it came to bedtime and Martha's insatiable jealousy took over. Fernandez had fallen asleep which left the two women together and exactly what happened next is pure conjecture. Martha who was already upset because her beloved had been showing Janet too much attention, bludgeoned the poor woman into unconsciousness with a ball-peen hammer and then strangled her using a scarf as a tourniquet.

When Raymond woke and found what Martha had done, he acted calmly and the couple cleared up the room. Next the wrapped the body in towels and a sheet and pushed into in a cupboard.

The next day they bought a large trunk and dumped the body inside and then took it over to Raymond's sister's house. They asked her to store the trunk in her basement for a few days. Raymond collected the trunk eleven days later and on January 15 buried it in the cellar of a rented house.

Their next victim was Mrs. Delphine Downing, a young widow with a two-year-old daughter. For several weeks Fernandez corresponded with the unsuspecting Delphine. He had told her that he was a successful businessman and that his name was Charles Martin. He arranged a visit to Byron Center, a suburb of Grand Rapids, Michigan, and Delphine seemed quite happy about the fact that he was bringing his sister along with him. Delphine seemed very impressed when she met 'Charles'. She liked his polite manner and his attitude towards her young daughter. Very soon they became lovers which left Martha seething with rage. However, Delphine's happiness was short-lived for one morning she spotted her lover in the bathroom without his toupee and seeing the bald head and ugly scar she immediately accused him of fraud and deception. Martha remained calm and convinced Delphine to take some sleeping pills hoping the situation would resolve itself. The child, Rainelle, began to cry, seeing her mother was not her normal self, and Martha grabbed the baby and started to choke her into unconsciousness leaving bruises on her neck. Fernandez was angry and said that if Delphine woke up and saw the baby she would report them to the police. Martha told him to do something about it, and Fernandez responded by going to get a handgun from the next room, wrapping it in a blanket and shooting Mrs. Downing in the head from very close range.

Between them they wrapped the body in sheets and carried it to the basement of the house. There they dug a large hole and buried the body. Fernandez covered the grave with cement, while Martha dutifully cleared up the murder scene.

For the next couple of days they made plans to escape, but they still had the problem of the child who refused to eat and constantly cried. They talked about what they should do, but neither of them could agree, until finally Fernandez told Martha to get rid of her. Although Martha pleaded that she couldn't do it, she knew she was already too heavily implicated and subsequently in an act of complete callous depravity, she held the baby's head under water until she was dead. A little while later there was an even smaller grave next to her mother's.

Although they were now free to leave town, the couple chose to wait until the next day and decided to go to the cinema. Later, when they were back at the apartment packing their bags, there was a knock at the front door. When they opened the door they found two stern-looking policeman who had been called to the apartment by some suspicious neighbours.

Beck and Fernandez were arrested and extradited to New York because Michigan could not issue the death penalty. Both prisoners confessed to the Fay and Downing murders, but denied any connection with a string of seventeen other deaths which the police felt were connected. The trial itself became headline news, not so much because of the murders, but because Martha kept writing to them telling about her sexual exploits with her lover Raymond Fernandez. Although serious doubts were expressed as to the sanity of Fernandez he was judged to be sane and found guilty on the charges of murder. Right up to the end they expressed undying love for each other and they were both executed by electric chair at Sing Sing prison on March 8, 1951.

Charles Starkweather and Caril Ann Fugate

Charles Starkweather, together with his companion Caril Ann Fugate, embarked on a murder spree in 1957 to 1958 which sent a shockwave over the entire United States. This scary rebel twosome killed eleven people before they were finally apprehended.

Charlie Starkweather was born on November 24, 1938 in Lincoln Nebraska. He was the third of seven children and he was raised in a poor, uneducated but hardworking family environment. Although the family were not well off they never went without food and Charlie had happy memories of his childhood. Although he was happy at home Charlie found school rather traumatic due to a minor speech impediment and his bow legs. He got teased by his classmates and preferred the security of his home. Another thing that made it hard for him during his lessons was that he had a condition called myopia, which went undetected until he was fifteen. This meant that he wasn't able to read anything that was written on the blackboard and consequently he got left behind in his studies. One thing he did excel at, however, was gymnastics and in this class he was strong and well co-ordinated. The only problem was that he used this strength to fight with his fellow class-mates on several occasions.

When he was in ninth grade Charlie made friends with a boy named Bob Van Busch. Bob later described his friend as a two-sided coin, and said that on the one hand he was kind and great fun to be around, but on the other he could be as mean as hell. They were both James Dean fanatics and loved to watch all of his movies.

CARIL ANN

Charlie's closest friend, Bob, started to date a young girl named Barbara Fugate in 1956. Barbara had a younger sister named Caril, who had only just turned thirteen, and Charlie turned his attentions on her. Caril was a pretty girl with dark brown hair, but she too had a streak of rebellion in her. The four of them used to go out on double dates, despite Caril's age, and gradually Charlie became totally obsessed with his child sweetheart.

Charlie left school when he was sixteen and went to work at the Western Newspaper Union un-loading and loading their trucks. The factory was near Caril's school which meant that Charlie was able to see her every day. He taught her how to drive but this caused a rift with his parents as they borrowed his father's car and they were involved in a minor accident. This caused a huge argument and Charlie was forced to move to the same house as his friends Bob and Barbara Fugate. Caril became the centre of Charlie's life, and he began telling people that they were getting married and that she was expecting his baby. This lie backfired when Caril's parents found out. Charlie gave up his job at the paper company and started working as a garbage man, purely so that he could be around when Caril came out of school. His wages were extremely poor and he got behind with his rent. He became depressed as he saw himself always being poor and never having enough money to support himself and his beloved Caril. He started to fantasize about robbing a bank or doing something dramatic to earn some extra cash to get himself out of the mess he was in.

THE VIOLENCE STARTS

Charlie Starkweather's reign of violence started on December 1, 1957 at a petrol station in Nebraska. It was a bitterly cold day and Charlie was carrying a 12-gauge shotgun. Charlie had a score to settle with the young man who worked at the station, twenty-year-old Robert Colvert. The day before Charlie had wanted to buy a soft toy for his girl-friend Caril, but he had no money and so he asked Robert if he could buy it on credit. The young lad refused and Charlie left vowing that he would get his revenge.

Charlie parked round the corner from the garage and put on his disguise which comprised of a bandana which covered much of his face and a hat to cover his very distinguishing red hair. Colvert was working on the engine of a car and didn't realize anyone was behind him until he felt the gun poked into his back. Charlie made the young man go back to the office and open up the cash drawer. Charlie scooped out the money and put it into a canvas bag that he was carrying. Then he demanded that Colvert opened the safe, but he said he wasn't allowed to know the combination and that only his boss could do that. Charlie seemed to believe him but that wasn't to be the end he forced Colvert to drive him out to the house owned by 'Bloody Mary'. Bloody Mary was a crazy old woman who would shoot anyone who trespassed on her property, using a shotgun full of rock salt. When they arrived at the house he made Colvert get out of the car and shot him directly in the head.

For a while Charlie felt elated by the fact that he had some money to spend, albeit only $100. He told Caril about the robbery but said that someone else must have killed the garage attendant. Caril was not fooled but someone the killing had formed an even stronger bond between the two of them. After a few days the euphoria wore off and Charlie realized that he no longer had a job, he had nowhere to live, it appeared as though Caril were really pregnant, and he had no chance of making her his wife as he had no prospects. Caril's parents were completely against the relationship and did everything possible to try and get their daughter to stop seeing Charlie.

Almost two months after the garage incident, on January 21, 1958, Charlie called round to Caril's parents' house. It was nothing fancy, in fact they lived in rather squalid conditions. Charlie had borrowed a .22 rifle and some ammunition, and armed with this he knocked on the back door. It was Velda, Caril's mother, who answered the door. Caril's stepfather, Marion, was also in the house along with their two-and-half-year-old daughter, Betty Jean. A loud argument broke out between Velda and Charlie, because she told him point blank that she did not want him to see their daughter any more. Charlie stormed out of the house allegedly leaving the gun behind. When he came back for it just a short while later, Marion literally kicked him back out of the door.

Charlie then waited near the house for Caril to get home from school. When she arrived he told her what had happened and what her parents had said. Caril was angry and the pair went back inside the house, where an argument broke out between Caril and her mother. Velda started hitting out at Charlie and shouting at him for making her daughter pregnant and then everything got totally out of hand. Charlie ended up by murdering Marion, Velda and Caril's baby sister. No one is quite sure what part Caril took in this massacre, because they were the only two left alive. However, what happened after the murder is totally unbelievable.

Velda's body was dragged to the old outhouse and pushed into the toilet opening, Caril's baby sister was shoved in a box and was also taken out to the outhouse, while the body of Marion was just dumped on the floor of the chicken coop. Charlie and Caril then went back inside the house, cleaned up the mess and sat down and had supper. They lived in the house, just a few yards away from the decomposing bodies, for nearly a whole week. They bought milk and bread from the milkman and Charlie went down to the local grocery store for any other essentials they needed. The couple turned any visitors away on the pretence that everyone was ill and Caril even put a sign on the front door 'Stay away Every Body is sick with the Flue'.

Gradually Caril's relatives became suspicious because they had heard nothing from the family, and eventually it was Caril's grandmother who called the police. When they arrived at the house Charlie and Caril had already fled, but a search of the house and its outbuildings soon confirmed their worst fears.

MORE KILLING

Charlie and Caril, having fled town, took refuge with an old family friend of Charlie's, seventy-two-year-old August Meyer. August was a kindly old bachelor who had known Charlie since he was a little boy and had never shown him anything but kindness. On their way up to his remote farm the couple's car got stuck in some mud and they ended up walking the rest of the way. From here the story is a little confused, because both Charlie and Caril gave a different version of the events, but August

Meyer was shot in the head. They carried his body to the outhouse and hid it under a blanket. Then they returned to Meyer's house, stole his money, his guns, ate his food and then fell asleep as if nothing had happened.

The next day the couple returned to their car and with the help of some neighbours managed to free it from the mud. However, further down the track they got stuck again and decided to abandon the car and go on foot. Hiding their guns they managed to cadge a lift from seventeen-year-old Robert Jensen and sixteen-year-old Carol King. The second they were inside the car Charlie held the gun at Robert's neck and forced him to drive back to Meyer's farm where there was an abandoned storm cellar. Once there Charlie killed the young couple by shooting them in the head. Carol was left half-naked with her jeans and pants around her ankles, and their were repeated stab wounds in her abdomen and pubic area, but no sign of sexual abuse. Caril, allegedly, was sitting in the car while all this happened, but of this there is no proof. Having emptied their pockets of any money Charlie returned to the car and they escaped.

By now there was a massive police hunt underway. Stupidly enough the couple now returned to Lincoln where they were well known, and it was here that they chose the house of a wealthy steel executive, C. Laur Ward. Charlie forced Mrs. Ward and her housekeeper upstairs where they were both tied to a bed and stabbed to death. When Mr. Ward returned home after work, he was confronted by

Charlie and he was shot as he entered his home.

Next Charlie and Caril stole the Ward's car and drove to Wyoming. They drove all night and crossed over into Wyoming the following morning, January 29, 1958. On their way they kept a look-out for a car to steal and came across a Buick that was parked up on the highway. When they stopped they found a man sleeping, Merle Collison, a travelling shoe salesman. Charlie woke up the salesman to tell him that they were going to swap cars, and then shot the poor man in the head. With Collison dead in the front passenger seat, and Caril in the back of the car, Charlie started the Buick but was unable to release the handbrake.

A couple of minutes later a young geologist, Joe Sprinkle, stopped to see if they needed help. Charlie immediately pointed his gun at the young man and threatened to kill him if he didn't help him release the brake. Suddenly Joe saw the slumped body of Merle Collison in the passenger seat and realized that if he were to stay alive he would have to get the gun from Charlie. They wrestled and while they were struggling a deputy Sheriff by the name of William Romer, came by and saw the fight.

When she saw the man Caril jumped out of the back seat and rushed up to him and started crying. She asked him to take her to the police because she yelled, 'He's killed a man'. The man replied that he was the police, but before he could take any action Charlie had run off to their original car and was driving back towards the town of Douglas. The Sheriff immediately ordered a roadblock and went off in pursuit. A chase ensued but Charlie was eventually apprehended and he and Caril chose Nebraska as the place to stand trial. Caril maintained that she was a hostage throughout the whole ordeal and she only stayed with him for fear that he would kill her family if she didn't.

Charlie and Caril were both charged with first degree murder and murder while committing a robbery. Charlie's trial started on May 5, 1958 and he did nothing to help himself, in fact he was quite unrepentant and tended to brag about his crimes. Initially he told the authorities that Caril had played no part in the crimes, but when he learned that she was trying to say that she was an unwilling hostage, he turned and tried to implicate her in the murders. The jury had no doubt about his guilt and sentenced him to death by electric chair. He was finally executed on June 25, 1959.

Caril's defence built upon her being a hostage and that she was forced by Starkweather to go along with him on his murdering spree. However, the jury were not convinced and she was also found guilty on November 28, 1958.

Due to the fact that she was only fourteen years old, she was given a life sentence instead of the death penalty. She was sent to the Nebraska Center for Women to serve her sentence and was paroled in 1977.

Fred and Rosemary West

*Fred and Rosemary West had a love affair with
violent pornography and every video they
owned reflected in some way their very own
depraved and perverted behaviour.*

This case study covers every sordid angle of a
team working in unison to satisfy their sadistic
fantasies – prostitution, drugs, kinky sex, incest,
paedophilia, suicide and murder. The house where
all this happened, 25 Cromwell Street, became
known as the House of Horrors and as you read on
you will see just why it received this name.

FRED WEST

Fred West was born in 1941 in the small village of
Much Marcle. He was the eldest of six children to
Walter and Daisy West and he began life as a
beautiful baby with blond curly hair and piercing
blue eyes. Fred was definitely his mother's
favourite but he also had a good relationship with
his father. His homelife was happy and suffered
none of the normal abuse that we find in many of
the killers that have been mentioned in this book.

As Fred reached puberty he started to lose some

of his baby good looks, and he became rather unkempt and scruffy. At school he was not a very promising student and was constantly being punished for insubordination. His mother, not happy with the constant caning her favourite son received, would go to the school and yell at his teacher. This only made matters worse for Fred and this earned him the nickname 'Mother's Boy'.

Virtually illiterate, Fred left school at the age of fifteen, and took a job as a farm hand. By sixteen Fred had started to tidy himself up so that he was able to attract the opposite sex. He appeared that he took any girl that caught his fancy and he was known to be a very aggressive lover.

When Fred was seventeen he was involved in a very serious motorcycle accident which left him in a coma for more than a week. The accident resulted in him having a metal plate in his head, and one leg that was permanently shorter than the other. This incident seemed to have a lasting effect on Fred and he was prone to violent outbursts of temper and had less control over his emotions. This may well have been the reason why his sexual fantasies became so perverse and resulted in him being a serial killer.

When Fred had recovered from his accident he met the pretty sixteen-year-old, Catherine Bernadette Costello, nicknamed Rena. She had been in and out of trouble with the police since early childhood and by the time they met she was already an accomplished thief. They became lovers but the affair ended when she returned home to Scotland a few months later.

In the year 1961, Fred was accused of getting a thirteen-year-old girl pregnant. She was a friend of the family, but Fred was adamant that he didn't see anything wrong with molesting minors, and his parents ordered that he move out and find somewhere else to live. Fred, still obsessed with sex and with young women in particular, stuck his hand up the skirt of a young woman standing on a fire escape outside the local youth club. She was so angry that she turned round and knocked the young Fred off the fire escape. Once again he was knocked into unconsciousness and this along with the damage from the motorcycle accident seems to have had a lasting impact on Fred West. He had no doubt suffered brain damage.

In 1962, Fred's parents relented and said that he could return home, which coincided with the return of Rena to Much Marcle. Immediately the affair started up again and in certain respects they seemed to be a good match. Rena was certainly somewhat of a delinquent and on her return was pregnant by another man. Fred and Rena married secretly in November 1962 and moved up to Scotland. Fred's parents presumed that the baby Rena was carrying was Fred's, but when Charmaine was born in March 1963, it was very obviously of mixed-race. They wrote to Fred's parents and told them their baby had died during childbirth and that they had decided to adopt a baby.

Despite the fact that Rena had been a prostitute she objected to Fred's obsessional sexual appetite, which included bondage, oral sex and other perversions. This drove Fred to satisfy his urges elsewhere and his job as the driver of an ice cream truck gave him unlimited access to young women. For some reason the image he portrayed to the outside world made him attractive to the young girls who surrounded his ice cream truck to hear his interesting stories. Even though Fred was unfaithful, he always remained totally possessive of both Rena and Charmaine.

Fred and Rena's second child, Anna Marie, was born in 1964. Their marriage certainly had many ups and downs and during this period they met Anna McFall, whose boyfriend had been killed in an accident. Fred was involved in an accident with the ice cream truck that had killed a young boy, and even though Fred was not at fault, they decided to move back to Gloucester, along with Anna McFall.

Fred took a job in a slaughter house and this only seems to have heightened his sexual perversions. He seemed to love to mutilate and dismember corpses and the sight of blood excited him even more. By now Fred and Rena's marriage was really on the rocks and Rena wanted to move back to Scotland with the children. Fred wouldn't allow the children to leave and so Rena returned to Glasgow on her own. However, Rena was so miserable without her daughters that she returned to Gloucester in July 1966 to find Fred and Anna now living in a trailer. Rena, desperate to get her children back, went to the police and told them that her husband was a sexual pervert and was unfit to raise their children.

In 1967, Anna McFall became pregnant with Fred's child. Anna was desperate to get Fred to divorce Rena so that they could marry, and Fred's response to this request was to kill her and her unborn baby. He buried the body near the caravan park, but not before dismembering the body. He had cut off her fingers and toes which were found to be missing at the gravesite, and this was to become his 'signature' for further crimes.

For a while Fred seemed nervous and unsettled, but Rena moved back into the trailer and Fred returned to his normal self. Rena went out to earn some money as a prostitute, and while she was away from home he started to fondle the young Charmaine.

Coincidentally around this time there were several sexual assaults committed in the Gloucester area, and one was pretty fifteen-year-old Mary Bastholm in January 1968.

In February of that year Fred's mother died following an operation, and it was about this time that he committed a series of petty thefts. He had many different jobs and it was while he was working as a driver for a baker, that he met Rosemary Letts. She was to become his lifetime soulmate and next wife.

ROSEMARY LETTS

Rosemary Letts was born in November 1953 in Devon. Her background was far more unstable than Fred's because her father was a schizophrenic and her mother suffered from severe depression.

When her mother, Daisy, was pregnant with Rose, she underwent several electrotherapy treatments for depression, and it is not known what effect this had on the unborn baby. After she was born, Rose developed a habit of rocking herself, and as she became a little older this developed into only head rocking. As a toddler she used to swing her head from side to side for hours on end until she appeared to have hypnotized herself into a form of semiconsciousness.

At school she was below average, and was often the butt of cruel jokes due to the fact that she was overweight. She would lash out at anyone that teased her and consequently became rather a bad-tempered loner. As a teenager she started showing signs of being sexually permissive and loved to climb into bed with her younger brother and start to fondle him. Her temper and chubbiness kept boys of her own age from being interested, and so Rose turned her attentions to the older men in the village.

In January 1968, Rose and other girls in the area started to worry about their safety, as a young girl named Mary Bastholm had disappeared from a bus stop in Gloucester. But as time went by she became less and less cautious and ended up by being raped by an older man.

In 1969, Daisy Letts became intolerant of her husband's cruelty and she took Rose, who was by this time fifteen, to stay with her other daughter Glenys and her husband. Rose spent most nights out with men and her brother-in-law, Jim Tyler, who even claimed that Rose once tried to seduce him. A couple of months later, much to everyone's surprise, Rose moved back in with her father. Rose's main aim in life seems to have been to find herself an older lover, and then she met Fred West.

THE PARTNERSHIP

Rosemary's father was not pleased when his daughter started having a relationship with Fred West. He considered that he was an undesirable boyfriend and took several measures to try and stop the affair. Meanwhile Fred was sent to prison for various thefts and failure to pay fines for previous offences. Rose went back to live with her father for a while, that is until he discovered that she was pregnant with Fred's child. She moved back to take care of Charmaine and Anna and also to cope with Fred, who was always in and out of trouble with the police.

Heather was born in 1970. Rose became short-tempered and was not happy about having to look after three children with very little money. She was not happy about having to look after Rena's children and she started to treat them badly. One day in 1971, Charmaine went missing. Rose told Anna Marie that Rena had come to fetch her, but it is believed that Rose lost her temper and went further than she normally did. Anna Marie described Rose as 'a woman entirely without self-control – when she lost her temper, she became a kind of maniac'.

Fred was in jail when Charmaine was murdered so the only part he probably played in this was to

548

bury her body under the kitchen floor of their home in Midland Road, where it lay undisturbed for over twenty years. Fred now had a hold over Rose and between them they kept the deadly secret.

Both Fred and Rose had no interest in normal sex they were only interested if it involved perverse acts like bondage, lesbianism or sadism, and for this purpose they used to invite members of the West Indian community to fulfil their fantasies. Fred would watch, take erotic pictures and even place adverts in magazines for willing participants. However, when Rose killed Charmaine she posed a new problem for Fred, his first wife Rena. It was only a matter of time before she came looking for her daughter. In August 1971 Rena did in fact come looking for Charmaine, but she went to Fred's father, Walter, to see if he knew what had happened. Fred realised that the only way out of this predicament was to kill Rena and after he had strangled the life out of her, he dismembered her body and mutilated it in the same way he had done with Anna McFall. He then put all her remains in a bag and buried them in the same place as that of Anna.

Rose and Fred had befriended a neighbour, Elizabeth Agius, who babysat for them on several occasions. She asked them one evening if they had had a nice evening and where they had been, to which they replied they had been cruising around in the car looking for young virgins. Elizabeth laughed because she thought they were joking, but it turned out that she was openly propositioned by

Fred and eventually drugged and raped.

Fred and Rose's second daughter was born in June 1972. They were now legally married and they decided they needed a larger house in which to raise their growing family. They also needed the room so that Rose could continue with her expanding prostitution business. Number 25 Cromwell Street seemed the ideal location. It was a nice large house with a good-sized cellar, and the West's took in lodgers to help them pay the rent. Fred told Rose that he had plans for the cellar and that he would either make it a place for her to entertain her clients, or alternatively he would soundproof it and use it as his 'torture chamber'. Unfortunately, his first client was to be his own daughter Anna Marie. Together Fred and Rose undressed Anna and tied her hands behind her back. Then Fred raped her, while Rose held her down. Apparently the pain from the rape was so bad that she was unable to go to school for several days. She was threatened that she would be beaten if she told anyone about their little secret. This was to happen on more than one occasion.

In December 1972, Fred and Rose picked up a seventeen-year-old girl called Caroline Owens, who they hired as their nanny. They promised her parents that they would take good care of her, but Caroline promptly left when Rose made sexual advances towards her. Foolishly, three weeks later, Caroline accepted a lift from the Wests. As soon as she was in the car Rose started to molest her while Fred drove the car and started asking kinky questions about Caroline's body. Back at Cromwell

Street the couple stripped, tortured and raped her. Although she had also been threatened with violence if she didn't keep her mouth shut, she did later go to the police and tell her story.

Even though Fred had a record, the couple were only fined a meagre £50 as the police didn't believe this nice couple could possibly be capable of such heinous acts.

Fred and Rosemary had for some while been friends with a girl named Lynda Gough. After several months Lynda moved into Cromwell Street to help take care of the children. Her mother was suspicious when she left a note to say she was leaving and traced her back to the Wests' house in Cromwell Street. When she knocked on the door it was answered by Rose who was wearing Lynda's slippers, and she told the anxious woman that her daughter had gone to Weston-Super-Mare. In truth her dismembered body was buried in the basement.

In August 1973 their first son, Stephen, was born. The next person to be abducted by the Wests was Carol Ann Cooper, in November of the same year. Her body was buried along with the growing number of others that were beneath 25 Cromwell Street. As normal her body had been dismembered and she had had her head and legs removed.

Fred decided he needed to enlarge the cellar of the house and started to demolish the garage to build an extension to the main house. He worked very strange hours on these improvements, sometimes into the early hours of the morning.

Over the next few years their killing and sexual

perversions continued with many more bodies buried under the cellar. In the year 1977, Fred decided the upstairs of the house needed to be re-designed to allow for some lodgers. One of these lodgers was eighteen-year-old Shirley Robinson, a former prostitute who had bisexual inclinations. Shirley had relationships with both Fred and Rose and she eventually fell pregnant with Fred's child. At the same time Rose had fallen pregnant to one of her black clients. Fred was delighted that Rose was carrying a child of mixed-race, but Rose was not happy that Shirley was having Fred's baby. Shirley very foolishly thought she could take Rose's place in Fred's life, but the three of them together did not work and Rose had Fred murder the very pregnant woman.

The cellar was by this time full and Fred had to bury Shirley in the garden. After he had killed and dismembered the body, Fred removed the unborn baby and then buried it alongside its mother.

In November 1978, Rose and Fred had another daughter, Louise, which made a total of six all living in the House of Horrors. It was a very un-savoury existence for children, and especially as Fred was already incestuous with his eldest girls. The children were aware of some of the things that were happening in the house, they knew that Rose was a prostitute and that Anna Marie was being raped by her father. When Anna Marie eventually moved away from home to live with her boyfriend, Fred turned his attentions to Heather and Mae and if Heather resisted her fathers advances she would be beaten into submission.

In June 1980, Rose gave birth to Barry, their second son. Then again, in April 1982, Rosemary junior was born, but she was not Fred's daughter. In July 1983, she gave birth to another half-black child who they named Lucyanna, just like Tara and Rosemary junior. The stress of so many children was certainly taking its toll on Rosemary and she regularly lost control of her temper, taking it out on her offspring. In 1986, Heather broke the code of silence and told her girlfriend about her father's advances, her mother's prostitution, and about the regular beatings she received. Her friend in turn told her parents, who happened to be friends of the Wests, and this put poor Heather's life in jeopardy. She was murdered along with all the other victims, and then her mutilated body was buried in the back garden.

THEIR LUCK RAN OUT

Rose's prostitution business was built up by putting advertisements in pornographic magazines. They were always on the lookout for women who were prepared to participate in their bizarre and perverse sexual activities. But the Wests' run of luck was about to run out. One of the young girls that Fred had raped with the assistance of Rose, had told a girlfriend what had happened. The girlfriend subsequently went to the police and the case was given to an experienced Detective Constable named Hazel Savage. Hazel knew Fred from old when he was married to Rena, and had learned from his ex-wife all about his perverse sexual preferences. On August 6, 1992, the police arrived at 25 Cromwell Street with a search warrant to look for pornographic material and any evidence of child abuse. They found far more pornographic literature than they expected and they arrested Rose for assisting in the rape and Fred for the rape and sodomy of a minor.

Hazel started a full-scale investigation and was more and more disturbed when she heard about the disappearance of Charmaine, Rena and Heather. The younger children were taken away from Rose and put into care, and with her beloved Fred in jail Rose attempted suicide by taking an overdose. Her son, Stephen, found her and managed to save her life. Fred, meanwhile, was not doing much better in jail. He was feeling depressed and very sorry for himself, until, that is, the case against the Wests was dropped. Two of the key witnesses were not prepared to testify against them, but Hazel Savage was not prepared to leave it there. Were the rumours true that perhaps their missing children were buried under the patio at 25 Cromwell Road?

Finally the police managed to get a search warrant and they started the unenviable task of digging up the garden at number 25. To make it even harder Fred had already built an extension over part of the garden, so it was going to be a very long and expensive search. Things started to go better for the investigation after Fred confessed to killing his daughter. Meanwhile back at the excavations they were starting to uncover bones that were other than the Wests' missing children, and they started to realise the enormity of the crime.

As Fred started talking freely about his murders, the police had the difficult job of trying to piece together the evidence. Lining up the various bodies with the names was not an easy task. More bones were discovered in the cellar, and Fred was not much use to them because he couldn't remember the names of the women that they had picked up. To protect Rose, Fred claimed full responsibility for the murders himself, and as the case developed Rose distanced herself from Fred to save herself. She tried to say that she was the victim of a murderous man, however, the police were not very convinced.

As Fred continued to co-operate with the police telling them of his burial places, the bodies of Rena, Anna McFall and Charmaine were discovered.

When they attended their joint hearing, Rose continued to reject Fred, telling the police that he made her sick. It appeared at last the great criminal partnership was over. Fred was totally devastated by Rose's rejection and on December 13, 1994, he was charged with twelve murders.

It was just before noon on New Year's Day at Winson Green Prison in Birmingham, that Fred ended his life by hanging himself with strips of bed linen.

Rose went on trial on October 3, 1995, and several witnesses testified to her sadistic sexual assaults on young women. The jury did not take very long to find Rose guilty of the murders of Charmaine, Heather, Shirley Robinson and the other girls buried at the house. She was sentenced to life imprisonment on each of the ten counts of murder. And then the House of Horrors was demolished.

Fred and Rosemary were perfect partners in crime. Their combined obsession with sex made a lethal combination. It has been suggested that perhaps they were working for a witches' coven because they use human digits as sacrifices, but there is no real evidence to back up this theory. Again, but it is only supposition, that perhaps it was Rosemary who was the driving force behind the team, but in my eyes I think they were both just as evil, and goaded each other into their evil acts.

The Papin Sisters

Surely something had gone terribly wrong, these were not hardened criminals, these were not even psychopaths. They were two ordinary housemaids. So what on earth had driven them to hack their employers to death?

The date was February 2, 1933, and the place was the town of Le Mans, in France. Two respectable, middle-class women, a mother and daughter, had been brutally murdered by their maids. The maids were sisters, Christine and Lea Papin. Christine was twenty-eight and Lea only twenty-one, and they lived in the same house as their employers Madame and Monsieur Lancelin, and their daughter Geneviève.

Monsieur René Lancelin was an attorney who had been away on business all day. He had arranged to meet his wife and daughter for dinner at the home of a friend, but when they didn't turn up he was concerned and returned home. When he arrived there the front door was locked and the house in darkness with the exception of a faint light coming from the maids' room upstairs. Monsieur Lancelin was unable to get into his house and so he called the police.

When the police entered the house the ground floor was empty, but on the first floor landing lay stretched out on the floor the frighteningly mutilated bodies of both Madame and Mademoiselle Lancelin. The body of Geneviève was laying face downwards with her coat pulled and and her knickers around her ankles. There were deep wounds on her buttocks and multiple cuts on the calves. Her mother's body was lying on its back. The eyes had been gouged out, her mouth was no longer visible and all her teeth had been knocked out. The full force of the attack seemed to have been directed at their heads and the victims were left literally unrecognizable.

The surrounding walls and doors were covered with splashes of blood to a height of more than seven feet which showed the height of frenzy of the attack. Surrounding the bodies were fragments of bone and teeth, one eye, some hair pins, a handbag, a key ring, an untied parcel, numerous bits of porcelain and a coat button. There were even more gruesome discoveries in the kitchen. A knife covered in blood, a damaged pewter pot and lid, and a blood-stained hammer. But the maids were nowhere to be found.

Added to this bizarre and horrifying scene, is the fact that the two maids had made no attempt to escape and were found huddled together in bed, naked. This added even more dimension to the weird case – were the maids having an incestual sexual relationship?

The two sisters, Christine and Lea, became famous overnight. The public were incensed by the brutality of the attack, while the tabloids started calling them colourful names like 'Monsters of Le Mans' and 'The Lambs Who Became Wolves and the Raging Sheep'. The name Papin became infamous throughout the land.

TRYING TO UNDERSTAND THE CRIME

What was so hard to understand was how two sisters with such a reserved demeanour could resort to such an horrific crime. They had worked for their employers for seven years and had always been quiet, hard working and very well behaved. They had no criminal record and at no time had their employers had cause for complaint. They always spent their spare time together, appeared to have no vices, and were both regular church-goers. And yet, seemingly overnight, these two honest, industrious and righteous young women had turned into monsters. It just didn't make any sense.

While most of the French population wanted to lynch the Papin sisters, others were intrigued to find out exactly what had happened. There was a gap of almost eight months before the trial, and so there was plenty of time for both speculation and fact finding. Psychoanalysts were called in to see what lay beneath the calm exterior of these two young maids. During their time in jail waiting for the trial, the eldest sister, Christine, spent much of her time crying out for Lea. She begged to be reunited with her sister and rolled around on the floor in sudden outbursts of sexual frenzy using sexually explicit language at the same time. She also used to experience hallucinations and visions, and during one such attack even attempted to gouge her own eyes out and had to be placed in a straightjacket.

For her part Christine tried to take the whole blame for the murders, saying that Lea took no part. She said that she had committed the acts during a kind of 'fit' which had come over her. But this theory was dismissed as just a sister's love trying to set the other one free, and anyway Lea had already admitted to taking part.

THE TRIAL

The trial started in September 1933 and was by now of national interest. It was attended by vast numbers of the public and press. The police had to be called in to control the crowds outside the packed court; and on several occasions the Judge had to threaten to clear the court when the crowd went out of control. The girls both denied any form of sexual relationship, but never made any attempt at denying the murders.

They were found guilty and Christine was sentenced to death on the guillotine. Lea was sentenced to ten years hard labour as they felt that Geneviève had been killed prior to the younger sister taking part. The jury also felt that Lea had been totally dominated by the very overpowering Christine. Christine's sentence was later commuted to life imprisonment, which was the normal procedure in the case of women.

Christine's condition deteriorated rapidly after

the sentencing, and she became profoundly depressed at being separated from her beloved Lea. She refused to eat and was eventually transferred to an asylum in the town of Rennes. She never improved and she died in 1937, the official cause of death was *cachexie*, which means wasting away.

On the contrary, Lea continued to be her normal, quiet, mild-mannered self and was released after eight years for good behaviour. Lea settled in the town of Nantes, south of Rennes, with her mother, Clemence. Lea worked as a chambermaid, using the name of Marie. As of December 2000, Lea Papin was said to be still alive in a hospice somewhere in France. She was half paralyzed and unable to speak as a result of a stroke, and would have been eighty-nine years old. Although this has never been confirmed, there has been no further news since that time.

PSYCHOANALYSIS

The Papin case is as much a psychological one as a criminal one, and it has already been said that psychoanalysts had a field day with the sisters while they were waiting to come up for trial. In the modern day, Christine Papin would definitely have been diagnosed as a paranoid schizophrenic. In the 1930s there would have been no effective medical treatment for her condition, but these days would probably have been treated with major tranquillizers and had a much better quality of life.

However, her sister Lea showed no signs of being psychotic and there is no reason to believe otherwise. She always appeared to be timid, a little anxious and rather prone to panic attacks, and may have suffered from a few anxiety disorders. She was definitely dominated by her sister and this may have been due to her rather low intelligence. Doctors who testified at the trial said that they felt Lea's personality had completely disappeared into Christine's own personality, so Lea's tragedy was that she was so overpowered by her elder sister. It is felt that if she had been separated from Christine at an earlier stage she would undoubtedly have led a much happier, and trouble-free life.

If we take a look at their family history, perhaps it will explain why the sisters had major problems. Their paternal grandfather was given to violent outbursts of temper and also suffered from epileptic fits. Other relatives had either been committed to asylums or taken their own lives. Their father, Gustave Papin, had had a severe drinking problem and was known to have raped their sister Emilia when she was only nine years old. It was this rape that had caused the rift in their parents' marriage, ending in divorce. Christine and Emilia were sent to live in an orphanage at Le Mans for several years, while Lea was looked after by an uncle until he died. Then she too was placed in an orphanage until she became of an age where she could work. Their mother had always paid them regular visits, but it was clear that there was some friction between her and Christine. About two years before the murders, there was a complete rift in the relationship between the girls and their mother, which was apparently caused over disagreements regarding money. Over the years their mother wrote trying to patch up their differences, but the letters were always ignored.

It seems that the one constant thing in the girls' lives was their devotion for one another. They always tried to work in the same place which was why they both ended up in the Lancelin household in 1926. It was Christine who started to work there first and then she persuaded her employers to take on her sister. Christine was employed as a cook and Lea as a chambermaid, and they shared a room on the top floor of the house. They went to church every Sunday but apart from that the girls seemed to have no other interests.

The girls seemingly shared a paranoid disorder, as the French would call it *folie a deux*, literally translated as 'madness in pairs'. This is a condition that occurs in small groups or pairs who become isolated from the outside world but who have a paranoid view of what it is like. It is also typical of this disorder that one partner dominates the other, and of this the Papin sisters were a perfect example.

Apparently, leading up to the months before the murders, Christine had become increasingly agitated and even manic in her behaviour. She gradually got worse until on the evening of February 2, 1933, her madness finally took the form of violence. She attacked the mother first and then the daughter, gouging at her face with her fingers like a woman possessed. At some stage during this outburst Lea joined in and they continued the attack with a hammer, a knife and a pewter pot.

The killing frenzy appears to have lasted for around thirty minutes, at the end of which time the victims were beyond recognition. Then the sisters washed the blood from themselves, retreated to their room, took their clothes off and climbed into bed and waited to be discovered.

David and Catherine Birnie

No one would have believed that this couple could be capable of multiple murders. It was only when their murderous campaign was uncovered did people really know the truth about Mr. and Mrs. Birnie.

The last story in this book takes us back to Australia. Killer couples were very rare, but the typical *folie à deux* has now become quite a common type of murder. Since the Birnie murders there have been several husband and wife teams, for example Fred and Rose West in England, and their case history was discussed earlier in this section. With couple killers, that is a man/woman team, the woman was always used to lure the victims to their death. Hitchhikers would gladly accept lifts from a friendly looking couple, feeling safe in the knowledge that there was a woman in the car. Unfortunately, women like Catherine Birnie are different from most women, and they loved to join in with the rape, torture and eventual killing of their victims. In most cases the capture of the couple is the undoing of their relationship, but this was no to be in the case of David and Catherine. Even to this day, although they are separated by law, they are still soulmates, they still love each other, and perhaps the most loyal act was the fact they never once tried to blame one another.

HOW THEY MET

Catherine and David had known one another since childhood, and at one time their families had lived next door to each other. David Birnie was born in 1951 in Wattle Grove and was the eldest of five children. His parents were both alcoholics and over the years one by one the children were taken away and put into foster care. David was a sickly child and was always being picked on at school. David left school at the age of fourteen and went to work as an apprentice jockey. Being of short stature the job suited him well, but he was sacked when he was caught stealing from his boss.

Catherine's mother died when she was only twenty months old, so she never really knew true maternal affection. After her mother's death, her father moved to South Africa, taking Catherine with him, but she was later shipped back to be brought up by her grandparents when news of her continued sexual and physical abuse by her father came to light. She was a lonely child, who rarely smiled and was not allowed to play with the other children in the neighbourhood. Catherine longed for love and affection and this craving haunted all her growing years. When David came into her life she found a kindred spirit, and someone with whom she could identify.

Catherine and David became close friends, and

she vowed she would do anything for him, even commit crime. In 1966 when they were both fifteen, Catherine met up with David once again. David was wilder and he already had a considerable criminal record for robbery and assault. Catherine was just what he needed and he drew her into his world of crime as his accomplice. By 1969, the couple found themselves in front of the magistrate being charged with breaking and entering with intent to steal. Both pleaded guilty and David received a nine month prison sentence. Catherine, who was already pregnant with another man's child, was placed on probation.

The couple hated being apart, and David broke out of jail on June 21, 1970, to be with his beloved Catherine. Together they committed another string of thefts and this added another two-and-a-half years to David's sentence. This time Catherine was jailed for six months and her newborn baby was taken away from her and put into care.

When they were released from prison the couple went their separate ways for a while. David married, had a daughter, and tried to settle down to married live.

Catherine was released on the condition that she no longer associated with David Birnie and she was once again reunited with her child. She found work as a live-in nanny for the MacLaughlan family, but fell pregnant by her employers' son, Donald. The couple were married on May 31, 1972, on Catherine's twenty-first birthday. Catherine was happy at last she had found a real family, and this was enhanced by the birth of their son,

Donny Jnr. However, Catherine's new-found happiness was not to last for long as her son Donny was crushed by a friend's car, and she witnessed the terrible accident. Luckily the couple survived the ordeal and went on to have six more children. Although they were never rich, Donald always provided enough money to support his family, that is until he injured his back and was no longer able to work. They were forced to live in an old, dilapidated house provided by the government and Catherine soon tired of the life of poverty.

Around this time David came back into her life. They began an affair that lasted for two years before she finally rang her husband and told him that she would not be returning. Donny was left in the shabby house with their six children, her father and her uncle.

THE DEPRAVITY STARTS

The couple were excited to be back together and they moved into a house in Willagee in Western Australia. Catherine changed her name by deed poll and became known as Birnie. They both had a very high sexual drive and would spend hours on end experimenting with new positions or even toys. However, with time, the couple became bored and they started talking about abducting women and raping them for sexual fulfilment. Catherine became excited at his talk and told him she would love to watch him do erotic things to a woman who was bound and gagged. David knew that with

Catherine as his accomplice all this was possible and he decided to act.

The first victim was almost stumbled upon by accident. On October 6, 1986, a young twenty-two-year-old student named Mary Neilson called round at their house. David had spoken to Mary earlier in the day at the spare parts factory where he worked and he had told her to come round after work to buy some tyres for her car. As she entered the house she was grabbed by David who held a knife to her throat. She was dragged to the bed, chained up and gagged. Catherine watched in delight as David repeatedly raped the petrified young girl. When he was satisfied and the ordeal was over, the couple knew that they had to do something to stop Mary from talking – the girl had to die. Later that evening they drove Mary to Gleneagles National Park, where David raped her once more and then strangled her with a rope hung from a tree branch. He then stabbed her repeatedly and then the couple buried her body in a shallow grave.

The pleasure they had achieved from the death of Mary Neilson kept the couple happy for a couple of weeks, and then they were out on the hunt for their next victim. Susannah Candy was a fifteen-year-old-girl who was hitchhiking alone on the highway. When the Birnies stopped along Susannah and offered her a lift she felt safe because there was a woman in the car. Little did she know how wrong she was. As soon as she was in the car they bound and gagged her and took her back to their house. Just like Mary, Susannah was chained to the bed, raped and sodomized, while Catherine watched. Once David's appetite was satiated he tried to strangle her with his hands, but she struggled so violently that they found it necessary to drug her with sleeping tablets. After she had fallen into a comatose sleep, David passed the rope to Catherine and told her to prove her love for him by killing the girl. Catherine quite willingly pulled the rope tight around the girl's throat until she had stopped breathing. They took the body to Gleneagles Forest and buried her alongside their other victim, Mary Neilson.

On November 1, thirty-one-year-old Noelene Patterson became the Birnie's third victim. Noelene already knew David and Catherine, in fact they had helped her wallpaper a room in her house a few weeks earlier. Noelene had been having a particularly bad day and to make matters worse her car had just run out of petrol. She was relieved when she saw her friends draw up beside her and offer a lift. However, this relief soon turned to horror when David held a knife to her throat and told her that she was to become their sex slave. They chained her to the bed, gagged her and once again David repeatedly raped her. Catherine felt a little more concerned this time because Noelene was very beautiful and she was worried that David may actually take a fancy to her, particularly as he didn't seem to keen on murdering her straight away. He kept putting off the evil deed and she was kept as a prisoner in their house for three days before Catherine forced David to give her some sleeping pills. Catherine was upset and held a knife to their victim's throat, shouting at David that he had to choose between the two of them. David strangled Noelene much to Catherine's delight, then the body was to the forest to join the others.

Just three days later, Denise Brown was picked up by the couple as she waited at a bus stop on the Stirling Highway. She was a happy girl, who was quite prepared to accept the lift rather than wait for the bus as originally planned. As she climbed into the car a knife was thrust at her throat and, like the others, she was taken back to the house to be used to fulfil their sexual pleasures. Catherine did not want to keep the woman in the house for too long and so they bundled her body into the boot of their car and drove to the Wanneroo Pine Plantation.

This was where the couple's actions became even more depraved and David plunged a knife into Denise's neck while he raped her once more. Denise did not die immediately and she just lay there making horrible gurgling noises. Catherine passed David an even bigger knife and this time he plunged it into the woman's chest. She stopped moving and the couple hastily dug a shallow grave. However, just as they were covering the body with sand, Denise started to move again and tried to sit up in her newly-dug grave. David grabbed an axe and swung it at her head, but once again she attempted to sit up, refusing to die. This time he turned the axe around and drove it into the woman's skull – this time she was dead.

Catherine was nauseated by what had happened

and told David that she didn't think she could go ahead with any further killings.

David did not allow Catherine any time to mull over what they had done and their final victim was abducted just three days later.

This time it was seventeen-year-old who was hitchhiking along Stirling Highway. She too was bound and gagged and taken back to their house. She was subjected to a day of sex and violence, after which she was untied and left on her own for a short while. The girl used this opportunity to escape, and with a clear head left her bag and cigarettes under the bed to prove that she had been there. How this young girl managed to think so sensibly after the ordeal she had been through, is all the more credit to her. She ran from the house, covering her body with the little clothing she had left, and stumbled into the nearby Fremantle Shopping Centre. The police were called and she was taken back to the station for questioning. She told them all about the kidnapping, the rape and abuse and that she would be able to prove she was at the house because they would find her bag and cigarettes underneath the bed.

When the police arrived at the house no-one was in, so they lay in wait. Catherine was the first one to come home and David was later arrested at his place of work.

THE END

The couple were sat in separate interview rooms and said nothing. The police tried everything they could think of to make them talk, but nothing worked. The police knew they had to get their admission to the rape and abduction before they could charge them. They also knew that there were other victims, because David had bragged about it to the young woman.

Totally exhausted and in a last effort to get some response from David, the policeman said, 'It's getting dark, why don't you show me where the bodies are, so that we can dig them up'. To his complete amazement, David responded, 'Okay, there is four of them'.

Immediately they started to make some headway in their investigations. Once David had confessed it wasn't long before Catherine broke her silence. The couple went with a cavalcade of police cars to the graves on Wanneroo Pine Plantation.

At first they had difficulty in locating the graves until David pointed out where Mary Nielson and Susannah Candy were buried. They then had to begin the arduous task of digging up the victims.

Catherine said that she wanted to point out the next one and indicated where Noelene Patterson lay. With complete contempt and lack of any remorse Catherine spat on the grave of Noelene. The fourth victim was unearthed at a nearby plantation and the couple were then taken back to the police headquarters.

They were held in cells until they were officially charged on November 12, on four counts of murder and one count of abduction and rape. No plea was entered.

At the hearing held on February 10, 1987 both

Catherine and David pleaded guilty to all charges. The Birnies were each imprisoned to life imprisonment and this meant a minimum of twenty years before they would be eligible for parole. However, the trial judge stated that the crimes were premeditated, planned and carried out so cruelly and relentlessly over such a short period of time, it was his suggestion that this couple should never be released from prison.

DID THEY REGRET THEIR ACTIONS?

After his arrest David Birnie claimed to be sorry, saying that he deeply regretted the suffering he had caused. Whether this was a genuine emotion, or whether he was just trying to gain some leniency, is a matter of opinion. His crimes certainly shocked the whole of Australia, and even his fellow inmates were disgusted by his crimes. In prison he was repeatedly beaten up and even tried to take his own life in 1987. He was moved to Fremantle Prison's old death cells for his own protection.

Catherine Birnie had signed a detailed statement admitting her direct involvement in all four of the murders. David said that his partner had only taken part because of her total and undying dedication for him, and to help him satisfy his desperate sexual desires. This is probably one of the worst cases of personality dependence that has ever come to light.

David and Catherine Birnie were certainly not insane and knew exactly what they were doing.

To this very day the couple still write love letters to each other constantly and both claim to still be very much in love. In fact in the first four years they were apart they exchanged a phenomenal 2,600 letters but they were denied the right to marry, have phone calls or indeed any contact visits. The authorities felt that David Birnie was such a bad influence on Catherine that the two should never be allowed to make contact as they felt he would further inflict his evil influence over his lover.

In 1990 David Birnie said that the denial of these rights was causing them both physical and mental torture. It went on to say that it would cause them to have a mental breakdown which would lead to inevitable suicide. In 1993 David Birnie had his personal computer confiscated when it was found to contain pornographic software.

Catherine's first husband died on January 22, 2000, who was the father of her six children. He was only fifty-nine and his death was rather sudden. Catherine made an application to attend her former husband's funeral but her request was denied.

Summing Up

The mind of the human being remains one of the last great enigmas of modern science. It is hard for the average person who aspires to such normal emotions as love, kindness, creativity, intelligence, wisdom, bravery, etc., to accept the depraved minds of others who love to harm, kill, torture or even mutilate a fellow human being. Throughout most of our case histories it becomes clear that most people that kill have several characteristics in common. Most of them appear to have had very difficult starts to their lives, or indeed been the victim themselves of unscrupulous adults. Events that have happened in their childhood seem to have an everlasting effect in the way they behave when they reach adulthood. It appears that two-thirds of all murderers who have been studied have been found to be suffering from either a mental illness, neurological damage or child abuse or indeed all three. It certainly seems true that abuse sets up an impulse towards violence that a normal, healthy brain can keep under control. However, if a brain that is already impaired by neurological damage or mental illness, then these violent impulses are not to easy to keep in check. The more we can learn about the brain and the way it functions the more successful we will be in truly rehabilitating offenders and preventing 'at risk' children from turning to lives of crime.